The Legal Construction of Identity

The LAW AND PUBLIC POLICY: PSYCHOLOGY AND THE SOCIAL
SCIENCES series includes books in three domains:

Legal Studies—writings by legal scholars about issues of relevance to
psychology and the other social sciences, or that employ social science
information to advance the legal analysis;

Social Science Studies—writings by scientists from psychology and the other
social sciences about issues of relevance to law and public policy; and

Forensic Studies—writings by psychologists and other mental health scientists
and professionals about issues relevant to forensic mental health science and
practice.

The series is guided by its editor, Bruce D. Sales, PhD, JD, ScD, University of
Arizona; and coeditors, Bruce J. Winick, JD, University of Miami; Norman J.
Finkel, PhD, Georgetown University; and Stephen J. Ceci, PhD, Cornell
University.

* * *

The Legal Construction of Identity

THE JUDICIAL AND SOCIAL LEGACY OF AMERICAN COLONIALISM IN PUERTO RICO

Efrén Rivera Ramos

AMERICAN PSYCHOLOGICAL ASSOCIATION
WASHINGTON, DC

First Printing January 2001
Second Printing October 2001

Published by
American Psychological Association
750 First Street, NE
Washington, DC 20002

Copies may be ordered from
APA Order Department
P.O. Box 92984
Washington, DC 20090-2984

In the U.K., Europe, Africa, and the Middle East, copies may be
ordered from
American Psychological Association
3 Henrietta Street
Covent Garden, London
WC2E 8LU England

Typeset in Times Roman by EPS Group Inc., Easton, MD

Printer: United Book Press, Inc., Baltimore, MD
Cover Designer: Berg Design, Albany, NY
Technical/Production Editor: Jennifer Powers

The opinions and statements published are the responsibility of the
authors, and such opinions and statements do not necessarily represent
the policies of the APA.

Library of Congress Cataloging-in-Publication Data
Rivera Ramos, Efrén, 1947–
    The legal construction of identity : the judicial and social legacy of American
colonialism in Puerto Rico / Efrén Rivera Ramos.
        p. cm.—(Law and public policy)
    Includes bibliographical references.
    ISBN 1-55798-670-3 (hardcover : alk. paper)
        1. Law—United States—Territories and possessions.   2. Law—Puerto Rico—
History.   3. Sociological jurisprudence.   4. Puerto Rico—Colonial influence.
5. Puerto Rico—Social conditions.   I. Title.   II. Series.

    KF4635 .R58 2000
    340′.115—dc21

                                                                            00-050272

British Library Cataloguing-in-Publication Data
A CIP record is available from the British Library.

Printed in the United States of America

For Esther and Ariel

CONTENTS

PREFACE

This book was born of two concerns. As a Puerto Rican, I have always felt the need to question how the relationship between the United States and Puerto Rico has been created and recreated during the last 100 years. And as a legal academician, I have asked myself what the role of law has been in that process. This book is my attempt to answer both questions.

I now realize that this combined inquiry has produced a look at the history of those relations from a new perspective. Although there exist a number of general, economic, political, and constitutional histories of Puerto Rico, none has undertaken to analyze the development of the relationship between Puerto Rico and the United States relying on the insights provided by recent studies on law and society. This is the endeavor I have undertaken here, and I hope that this text will be of use to psychologists and other social scientists as well as to legal scholars interested in the intersection of social sciences and the law. I also hope that the book will be useful to academics in various disciplines who teach aspects of Puerto Rican history in the context of American colonialism. As a professor at the University of Puerto Rico, I count myself among those academics as well as among the members of the people about whom I write in this volume.

As I grew up in a town in western Puerto Rico in the late 1950s, I started to become slightly aware of some of the problems facing Puerto Ricans in our relationship with the United States. I remember distinctly my perplexity at the sea of American flags in Puerto Rican Republican Party public meetings. I recall the fear and hidden admiration provoked by the caravans of independence supporters as they passed by the public housing project where I lived with my family during a good part of my childhood. I recollect the attraction generated by the socially conscious language of Popular Democratic Party leaders, because it spoke to the realities lived by those closest to me. But I also remember the mystification produced by their sinuous descriptions of the "new" political relationship with the United States they had helped to create.

In retrospect, I understand now that many of the problems faced by Puerto Ricans during those years were similar to the conundrums encountered by Isabella González, Adolfo Marín, Rafael Ortiz, and the rest of their compatriots at the beginning of the century, whose stories are told in the introduction to this book. Puerto Rico has changed in the 100 years since its acquisition by the U.S. Significant social, political, and economic transformations have been made. Yet the same issues persist today.

These personal experiences have influenced my approach to the topic as a Puerto Rican. My approach to the topic as a scholar has been influenced by several additional factors.

First of all, although I have been a long-time supporter of independence for Puerto Rico, I cannot deny the fact that, for several decades, the vast majority of Puerto Ricans have shown their preference for some sort of close political connection to the United States. I have grown increasingly skeptical about explanations that reduce the underlying reasons for this attitude either to strictly economic motivations or to the sole effect of political persecution and repression of the independence movement. Both sets of factors have certainly played an important role in the reproduction of U.S. hegemony over Puerto Rican society. But they are far from constituting the whole answer. Intertwined with them are social and ideological phenomena that have buttressed a generalized acceptance of U.S. constitutional, legal, and political institutions and values. This acceptance, on the other hand, cannot simply be attributed to a state of "false consciousness" somehow afflicting the majority of the Puerto Rican population.

By the term "false consciousness" I mean a mental state in which people fail to perceive their true interests because they are under the effects of an ideological delusion. Some currents of critical social theory have used the notion of false consciousness to explain why subordinated groups seem to accept their condition of subordination. However, the concept of false consciousness does not capture the complexities of the power relationship between the U.S and Puerto Rico, nor does it capture the many nuances of the responses of the Puerto Rican people to that relationship.

It seems to me that one has to look for explanations that achieve at least two objectives. First, such explanations must not conceal the unequal balance of power between the United States and Puerto Rico as political communities. At the same time, they must take into account the capacity of Puerto Ricans for agency. In other words, these explanations must describe the many ways in which Puerto Ricans have tried, with varying degrees of success and regardless of political affiliation, to confront the challenges posed by having become the main colony of the dominant political, economic, and military power during most of the 20th century.

Second, over the years, my understanding of the operation of law in society has evolved to embrace what has become a distinct paradigm in the social theory of law. I refer to the notion that law must be regarded as constitutive of society. According to this view, law is not just a product of social processes. It is also an important producer of social experience. It helps to shape social relations and to influence historical and cultural contexts. This has led me to examine how legal discourse has become one of the forces at work in the construction of U.S. policy toward Puerto Rico and in the production of a particular social and cultural experience within Puerto Rican society itself. The fruitfulness of this inquiry became clear to me as more and more studies documented the centrality of law in U.S. political history and as I realized that throughout the past century Puerto Rican society had increasingly become attuned to the intricacies of the discourse of law and rights.

Guided by these general concerns, I decided to look at two different dimensions of the question. One is the legal characterization made by the U.S. judiciary of the nature and extent of the power that the federal government may exercise over acquired territories such as Puerto Rico. This inquiry has the objective of unveiling how the United States legitimated the exercise of such power and how it has attempted to justify that process in the context of its political and constitutional traditions. The other dimension explored is the ways in which Puerto Ricans have managed the different legal conceptions and categories devised to rule them in order to cope with the reality of political subordination that has characterized the relationship until now. The decision to examine these two dimensions stems from the conviction that the relationship between the two societies is not a unilateral affair. It involves varying degrees of imposition, resistance, negotiation, willful acceptance, fatalistic resignation, and realistic accommodation.

I have drawn from insights furnished by several contemporary currents of social and legal thought. The book consciously relies on contributions made by critical Weberian, Foucauldian, Marxist, post-Marxist, feminist, postmodernist, and postcolonial theories of law and society, as well as on recent developments within analytical and normative jurisprudence. I have attempted to follow a transdisciplinary approach that benefits from these multiple traditions and perspectives. I have tried to appeal to a wide audience of readers interested in the history of Puerto Rico, Latin American studies, political science, social psychology, and the sociology of law, among others.

The main contribution I hope to make with this book is to shed light on the history of the relationship between the United States and Puerto Rico from the perspective of social legal theory. I believe that such historical understanding is necessary to better grasp the alternatives open to Puerto Rico and the United States in their future dealings. Moreover, I am convinced that the effects of that history will be apparent even in a "postcolonial" Puerto Rico. In this sense, this review of the past century may provide a glimpse of the century to come. As a secondary objective, I hope that the insights drawn from this study may illuminate broader questions regarding the workings of law in society, particularly its role in the construction of relationships of subordination.

ACKNOWLEDGMENTS

Many people contributed to making this book possible. I thank all of them. I particularly appreciate the encouragement given by Dean Antonio García Padilla and the members of the Personnel Committee of the University of Puerto Rico (UPR) School of Law. I am grateful to the staff of APA Books, especially to Jennifer Powers, Technical/Production Editor; Chris Davis, Supervisor of Technical Editing and Design; Vanessa Downing and Shelly Wyatt, Development Editors; Susan Reynolds, Acquisitions Editor; and the two anonymous reviewers who offered insightful recommendations. Michael D. A. Freeman, of University College London, provided invaluable guidance during the early stages of this project. William Twining, Francis Snyder, Peter Fitzpatrick, Hugh Collins, John Brigham, David Wexler, Bruce Sales, and Esther Vicente made useful suggestions. José Rodríguez, María del Mar Ortiz, Carmen Márquez, Marta Santiago Ramos, Larissa Maldonado Carrasco, Karen Rivera Turner, and Olivette Rivera Torres were effective research assistants at different periods. Roxana Varela Fernós was extremely helpful in the final phase of the process.

For their support in a variety of ways I would like to thank Fernando Agrait, Manuel Saldaña, Víctor Pons, Efraín González Tejera, Michel Godreau, Rafael Escalera Rodríguez, Luis Agrait, Annie Santiago de Curet, Arcadio Díaz Quiñones, Francisco Catalá, Josefina Pantojas, Evelyn Vicente, Zoraida Pacheco, Lizzette Ramos, Arlene Agosto, the library staff of the UPR School of Law, and the editors of the *Revista Jurídica de la Universidad de Puerto Rico*. I am also indebted to many colleagues and students who commented on some of the ideas contained here during academic meetings.

Finally, my deepest appreciation goes to my wife, Esther Vicente, and our son, Ariel Cacimar, for their unswerving solidarity throughout this endeavor and for the many sacrifices they were willing to endure to see its completion. This book is theirs as much as it is mine.

The Legal Construction of Identity

INTRODUCTION

Puerto Rican artist Adolfo Marín Molinas woke up one morning with a changed legal identity. He was residing temporarily in the French city of Biarritz. It was April 11, 1899. On that date the Spanish Crown officially ceded the Caribbean island of Puerto Rico to the United States. Marín Molinas had ceased to be a Spanish subject. What should he be considered now? Was he a citizen of the United States? Was he a subject of the emerging imperial power? Was he an American national? How would this well-to-do Puerto Rican cope with these new circumstances?

The matter of the Puerto Rican artist's newly acquired identity surfaced three years later to create an important legal precedent. In 1902 Marín Molinas decided to send some of his paintings to his friend Federico Degetau, who was then living in Washington, DC, as resident commissioner for Puerto Rico in the United States. The U.S. Treasury Department sought to recover duties on the imported paintings, in accordance with federal tariff laws. Degetau objected. He relied on a provision exempting from such exactions the works of art produced by "American artists" residing temporarily abroad. The question arose, Was Marín Molinas, the Puerto Rican painter, an American artist? The secretary of the treasury had doubts. He referred the query to the attorney general of the United States.[1]

The same year that Marín Molinas shipped his works of art to Washington, a compatriot of his from a very different social background also forced the highest officials of the U.S. government to face the question of the legal identity of Puerto Ricans. Isabella González, an unmarried woman presumably of working-class origin, was prevented from landing and detained in the port of New York as she arrived from Puerto Rico. Immigration officials intended to exclude her from the United States as an "alien immigrant," alleging that she was "likely to become a public charge." A writ of habeas corpus seeking her release was filed on her behalf. Several basic questions emerged. As a Puerto Rican, was Isabella González an alien? What was her legal relationship to the United States? Was she a part of the American body politic? Could she freely enter the United States? Eventually, the answers had to be provided by the U.S. Supreme Court.[2]

Meanwhile, back in Puerto Rico, another personal drama with collective implications had been unfolding. A 21-year-old cab driver from the mountain city of Caguas had been sentenced to death by a U.S. "military commission" during the American occupation of Puerto Rico. Rafael Ortiz was charged with killing an American soldier in a workers' club apparently because of the soldier's offensive conduct toward Ortiz and his girlfriend.[3] The incident occurred on February 24, 1899. Because he was tried

---

[1] 24 Op. 40 (1903). Very little is said about Adolfo Marín Molinas in the official documents relating to his case. In fact, he is referred to only as Mr. Molinas. His full name and other biographical details have been obtained through the meticulous and generous search conducted by Puerto Rican historian Annie Santiago de Curet upon the author's inquiry.

[2] *See* González v. Williams, 192 U.S. 1 (1903).

[3] The Rafael Ortiz story has been recently discovered by Puerto Rican scholar Arcadio Díaz

by a commission, he was not tried by jury. The American military governor of Puerto Rico commuted his death sentence to life imprisonment shortly before the official proclamation of the Treaty of Paris, which formally ceded Puerto Rico to the United States. Ortiz was sent as a federal prisoner to a jail in Minnesota. A habeas corpus petition filed on his behalf failed. Among other things, his American lawyer had alleged that as a "U.S. citizen" Ortiz had the right to be tried by jury.

On June 14, 1902, one month and one day after the attorney general rendered his opinion declaring Adolfo Marín Molinas an "American artist," the first American civilian governor of Puerto Rico commuted Rafael Ortiz's life sentence to five years in prison. Two months later, on August 24, Isabella González was being held in New York. On January 4, 1904, the Supreme Court decided that although González was not a citizen, she was a "national" of the United States, with the right to freely enter the country. Chief Justice Melvin Weston Fuller cited the opinion of the attorney general in the Marín Molinas case. The court ordered her discharge from detention. Six months later, Ortiz, now 26 years old, regained his freedom and returned to Puerto Rico.

The Legal Construction of Social Reality

The history of Puerto Rico under the rule of the United States illustrates the axiom that law has the capacity to define, within limits, social reality. To understand the individual and collective psychology of the people of Puerto Rico, therefore, requires an understanding of both the history of its colonization and the U.S. laws that have helped shape the social world of the Puerto Rican people, both in the United States and in the colony itself. This introduction paints in broad strokes the framework of understanding that guided my analysis and the conclusions I have drawn about the social reality of Puerto Rico.

Psychologists and other social scientists interested in the psychological and social forces that shape and are shaped by legal considerations may be more interested in my description of how law and social forces combine to influence collective behavior in unequal power relationships. Legal scholars may be more interested in my understanding of how social forces influence the development of legal categories and how those categories are used by different social actors to attain different goals. My hope is that all will find in this analysis not only a point of departure for considering the individual and collective character of this specific people, but also a way of looking at power relations in the national and international sphere in a broader sense.

Puerto Rico Under U.S. Rule: Persistent Issues

Early History

U.S. troops occupied Puerto Rico on July 25, 1898, during the course of the Spanish American War. As a prize for its victory, along with Puerto Rico, the United States

---

Quiñones. *See* Arcadio Díaz Quiñones, *Once tesis sobre un crimen de 1899*, 11 Op. Cit. Rev. del Centro de Inv. Hist. 109 (1999). The account offered here relies on the cited article and accompanying appendix, as well as on personal conversations with Díaz Quiñones and documents provided by him.

acquired the islands of Guam and the Philippines in the Pacific Ocean. The peace treaty was signed on December 10 in Paris, France, the country Puerto Rican painter Marín Molinas had chosen as his temporary abode. The treaty was ratified by the U.S. Senate on February 6, 1899, two weeks before the Caguas killing that sent Rafael Ortiz to Minnesota as the first Puerto Rican federal prisoner.[4] The Treaty of Paris was finally proclaimed on April 11, 1899, five days after Ortiz's death sentence had been commuted.

The U.S. acquisition of Puerto Rico had a dual transforming impact. At one level it shaped the collective experiences of the two political communities involved. Thus, the United States emerged as an imperial power on the world stage. It started to draw into its orbit entire communities that posed complex legal, economic, and social challenges. Puerto Rico, on the other hand, shed an old colonial master and faced a new stage in its colonial history.

At another level, these developments had immediate effects on individual Puerto Ricans and Americans of all walks of life, as illustrated by the three cases that introduced this chapter. These cases demonstrate the interrelations between the personal and the political. Personal lives were transformed by larger historical and political forces. At the same time, these individual histories shed light on the collective responses, in terms of law and politics, that the new situation was to generate.

The story of the relationship between the United States and Puerto Rico during the 20th century cannot be fully understood without taking into account those two levels of experience, not only in the past but in the present as well. The situations involving Adolfo Marín Molinas, Isabella González, and Rafael Ortiz at the dawn of the U.S. colonial project in Puerto Rico raised issues that persist to this day.

For example, the three cases expressly brought out the question of personal worth and collective identity in situations of unequal power. What effects did the change in colonial master have on the individual and collective self-perceptions of Puerto Ricans? How were they to be regarded by the United States, which was, in effect, a metropolitan state?[5] For example, was Marín Molinas an American artist or a Puerto Rican artist? What did it mean that González was a U.S. national? Was Ortiz a U.S. citizen back in 1899?

These questions are closely related to the ties that were thought to link individual Puerto Ricans with the metropolitan state. They trigger questions about the meaning of citizenship. This consideration, in turn, pushes to the surface the query about the location of Puerto Rico, as a collectivity, within the American body politic. Then, there is the question of rights. What rights accrued to Puerto Ricans collectively and individually? (Could they move freely to continental territory? Would they be exempted from the treatment extended foreigners, as their persons, goods, and creations crossed U.S. borders? Were they to enjoy all the safeguards enshrined in the U.S. Constitution for those subjected to criminal proceedings? Were they "within" or "without" the Constitution?[6]

The case of Rafael Ortiz also highlights the role of the U.S. military in that first

---

[4] Díaz Quiñones, *supra* note 3, at 109.

[5] The term "metropolitan state" is used in this book with the meaning commonly attributed to it in the literature on colonialism. It refers to the colonizing power as opposed to the colonial territory.

[6] *See, e.g.,* WINFRED LEE THOMPSON, THE INTRODUCTION OF AMERICAN LAW IN THE PHILIPPINES AND PUERTO RICO: 1898–1905 213 (1989).

Exhibit 1—*Questions Regarding the Effects of U.S. Law on Puerto Ricans*

- What has been the place of law in the imperial administration of the colonial possessions?
- How much of the Puerto Rican experience within the American regime has been influenced by law and legal discourse?
- How have Puerto Ricans managed the legal machinery of the United States to achieve their goals?
- How have these legal experiences contributed to the shaping of Puerto Rican attitudes toward the metropolitan state?

encounter with the Puerto Rican population.[7] That role is still the center of heated controversy. His story showcases the role of violence and the interplay between repression and mercy in the construction of a governable political space. The case of Isabella González foreshadowed the crucial fact of migration to the United States in the historical experience of being Puerto Rican in the 20th century. Her situation illustrated deep social and economic issues that continue to this day. What alternatives were opened for the poorer among Puerto Ricans when the United States became their sovereign master? How would the metropolitan state respond to their economic and social plight?

The social contrasts between Isabella González, the unemployed migrant woman, and the cosmopolitan male artist Adolfo Marín Molinas remind us that Puerto Rico was not then and has never been a homogenous society. Yet all its social sectors have been touched by the rough and benevolent edges of colonialism. All three cases pose the question of how different social groups have positioned themselves vis-à-vis the power embodied in the behavior of the United States. They illustrate how acceptance, resistance, accommodation, and negotiation have shaped the individual and collective identity of Puerto Ricans.

The actions of those three Puerto Ricans also reveal important clues about their attitudes toward the legal, economic, and social conditions resulting from the invasion of 1898. How did they respond to the restraints and opportunities created by the American presence in their country? How did they manifest their Puerto Rican identity in the process?

Finally, there was the question of law. These three stories eventually became cases in the legal sense. All three individuals became entangled in the legal processes and the legal culture of the United States. Their situations were handled through legal discourse. Their lives, their work, and their personal freedom were directly affected by decisions made at the highest levels of the legal apparatus of the United States. From these, many other questions emerge, as shown in Exhibit 1.

The Modern Era

The 1950s was a watershed decade for relations between Puerto Rico and the United States. Nationalists staged a revolutionary uprising in Puerto Rico, and young independence advocates fired on the U.S. Congress and the president's house in Wash-

---

[7] *See* Díaz Quiñones, *supra* note 3, at 109.

ington. New Puerto Rican prisoners landed in American jails for those actions. A charismatic leader named Luis Muños Marín, who as a young man lived in the U.S., asked Puerto Ricans to put aside the political status question in order to concentrate on social and economic reform aimed at modernizing Puerto Rico and bringing its people out of dire poverty. Migration to the United States reached new heights—nearly half a million Puerto Ricans moved to the U.S during that decade. These years also witnessed able pro-statehood political leaders persuading their opponents to include language in the Puerto Rican Constitution highlighting the virtues of U.S. citizenship during an epoch of a heightened official emphasis on the uniqueness of Puerto Rican culture.

While these paradoxes were made manifest, legal reform flourished, resulting in a new constitution for Puerto Rico. It also resulted in social legislation and more efficient mechanisms for the internal protection of human rights. For example, the Puerto Rican legislature passed laws reorganizing the judicial system; creating new administrative agencies, and barring discrimination in employment based on age, race, color, religion, social origin, or condition, and political affiliation. The governor appointed a special committee to render a report on the state of civil rights in Puerto Rico. The committee's recommendations led to the abolition of a Puerto Rican gag law used to persecute political opponents, to the commutation of the sentences of independence advocates convicted under that law, and to the creation of the Puerto Rico Civil Rights Commission.

Finally, this decade heralded the institutionalization of an arrangement called the *Estado Libre Asociado de Puerto Rico* (the ELA). Its English name, the Commonwealth of Puerto Rico, had nothing to do with the Spanish original. The ELA was first touted as a provisional break in the debate over political status that did not preclude choosing either independence or statehood for Puerto Rico in the future. Later, it developed its own force and became one more among the "solutions" to the question of political status proposed by the different factions in Puerto Rico.

Thus, half a century after the occupation, issues of identity, resistance, accommodation, repression, mobility, social and economic opportunity, culture, and legality were still central to the Puerto Rican colonial experience.

Entering a New Century

The summer of 1999 was a particularly revealing time. A century of U.S.– Puerto Rican relations in the political, economic, and social spheres had played itself out. It seemed that old issues were being revived in new settings. One morning the newspapers brought the news that Abelardo Díaz Alfaro, a prominent Puerto Rican writer, had died. Díaz Alfaro became famous for his stories emphasizing the clash between U.S. culture and Puerto Rican traditional values. A sizable crowd accompanied his body to an Old San Juan cemetery to be buried alongside other stalwarts of Puerto Rican culture and politics. His casket was carried in an oxcart, reminiscent of a way of life that had long disappeared in Puerto Rico. A large sign bore the name *El Josco*, the title of his best known short story, a tale about a dark-colored Puerto Rican bull who preferred suicide to being subjected to the yoke. The crucial question of Puerto Rican identity the writer poignantly posed was being theatrically reenacted in the streets of modern San Juan as his remains were carried to rest.

On the opposite side of the page on which his obituary appeared, one of the leading San Juan dailies carried a large photo of a crowd of angry Puerto Ricans shouting slogans against the U.S. Navy. The protest was one of many motivated by the death of a Puerto Rican civilian guard accidentally killed in the Navy's training ground in the nearby island of Vieques during air-to-ground bombing exercises. A solid consensus within Puerto Rican society, expressed by the leaders of all political parties, religious denominations, and numerous civic groups, called for the cessation of Navy activities in Vieques. This tragedy inspired the people once again to publicly question the role of the U.S. military in Puerto Rico. And, once more, as in the first years after the invasion, the matter of life and death, and its legal and political implications, was being played out in the context of the U.S. military occupation of Puerto Rico.

As Washington was prodded to respond, President Bill Clinton appointed a Blue Ribbon Commission to investigate. Several members of Congress demanded that the Navy cease its live ammunition training exercises in the island. New York Representative Charles Rangel, whose constituency is largely Puerto Rican, reminded his colleagues that Puerto Rico was not just some island in the Caribbean. It was a community of U.S. citizens, an argument made by Rafael Ortiz's lawyer in 1899.

While visiting Puerto Rico to show his support for the Vieques cause, the Reverend Jesse Jackson met with a group of Puerto Rican athletes to discuss their situation within U.S. sports circles. Puerto Rico has its own international sports representation. Are Puerto Rican athletes "American athletes"? From a cultural perspective, the question sounds eerily similar to that posed about the Puerto Rican artist Adolfo Marín Molinas in 1902.

Puerto Rican politicians and activists in New York asked U.S. Senate candidate Hillary Clinton to take a stance in favor of their Vieques compatriots. They viewed the plight of Vieques as part of the problems of their community. Speaking on behalf of the Puerto Rican community, many of those leaders pressed for the release of 17 Puerto Rican independence advocates jailed in U.S. federal prisons. In early August, the White House announced that it had decided to commute the sentences of all except one of the Puerto Rican pro-independence prisoners, provided they signed agreements renouncing the use of violence and adhering to other conditions.[8] These were denounced as mean and oppressive.[9]

It appeared that the nature of the ties that bind Puerto Ricans, individually and collectively, to the United States was clearly still a contested site for meaning at the end of the 20th century. The questions of coercion, mercy, governability, and colonialism were still haunting the United States nearly a century since they were first raised.

As in previous years, on July 25, 1999, independence supporters gathered in the southern town of Guánica, Puerto Rico, to decry the U.S. invasion of 1898. That same day, followers of the Popular Democratic Party held a massive rally in the opposite side of the island to celebrate the adoption of the 1952 Constitution and the establishment of the *Estado Libre Asociado*. Two days later, thousands of pro-statehood partisans flocked to a town near San Juan in remembrance of José Celso

---

[8] *Clinton Offers Release to P.R. Prisoners*, SAN JUAN STAR, Aug. 12, 1999, at 5.
[9] John McPhaul, *President's Clemency Conditions Blasted*, SAN JUAN STAR, Aug. 13, 1999, at 4.

Barbosa, the Puerto Rican Black physician who founded their movement in the early part of the 20th century. The political future of the country was clearly still at stake.

After more than 100 years of U.S. rule and presence in Puerto Rico, the United States and the Puerto Rican community are still grappling with problems that sprang from the early decision to acquire Puerto Rico as part of an imperial war. Since then, both countries have changed significantly. The United States is now the strongest military and economic power in the world. Its popular culture penetrates the remotest corners of the globe. Formerly marginalized groups are making their way into mainstream American society. Some consider the American life world the epitome of a "postmodern" way of life.

Puerto Rico, in turn, has become a heavily populated, urban, (perhaps) postindustrial, colonial society. Its almost 6 million "nationals" are distributed between the territory of Puerto Rico and the mainland United States. Its social and cultural environments combine elements of its complex Spanish and American colonial experience as well as influences from increasingly "globalized" cultural forms.

Despite these transformations, the codes used to interpret the political and constitutional relationship between the countries are remarkably identical to those generated in the early days of their encounter. Legal decisions made in its initial stages continue to heavily influence the relationship. The questions of legal identity posed 100 years ago have not entirely washed away. The analysis provided in this book will seek to prove these points.

One salient historical development, however, should be noted. In spite of the conflicted nature of the relationship, a century after the invasion most Puerto Ricans appear to accept on some level the American presence in Puerto Rico. In one way or another, the vast majority of Puerto Ricans have expressed their wish to preserve their ties to the United States. This has become evident from results at the polls and from intense discussions about the political future of Puerto Rico generated during the 1990s. The debate hinges, mostly, on the nature of those ties. An increasing number of Puerto Ricans appear to be dissatisfied with the current arrangement. Yet the solutions supported by more than 90% of the population are predicated on continued association with the United States and preservation of U.S. citizenship.[10]

This phenomenon appears to involve three interrelated concerns: economic survival, cultural identity, and political empowerment and dignity. The latter includes the aspirations of Puerto Ricans of gaining a larger degree of control over their own affairs, maintaining or enlarging their rights as legal and political subjects, and finding a more dignified place under the sun as a political community. The three political alternatives traditionally considered have been statehood (becoming a state of the Union), independence (becoming a separate, sovereign state), and some version of the present Commonwealth status. The differences in support for each alternative

---

[10] In three of the four referenda on the status issue held in Puerto Rico during the past 50 years, Puerto Ricans have expressly supported the *Estado Libre Asociado*. On this point, see Ediberto Román, *The Alien–Citizen Paradox and Other Consequences of U.S. Colonialism*, 26 FLORIDA STATE UNIV. L. REV. 1, 39–40 (1998). Román argued that despite indicating a wish to preserve the ties with the United States, the results in those three referenda also are evidence that Puerto Ricans sought enhanced rights. *Id.* at 40–41. In the fourth such electoral event, held in 1998 (after publication of Román's article), voters preferred a "None of the above" option advocated by the pro-Commonwealth party. The immediate effect was to withhold authorization from the government to make a formal request to the United States in favor of any specific change in status.

Exhibit 2—*Questions Providing the Framework for This Book*

- How did the United States end up constructing its colonial project in Puerto Rico?
- By what means was this complex experience of relations and practices engendered?
- What was the perspective of those who framed the initial policies?
- What is the basic conceptual framework through which the U.S. Congress and Supreme Court view the relationship of Puerto Rico and the United States?
- How was that framework constructed?
- What role did law play in that process?
- What legal doctrines and categories did the U.S. legal system deploy to confront the many issues that the new situation generated?
- How were the questions of identity, citizenship, rights, migration, governance, democracy, and others handled through the dominant legal discourse?
- How were the demands of concrete legal agents satisfied?
- What have been the constraining effects of those legal constructs?
- To what extent is that basic conceptual and legal structure operative today?
- How was Puerto Rican identification with American rule and presence engendered?
- What were the factors contributing to that result?
- How have Puerto Ricans reacted to the legal framework devised to govern them, including those laws passed without their initial consent and others with their active collaboration?
- What role does legal discourse play today in Puerto Rican society?
- To what extent does that role contribute to the continuance of U.S. hegemony?
- How are the questions of identity, citizenship, subjectivity, and democracy handled in that hegemonic context?
- What do those issues have to do with hegemony itself?

---

among the population of Puerto Rico depend largely on assessments of the strengths and weaknesses of each alternative with regard to economic viability, emphasis on cultural identity, and degree of political empowerment desired and on the relative weight accorded by individual Puerto Ricans to each of those factors. So far, the majority appears to have concluded that at least two of those aspirations, economic survival and political worth, are best secured through some type of association with the United States. Also, it seems that most prefer a type of connection that would allow room for what most Puerto Ricans perceive to be a distinct cultural identity. This generalized acceptance of U.S. rule and presence in the island amounts to a situation of hegemony (to be explored later in the Introduction).

This framework for understanding has guided my inquiries, as developed in this book. A number of key questions have more specifically informed my exploration. These are listed in Exhibit 2. As the questions multiply, their interrelationships become clear. What ties them together are the two basic dimensions of the colonial experience: the larger, historical context of Puerto Rico as a collectivity and the particular experiences of specific Puerto Ricans as their identities are shaped as individuals and as families. The law has influenced both spheres.

The Legal Construction of Puerto Rican Reality

To tease out this influence, I decided to look at three key legal developments that have played central roles in the relationship between the United States and Puerto

Rico throughout the past century. The first is a series of decisions by the U.S. Supreme Court issued from 1901 to 1922. They are collectively known as the *Insular Cases* and provide the basic legal framework for U.S. actions since the acquisition of Puerto Rico in 1898. The second development, the extension of U.S. citizenship to Puerto Ricans in 1917, has probably been the most important decision made by the United States regarding the political future and the lives and struggles of Puerto Ricans. The third development is the gradual establishment in Puerto Rico of a system of partial democracy based on the notion of the rule of law and the discourse of rights. The operation of that system within a relationship of political subordination to the United States has proved to be one of the most interesting features of American colonialism in Puerto Rico.

I use these legal developments and their effects to analyze the process of production of American hegemony in Puerto Rico and the shaping of conflicts over legal, political, and cultural identities and subjectivities. To develop my argument, I have relied on several theoretical perspectives and assumptions that are briefly explained below and then developed more fully in later chapters.

Puerto Rico as a Nation

The first assumption relates to the debate about whether Puerto Rico should or should not be considered a nation, which in turn hinges on one's conception of what constitutes a nation. Nations do not have essences, in the sense of immutable constitutive traits. *Nation* is rather a sociocultural construct used to refer to certain collective phenomena, which usually consist of groups or communities of people with perceptible common characteristics and a sense among its members of belonging to the collectivity.[11] Beyond that basic notion, there may be great disagreement over the nature of the common elements necessary for a nation to be said to exist. There may also be discrepancies regarding the weight that should be accorded so-called objective and subjective criteria. The debate may be of an academic nature. But, as the case of Puerto Rico shows, it is also a political polemic in which participants take positions influenced by their preferred visions of the community's future.

A source of confusion is the fact that the term "nation" has been used by many people to mean "nation-state." Because Puerto Rico is not a sovereign state, it cannot be properly called a nation, the argument goes.[12] Others insist that a nation can exist

---

[11] *See* NANCY MORRIS, PUERTO RICO: CULTURE, POLITICS, AND IDENTITY 12–13 (1995). Centering on subjective criteria, Morris defined a nation as a "self-defined community of people who share a sense of solidarity based on a belief in a common heritage and who claim political rights that may include self-determination," *Id.* at 15. She pointed out that the "group's self-recognition as a nation is usually based on some combination of objective characteristics of history, language, culture, and territory," and clarified that, "the claim to political self-determination is not necessarily tantamount to a desire for political independence." *Id.*

[12] *See* Alaska Rep. Don Young's statement that "Puerto Rico is not a nation" and his suggestion that it would become so only if it became an independent country. Rep. Young supports statehood for Puerto Rico. *See also,* the assertion by Carlos Romero Barceló, Puerto Rico's resident commissioner in Washington, that "Puerto Rico is not a nation. Puerto Rico is a community," adding that "there is no such thing as a nation in Puerto Rico." Romero Barceló, who is an ardent statehood advocate, clarified, nevertheless, that, although in "geo-political" terms it is not, maybe "sociologically" Puerto Rico could be considered "a nation." U.S. CONGRESS, 144 CONG. REC. H823, H822, H829 (daily ed. March 4, 1998) (statements by Rep. Young; Res. Comm. Romero Barceló).

without being a sovereign state. They point to the Basques, the Catalans, the Scots, and other "national" groups that live within larger multinational states.

Academic, political, and popular opinions weightily indicate that most Puerto Ricans view themselves as a distinct national group. In her 1995 study on Puerto Rican culture and identity, Morris arrived at the conclusion that "Puerto Rico is a nation—a self-defined community of people who share a sense of solidarity based on a belief in a common heritage, and who claim the right to political self-determination." [13] She reported that many of her interviewees, across all status preferences, "contended that Puerto Rico was itself a nation, defining the term with references to Puerto Rico's distinct history and culture." [14] Some of her pro-statehood respondents clarified that Puerto Rico was a "sociological nation," presumably to explain the strong feeling of nationality evident within the Puerto Rican population despite the fact that Puerto Rico is not a sovereign state. [15]

Analogous perceptions were reflected in a study conducted in 1993 for Ateneo Puertorriqueño, one of the leading cultural institutions in Puerto Rico. [16] Its authors reported that 97.3% of those interviewed answered that they regarded themselves as Puerto Ricans. The same study showed that a majority (56.2%) believed Puerto Rican culture to be "very different" from American culture. Thirty percent thought that the two cultures were "somewhat different." An overwhelming majority (78.3%) held the opinion that it was "extremely important" for Puerto Ricans to preserve their national identity. And close to the same proportion (74.5%) expressed that they considered themselves to be "Puerto Rican first, and American next." Asked to select from a series of alternative courses of action if Puerto Rico ever became a state of the union and the United States required English as the "official language" of Puerto Rico, 93.3% answered that they would not relinquish Spanish as their language. All these reactions clearly point to a very strong sense of national identity among those surveyed. [17]

This subjective feeling among Puerto Ricans is based on centuries of intensely shared experiences. Those experiences have been lived within the territorial boundaries of the islands known as Puerto Rico and, during this century, inside larger

---

[13] Morris, *supra* note 11, at 15.

[14] *Id.* at 76.

[15] *Id.* at 76–77. Morris quoted from a statehood advocate: "Basically what we're saying is that sociologically, Puerto Rico has a distinct culture and to a certain extent a distinct sociological nationhood. In terms that you have a distinct people, in a distinct geographic locality, with a distinct language, distinct dialect within that language, with its own literature, its own music, its own everything. And in that sense, sociologically speaking we are a nation." *Id.* at 77.

[16] HISPANIA RESEARCH CORPORATION, MEMORANDO ANALÍTICO SOBRE EL ESTUDIO DEL IDIOMA EN PUERTO RICO—SOMETIDO A: ATENEO PUERTORRIQUEÑO 56, 58, 59, 60 (1993).

[17] Even Puerto Rican "postnationalist" intellectuals who have severely questioned traditional nationalist discourse highlight the fact that the majority of Puerto Ricans view themselves as a "nation" without a state. They refer to the existence of a "national subjectivity" and to how the *Estado Libre Asociado* managed to resignify the meaning of the "national" in Puerto Rico and to "reproduce a discourse that has effectively constituted 'national' subjects (at least culturally)." In their view, Puerto Ricans perceive themselves both as a nation and as an ethnic group, depending on the context. For that reason, they conclude that Puerto Ricans must be considered to constitute an "ethno-nation." PUERTO RICAN JAM: ESSAYS ON CULTURE AND POLITICS 11–12, 17–19 (Frances Negrón-Muntaner & Ramón Grosfoguel Ed. 1997). For the suggestion that Puerto Ricans in the United States may be considered an ethnic group, while those in Puerto Rico would constitute a nation, see Morris, *supra* note 11, at 12.

communities in the United States, where Puerto Ricans have kept close associations among themselves based on their own, or their parents', national origin.

These realities warrant reference to Puerto Rico as a nation, albeit a nation without its own sovereign state. More to the point, it may be described as a nation in a relationship of political subordination to a metropolitan state.

Puerto Rico as a Colony of the United States

The above definition of Puerto Rico as a nation brings forth the second assumption underlying my work. I proceed from the premise that the relationship between the United States and Puerto Rico is still colonial in nature. This notion has gained increasing acceptance throughout the Puerto Rican political spectrum.[18] My position is based on a number of considerations.

Puerto Rico is considered "unincorporated territory" by the United States. This means that it is deemed to "belong to" the latter, without being a part of it. According to American constitutional doctrine, this legal and political status implies that the U.S. Congress may exercise "plenary powers" over Puerto Rico. Plenary powers is the exclusive authority to legislate over Puerto Rican affairs, subject only to the restrictions imposed by fundamental individual rights as interpreted by the U.S. Supreme Court. By virtue of that power Congress legislates over many fundamental aspects of Puerto Rican life, including citizenship, the currency, the postal service, foreign affairs, military defense, communications, labor relations, the environment, commerce, finance, health and welfare, and many others. The executive branch of the U.S. government performs important governmental functions in Puerto Rico. The U.S. military possesses numerous installations and carries out multiple operations in Puerto Rican territory. When in force in the United States, the military draft has been extended to Puerto Rico residents.

Many provisions of the U.S. Constitution apply to Puerto Rico. These include the supremacy clause of Article VI, that prescribes that the Constitution, laws, and treaties of the United States shall be the supreme law of the land; the territorial clause of Article IV, granting the U.S. Congress the power to make rules and regulations for the territory or other property of the U.S.; and many of the guarantees of the Bill of Rights. Decisions of the U.S. Supreme Court are binding on the island. In certain circumstances, that court may review decisions rendered by the Supreme Court of Puerto Rico. The U.S. District Court for the District of Puerto Rico and a U.S. Court of Appeals pass judgment over a variety of legal controversies that affect the country's government and population.

Despite the overwhelming power the United States exercises over Puerto Rico, the latter does not participate directly in decisions taken on the many matters mentioned above. Neither does it elect those responsible for making the decisions. Residents of Puerto Rico do not vote for the president of the United States or send

---

[18] A former secretary of justice and former chief justice of the Supreme Court of Puerto Rico has referred to Puerto Rico as the "oldest colony in the world." *See* JOSÉ TRÍAS MONGE, PUERTO RICO: THE TRIALS OF THE OLDEST COLONY IN THE WORLD (1997).

representatives to the U.S. Senate or House of Representatives, except for a non-voting resident commissioner for Puerto Rico, who sits in the latter body.[19]

In sum, Puerto Rico can be considered an overseas possession of the United States, to which it is legally, politically, militarily, and economically subordinate. At the same time, as we saw before, Puerto Ricans constitute a distinct nationality, with their own national culture and traditions.[20] Since Puerto Rico's emergence as a distinct sociocultural entity, its history has been that of a subordinated nation. This book explains the legal and social construction of that subordination under American rule.

The Concept of Hegemony

The pervasive acceptance of U.S. rule and the American presence within Puerto Rican society poses a crucial question. How has this adhesion been produced? This phenomenon is best understood through the theoretical concept of hegemony. In this book I use the concept in the basic sense given it by Italian Marxist philosopher Antonio Gramsci and by theorists who have elaborated upon his analysis.[21] Gramsci used the theoretical category *hegemony* to explain the process by which a social class

---

[19] The resident commissioner can vote in congressional committees to which he is assigned, but he cannot cast a final vote on legislation proposed in the House.

On January 5, 1993, the House of Representatives amended its rules to allow resident commissioners and delegates from the territories to vote in the "Committee of the Whole." This is the name given to the House when it considers amendments to most bills reported out of the standing or select committees. However, as adopted, the amended rules required that a new vote be taken if the votes cast by the commissioners or delegates in the Committee of the Whole had made the difference. This new vote was to be taken technically in the full House itself. The commissioners or delegates could not participate in the decisive second round. Rules of the House of Representatives, Rules XII (2) and XXII (2) (d), as amended by H.R. 5.

This rule change survived an attack on its constitutionality by Republican members of the House of Representatives. The Republicans alleged that granting the delegates and the resident commissioner the prerogative to vote in the Committee of the Whole endowed them with legislative power, in violation of Art. I and other provisions of the U.S. Constitution. *See* Michel v. Anderson, 817 F. Supp. 126 (1993), *aff'd* 14 F.3rd 623 (D.C. Cir. 1994). Judge H. H. Greene, rendering the opinion of the district court, characterized the new rules as "meaningless," as they failed to grant the representatives from the territories any effective legislative power.

After the Republicans gained a majority in the House following the 1994 congressional elections, the applicable rules were amended once again, this time to revoke the right of the delegates and resident commissioners to vote in the Committee of the Whole, thus returning to the situation that existed prior to the rule amendment of 1993. *See* H.R. 6, 104th Cong., 1st Sess. (1995).

[20] For a brief, but cogent, argument that Puerto Rico fits the definition of a colony accepted by the international community, see Ediberto Román, *Empire Forgotten: The United States' Colonization of Puerto Rico*, 42 VILLANOVA L. REV. 1119, 1137–39 (1997).

[21] *See* ANTONIO GRAMSCI, SELECTIONS FROM THE PRISON NOTEBOOKS (Q. Hoare & G. N. Smith Eds. & Trans. 1971), *and, among others*, HEGEMONÍA Y ALTERNATIVAS POLÍTICAS EN AMÉRICA LATINA (J. Labastida Martín del Campo Ed. 1985); ROBERT BOCOCK, HEGEMONY (1986); Maureen Cain, *Gramsci, the State and the Place of Law*, in LEGALITY, IDEOLOGY AND THE STATE (David Sugarman Ed. 1983); Eugene D. Genovese, *The Hegemonic Function of Law*, in MARXISM AND LAW (P. Beirne & R. Quinney Eds. 1982); A. S. Sassoon, *Hegemony, in* A DICTIONARY OF MARXIST THOUGHT (T. Bottomore et al. Eds. 1983); Bob Jessop, *On Recent Marxist Theories of Law, the State and Juridico-Political Ideology*, 8 INT'L J. SOC. LAW 339 (1980); Austin Sarat & Thomas R. Kearns, *Beyond the Great Divide: Forms of Legal Scholarship and Everyday Life*, in LAW IN EVERYDAY LIFE (Austin Sarat & Thomas R. Kearns Eds. 1993); ROGER COTTERRELL, THE SOCIOLOGY OF LAW 3 (2nd ed. 1992).

or bloc of social groups wins consent to its historical project from other classes or groupings in society relying mostly on noncoercive mechanisms.[22] He defined *hegemony* as

> the "spontaneous" consent given by the great masses of the population to the general direction imposed on social life by the dominant fundamental group. This consent is "historically" caused by the prestige (and consequent confidence) which the dominant group enjoys because of its position and function in the world of production.[23]

In Gramsci's theoretical system, hegemony is both a strategy of domination and the kind of domination resulting from its successful realization.[24] The production of hegemony requires several conditions. It depends on the dominant group's capacity for intellectual, political, and moral leadership, as well as on its willingness to incorporate the demands of other groups and satisfy them, at least partially. This leaves room for subordinated sectors to obtain some advantages in exchange for their willingness to submit to the rule of the dominant group. Furthermore, the dominant group's hegemonic position rests on the perception by others that it has the requisite knowledge, resources, and experience to manage the general affairs of society. The group's hegemonic position is possible to the extent that the "common sense" prevailing in the general population can be shaped by the group's worldview.[25]

Hegemony, therefore, has both an ideological and a material foundation. The material foundation is what Gramsci called the "decisive nucleus of economic activity."[26] In this sense, the Gramscian notion of hegemony resembles German philosopher and social theorist Jürgen Habermas's contention that in advanced capitalist societies the legitimation of political systems cannot be separated from the satisfaction of needs.[27]

The widespread adherence to American rule and presence in Puerto Rico is the

---

[22] The concept of hegemony is also used, especially in international studies, to refer to the domination of one country over another. Sassoon, *supra* note 21, at 201. Thus, historians of American imperialism speak of the "hegemony" of the United States over countries in the Caribbean. *See, e.g.,* DAVID HEALEY, DRIVE TO HEGEMONY: THE UNITED STATES IN THE CARIBBEAN, 1898–1917 (1988). This meaning and the sense given the term in Gramscian approaches may well converge in the context of situations of "modern colonialism," like those prevalent in Puerto Rico and other countries of the Caribbean. This book is concerned, to a great extent, with that convergence. However, most of the time, the concept will be used in the Gramscian sense.

[23] GRAMSCI, *supra* note 21, at 12.

[24] For a critique of the use of the concept "hegemony" as equivalent to domination, see Nancy A. Weston, *The Fate, Violence, and Rhetoric of Contemporary Legal Thought: Reflections on the Amherst Series, the Loss of Truth, and Law*, 22 L. & SOC. INQ. 733 (1997).

[25] Subordinated groups may also exercise their hegemony over other groups in their struggle to become the dominant groups in society. GRAMSCI, *supra* note 21, at 53.

[26] "Undoubtedly the fact of hegemony presupposes that account be taken of the interests and the tendencies of the groups over which hegemony is to be exercised, and that a certain compromise equilibrium should be formed—in other words, that the leading group should make sacrifices of an economic–corporate kind. But there is also no doubt that such sacrifices and such a compromise cannot touch the essential; for though hegemony is ethical–political, it must also be *economic*, must necessarily be based on the decisive function exercised by the leading group in the *decisive nucleus of economic activity*." *Id.* at 161 (emphasis added).

For a critique of "neo-Gramscian" approaches to hegemony that privilege its politico-ideological dimensions in detriment of its "decisive economic nucleus" or its relationship to the "structural sources of power," see Jessop, *supra* note 21, at 109–24.

[27] *See* JÜRGEN HABERMAS, LEGITIMATION CRISIS (1988).

result and manifestation of American hegemony. That hegemony has been produced by conditions similar to those described by Gramsci and has been based on both ideological and material factors.

A problem with Gramsci's theory of hegemony is his apparent overemphasis on the role of civil society as compared to the state in the production of consent.[28] That slant may be due to the fact that he wrote before the massive development of the welfare state. He did indicate, however, that the division between state and civil society was only "methodological," and he was careful to stress the "overlaps" to be found in actual societies.[29] The matter, however, is of more substance than that. Contemporary states cannot rely simply on forced compliance. They must be able to persuade. The legitimation needs of the welfare state—despite its apparent retrenchment in the age of neo-liberalism—still require the production of persuasion through various mechanisms.[30]

Furthermore, the claims of superior technical knowledge on which the dominant groups frequently justify their rule are tested through their performance in the direct or indirect management of the state apparatus for the satisfaction of needs and demands. A theory of hegemony that takes account of the realities of the modern state would have to ponder the many economic, political, and ideological practices whose source is primarily the state and that contribute to the production of consent. My analysis of the Puerto Rican situation will focus on state-generated policies that have been able to secure hegemony.

Hegemony and the Dynamics of Power

Despite its theoretical difficulties, the concept of hegemony provides a solid starting point from which to construct explanations of the ways power is exerted in contemporary societies. The concept enables one to explain power relationships defined by class, gender, race, ethnicity, nationality, sexuality, belief, or geography. The specific question arises, however, whether the concept is applicable to the relationship between a metropolitan state and the population of its colonial dependency. Is not colonialism primarily the product of force, rather than persuasion? Is it adequate to speak of the hegemonic project of the metropolitan state? Should we refer, rather, to the hegemonic strategy of the dominant groups within that state? In the colonial context, is hegemony realized to a greater degree through the activities of the state? Is the "colonial population" the subordinate group? Or should we make distinctions among groups within the colonial society itself? Is the "American colonial project" distinct from the economic project of capitalist expansion and penetration? Many of these questions will be addressed in the chapters that follow in the context of the analysis of concrete situations.

At this point, however, the following propositions are put forth to support the view that modern colonial relationships in general, and the relationship between the

---

[28] Gramsci inherited the distinction between civil society and the state from Hegel and Marx. In this formulation, civil society is the sphere of "private" action. *See, e.g.,* KARL MARX, CRÍTICA DE LA FILOSOFÍA DEL ESTADO DE HEGEL (P. A. Encinares trans. 1961). The institutions of civil society include churches, schools, labor unions, and so forth. GRAMSCI, *supra* note 21, at 56, editors' n.5.

[29] Sassoon, *supra* note 21, at 202.

[30] HABERMAS, *supra* note 27; Sassoon, *supra* note 21, at 202.

United States and Puerto Rico in particular, are susceptible to analysis using the Gramscian notion of hegemony.[31]

In its origins, the U.S. colonial project in the Caribbean region was tied to military concerns and to the need for new markets for the realization of capital.[32] U.S. colonialism was a project that involved social and economic class considerations as much as particular military objectives. Therefore, the hegemonic strategies that ensued were related to the perceptions that the dominant economic groups and the military establishment entertained about the usefulness of those strategies to their short- or long-term interests.

Throughout the 20th century, the relative weight of those perspectives may have shifted at different moments, but those two fundamental considerations—economic and strategic—have remained constant. In sum, the project has responded to the perceived needs and power objectives of specific dominant groups within American society. (This will be discussed further in chapters 1 and 3). It is fitting, then, to tie the resulting type of colonial domination to the interests and strategies of such groups, and the Gramscian theory of hegemony provides us the framework to do that.

Moreover, in the specific context of Puerto Rico, acceptance of the colonial regime has been directly linked to the emergence of a common sense that has seen as natural the development of a capitalist economy and a liberal democratic state. In this regard, class domination and colonial rule are intertwined, so that hegemonic strategies designed to preserve class rule are integral parts of the colonial project. Furthermore, as will be demonstrated in chapters 7 and 8, the colonial project in Puerto Rico has relied on eliciting consent from substantial segments of the Puerto Rican population to its close association with the United States. The Gramscian notion of hegemony, therefore, is appropriate to examine the dynamics whereby this type of consent is secured and reproduced.

When viewed from the perspective of the internal dynamics of Puerto Rican society, there are three senses in which the question of hegemony and colonialism are related. First of all, for some time, the majority of Puerto Ricans obviously has acquiesced to what has been a colonial relationship. The *Estado Libre Asociado* commanded overwhelming electoral support. Even many of those who aspired to enhanced autonomy or even statehood were satisfied that the arrangement could be accepted as a provisional status until a "better" blueprint could be found. That is still the case with many people. This is what some authors have called "colonialism by consent."[33]

Second, American hegemony has been constructed within colonialism. Acceptance of the American presence and American rule has been produced within the

---

[31] For an early, succinct, and perceptive analysis of the production of American hegemony in Puerto Rico in the Gramscian sense, with a particular reference to the role of civil rights in the process, see Wilfredo Mattos Cintrón, *La hegemonía de Estados Unidos en Puerto Rico y el independentismo, los derechos civiles y la cuestión nacional*, 16 EL CARIBE CONTEMPORÁNEO 21 (1988); *see also* Efrén Rivera Ramos, *Self-Determination and Decolonisation in the Society of the Modern Colonial Welfare State, in* ISSUES OF SELF-DETERMINATION (William Twining Ed. 1991). For more recent applications, see Román, *supra* note 20; Román, *supra* note 10; HÉCTOR MELÉNDEZ, GRAMSCI EN LA DE DIEGO: TRES ENSAYOS SOBRE CULTURA NACIONAL, POSMODERNIDAD E IDEOLOGÍA (1994).

[32] This matter is discussed in detail in chapter 1.

[33] *See, e.g.,* Rivera Ramos, *supra* note 31, at 121; Román, *supra* note 20, at 1177.

confines and dynamics of a colonial relationship. Third, the "solution" to colonialism is increasingly viewed by a substantial number of people as occurring within close ties with the United States. This means that if the current specific institutional arrangement—the *Estado Libre Asociado*—were to be superseded by another that implied either legal incorporation into the United States or some other type of semiautonomous link to the metropolitan state, it will be done under conditions of hegemony.

Finally, in all modern colonial cases the metropolitan state has been the fundamental coordinator of strategies, policies, and actions regarding the control of the colonial territory. In this sense, it is appropriate to refer to the hegemonic practices of the metropolitan state. In the type of colonialism that survived the post-World War II decolonization wave, of which Puerto Rico is a typical example, state-directed hegemonic practices have been a central component of the colonialist project.

Because of this state direction, it is important to consider the heterogeneous nature of the metropolitan state. The dominant groups in the state are not constituted homogeneously. There are diverse interests, views, and strategies pursued within the state. Sometimes they conflict, as will be readily seen in the discussion of the *Insular Cases* in chapters 4 to 6. It has been necessary in this book, therefore, to identify the conflicting trends and perspectives, as well as the compromises, within the various forces that control the metropolitan government. Moreover, in the United States, the principle of separation of powers produces a particular governing logic that must be taken into consideration when analyzing the processes by which colonial policies are developed, justified, and implemented.

The chapters in Part II, on the judicial construction of colonialism, and chapter 7, on the effects of the decision by the U.S. Congress to extend U.S. citizenship to Puerto Ricans, will bring to light the roles played by the different branches of the federal government in this process. They will illuminate the distribution of powers devised to deal with the situation of the territories. The internal governing logic of each branch, although relatively autonomous, is not totally independent of the entire institutional framework. Nor is it, in practice, divorced from the larger interests of the metropolitan state and the shared ideological perspectives of its dominant governing groups. Despite the differing views with respect to specific policy decisions, in the final analysis there has always been a remarkable consensus regarding the need to reaffirm the power of the United States over the territory of Puerto Rico.

The relationship of colonial domination is frequently mediated through an internal state apparatus in the colonial territory. Thus, in the case of Puerto Rico, one may speak of the state as composed of two closely intertwined levels. One level—the dominant one—is the "metropolitan state" properly called, and the other—in a relation of subordination—is the "internal," "local," or "territorial" state apparatus. In Puerto Rico, this internal level was for a long time referred to as the "insular government." Since the establishment of the Commonwealth of Puerto Rico in 1952, it is frequently referred to as "the government of Puerto Rico," or simply, "the Commonwealth government."

The colonial state, then, is constituted by the sets of institutions, functions, practices, and relationships that result from the interaction between the two levels. This is crucial for a better understanding of the question of hegemony. In Puerto Rico, there is a degree of relative autonomy of this internal government, especially regarding some areas of governance. The "local" level is an arena for the internal conflicts of the colonial society. In many ways, it is also constituted through conflict and compromise, as the creation of the Commonwealth in 1952 exemplified. Since the early days of the American occupation, Puerto Rican subhegemonic groups have vied for the control of this internal institutional space. The hegemonic effects of how it has been organized and administered will be explored in chapter 8.

As in similar colonial situations, the specific forms of the relationship of subordination between the United States and Puerto Rico are shaped by three types of forces. First and foremost, the relationship is molded by the efforts of the metropolitan state and its dominant groups to consolidate or maintain their rule. Second, it is influenced by the mediating activities of groups and individuals within the colonial society that enjoy subhegemonic positions or benefit in one way or another from the relationship with the metropolitan state. Finally, the relationship is affected by the acquiescence, struggle, and resistance of the various sectors of the people in the colonial territory. Those struggles and forms of resistance are varied and have varied effects. They are not always identical with the proindependence movement. Part III, more directly concerned with the problem of hegemony, examines some of those responses in the context of the analysis of the effects of U.S. citizenship and the discourse of rights.[34]

The question of American hegemony in Puerto Rico points to what may be regarded as a paradox. How is it that Puerto Ricans, subjected to American colonial rule for a century, profess such attachment to the U.S. economic, legal, and political system? Part III is entirely dedicated to answering that question. In my case, however, raising the question does not rest on any essentialist or naturalistic claim that it is the "destiny" of nations or nationalities to have their own independent nation-states. After all, some national communities in the contemporary world do not express such aspiration. In fact, international law recognizes diverse ways in which colonized nations may resolve their colonial problem.

What I raise is a historical question. It is based, first of all, on the historical fact that during the 20th century most colonial societies sought to realize their self-determination claims through independence. Why, despite this overwhelming historical tendency, has the Puerto Rican population not opted for that route? In Chapters 7 and 8 I provide historical and sociological explanations for this. However, the historical puzzle is incomplete without understanding how the colonized society has come to associate its present and future welfare with its ties to the colonizer.

During the past decades there has been a growing awareness among the population that its relationship to the United States is colonial in nature. There has been a swelling feeling among Puerto Ricans that the United States is denying them their fundamental right of self-determination. There have been many instances of massive rejection of the concrete consequences of colonialism, such as the harm being caused

---

[34] I do not subscribe to the notion that the theory of hegemony precludes explanations based on the capacity of subordinate cultures for resistance. *See, e.g.,* Román, *supra* note 20, at 1178, discussing T. J. Jackson Lears, *The Concept of Cultural Hegemony: Problems and Possibilities*, 90 AMER. HIST. REV. 567 (1985). In fact, Román's analyses, based on the notion of hegemony, point to important manifestations of resistance on the part of Puerto Ricans to colonial subordination, such as "the well-publicized armed conflicts against the U.S. government from the 1950s to the 1980s" and the many efforts at gaining "greater citizenship rights." Román, *supra* note 20, at 1179; Román, *supra* note 10, at 41. The questions of hegemony, coercion, resistance, and rights are discussed in detail in chapter 8.

to the island of Vieques or the punishing attitude taken toward Puerto Rican political prisoners.

But none of this refutes the fact that Puerto Rico still desires to keep its ties to the United States. It only deepens the paradox that such growing dissatisfaction with its colonial condition has been accompanied by an increasing acceptance of the desirability of preserving the link with the metropolitan state.

The explanation of this phenomenon rests on a crucial distinction. One part of this distinction rests on the acceptance or rejection of the present arrangement— another part is defining the extent to which American presence and rule are deemed desirable. Puerto Ricans may come to overwhelmingly decry the *Estado Libre Asociado* as a colonial deal that does not meet their critical needs. Yet, they may decide that the future is better guaranteed by remaining in a close relationship, no matter what the version, with the United States.

This would, in fact, be the fullest realization of American hegemony. The analysis in this book provides the explanation to that eventuality. The legal framework developed during the past 100 years contributes to and supports this paradox and, in that sense, helps to understand the social and psychological underpinnings of the power relations between the United States and Puerto Rico.

The Legal Construction of Hegemony

Law contributes to the reproduction of hegemony and colonialism. This is the basic theoretical claim regarding law made in this book. It relies on the assumption that law possesses the capacity to construct social realities. In this regard, the analysis draws from insights developed by a substantial body of literature that has forged what can be considered a new theoretical paradigm in social and legal studies: the "constitutive theory of law." [35]

As a general theoretical proposition, law can be considered constitutive of the

---

[35] This body of literature has emerged from different traditions of thought and spans a wide range of cultural and geographical contexts. *See, e.g.,* Robert W. Gordon, *Critical Legal Histories,* 36 STAN. L. REV. 57, 102–09 (1984); Andrew Fraser, *The Legal Theory We Need Now,* 8 SOC. REV. 147, 147–54 (1978); MARK KELMAN, A GUIDE TO CRITICAL LEGAL STUDIES 253–57 (1987); Pierre Bourdieu, *The Force of Law: Toward a Sociology of the Juridical Field,* 38 HASTINGS L. J. 805, 839 (1987); Richard Terdiman, *Translator's Introduction* in Bourdieu, *The Force of Law, supra* at 805–06; Susan S. Silbey & Austin Sarat, *Critical Traditions in Law and Society Research,* 21 L. & SOC. REV. 165 (1987–88); LAW IN EVERYDAY LIFE, *supra* note 21; Sarat & Kearns, *supra* note 21; Lisa E. Sánchez, *Boundaries of Legitimacy: Sex, Violence, Citizenship, and Community in a Local Sexual Economy,* 22 LAW & SOC. INQ. 543 (1997); Dianne Otto, *Subalternity and International Law: The Problems of Global Community and the Incommensurability of Difference,* 5 SOC. & LEG. STUD. 337, 351 (1996); and the collection of essays by authors from "First" and "Third" World countries in LABOUR, LAW AND CRIME: AN HISTORICAL PERSPECTIVE (F. G. Snyder & D. Hay Eds. 1987). Most of the works cited above fall within the fields of sociolegal studies, the social history of law, or the sociology of law. For some relatively recent scholarship in analytical jurisprudence that emphasizes that law must be viewed as forming part of the human and social world, that is, as a constitutive part of reality, *see, e.g.,* NEIL MACCORMICK & OTTA WEINBERGER, AN INSTITUTIONAL THEORY OF LAW: NEW APPROACHES TO LEGAL POSITIVISM (1986); PETER NERHOT, LAW, INTERPRETATION AND REALITY (1989); WILLIAM TWINING & DAVID MYERS, HOW TO DO THINGS WITH RULES (2nd ed. 1982). For a critical assessment of the constitutive theory of law as well as a discussion of some of the differences in meaning that have been assigned to the conception of law as constitutive of society, see Weston, *supra* note 24.

social world in at least two senses: first, because of the nature of legal acts, and second, because of the social effects of those acts. Legal acts form part of a particular type of discourse: legal discourse. *Discourse*—meaning a series of speech acts and their related practices[36]—has a certain materiality, the materiality characteristic of events.[37] An event is something that happens. In that sense it is part of reality. Legal acts, then, must be considered "events" that become part of the social world. Judicial decisions, legislative acts, and the actions taken by bureaucratic officials are events that become part of individual histories and of the history of a given community.[38]

Legal events tend to be recorded in various ways. When recorded, they acquire the materiality of texts. The interpretations of legal events and legal texts by the legal and general community also form part of the discourse of law. Those interpretations, too, constitute "events" whose records become texts that enter the current of reality. This continuous self-reproducing dynamic of legal events and legal texts, through particular practices, provides its materiality to a given legal culture. In all these senses, law—as event, text, and practice—becomes part of reality.

Legal events, moreover, can have certain effects. Therefore, law is constitutive of society also because of the effects it produces in the social world.[39] Again, as a general proposition, those effects are potentially diverse. Thus, law tends to become part of the social understandings within which people operate.[40] To express it in Gramsci's terms, law is constitutive of the common sense with which people interpret their lives and reproduce their social existence.[41] This amounts to asserting that law plays a role in the construction of subjectivity.

Law also helps to "structure the most routine practices of social life"[42] by either eliciting compliance or generating acts of resistance. In addition, in most instances, it provides the framework for legitimate discourse and action. In doing so, it proffers explicit justifications for the exercise of power; it defines what are to be considered legitimate needs, claims, and aspirations and circumscribes the array of legitimate means for their satisfaction and fulfillment.[43] Finally, law imposes constraints and affords opportunities for individual and collective action. In all these ways law becomes a context for social practice and action. To that extent, it becomes part of the "reality" within which social actors must live their lives and conduct their struggles.

---

[36] For this conception of discourse see MICHEL FOUCAULT: LA VERDAD Y LAS FORMAS JURÍDICAS 162–63 (Enrique Lynch trans. 3rd ed. 1988).

[37] *Id.* at 157.

[38] The legal decisions taken in the cases of Adolfo Marín Molinas, Isabella González, and Rafael Ortiz became part of their personal histories (in fact, they shaped their lives with varying degrees of force). They also have become part of the legal, political, and cultural history of Puerto Rico and the United States (also with different types of impact).

[39] The basic proposition, then, is that legal pronouncements—to the extent that they can be considered "speech acts" in the sense the term is used by philosophers like Austin, Foucault, and Lyotard—can be studied as events that have certain effects.

[40] As Fraser put it, law is related to the "intersubjective meanings" that go into the construction of social life. Fraser, *supra* note 35, at 147. Intersubjectivity, according to Fraser, is composed of the meanings rooted in social practice (and not merely of a convergence of individual beliefs). *Id.* at 185 n.4.

[41] Gordon argued that law is constitutive of society to the extent that it is constitutive of social consciousness. Gordon, *supra* note 35, at 125.

[42] *Id.*

[43] *See* Fraser, *supra* note 35, at 180.

In sum, law must be viewed as a dimension of social life overlaid or imbricated with the many aspects that converge in the constitution of a multidimensional reality.[44]

To affirm that law is constitutive of society, however, is not to assert that it is totally determinative of reality. Other determinants or conditioning factors may exert a greater weight. In many instances what law possesses is a limiting or conditioning capacity. In others, it may serve only as a generator of possibilities. Law may have the effect of constraining social action and of opening up alternatives for such action. The relative weight of diverse social factors in the constitution of law and of law in the constitution of reality is to be determined by detailed research for each society in each historical moment.[45] This book is such an exploration: an attempt at discerning how law—or a particular set of legal events—has contributed to the construction of a particular social reality. In this case, it is the reality embodied in the colonial relationship between the United States and Puerto Rico.

I have used the concept of legal events to refer to the set of decisions known as the *Insular Cases*, to the act extending U.S. citizenship to Puerto Ricans and, in a more generalized fashion, to the development of a social discourse that emphasizes the importance of rights, the rule of law, and democratic participation in Puerto Rican society. Those legal events, I argue, have had important social, cultural, and political effects. Furthermore, because those events are also social and historical products, I have offered my interpretation of the processes that have converged to produce them.

The main proposition is that law has become a constitutive part of the relationship between the United States and Puerto Rico and has had a significant role in the production of American hegemony in Puerto Rican society. It has contributed to shape and reshape identities and subjectivities. More specifically, legal categories and concepts like "unincorporated territory" and "plenary powers" have supported efforts to legitimate the exercise of colonial power. My analysis will demonstrate how categories like "U.S. citizen" have played a central role in the constitution of legal and political subjects over which the United States can exercise its power. Those subjects, in turn, have felt legitimated to place demands on the government of the United States.

I conclude that metropolitan law has created a discursive context that has set constraints on and provided opportunities for collective and individual actions of Puerto Rico and the United States. Moreover, law has been at the heart of the struggles for the definition of a Puerto Rican identity. Those struggles involve the tension between claiming rights of American citizenship and participation, on one hand, and asserting a separate cultural reality, on the other. In this sense, law has been crucial for issues of self-definition and self-perception, as many Puerto Ricans strive to harmonize their condition as American citizens with the perception that they form a distinct national group with particular characteristics. Finally, as the book ends, I argue that the development of legal consciousness and reliance on the discourse of rights influence the way Puerto Ricans conceive of alternatives to their present political, socioeconomic, and cultural situation.

---

[44] For similar ideas, see KELMAN, *supra* note 35 (there is an interpenetration of law and other aspects of social life); Silbey & Sarat, *supra* note 35, at 173 (law is "fused with and thus inseparable from all the activities of living and knowing"); LABOUR, LAW AND CRIME, *supra* note 35, at 10 (law is "a fundamental constitutive element in virtually all, if not all, socio-economic relations").

[45] *See* LABOUR, LAW AND CRIME, *supra* note 35, at 10–11.

Plan of the Book

The book is divided into three parts. Part I provides a historical overview of Puerto Rico and its relationship to the United States. The purpose is to provide a comprehensive backdrop against which to gauge the specific social and legal events and developments described in Parts II and III.

Chapter 1 describes the main forces behind the expansionist movement of the United States at the end of the 19th century. The story begins with the founding of the United States and continues to the Spanish American War. It looks at the way in which racism and such ideologies as Manifest Destiny and Social Darwinism combined with strategic, economic, and political concerns to give the movement its character. It provides several clues to fathoming the ensuing legal construction of American colonialism. Chapter 2 looks at the history of Puerto Rico before 1898 as a Spanish possession. It offers a picture of the community encountered by the invading U.S. forces and of some of the conditions that predisposed the Puerto Rican population to initially welcome the symbols and practices associated with American democracy. It also helps explain the conflicts over identity that have plagued the relationship between the United States and Puerto Rico. Chapter 3 sketches the main transformations experienced by Puerto Rico under the American regime. It supplies evidence for the assertion that Puerto Rico is, in effect, a modern colonial welfare state. It should help readers understand the situation the two countries face at the turn of the 21st century.

Part II, The Judicial Construction of Colonialism, scrutinizes the *Insular Cases* in three chapters. Chapter 4 describes how the Supreme Court elaborated the category of "unincorporated territories" to name the new territorial acquisitions. It explains the legal and constitutional meaning accorded the term. It highlights the debates within the Court and how they were eventually settled. In chapter 5, I discuss the legal theories the justices used to construct the doctrine of incorporation and the ideological perspectives that informed them. Those theories and ideologies, in turn, are connected to the ideological currents suffusing the expansionist movement discussed in chapter 1. Finally, chapter 6 explores the social, cultural, and political effects that have flowed from the legal doctrine established by the *Insular Cases*. I show how colonialism was constitutionally legitimated and the colonial project facilitated by the opinions of the Court. The analysis clarifies how the legal framework formulated by the Court still constrains possibilities for action and conditions self-determination processes.

Part III is dedicated to the ways in which hegemony has operated in Puerto Rican society and the place of law in that process. Chapter 7 studies the effects of extending U.S. citizenship to Puerto Ricans in 1917. After surmising the historical and political motives for the decision, I explore how U.S. citizenship has been intertwined with conflicts over identity, loyalty, and subjectivity. I argue that the status of U.S. citizen has become one of the key factors in the production of American hegemony because it is associated with tangible benefits and values.

In chapter 8, I venture into relatively uncharted terrain in the study of U.S.–Puerto Rican relations. I survey the roles of the discourse of rights, representative democracy, and the ideology of the rule of law in the production of American hegemony. This chapter most clearly reveals the distinct fashion in which modern colonialism has managed to bring the colonized into the colonizers' fold.

The book concludes with some general observations about the operation of law in modern colonial societies. After reviewing major specific findings regarding the evolution of Puerto Rican society in the context of colonialism, I speculate about the potential much longer term effects of those processes as they could manifest in a "postcolonial" Puerto Rico.

In telling this story and proffering my interpretation of these events, I have relied on abundant legal, historical, and sociological sources. However, there are narratives found in Puerto Rican literature, music, and the visual arts, to which I have been exposed since I was a child, that are not cited. They are deeply ingrained in my way of thinking and have probably influenced more than I know the account given in this book. The same may be said for the daily contact I have had with other Puerto Ricans living in Puerto Rico during most of my life and in the United States during much shorter periods. That firsthand knowledge, not reducible to notes or citations, is inevitably present in my interpretation of Puerto Rican history.

At a more conscious level, I have attempted to infuse my theoretical explanations with episodes that provide the names, locations, circumstances, and perspectives of the individuals involved. I hope that the generality of the discourse of theory is thus sufficiently nuanced by these particulars and by the insight I have gained from direct exposure to a culture that I, as a Puerto Rican, consider my own.

Part I

Essential History

Chapter 1
THE U.S. EXPANSIONIST DRIVE

The acquisition of the islands constituting the territory of Puerto Rico by the United States in 1898 was part of a process of expansion that had been initiated long before in American history. The factors that gave impulse to American expansionism and the cultural understandings that suffused it with meaning helped to construct the phase of Puerto Rico's colonial experience inaugurated with the Spanish American War. This chapter describes that crucial process.[1]

From Continental to Overseas Expansion

The U.S. expansionist drive and eventual emergence as a world imperial power must be explained in terms of a complex articulation of forces, motives, and determinants whose development, precise configuration, and relative weight have varied since the early days of the Republic. Economic, political, social, cultural, and ideological forces, as well as international and domestic concerns, all play a role.

The United States of America was born and constituted through expansion. In fact, expansion throughout the North American continent and beyond was envisioned even before the Republic was established. The Articles of Confederation authorized the admission of Canada and other colonies if such admission were agreed to by nine states. In the Treaty of Alliance, which Benjamin Franklin concluded with France in 1778, there was a provision to the effect that in the event that the United States succeeded in the "reduction" of the British empire in northern America or the islands of Bermudas, such territories should be confederated with or made dependent upon the United States.[2] As Justice Fuller expressed it in his dissenting opinion in *Downes v. Bidwell*, "The rising sun to which Franklin referred at the close

---

[1] The main sources consulted for this chapter have been JULIUS W. PRATT, EXPANSIONISTS OF 1898: THE ACQUISITION OF HAWAII AND THE SPANISH ISLANDS (1936); AMERICAN IMPERIALISM IN 1898 (T. P. Greene Ed. 1955); E. R. MAY, AMERICAN IMPERIALISM: A SPECULATIVE ESSAY (1968); J. A. HOBSON, IMPERIALISM: A STUDY (1972); ROBIN F. WESTON, RACISM IN U.S. IMPERIALISM: THE INFLUENCE OF RACIAL ASSUMPTIONS ON AMERICAN FOREIGN POLICY, 1893–1946 (1972); GEORGE LISKA, CAREER OF EMPIRE: AMERICA AND IMPERIAL EXPANSION OVER LAND AND SEA (1978); 1 JOSÉ TRÍAS MONGE, HISTORIA CONSTITUCIONAL DE PUERTO RICO (1980); JUAN BOSCH, DE CRISTÓBAL COLÓN A FIDEL CASTRO: EL CARIBE, FRONTERA IMPERIAL (1983): DAVID HEALEY, DRIVE TO HEGEMONY: THE UNITED STATES IN THE CARIBBEAN, 1898–1917 (1988); MARÍA EUGENIA ESTADES FONT, LA PRESENCIA MILITAR DE ESTADOS UNIDOS EN PUERTO RICO 1898–1918 (1988); J. P. NEDERVEEN PIETERSE, EMPIRE AND EMANCIPATION: POWER AND LIBERATION ON A WORLD SCALE (1990); Warren Zimmermann, *Jingoes, Goo-Goos, and the Rise of America's Empire*, WILSON Q. 42 (Spring 1998). For a commentary on the American historiography on American imperialism, see CARMELO DELGADO CINTRÓN, DERECHO Y COLONIALISMO: LA TRAYECTORIA HISTÓRICA DEL DERECHO PUERTORRIQUEÑO 11–16 (1988).

[2] *See* Argument of the Solicitor General of the United States *in* De Lima v. Bidwell, 182 U.S. 1, 141–42 (1901).

of the convention, they well knew, was that *star of empire*, whose course Berkeley had sung sixty years before."[3]

Thus the expansionist course throughout the continent was launched. First there was the search for lands, furs, and gold, and then came efforts to extend the plantation economy and the slave trade. Throughout, the process was consummated at the expense of the European powers (Great Britain, France, Spain) and Mexico and, above all, of the indigenous populations of North America. But the vision of empire extended beyond the continent as well. By the mid-1850s Thomas H. Benton, ex-senator from Missouri, referring to the process of expansion, summarized what some may have considered an extreme view, but which was not at all uncommon:

> Vast and varied accessions are still expected. Arizona has been acquired, fifty millions were offered to Mexico for her northern half, to include Monterey and Saltillo; a vast sum is now offered for Sonora and Sinaloa, down to Guaymas; Tehuantepec, Nicaragua, Panama, Darien, the Spanish part of Santo Domingo, Cuba, with islands on both sides of the tropical continent. Nor do we stop at the two Americas, their coasts and islands, extensive as they are, but circumvolving the terraqueous globe, we look wistfully at the Sandwich Islands, and, on some gem in the Polynesian group, and plunging to the antipodes pounce down upon Formosa in the China Sea. Such were the schemes of the last administration, and must continue, if its policy should continue. Over all these provinces, isthmuses, islands, and ports, now free, our Constitution must spread . . . overriding and overruling all anti-slavery law in their respective limits, and planting African slavery in its place, beyond the power of Congress or the people there to prevent it.[4]

Interest in the Caribbean Region

American statesmen and politicians had manifested specific interest in the Caribbean region even before the constitution of the Republic. Before the American War of Independence, Benjamin Franklin had advised England to take possession of the island of Cuba.[5] After independence, five of the first six presidents of the Republic (the exception was Washington) were actively concerned with the question of the desirability of acquiring that island.[6] Worries about the possibility of Cuba's falling into the possession of one of the rising European powers, notably England or France, figured prominently in the factors that led to the proclamation of the Monroe Doctrine in 1823.[7] John Quincy Adams, Monroe's successor to the presidency, referred to the Caribbean islands as the "natural appendages" of the North American continent.[8] But it was Adams himself who expressed most clearly that, desirable though the

---

[3] Downes v. Bidwell, 182 U.S. 244, 374 (1901) (emphasis added).

[4] THOMAS H. BENTON, HISTORICAL AND LEGAL EXAMINATION OF THE DRED SCOTT CASE (1857), *quoted in* Argument of the Attorney General of the United States *in* De Lima v. Bidwell, *supra* note 2, at 29. Senator Benton's statement reflects the degree to which the expansionist movement and mood in the United States in the years preceding the Civil War were related to the slavery question.

[5] TRÍAS MONGE, *supra* note 1, at 135.

[6] *Id.*

[7] *Id.* at 136.

[8] LISKA, *supra* note 1, at 123.

annexation of Cuba, and perhaps other islands in the region, may have been, the United States was not ready still to tackle the overseas annexationist venture.[9]

Just before the Civil War, however, the United States completed its continental expansion.[10] After the war a renewed interest toward the Caribbean, as well as the Pacific, emerged among merchants, financiers, statesmen, and members of the military elite. This interest was buttressed by the vast sums of capital accumulated by the steel and arms manufacturers and traders during the war, a situation that fostered the search for new sites for investment and expansion.[11] A steady stream of private investment started to move toward the Caribbean region, leading to the establishment of agricultural, manufacturing, financial, and commercial concerns belonging to American corporations or individuals.

The U.S. government also made efforts to implant an American presence in the region through the possession of territories or bases. Early attempts at acquiring possessions in the Caribbean included (a) new bids by several U.S. presidents to purchase Cuba from Spain, (b) a treaty signed by Secretary of State William H. Seward to buy the Danish West Indies in 1867 (not ratified by the U.S. Senate), (c) a proposal to authorize the establishment of protectorates over Haiti and the Dominican Republic in 1869 (defeated in the House of Representatives), (d) an effort by President Ulysses S. Grant to annex the Dominican Republic in 1870 (rejected by merely a few votes in the Senate), and (e) attempts to establish military bases in Mole St. Nicholas in Haiti and Samaná Bay in Santo Domingo (halted by adverse popular reaction in those countries).[12] Repeated actions were also taken to secure the construction of an isthmian canal under the control of the United States.[13]

The expansionist drive gained momentum in the 1890s. By that time U.S. economic interests in the Caribbean region were substantial. In 1893 trade between the United States and Cuba alone amounted to over $100 million.[14] By 1897 U.S. investment in the West Indies and Central America rose to nearly $70 million. The economic interests of the United States in the region included agricultural enterprises (especially sugar and bananas), banking and finance, widespread participation in railroad building, and merchandising. In 1894, for example, Cuba sent 87% of its exports to and received 38% of its imports from the United States.[15]

Economic Penetration Versus Colonialism

Against that background of intentions and growing investment a convergence of factors gave the final impetus to the overseas territorial expansion of the American empire. One note, however, is warranted. Although related, a distinction must be

---

[9] See TRÍAS MONGE, *supra* note 1, at 136.

[10] Louisiana was purchased from France in 1803 and Florida from Spain in 1819, in 1845 the Republic of Texas was annexed, in 1846 Great Britain ceded the Oregon territory, and Mexico lost part of its territory to the United States through successive treaties in 1848 and 1853.

[11] See BOSCH, *supra* note 1, at 636.

[12] See HEALEY, *supra* note 1, at 30–31; BOSCH, *supra* note 1, at 635–36; Zimmermann, *supra* note 1, at 46.

[13] HEALEY, *supra* note 1, at 29; Zimmermann, *supra* note 1, at 46.

[14] Charles A. Beard, *Territorial Expansion Connected with Commerce*, in AMERICAN IMPERIALISM IN 1898, *supra* note 1, at 21.

[15] See HEALEY, *supra* note 1, at 9–13, 15.

made between expansion through economic penetration overseas, which had begun well before the 1890s, and the formulation of a colonial project that entailed the acquisition of extracontinental territory. The two modalities of expansion shared some common determinants. For example, the ever-increasing accumulation of capital fuelled an expanding economy that, despite its recurrent crises, was reaping the benefits of rapid technological advances and that had been transformed, particularly after the Civil War, from a predominantly agricultural, land-based economy to an industrial and financial one.

However, as some opponents of overseas territorial acquisitions would argue later, economic expansion did not necessarily require the establishment of colonies. The advocates of "free-trade imperialism" would have preferred the benefits of economic hegemony without the costs and risks of direct colonial control. But this was not the view that finally prevailed within the dominant political groups in the United States at the end of the 19th century. The country soon found itself competing with European powers, Japan, and Russia in the fin-de-siècle scramble for colonial possessions.

Several factors led to the success of those promoting colonialism. First, there was the overarching preoccupation with the search for new markets. A crisis of overproduction had hit the country since the early 1890s, and many leading businesspeople and government officials perceived that the only solution was the opening up of new markets for American products beyond the North American continent. The leading European countries were undergoing a new current of protective nationalism, which included the imposition of tariffs on foreign products. Many parts of the world, especially Africa and the Middle East, had come under, or were targeted for, European influence. The United States, therefore, came to regard the Far East and Latin America, including the Caribbean, as the "natural" outlets for the increasing stock of American commodities and as sites for further investment.[16]

A second, interrelated factor was precisely the intense competition that ensued in the international field as a "new imperialism" emerged in Europe, Japan, and Russia for generally similar reasons. Great Britain, France, and Germany were expanding their power and influence throughout the world through various mechanisms, including the acquisition of territories and ports in Africa, parts of China, and other regions. Policy makers and expansionists of various sorts in the United States repeatedly expressed fears that the country would be left behind economically, politically, and militarily if it did not embark on a similar course.[17]

Adding to these fears was the argument that, if abandoned to the Europeans, particularly the Germans, the West Indies and Central America could be used as platforms from which to launch an eventual attack on the United States. This perceived threat, however real or imaginary, probably served as a powerful instrument of persuasion in a country whose dominant classes had apparently undergone a crisis of self-confidence—transmitted to the population at large—during the economic

---

[16] See id. at 35.

[17] Senator Henry Cabot Lodge, a prominent promoter of the imperial venture of the United States, expressed it in so many words: "We must not be left behind. ... In the economic struggle the great nations of Europe for many years have been seizing all the waste places, all the weakly held lands of the earth, as the surest means of trade development." Quoted in Zimmermann, supra note 1, at 46.

jolts of the early 1890s.[18] Taking into consideration this international factor, Liska argued that U.S. expansion into the Caribbean and the Pacific at the end of the century, in addition to its predatory character related to the economic determinants of expansion, had a markedly preemptive nature, that is, it responded, from a "security" perspective, to the perceived need to exclude other powers from the region.[19] In the end, the West Indies and Central America were to become new pawns in the imperialist chess game of the more industrialized countries, and the United States was to assume the principal role as a hegemonic force in the region.

Military Interest

The 1890s also witnessed in the United States the emergence of a new navalist ideology with very articulate and influential advocates. The most prominent among these was Captain Alfred T. Mahan, a former president of the Naval War College. In his books and numerous articles he urged the United States to strive for naval supremacy in the world. Mahan's theory propounded, in essence, that foreign commerce was essential to the welfare of any great nation; that to protect maritime routes, a world power needed to have a strong naval force; that to make viable such a force it was necessary to secure overseas bases and coaling stations; and that the possession of colonies would facilitate control over such installations.[20] Mahan pointed to the Caribbean and the Pacific as the most suitable places for the establishment of naval bases and coaling stations. By the 1890s Mahan's strategic program included (a) the construction of an interoceanic canal in the Central American isthmus, (b) the establishment of a chain of naval bases in the Caribbean and Central America, and (c) the growth of the U.S. Navy.[21] He also supported the annexation of Hawaii as essential for the defense of U.S. commercial and strategic interests in the Pacific.[22]

Mahan had very close connections with prominent expansionists of the time, such as Theodore Roosevelt and Senator Henry Cabot Lodge, whose own proposals were to reflect Mahan's principal theses.[23] In 1895 Senator Lodge called for a much-enlarged

---

[18] Richard Hofstadter referred to the "psychic crisis" of the 1890s in an attempt to explain the expansionist drive that led to the taking of the Philippines during the Spanish American War. See Richard Hofstadter, *Manifest Destiny and the Philippines*, in AMERICAN IMPERIALISM IN 1898, *supra* note 1, at 54–70. Although it is doubtful that such a "crisis," if in fact it was as pervasive as Hofstadter argued, had decisive impact in the development of the imperialist policies of the times, it can be argued that the public mood resulting from the economic difficulties of the decade provided fertile ground for the arguments of the proannexationist camp that imperialist expansion was necessary to cure the ills of the nation.

[19] LISKA, *supra* note 1, at 117 *ff.* "Extending American possessions into the Caribbean and Central America," stated Liska, "was anticipated from the early nineteenth century on, in opposition to European designs on the continent's 'natural appendages' to the 'American seas', illustrated by the French in regard to Cuba, the British in Central America, and, in due course, Imperial Germany in Haiti and the Danish West Indies." *Id.* at 118.

[20] *See* PRATT, *supra* note 1, at 12–17, 22; HEALEY, *supra* note 1, at 29; ESTADES, *supra* note 1, at 26–31; Zimmermann, *supra* note 1, at 51–52.

[21] ESTADES, *supra* note 1, at 31.

[22] PRATT, *supra* note 1, at 152–154, 319.

[23] For the personal and political relationship among Alfred T. Mahan, Theodore Roosevelt, Henry Cabot Lodge, Elihu Root (secretary of war under Presidents McKinley and Roosevelt), and John Hay (secretary of state under the same presidents) and the prominent roles they individually and jointly played in the American imperialist project of the turn of the century, see Zimmermann, *supra* note 1.

navy, acquisition of a naval base in the West Indies, some form of U.S. dominion over Cuba, and construction of an isthmian canal under the control of the United States.[24] The Republican Party's platform of 1896 advocated the construction of an isthmian canal, the continued enlargement of the U.S. Navy, and a complete system of harbor and coast defenses.[25] The newly organized National Association of Manufacturers also backed the idea of an American-controlled isthmian canal.[26]

Mahan's theses and the related proposals put forward by business, government, and military figures and organizations evidence the inter-relationship between economic and military interests regarding the expansionist movement in the Pacific and the Caribbean. However, in the Caribbean military objectives seem to have had a heavier relative weight than in the Pacific, where the concern appeared to be more centrally economic. In any event, military considerations can be considered to have been the main determinant in the decision to acquire specific territories and, eventually, in the establishment of direct colonial control as opposed to informal, or indirect, economic or political hegemony.

Such was the case with Puerto Rico. As Puerto Rican historian María Eugenia Estades has noted, acquiring direct control of Puerto Rico was to provide the United States uninhibited access to its territory, its resources, and even its people for military purposes.[27] The extent to which military objectives were related to colonialism in the Caribbean was to be demonstrated, in part, by the number of American military and defense departments and agencies that, after the Spanish American War, were entrusted with the direct handling of administrative, diplomatic, and political affairs in the region.[28]

Social and Political Factors

Two additional sets of domestic factors contributed significantly to the expansionist impetus: the internal conflicts within the most influential social and political groups in the country and the growing social unrest fuelled by the economic crises of the 1890s.

The dominant political and social groups in the United States at the end of the 19th century shared long-term interests but diverged on their perceptions of their immediate needs and of the strategy and means to achieve the objectives of continued economic growth and maintenance of power. These groups included large-scale farmers, industrialists, financiers, merchants, a rising military and bureaucratic elite, and what amounted to what Liska called a "self-perceived hereditary aristocracy,"[29] whose roots went back to the landowning and mercantile elites that had shaped the nation during the revolutionary and postrevolutionary period. Closely connected to these dominant groups were an influential and highly visible group of professionals and intellectuals who helped to articulate and mold the prevailing and competing views.

---

[24] See HEALEY, *supra* note 1, at 36.

[25] *Id.*; BEARD, *supra* note 14, at 22–23.

[26] HEALEY, *supra* note 1, at 36.

[27] ESTADES, *supra* note 1, at 219.

[28] For a detailed analysis of the "agents of [American] hegemony" in the Caribbean and Central America from 1898 to 1917, see HEALEY, *supra* note 1, at 238–259.

[29] See LISKA, *supra* note 1, at 183.

Varying degrees of cooptation and fusion among the groups sometimes blurred the distinctions and operated to establish links and to facilitate the sharing of attitudes and insights. Perceptions of the past and future of the nation differed even within these dominant subgroups, as did their reaction to the growing demands from the subordinated classes.

The main actors within the subordinated groups, defined in terms of social class, included a restless rural population and a largely immigrant, non-Anglo-Saxon, non-Protestant urban proletariat.[30] Women and the descendants of former slaves were also struggling against the patriarchal and racist structures and power relationships that characterized a society divided along class, gender, race, ethnic, religious, and other lines.

According to Liska, what he called the "plutocrats" (the industrial, commercial, and financial bourgeoisie), while entertaining differences among themselves, generally preferred informal economic expansion, that is, the exporting of American capital and goods to foreign lands, without territorial acquisition or direct political meddling.[31] The "neo-aristocrats" predominantly favored territorial expansion and direct colonial administration.[32] Included in the latter group were the "naval aristocracy" (of which Mahan was a prime example) and a "younger 'Tory' generation" (whose "conservative" and "progressive" tendencies were represented by Henry Cabot Lodge and Theodore Roosevelt, respectively) that "mixed domestic reformism and foreign policy expansionism."[33]

According to Hofstadter, the expansionist statesmen and intellectuals "were largely drawn from a restless upper-middle class elite that had been fighting an unrewarding battle for conservative reform in domestic policies and that looked with some eagerness toward a more spacious field of action" or "larger stage."[34] Pratt asserted that "the need of American business for colonial markets and fields for investment was discovered not by businessmen but by historians and other intellectuals, by journalists and politicians."[35] Although stating only a partial truth, for a good number among the business barons did portray expansion as a necessary step both before and after the Spanish American War, the statement reflects the degree to which the colonial venture of the United States was theorized, articulated, promoted, and even organized by a powerful group of what in Gramscian terms could be called "organic intellectuals" of the American dominant social classes of the time.

Whatever initial opposition to direct colonial acquisitions there was among sectors of the business community during the 1890s was soon to be overcome after the outbreak of the Spanish American War, as many rushed to seize the opportunities for economic gain opened to them by the capture of the new territories.[36] As Liska

---

[30] *See id.* at 179.

[31] According to Zimmermann, "Steel baron Andrew Carnegie's opposition to expansion combined his pacifist leanings with his belief that war was destructive to commerce." Zimmermann, *supra* note 1, at 57.

[32] LISKA, *supra* note 1, at 175. Liska's argument finds support in Pratt's analysis of expansionist views during the period. See PRATT, *supra* note 1, at 230–278; *see also* Zimmermann, *supra* note 1, at 56–58.

[33] LISKA, *supra* note 1, at 179.

[34] Hofstadter, *supra* note 18, at 68, 60.

[35] *Quoted in* Hofstadter, *supra* note 18, at 60.

[36] *See id.* at 61 *ff.*

explained it, the "composite ruling class" made a transaction whereby the aristocrats would help contain domestic instability and promote the search for new markets through expansion:

> The American aristocracy would extend support for the survival of the American plutocracy via expansion of foreign markets and containment of the domestic popular mass; in exchange the economic elite would support the political revival of the social elite via effective empire-building and reform-boosting action and rhetoric.[37]

The expansive foreign policy pursued thereafter would be justified as the "morally superior alternative to stagnation and remedy against the dangers of sociopolitical anarchy."[38]

The 1890s were years of increasing militant popular action, which included labor organizing and the rising influence of rural populism, socialism, anarchism, suffragism, and other resistance and transformative struggles and movements. The relationship between the justification for a policy of expansion and the objective of placating social unrest at home was evident throughout the public discussions of the issue. As the editor of the Louisville *Courier-Journal* expressed it,

> From a nation of shopkeepers we become a nation of warriors. We escape the menace and peril of *socialism* and *agrarianism*, as England has escaped them, by a policy of *colonization and conquest*. From a provincial huddle of petty sovereignties held together by a rope of sand we rise to the dignity and prowess of an *imperial republic* incomparably greater than Rome. . . . We risk Caesarism, certainly, but even Caesarism is preferable to *anarchism*. We risk wars; but a man has but one time to die, and either in peace or war, he is not likely to die until his time comes. . . . In short, anything is better than the pace we were going before these present forces [the acquisition of colonial territories] started into life.[39]

The Spanish American War

By the end of the 1890s public discussion and political and bureaucratic planning had already given shape to a relatively coherent project for expansion. This project included the enlargement of the U.S. Navy, the acquisition of colonies, the establishment of bases and coaling stations in the Caribbean and the Pacific, and the construction of an interoceanic canal in the Central American isthmus. The opportunity for territorial expansion came with the outbreak of the Spanish American War in 1898.

The explosion of the American warship USS *Maine* on February 15, 1898, in the port of Havana is generally regarded as the starting point of the war. However, evidence unearthed by historians has established that planning and preparation for the conflict had started in the U.S. Naval War College as early as 1894. Between 1896 and the summer of 1897, American naval officers had elaborated three successive war plans whose common elements included a blockade of Cuba and Puerto Rico, a land operation directed to Havana, the occupation of Puerto Rico, a blockade

---

[37] LISKA, *supra* note 1, at 185.
[38] *Id.*
[39] *Quoted in* Hofstadter, *supra* note 18, at 67–68 (emphasis added).

or direct assault on Manila in the Philippines (also a Spanish colony at the time) and naval incursions in Spanish waters.[40] On December 24, 1897, the undersecretary of the War Department sent instructions to Army General Nelson A. Miles, who was to become the chief commander of the armed forces during the war, concerning his "political mission" upon the outbreak of the programmed hostilities. He advised Miles that the campaign would probably commence in October 1898, unless events forced the United States to precipitate the action.[41]

Cuban insurrectionists had been waging a prolonged war of independence against Spain. Their representatives had been actively mobilizing support for their cause in the United States. As the decade ended, there were repeated calls in the American press for an American intervention to expel the Spaniards from Cuba. The motives, however, varied. Largely as a result of the successful propaganda effort of the Cuban revolutionaries, many Democrats and Populists favored intervention to help secure the independence of Cuba. On the other hand, the Republicans, with some exceptions, saw it as an opportunity to initiate the process of expansion and exert the longed-for control over the largest of the Antilles.

The explosion of the USS *Maine*, which resulted in the death of scores of U.S. crewmen, was blamed on the Spaniards by the American sensationalist press. A feverish, jingoistic campaign for American armed intervention developed.[42] On April 19, 1898, the U.S. Congress demanded Spain's withdrawal from Cuba and authorized the president's use of force to achieve that objective. On April 22, the U.S. blockaded Cuba, on April 24, Spain formally declared war on the U.S., and the next day, the U.S. issued a declaration of war made retroactive to April 21.[43] The war came to a swift end after the American forces occupied Cuba, Puerto Rico, the island of Guam (in the Marianas), and Manila. The peace treaty was signed on December 10, 1898, in Paris. The prizes for victory for the United States included the acquisition of Puerto Rico, Guam, and the Philippines and, for all practical purposes, effective political control over the soon to be formally independent Republic of Cuba. The United States had entered the world stage as an imperialist power.

The Ideology of Expansion

A certain rhetoric; a particular discourse of power; and distinctive notions of history, society, order, and progress and of the relations among peoples served as justifications and provided impetus to the U.S. expansionist drive at the end of the 19th century. *Ideology*—the set of perceptions, assumptions, ideas, beliefs, explanations, and values dominant at a given time and place or within particular social groups or movements—is not just an epiphenomenon, a mere distortion or reflection of underground material forces. As Marx pointed out, when ideas grasp the imagination

---

[40] ESTADES, *supra* note 1, at 40–41.

[41] BOSCH, *supra* note 1, at 621–622.

[42] For the role of the press in precipitating American intervention in the war, see Zimmermann, *supra* note 1, at 47–48.

[43] *See* BOSCH, *supra* note 1, at 624–627.

of the masses, they become a powerful material force in themselves.[44] In this sense, the ideology of expansion in the United States—as a "power in the domain of consciousness"—must be included among the factors that converged to produce the imperial enterprise.[45]

As with all ideology, the ideology of expansion was not necessarily coherent. It had contradictory elements, it was not universally accepted, and diverse groups in American society, including the various dominant factions, related to that ideology in different ways. Nevertheless, it is possible to identify some of its most important constituent elements, many of which were widely shared or forcefully propounded by the advocates of expansion in one form or another.

The Right to Expand

One assumption underlying the variety of arguments for continued expansion that seems to have been a fundamental feature of the ethos of the times was a certain ingrained notion of an inherent "right" to expand that had accrued to the American people.[46] This assumption was probably rooted in a perceived "tradition of expansion," developed through a century of almost continuous territorial enlargement throughout the continent. The collective *habitus*[47] of expansion had created its own justificatory principles. They constituted an imperial "common sense" that was most prevalent among the self-perceived hereditary aristocracy.

More than any other group, the members of this aristocracy felt attached to the origins of the expansion tradition through very concrete ancestral and material ties. The renewed political ascendance of this aristocratic element at the end of the century, with new and vigorous intellectual spokesmen, provided the needed justificatory discourse that both related to the past and articulated a vision of the future. That future was now projected as linked intimately to the newly found powers of an expanding industrial, commercial, and financial society.

The Inequality of Peoples

This "right to expand" was in turn predicated on a very strong belief in the principle of the inequality of peoples.[48] Many thought that this belief was buttressed by History

---

[44] R. J. LUSTIG, CORPORATE LIBERALISM: THE ORIGINS OF MODERN AMERICAN POLITICAL THEORY 1890–1920 xi (1982). Referring to the economic theories of Adam Smith, Marx asserted that they "can be considered both a product of modern industry and a force which has accelerated and extolled the dynamism and development of industry and had made it a power in the domain of consciousness." KARL MARX, PARIS MANUSCRIPTS, *quoted in* DAVID MCLELLAN, MARX BEFORE MARXISM 181 (2nd ed. 1980).

[45] For a similar argument, see Zimmermann, *supra* note 1, at 46–47.

[46] Zimmerman remarked that Senator Cabot Lodge, for example, "was driven by the conviction of America's superiority and its *right* to 'conquest, colonization, and territorial expansion.'" Zimmermann, *supra* note 1, at 54.

[47] The notion of *habitus* is taken from Bourdieu, who defined it as a system of durable dispositions, structured through collective practice, to act in certain ways that in turn reproduce the very collective practices that generated the habitus in the first place. Those practices, however, do adjust to the "demands inscribed as objective potentialities" (e.g., for change) as defined by the cognitive and motivating structures making up the habitus. *See* PIERRE BOURDIEU, *Structures and the Habitus, in* OUTLINE OF A THEORY OF PRACTICE (1977).

[48] *See* HEALEY, *supra* note 1, at 288.

itself. After all, was not the world replete with contemporary examples of peoples living in patent conditions of inequality, and were not the Anglo-Saxon Americans one of the few privileged groups who, through hard work, dedication, special "natural" endowments and, above all, divine design, were enjoying the blessings of the most advanced economic and political institutions? The dominant view was articulated in a series of binary oppositions: the civilized and the barbarous, the prosperous and the stagnant, the rational and the irrational, the hard-working and the indolent, the self-disciplined and the disorderly, the meritorious and the undeserving. The categories were constructed in direct reference to race: the White, Anglo-Saxon race was the privileged pole in the discourse of power; the "others," the non-White peoples and non-Europeans, as well as those of mixed races, were to be on the receiving end of the exercise of that power. Those "others" were the barbarous, the stagnant, the irrational, the indolent, the disorderly, and the undeserving, more fit to be governed than to govern. There was also a geography of power. Whereas the temperate zones were thought to be more conducive to hard work, self-discipline, and therefore capacity for self-government and economic and scientific progress, the "tropics" were considered breeders of lazy, ignorant, and inferior populations incapable of self-government and condemned to be governed from outside for progress and civilization ever to flourish in their midst.[49]

The Notion of Racial Superiority

The notion of racial superiority had been present in American life since colonial times. The male, White, Anglo-Saxon elites had had ample occasion to put in practice domestically what was later to become the guiding ideology of the nation's imperial career. As Weston has pointed out, the attitude that would permeate the metropolitan state's dealings with the peoples of its insular possessions after 1898 had been shaped through White America's experience with, and treatment of, Native Americans, African Americans, and Chinese and Japanese immigrants.[50] We may add to the list Mexicans and, to varying degrees, non-Anglo-Saxon European immigrants of working class and peasant origin. Furthermore, in a convenient interplay of dialectical reinforcement, the policies sustained abroad would, in turn, be used as justification for the continued subjugation, on racial, ethnic, and social grounds, of the various subordinated groups at home.

John W. Burgess, a leading political and constitutional theorist of the times, whose classes at Columbia University were attended by, among others, Theodore Roosevelt, would express it patently:

> The North is learning every day by valuable experiences that there are vast differences in political capacity between the races, that it is the white man's mission, his duty, and his right to hold the reins of political power in his own hands for the civilization of the world and the welfare of mankind.[51]

For Burgess, "the Teutonic nations" were "intrusted, in the general economy of

---

[49] *See id.* at 65–66.

[50] WESTON, *supra* note 1.

[51] JOHN W. BURGESS, RECONSTRUCTION AND THE CONSTITUTION 1866–1876 ix (1902), *quoted in* WESTON, *supra* note 1, at 16.

history, with the mission of conducting the political civilization of the modern world" by taking that civilization "into those parts of the world inhabited by unpolitical and barbaric races; i.e., they must have a colonial policy."[52] "Right," "duty," "mission" —those were the key concepts in the ideology of Manifest Destiny, that special calling of the "superior Anglo-Saxon race" to spread the gospel and practices of civilization throughout the world.

Social Darwinism also added to the discourse on imperial power. In the struggle for international survival and supremacy only the strong would prevail. Darwin himself had encouraged the notion with his characterization of the American as "the heir of all the ages, in the foremost files of time" and with his statement in *The Descent of Man* that there "is apparently much truth in the belief that the wonderful progress of the United States, as well as the character of the people, are the results of natural selection."[53] The United States must do as the other imperial powers, Social Darwinists argued, lest it become threatened with eventual extinction. The Social Darwinist perspective included a peculiarly American corollary, according to Liska, that had been present since the early days: Weak powers must be unavoidably replaced by a stronger power. This postulate served to "justify interposing the United States in the chain of succession," as would be shown with regard to Spain in the insular territories in the Pacific and Caribbean.[54]

As Liska noted, underlining the American justification of expansion was a peculiar conception of security: one that equated self-preservation with self-aggrandizement, safety with total immunity, and sustenance with unlimited growth.[55]

Belief in Free Enterprise, Progress, Rationality, and Control

Present throughout, particularly among the new industrial, commercial, and financial elites and their organic intellectuals, was the unquestioned belief in "free enterprise" and the promotion of the idea that investment in foreign lands would necessarily be beneficial for the investor and the "host" country alike. Experience would later refute this axiom, as it would become more and more evident that in the case of the poorer countries of Latin America and other regions, the greatest beneficiaries by far would almost invariably be the foreign investors and, to a lesser degree, perhaps the local economic and political elites. Of course, the coupling of economic expansion and colonial acquisitions at the end of the century proceeded regardless of the fact that there might be a certain contradiction between the notion of free trade and the imposition of economic and political control. But those were finer distinctions that could not stand in the path of U.S. national growth and development.

The ideology of expansion at this stage was predicated on a certain vision of order, tied to the rationality of capital and the market and to the institutions of liberal government. It was a vision obsessed with stability as the cornerstone of progress, but stability conceived as the unquestioned acceptance of hierarchy and subordination under the normalizing control of the institutions of capital, patriarchy, racism, and elitist representative politics. This notion of order would be used repeatedly as a

---

[52] *Quoted in* PRATT, *supra* note 1, at 8–9.
[53] *Quoted in id.* at 3, 4.
[54] Liska, *supra* note 1, at 115.
[55] *Id.*

justification for outright intervention in the internal affairs of the Caribbean and Central American countries and even for the establishment of diverse forms of prolonged political and military control.

Just as the American Revolution and the founding of the nation had been permeated by the early rhetoric of the Enlightenment, with its emphasis on a particular conception of freedom, reason, and progress, so the new phase of imperial republicanism, very much like its European counterpart, was to incorporate the consummate discourse of latter-day Enlightenment culture: a true "imperial culture . . . whose forward march of power and knowledge, of rationality and control led spatially across the globe while penetrating internally with new modes of regimentation."[56] As the author of this quote perceptively suggested, this discourse is inevitably linked to the question of hegemony. Both Liska and Healey have made the point that although in many respects the American ideology of expansion was not unlike that of European imperialism,[57] the former was marked by an added intensity and poignancy due to the deep-seated belief in the uniqueness of the American polity and the experiment it was thought to represent.[58]

The Anti-Imperialist Position

The acquisition of new territories overseas opened up an intense controversy in the United States regarding the desirability and constitutional legitimacy of holding colonies. The polemic took place in academic journals, the public press, Congress, and eventually the courts.[59] In the course of the debate, a group of self-denominated "anti-imperialists" took it upon themselves to campaign against the U.S. pursuance of a policy of overseas territorial expansion. Many of its members had been actively engaged in the successful opposition to previous attempts at extracontinental territorial enlargement, such as the proposed annexation of the Dominican Republic in 1869–1870. The anti-imperialist camp included businessmen, trade unionists, writers, academicians, and notable members of Congress.[60]

Prominent among this group was Carl Schurz, a liberal German-American with a long involvement in journalism and politics, including stints as senator from Missouri and secretary of the interior under President Rutherford B. Hayes.[61] In 1899

---

[56] NEDERVEEN PIETERSE, *supra* note 1, at 21.

[57] For a detailed analysis of the influence of European, especially British, imperial thought on the American statesmen and intellectuals of the late 19th and early 20th centuries, see MAY, *supra* note 1.

[58] LISKA, *supra* note 1, at 115; HEALEY, *supra* note 1, at 288.

[59] A survey made by this author of the U.S. *Index for Legal Periodicals* for the years immediately following the Spanish American War yielded well over 100 titles of articles published in American law journals, including the most prestigious ones, concerning the legal and constitutional problems raised by the acquisition of the new territories. For summaries of the different positions expounded during the discussions in Congress, the press, and the courts, see, among others, AMERICAN IMPERIALISM IN 1898, *supra* note 1, esp. chaps. 7–10; JUAN R. TORRUELLA, THE SUPREME COURT AND PUERTO RICO: THE DOCTRINE OF SEPARATE AND UNEQUAL (chaps. 2–3) (1985); RAÚL SERRANO GEYLS (Demetrio Fernández Quiñones & Efrén Rivera Ramos, contributors), DERECHO CONSTITUCIONAL DE ESTADOS UNIDOS Y PUERTO RICO: DOCUMENTOS–JURISPRUDENCIA–ANOTACIONES–PREGUNTAS 449–50 (1986).

[60] *See* Zimmermann, *supra* note 1, at 56–58.

[61] *Id.* at 57.

Schurz delivered a lecture at the University of Chicago that contained an archetypical statement of the anti-imperialist stance.[62] For that reason it is worth summarizing.

The decision to expand or not, argued Schurz, would affect the future and character of the nation, which had so far been dominated by the idea of government by popular consent. There was a difference between the new and the old territories. All the former acquisitions were on the continent and, except Alaska, contiguous to American borders; had been thinly populated and were situated in the temperate zones ("where democratic institutions thrive[d]" and where Americans could emigrate en masse); could be organized as territories expected to become states, with populations "substantially homogenous" to that of the United States; and did not require an increase in the army or the navy either for their subjection or defense. The new territories, on the other hand, were beyond the seas and not contiguous to the continent; were situated in the tropics, where Germanic peoples had not migrated en masse to stay; were densely populated with races "to whom the tropical climate is congenial—Spanish creoles mixed with negroes in the West Indies, and Malays, Tagals, Filipinos, Chinese, Japanese, Negritos, and various more or less barbarous tribes in the Philippines."

The question, as Schurz put it, was, What shall the United Sates do with such populations? To keep the new territories, there were only two alternatives: accept them as states or govern them as colonial dependencies. The fundamental objection to bringing them in as states was that they would then participate in the government of the Republic:

> If they become states on an equal footing with the other states they will not only be permitted to govern themselves as to their home concerns, but *they will take part in governing the whole republic, in governing us,* by sending senators and representatives into *our* Congress to help make *our* laws, and by voting for president and vice-president to give *our* national government its executive. The prospect of the consequences which would follow the admission of the *Spanish creoles and the negroes* of West India islands and of the *Malays and Tagals* of the Philippines to *participation in the conduct of our government* is so *alarming* that you instinctively pause before taking the step.[63]

On the other hand, opposition to governing the new possessions as mere dependencies was grounded on different arguments. A colonial policy was contrary to American principles of government: For the first time since the abolition of slavery, there would be two kinds of Americans, first- and second-class Americans, which would result in a government where one part of the people, the stronger, would rule another, the weaker. This would lead to the production of "ways of thinking" and "habits of action" that would revert domestically, especially to the detriment of the "least powerful classes" in American society. Imperialism, in other words, would pose a threat to internal democracy by the abandonment of the principle of "equality of rights."[64]

---

[62] *See* Carl Schurz, American Imperialism, The Convocation Address Delivered on Occasion of the 27th Convocation of the University of Chicago (Jan. 4, 1899), *in* AMERICAN IMPERIALISM IN 1898, *supra* note 1, at 77–84.

[63] *Id.* at 79.

[64] Of course, these arguments presupposed that the American polity was effectively ruled on the basis of equality and that the existing racial, gender, and social cleavages did not prevent "equal participation" by Native Americans, African Americans, ethnic minorities, women, and poor people.

In addition, according to the anti-imperialists, a colonial policy would produce an increase in militarism and a danger of involvement in imperialist wars. Further, to expand commerce, there was no need for colonies; the penetration of new markets could be achieved by an increase in the efficiency of production and trade methods, and coaling stations for the navy could be secured without the need of owning the countries where they would be established. Finally, they argued, the "duty to civilize" other peoples should be accomplished not by ruling them, but by "helping" them.

In programmatic terms Schurz advocated granting independence to the newly acquired territories, with institutions of government corresponding to their own character and interests; obtaining from the European and Asian powers a guarantee of neutrality toward the Philippines; promoting the creation of a Confederacy of the Antilles that included Cuba and Puerto Rico, with agreements as to open ports and free trade with the United States; and a program of "assistance" to those countries involving economic aid and the introduction of popular education and other "civilising agencies."

There were obvious differences between the position of the expansionists and the so-called anti-imperialists. But there were also shared assumptions and objectives. In the first place, it was clear that many among the anti-imperialist group were not opposed to overseas economic expansion, nor would they object to the enlargement of the country's military and naval capabilities. What they opposed was the actual acquisition of overseas territories because of what they perceived as the complications of pursuing a direct colonial policy. Schurz and others were in effect proposing an alternative hegemonic strategy, based principally on the modernizing effects of the penetration of capital and geared more toward the eliciting of consent than subjection through coercion.

A second striking similarity characterizes the basic assumptions and values of both camps. The anti-imperialists' discourse was constructed with many of the same binary categories used by the territorial expansionists. They reproduced the racist notions and arguments of their adversaries, as the quoted passage from Schurz's address clearly demonstrates.[65] This fact had been evident since the mid-19th century debates over territorial expansion. In 1870 House Democrat Fernando Wood, from New York, stated that he opposed annexation of the Dominican Republic because it would add to the country's Negro population.[66] Representative John F. Farnsworth of Illinois scolded his colleagues for considering inviting "semi-civilized, semi-barbarous men who cannot speak our language, who are unused to our laws and institutions, to vote with us, to help legislate for us."[67] A similar stance was taken by Senator Charles Sumner of Massachusetts, who deplored the danger posed by "tak-

---

[65] Senator Bates of Tennessee, an anti-imperialist, opposed the incorporation into the United States of "millions of savages, cannibals, Malays, Mohammedans, head hunters, and polygamists," which he contended inhabited the Philippines. "Let us beware of those mongrels of the East, with breath of pestilence and touch of leprosy," he warned. And he added, "Do not let them become a part of us with their idolatry, polygamous creeds, and harem habits." José Cabranes, *Citizenship and the American Empire*, 127 U. PA. L. REV. 391, 431–32 (1978). Analogous sentiments were expressed by Representative John F. Fitzgerald, when he asked, on the floor of the House, "Are we to have a Mongolian state in this Union?" Zimmermann, *supra* note 1, at 57.

[66] MAY, *supra* note 1, at 100.

[67] *Quoted in id.* at 100–01.

ing into this country any of the Latin race, with its treacherous blood and its notions of superstition and bigotry."[68] As May pointed out, "both Sumner and Carl Schurz . . . argued [in 1870] that Manifest Destiny ran only on the continent and that expansion beyond the water's edge would involve dangers such as the republic had never faced before."[69]

In 1901 David Star Jordan, author of a book entitled *Imperial Democracy* and well within the anti-imperialist camp, argued that whenever the United States had "inferior and dependent races" within its borders, the country found itself with a political problem (referring to "the Negro problem, the Chinese problem, the Indian problem"). He warned that if the United States insisted on governing other peoples, then those peoples would in turn claim a right to participate in the governing of the people of the United States.[70]

The anti-imperialists eventually lost out to those who advocated the acquisition of overseas territories. But, as will be seen later, their arguments would have an impact on U.S. policy toward those territories and in the production of new legal theories that would in effect exclude from participation in the American polity those peoples subjected to direct political rule by the U.S. government after 1898.

Strategy and Mechanisms for Hegemonic Control

The U.S. strategy to extend its hegemony[71] over the Caribbean after 1898 would involve extensive economic penetration, effective political and military control— either directly or indirectly—and attempts at cultural transformation. The mechanisms for securing control or allegiance would vary in time and from country to country. The variations would depend on, among other factors, the dynamics of international and domestic politics and the nature and degree of acceptance or resistance within the countries of the region.

In the early part of the 20th century mechanisms for securing control or allegiance included massive private investment, special trade ties, financial supervision of local governments, formal protectorate arrangements, direct political (or formal colonial) control, armed interventions, the establishment of military bases, the imposition of blockades, interference with local electoral processes, and outright reform of legal and political institutions in those countries more directly under American rule (including the colonial territories, the protectorates, and those temporarily occupied by the U.S. military). In later decades, other means would be added to or substituted for the above: military coups, financing and supporting counterrevolutionary movements, control of regional organizations, debt manipulation, the imposition of models and strategies for development, arming and training local constabularies and military forces, the joint persecution of revolutionary and reformist

---

[68] *Id.*

[69] *Id.*

[70] *See* WESTON, *supra* note 1, at 17–18.

[71] *Hegemony* is used here in its dual meaning of "domination of one country over another," as it is used in studies on international relations and history, and as used in social theory to refer to the process by which the rulers obtain consent to their rule. *See supra* the Introduction to this book.

movements, and cultural penetration through advanced communications technology.[72]

The end of the Cold War and the formation of regional trade blocs in Europe, Asia, and Latin America and the Caribbean, as well as the general globalization processes that have characterized these later times, have given an impetus to economic coordination and penetration, with the revival of proposals and actual programs for special trade linkages, as ways of securing U.S. hegemony in the region. These have been combined with joint military arrangements and, interestingly enough, with new proposals for sweeping legal and institutional changes. The latter include the profusion of projects for judicial and political reform put in place in many Latin American and Caribbean countries with the financial support and guidance of U.S. and international agencies.[73]

The combination of military coercion with "persuasive" practices throughout the century attests to the complexities of the process as well as to the will and determination to guarantee U.S. control and hegemony in the region at whatever cost. U.S. policies toward Puerto Rico have to be understood within this context.

---

[72] For more detailed analyses and historical documentation of some of these mechanisms, particularly from 1898 to 1917, see HEALEY, *supra* note 1; ESTADES, *supra* note 1.

[73] *See, e.g.* Jorge Correa Sutil, *Acceso a la justicia y reformas judiciales en América Latina ¿Alguna esperanza de mayor igualdad?*, 2000 REV. JUR. UNIV. DEPALERMO 293 (2000); Boaventura de Sousa Santos, *The Gatt of Law and Democracy: (Mis)Trusting the Global Reform of Courts, in* GLOBALIZATION AND LEGAL CULTURES: OÑATI SUMMER COURSE 1997 (Johannes Feest Ed. 1999); *Informe Especial: Reforma Judicial*, 26 BIDAMÉRICA 9 (1999); Efrén Rivera Ramos, *La Reforma Judicial en la América Latina y el Caribe*, DIÁLOGO, January 1995, at 44.

Chapter 2
PUERTO RICO BEFORE 1898

When the United States invaded Puerto Rico in 1898, it encountered a long-established community of people who had a particular history; a distinctive culture; and a certain type of legal, political, and economic organization. This community also had its own share of internal problems, its own brand of social cleavages, and its own set of conflicting discourses about its past and its present and about desirable aspirations for its future. That historical and cultural reality would often produce clashes whose repercussions have been felt to this day.

The Puerto Rican territory is constituted by several islands, the largest of which bears the name of Puerto Rico.[1] It is located between the Caribbean Sea and the Atlantic Ocean, to the east of the island known as Hispaniola—which contains the independent countries of Haiti and the Dominican Republic—and to the northwest of the Lesser Antilles. It has an extension of slightly more than 3,500 square miles.[2]

A Convergence of Peoples

The island of Puerto Rico was known as Boriken to the Taínos, its last group of indigenous inhabitants in pre-Columbian days. From the description of early Spanish colonizers and the study of archeological data, it is known that the Taínos were grouped in relatively small, hierarchically organized communities. They derived their sustenance from subsistence agriculture, fishing, and hunting; had developed relatively advanced techniques for stone, gold, and wood crafting; and professed animist beliefs. Occasional hostile incursions from groups living in the nearby islands, especially to the east, had whetted their battle skills, a fact that led some Spanish conquerors to describe them as more warriorlike than their counterparts in Hispaniola and Cuba.[3]

The Taínos' first contact with Europeans occurred in 1493, when Christopher Columbus disembarked on the southwestern coast of the island during his second voyage to the "New World." Spanish colonization effectively started in 1508. The first settlement was established in the town of Caparra, located in the northern part of the island, close to what later became San Juan, the capital city. Forced to work as slaves, the Taínos were virtually extinguished in a relatively short time as a result of sickness, the hardships of coerced labor, armed rebellions, high suicide rates, and flight to other islands. However, some significant imprints of their life and interaction in the island are still visible in Puerto Rican culture. For example, hundreds of Taíno words are commonly used: towns, regions, and rivers bear indigenous names; many items of Puerto Rican food, musical instruments, and rhythms have Taíno origins;

---

[1] The other two populated islands, much smaller in size, are Vieques and Culebra and are located off the southeastern shore of the larger island of Puerto Rico.

[2] The current population of Puerto Rico is 3.8 million. More than 2 million more Puerto Ricans live in the U.S. mainland.

[3] FERNANDO PICÓ, HISTORIA GENERAL DE PUERTO RICO 27 (1986).

and some physical features of many Puerto Ricans can arguably be traced back to the Taíno phenotype.

The Spaniards brought large numbers of Africans to work as slaves in the new colony. In fact, by the year 1530 African slaves constituted the majority of the population.[4] Subsequent migrations, especially from the Canary Islands, and the arrival of fugitive and imported slaves augmented the population during the 17th and 18th centuries.[5] New immigrant waves during the 19th century contributed further to the demographic configuration of the country. They included Spaniards, Corsicans, Irish, Scots, Germans, Italians, and others of European ancestry, including a strongly conservative contingent of French and Spanish loyalists fleeing the independence wars of Latin America and the Caribbean. There were also Creoles from the other Antilles, especially Santo Domingo, and settlers who came from the United States, often with their own slave force.[6]

Throughout these first centuries of Puerto Rican history, racial mixtures became common, especially among the popular classes.[7] Despite this fact, racial differences and the tones of skin color were socially and economically relevant in Puerto Rican society. The White elites claimed the prerogative of cultural preeminence and of providing the fundamental codes for the interpretation of Puerto Rican culture. This emphasis on Whiteness resulted in a prolonged negation of the importance of Blackness in Puerto Rican culture and society.[8] Class and gender also constituted the bases for fundamental cleavages and for the differentiated distribution of opportunity, power, and privilege.

Economy

Mineral deposits susceptible to exploitation with the technology of the times were exhausted in the early 16th century.[9] During the 17th and 18th centuries, the Spaniards were to regard Puerto Rico basically as a military outpost to help guard their empire's possessions in the region against the predatory incursions of the other European powers, particularly the French, English, and Dutch. This military emphasis was due to the island's strategic position as the gate and key to all the other Antilles.[10] During this period, Spain imposed strict controls on economic and commercial activity in Puerto Rico. The scarce opportunities resulting from those limitations encouraged many of the island's inhabitants to turn to contraband as a way of living.

---

[4] FRANCISCO A. SCARANO, PUERTO RICO: CINCO SIGLOS DE HISTORIA 192–94 (1993).

[5] *Id.* at 285–86.

[6] *Id.* at 408–09. For an interesting analysis of the various historical "layers" of race, ethnicity, and class that have gradually contributed to the formation of Puerto Rican society, *see* JOSÉ LUIS GONZÁLEZ, EL PAÍS DE CUATRO PISOS Y OTROS ENSAYOS (1980). *See also* PICÓ, *supra* note 3, esp. chap. 9; JAMES L. DIETZ, HISTORIA ECONÓMICA DE PUERTO RICO 70–74 (1989).

[7] *See* SCARANO, *supra* note 4, at 330–32.

[8] *See generally* GONZÁLEZ, *supra* note 6. A recent commentary on contemporary racism in Puerto Rican society is found in Raquel Z. Rivera, *Rapping Two Versions of the Same Requiem*, in PUERTO RICAN JAM: ESSAYS ON CULTURE AND POLITICS 243–56 (Frances Negrón-Muntaner & Ramón Grosfoguel Eds. 1997).

[9] *See* SCARANO, *supra* note 4, at 191–92.

[10] *See* TOMÁS BLANCO, PRONTUARIO HISTÓRICO DE PUERTO RICO 39–42 ([1935] 1981); DIETZ., *supra* note 6, at 24–25.

A renewed economic interest in the colony, partly due to its declining hold in other parts of the Empire, drove the Spanish Crown to liberalize migration to the island and to ease restrictions relating to economic activity at several junctures during the 19th century. These policies led to significant developments in agriculture and commerce. By the end of the century, Puerto Rico was producing coffee; tobacco; cane sugar; and a variety of fruits, grains, and vegetables for internal consumption and for export. It also possessed a small but meaningful manufacturing sector based on small- and medium-scale factory operations in the main cities.[11]

The mode of production based on slavery coexisted with production by small farmholders and *agregados*[12] from the 16th to the 18th centuries. However, the slave economy, tied principally to the sugar plantations, became the dominant mode of production toward the end of the 18th and during the early 19th centuries, with independent economic activity and an incipient sector based on wage labor assuming subordinate positions.[13] During this period, sugar became Puerto Rico's main crop. By 1840, the island had become the tenth largest sugar producer in the world market.[14]

The invention of new machinery gradually made the old plantation methods of production obsolete. Additionally, sugar production was a seasonal operation and the plantation owners began to feel the pressures of the high cost of maintaining large numbers of slaves whom they had to feed and house throughout the year. The adoption of more efficient methods of production and the successful switch to wage-labor in other sugar-producing countries like Cuba placed Puerto Rican producers at a disadvantage. Moreover, Puerto Rican coffee planters, who operated their farms on a smaller, more efficient scale using family members, wage laborers, and *agregados* rather than slaves, began to displace sugar growers in economic importance. The increasing inefficiency of the slave economy, the political pressures of the more liberal sectors of Puerto Rican society, and the struggles and rebellions of the slaves cleared the way for the abolition of slavery in 1873. Former slaves became *agregados*, wage-laborers, or artisans.[15]

These developments led to an economic transformation toward the end of the 19th century. A strengthened wage-labor mode of production competed for preeminence with the traditional economy based mainly on the use of *agregados*, while the independent productive activity of small farmers declined.[16]

Political Institutions

Political institutions throughout most of the colonial period were extremely centralized.[17] In Spain itself, until the 19th century, absolute military and civilian authority

---

[11] For a more detailed description of the economic structure and development of Puerto Rico during the Spanish colonial period, see DIETZ, *supra* note 6, at chap. 1.

[12] The *agregados* were peasants who lived and worked on land that usually belonged to a large- or medium-scale landowner. *Agregados* were bound to the landowner by certain types of obligations, such as surrendering part of their crop or providing specified services.

[13] DIETZ, *supra* note 6, at 85–86.

[14] LYDIA MILAGROS GONZÁLEZ & ANGEL G. QUINTERO-RIVERA, LA OTRA CARA DE LA HISTORIA 19 (1984).

[15] *See id.* At 24–32; DIETZ *supra* note 6, at 76–79.

[16] DIETZ *supra* note 6, at 85–86.

[17] *See* 1 JOSÉ TRÍAS MONGE, HISTORIA CONSTITUCIONAL DE PUERTO RICO 12–30 (1980).

rested with the Castilian monarchs, while the Cortes (or Parliament) exercised very little power, and even then at the Crown's discretion. From 1524 to 1834, a Royal and Supreme Council for the Indies counseled the monarch—with varying degrees of influence throughout the centuries—on matters concerning the legislative, executive, judicial, military, commercial, and ecclesiastical affairs of the colonies.[18]

In the colonies themselves executive, legislative, judicial, and military functions were carried out by a captain general or governor, who operated as the Crown's representative. In Puerto Rico the creole elite participated very little in the government of the colony, except for a limited influence exerted at the municipal level.[19] During the 19th century Puerto Rico had a Provincial Delegation, a body with largely advisory and administrative functions. In effect, however, it was subordinated to the governor.[20]

Starting with the Cádiz Constitution of 1812, 19th-century Spain witnessed several attempts at introducing constitutional government. Such efforts had varying degrees of temporary success, depending on the shifts in the balance of power between the conservative monarchists and the liberal reformers. New constitutional charters were adopted in 1834, 1837, 1845, 1869, and 1876. The most liberal of the constitutional reforms was that of 1869. The reforms usually sought to reestablish the power of the Cortes and increase political and civil liberties at home. Some of them also purported to liberalize the colonial regime. However, in practice, constitutional changes in the metropolis normally had very little impact on colonial institutions. Except for brief periods, the latter remained largely untouched.

In Puerto Rico, much of the political activity of the Creole elites was directed at gaining concessions from Spain regarding self-government and the liberalization of the strictly regulated economic and commercial fields. In 1868 a radicalized sector of that elite, with some support from the peasantry and rural laborers, led an armed insurrection in the mountain towns of Lares and Pepino (now San Sebastián) and proclaimed the Republic of Puerto Rico. The revolution, known as the *Grito de Lares*, was suppressed rather swiftly by the Spaniards but was to become a symbol of resistance and struggle for the independence movement even to our days.

Class Structure

The class structure in late 19th-century Puerto Rican society exhibited a considerable degree of complexity. In general, the upper classes included a substantial group of landowners (*hacendados*), made up mostly of established Creole families and, to a lesser extent, of recently arrived immigrants of European origin; a group of merchants, many of whom were Spaniards; a smaller group of city factory owners; cadres of government bureaucrats, military officers, clergy, and others closely linked to the colonial administrative apparatus; and a small group of independent professionals (lawyers, doctors, teachers, etc.). The popular classes comprised artisans, a small but growing urban proletariat, agricultural free-wage laborers and *agregados*, peasants,

---

[18] RAÚL SERRANO GEYLS (Demetrio Fernández Quiñones & Efrén Rivera Ramos, contributors), DERECHO CONSTITUCIONAL DE ESTADOS UNIDOS Y PUERTO RICO: DOCUMENTOS–JURISPRUDENCIA–ANOTACIONES–PREGUNTAS 428–29 (1986).

[19] *See id.* at 429.

[20] *Id.*

and groups of middlemen.[21] Many of the artisans and agricultural laborers were former slaves. Throughout the entire structure of social stratification, women were subordinated and were legally and effectively excluded from many areas of economic, political, social, and cultural life.[22]

How class interests were expressed in the political and ideological movements of the times has been subjected to revision by Puerto Rican historians recently.[23] Social historians writing in the 1970s tended to portray the major 19th-century political struggles in the country as a clash between two sets of interests. On one hand, the landowners, mostly of Creole origin, made claims for self-government with the support of allied groupings of liberal professionals and intellectuals and, on the other, the so-called Spanish unconditionals, mostly merchants and bureaucrats, defended the colonial regime and the preservation of the political and economic privileges of their members.[24]

It is clear that many Creole landowners did support a greater degree of autonomy for Puerto Rico, and many Spanish merchants and bureaucrats were definitely on the side of the Spanish central government. But new research has called attention to the complexities of the matter, unearthing evidence about the role of Spanish liberal autonomists and Puerto Rican conservative unconditionals in those political struggles.[25] Moreover, there was no clear-cut separation between autonomist and assimilationist demands. For example, in addition to greater local self-government, some autonomists would petition for more participation in the legislative organs of the Spanish central government.[26]

What seems uncontroversial is that there was a strong liberal bent among sectors of the upper classes. Programmatically, such liberalism translated into claims for free economic exchange and political autonomy. The former was aimed at easing the strict commercial restrictions imposed by the Spanish Crown and the latter at combating the political absolutism of the central government. Demands for freedom of expression and association and male universal suffrage were also usually part of the liberal program.[27] This ideological formulation was very much in line with the worldview of the

---

[21] See DIETZ, *supra* note 6, at 74–76; ÁNGEL G. QUINTERO RIVERA, CONFLICTOS DE CLASE Y POLÍTICA EN PUERTO RICO (1976) [hereinafter QUINTERO, CONFLICTOS DE CLASE]; GONZÁLEZ, *supra* note 6. Many times there were no clear-cut boundaries among these groups. For example, there were landowners who were also merchants. See ÁNGEL G. QUINTERO RIVERA, PATRICIOS Y PLEBEYOS: BURGUESES, HACENDADOS, ARTESANOS Y OBREROS 313–24 (1988) [hereinafter QUINTERO, PATRICIOS Y PLEBEYOS]. Nevertheless, it is still useful to use these categories to refer to the shared experiences and identities, however nebulous or fluid at times, that emerged from social situations conditioned by existing relationships to the means and processes of production.

[22] The complex theoretical issue of class attribution or classification in the case of women cannot be discussed here. Suffice it to say that the common practice of categorizing women in class terms in reference to the class attributed to their husbands, fathers, or other male members of their households is, to say the least, extremely problematic. I am indebted to Esther Vicente for raising this point.

[23] For a review of the most recent historiography on the subject, *see* María de los Ángeles Castro Arroyo, *El 98 incesante: Su persistencia en la memoria histórica puertorriqueña*, in ENFOQUES Y PERSPECTIVAS: SIMPOSIO INTERNACIONAL DE HISTORIADORES EN TORNO AL 98 (Luis González Vale Ed. 1997).

[24] See, e.g., QUINTERO, CONFLICTOS DE CLASE, *supra* note 21; QUINTERO, PATRICIOS Y PLEBEYOS, *supra* note 21.

[25] Castro Arroyo, *supra* note 23, at 20–23.

[26] *Id.*

[27] See QUINTERO, CONFLICTOS DE CLASE, *supra* note 21, at 17–18; Castro Arroyo, *supra* note 23, at 22–23.

independent professionals, many of whom had studied in Europe or the United States and had absorbed the liberal ideas circulating in those societies at that time.

Although there is controversy over the matter, it seems that the landowners and the liberal professionals, who undoubtedly were politically subordinated to the metropolitan government, enjoyed a relative social hegemony over many sectors of the subordinated classes and social groupings.[28] In fact, at different moments during the course of the 19th century, both groups, related to each other in many ways, were able to draw support from sectors of the popular classes. They succeeded to a relative degree in presenting theirs as the general interests of the country, in conflict with the economic and political power of the Spanish government.[29]

Nonetheless, the popular sectors had their own traditions of political struggle. Those historical experiences included the Taíno rebellions, the slave revolts, the eruptions of localized social upheavals against the oppressive practices of the merchants, the many forms of resistance against attempts at disciplining the labor force (for example, through the infamous *libretas de jornaleros*[30]), and the emerging agitation and economic and political organization of the artisans and urban workers, with their support for anarchist and socialist ideas at the end of the 19th century. In those struggles their opponents had been, at different moments and for different reasons, both the Spanish colonizers and the Creole elite, the landowners and the merchants as well as the colonial bureaucrats, the liberal autonomists as much as the conservative unconditionals.

The incipient feminist movement represented another important area of social and political struggle at the end of the century. Its demands included the extension of voting rights to women, a claim that found strong opposition from the male-dominated class formations and political institutions of the times.[31]

Legal System

The normative structure of the legal system during most of the Spanish colonial period was provided by a series of charters, laws, decrees, and orders known col-

---

[28] For a brief discussion of the controversy, see QUINTERO, PATRICIOS Y PLEBEYOS, *supra* note 21, at 313–24. The situation, as Quintero explained it, is that the *hacendados* had predominant control of the means of production; yet, due to the colonial situation, they did not control either the macroeconomic or the political structure of society. This made it difficult, in his opinion, for the landowners to extend clearly their cultural dominance over the rest of the population. But, he seemed to imply, that fact did not prevent them from exercising a relative degree of influence in the production of consciousness among the subordinated groups. This moderate ascendancy over the way other groups ended up interpreting the world is what I have called here "relative social hegemony."

[29] See Efrén Rivera Ramos, *The Supreme Court of Puerto Rico and the Separation of Powers Doctrine: Notes on Constitutional Argument and Social Conflict* 31 (1981).

[30] The *libretas de jornaleros* were part of a system designed to force "free" laborers to work for the landowners or the municipal authorities. Each person considered a *jornalero*, or free laborer, was required to carry a special notebook or register to keep record of labor contracts and other related information. If caught without the notebook, the laborer was punished with forced labor for a public authority at a reduced wage. The *jornaleros* devised many ways to circumvent the system and on occasion burned the notebooks as a form of protest.

[31] See Esther Vicente, *Las mujeres y el cambio en la norma jurídica*, 56 REV. JUR. U.P.R. 585, 590 (1987), *esp.* nn.10–13 and works cited therein.

lectively as *Derecho Indiano*, enacted especially for Spain's overseas possessions. The most salient institutional feature of the system was the fusion of judicial, administrative, and military functions, which were exercised by the same officers, from the lowest level of the colonial apparatus to the governor, who sat at the top of the pyramid. Appeals could be made to the *Real Audiencia*, a body with judicial and administrative functions. But because Puerto Rico did not have an *Audiencia* of its own until 1832, appeals from the island were heard by the *Audiencia* of Santo Domingo and, later, that of Cuba. Since 1524 reviews of the decisions of that body could be sought in the *Consejo Real de Indias*, in Spain and, starting in 1834, in the Supreme Court of Spain and the Indies, which superseded the *Consejo*. However, appeals proceeded very slowly and, in effect, for most of the period the power of the governor tended to go unchecked.

Starting in 1832, successive reforms gradually transformed the normative, institutional and, to a lesser extent, practical features of the system. An important development was the movement to separate the judicial function from the executive and legislative powers. This was accompanied by an attempt at establishing the judiciary career. In 1832 Puerto Rico acquired its own *Audiencia Territorial*. In 1861 the *Audiencia* was formally freed from direct intervention by the governor. A further reform in 1855 left this body with appellate jurisdiction in civil and criminal cases, original jurisdiction in some controversies, the faculty to issue advisory opinions at the request of the governor, the general supervision of the judicial system, and the power to administer examinations to those aspiring to the legal profession.

The Spanish Constitution of 1876 finally established the principle that the overseas territories were to be governed essentially by the same body of laws governing the metropolis, with the modifications required by their particular circumstances. This provision, in conjunction with previous legal developments, allowed for the extension to Puerto Rico of the basic codes and procedural legislation in effect in Spain. These included the Civil, Commercial, and Criminal Codes; the Codes of Civil and Criminal Procedure; the *Ley Hipotecaria*[32]; and the Organic Law for the Court System. A unified Bar Association was established in 1840. Procedures were also established for the provision of free legal assistance to those without means.[33]

By the early 1890s Puerto Rico had in place—at least in terms of its normative and institutional structure—a relatively modern legal system based on the continental European civil law tradition. Whether this formal structure represented an advance in the dispensation of justice in the country can be debated. José Trías Monge, a leading Puerto Rican constitutional historian and former president of the Supreme Court of Puerto Rico, has argued that the formal developments in this field in the late 19th century were not matched by changes in the basic attitudes, values, and practices that had characterized the legal process in previous times. Authoritarianism

---

[32] The *Ley Hipotecaria* is an important feature of the civil law tradition. It is a comprehensive body of norms regulating the registration of title and diverse procedures concerning the protection of property-related rights.

[33] For a fuller account of the origins and development of the judicial system in Puerto Rico, *see* JOSÉ TRÍAS MONGE, EL SISTEMA JUDICIAL DE PUERTO RICO (1978), from which most of the above information has been taken. For the period under discussion, *see esp.* chaps. 1–3 of the cited work. For a more succinct description, highly laudatory of the Spanish legal system in operation in Puerto Rico, see CARMELO DELGADO CINTRÓN, DERECHO Y COLONIALISMO: LA TRAYECTORIA HISTÓRICA DEL DERECHO PUERTORRIQUEÑO 45–72 (1988).

and even violent repression of dissidents were still prevailing features of the colonial regime. Judges, many of whom were foreigners, did not show much enthusiasm for righting the wrongs of the authorities and protecting the basic rights of the population. Judicial independence, Trías Monge concluded, was more an ideal than a consummate fact during this time.[34] The repressive nature of the Spanish state apparatus at the end of the century has also been noted by social historian Mariano Negrón Portillo, who pointed to the fact that after 1870 the notorious Spanish Civil Guard became an important instrument for the surveillance of the restless rural population and the suppression of dissidence.[35]

As for the popular perception of judges and the judicial system, it seems that the reforms did not do much to eradicate the idea that the legal system was an instrument more for oppression than for the vindication of rights. Trías Monge quoted one of the leading representatives of the Creole elite, who complained that peasants thought that "laws are something mysterious elaborated not with the purpose of protecting [them], but with the aim of oppressing [them]." The result, Trías concluded, was a state of alienation and indifference to the law and its representatives.[36] Trías's analysis is predicated on the judgment that this distrust of law was based on the despotic nature of colonial authorities and on the gap between what the law dictated and what was implemented. This is certainly a plausible interpretation. However, similar sentiments would most likely have prevailed even if the law had been complied with to the letter. After all, what substantial remedy would have been available to the economically and socially oppressed sectors of this colonial society in codes that enacted into legal norms the class-, race-, and gender-biased worldview of the far-away 19th-century European bourgeoisie? These considerations would be overlooked by many who, in later times, were to look back to the institutions of the Spanish regime with nostalgia as a reaction to the new domination that descended upon Puerto Ricans with the military occupation of 1898.

During the 19th century, reforms also took place in the sphere of political relationships with the metropolis. Partly as a result of the Cuban insurrection of the 1890s, and partly due to pressures from the United States and to political maneuvering by Puerto Rican autonomists, Spain conceded Cuba and Puerto Rico an Autonomous Charter in 1897. The charter is regarded by many as a significant step forward in the obtaining of self-government for Puerto Rico.[37] It provided for the continued representation of Puerto Ricans and Cubans in the Spanish Cortes; the equality of rights between Spaniards and Antilleans; universal suffrage; the establishment of an insular parliament (with an elected Chamber of Representatives and an Administrative Council); and the formation of a parliamentary government, with ministers accountable to Parliament. The insular government was delegated important powers. At the same time, however, its effective scope of action was restricted with countervailing limitations both in theory and in practice.[38] Following elections, the insular Parliament was inaugurated on July 17, 1898. Two days later it held its first

---

[34] See TRÍAS MONGE, supra note 33, at 43–44.

[35] MARIANO NEGRÓN PORTILLO, CUADRILLAS ANEXIONISTAS Y REVUELTAS CAMPESINAS EN PUERTO RICO, 1898–1899 3–5 (1987).

[36] TRÍAS MONGE, supra note 33, at 44.

[37] See 1 TRÍAS MONGE, supra note 17, at 131–34.

[38] See id.

ordinary session. The Spanish American War, however, was already under way. On July 25, 1898, U.S. troops invaded Puerto Rico.

Relations With the United States Prior to 1898

The United States and Puerto Rico were not unknown to each other at the moment of the invasion. Significant links had developed prior to that event.

The main ties had been economic in nature. Since 1815 the United States had a "commercial agent" in San Juan.[39] In 1829 this officer became known as the U.S. Consul.[40] His duties, nonetheless, remained principally related to the promotion of American economic relations with Puerto Rico. By the mid-1800s Puerto Rico already exported a substantial amount of its sugar production to the United States and was importing a considerable number of American goods. However, exports declined later in the century as sugar was replaced by coffee and tobacco as principal crops. At that point Puerto Rican coffee had its main markets in Europe and Latin America.

American statesmen and military strategists had envisioned the possibility of acquiring Puerto Rico as a military base early in the final decade of the 19th century. In 1891 President Benjamin Harrison wrote to Secretary of State James G. Blaine about the need for overseas bases. Blaine advised him that only three overseas locations were of sufficient importance for the United States to acquire them: Hawaii, Cuba, and Puerto Rico.[41] One author has argued that during the Spanish American War the United States became interested in Puerto Rico "almost as an afterthought."[42] However, the evidence quoted by him and by others suggests otherwise.

As discussed in chapter 1, beginning in 1894 the U.S. Naval War College had prepared several war plans, some of which included blocking and occupying Puerto Rico in the event of an armed conflict with Spain in the region.[43] According to Healey, General Nelson Miles, the commanding general of the Army, had from the start given priority to the conquest of Puerto Rico, preferring an opening campaign there rather than in Cuba (although in this regard he was overruled).[44] In April of 1898, P. C. Hanna, the U.S. Consul in San Juan, moved to the nearby island of St. Thomas with other countrymen in anticipation of the imminent war. From there he insisted on the desirability of invading Puerto Rico and even suggested a plan to that effect.[45]

In May 1898, Theodore Roosevelt, then commanding a group of Army volunteers, wrote to his friend Senator Henry Cabot Lodge, "Do not make peace until we

---

[39] Gervasio Luis García, *Strangers in Paradise? Puerto Rico en la correspondencia de los cónsules norteamericanos (1869-1900)*, 9 REV. DEL CENTRO DE INV. HIST. 27, 31 (1997).

[40] *Id.*

[41] DAVID HEALEY, DRIVE TO HEGEMONY: THE UNITED STATES IN THE CARIBBEAN, 1898–1917 29–30 (1988). Others, like Secretary of the Navy Benjamin Tracy, thought that the United States needed a larger number of bases. *Id.* at 30. *See also* the discussion about Alfred Mahan's position supra in chapter 1.

[42] JUAN R. TORRUELLA, THE SUPREME COURT AND PUERTO RICO: THE DOCTRINE OF SEPARATE AND UNEQUAL 18 (1985).

[43] *See* chapter 1, nn.40–41 and accompanying text; García, *supra* note 39, at 29.

[44] HEALEY, *supra* note 41, at 47.

[45] García, *supra* note 39, at 45–46.

get Porto Rico [sic]. . . ." Lodge responded that the administration had given him assurances that Puerto Rico would not be forgotten.[46] In June, Whitelaw Reid, editor of the *New York Tribune*, who was later appointed to the U.S. peace delegation, declared that "the judgment of the American people" was so intent on acquiring Puerto Rico that the administration "could not make peace on any other terms if it wanted to."[47]

Ideological beliefs of the island's residents would facilitate the American conquest of Puerto Rico. Many members of the Puerto Rican elite, particularly the intellectuals and independent professionals, had been steeped in the liberal ideology of the time. Their political ideals hinged on the notions of liberty, equality before the law, and representative democracy. Some regarded the American political system as the most advanced of its time. This admiration was compounded by a shared faith in science and education as the hallmarks of progress. Theirs was an "enlightened" creed, whose realization, they thought, was only hindered by the backwardness of the Spanish regime. This view would eventually contribute to a warm welcome of the American intervention in 1898 on the part of many islanders.[48]

---

[46] JULIUS W. PRATT, EXPANSIONISTS OF 1898: THE ACQUISITION OF HAWAII AND THE SPANISH ISLANDS 231 (1936); HEALEY, *supra* note 41, at 47; TORRUELLA, *supra* note 42, at 20; 1 TRÍAS MONGE, *supra* note 17, at 144.

[47] HEALEY, *supra* note 41, at 47–48.

[48] For a revealing fictionalized account of the reception of the occupying American forces, see JOSÉ LUIS GONZÁLEZ, LA LLEGADA (1980). For a historian's account, see García, *supra* note 39, at 48–55. *See also* Jaime B. Fuster, *The Origins of the Doctrine of Territorial Incorporation and its Implications Regarding the Power of the Commonwealth of Puerto Rico to Regulate Interstate Commerce*, 43 REV. JUR. U.P.R. 259, 292 n.101 (1974). For a stinging critique of the "idyllic view" of the United States that many Puerto Rican liberals entertained, see BLANCO, *supra* note 10, at 94–95.

Chapter 3
PUERTO RICO UNDER THE AMERICAN REGIME

This chapter provides a general outline of the relationship between the United States and Puerto Rico to contextualize the specific legal events bearing on that relationship. This overview has been broken into five parts: (a) constitutional and political developments, (b) economic and social transformations, (c) strategic importance, (d) cultural transformation and resistance, and (e) the legal system.

Constitutional and Political Development

Upon occupying the island, the United States installed a military regime. Three successive military governors administered the territory, introducing from the start, by decrees or general orders, many reforms of the legal and institutional structure of the country. The U.S. Supreme Court, reaffirming doctrines previously adopted in other contexts, later validated the authority of the military government.[1]

After an extensive debate, in 1900 the U.S. Congress passed the Foraker Act,[2] which replaced the military regime with a civilian government. This Organic Act[3] provided for a civilian governor and a Legislative Assembly. The latter would exercise legislative power over vaguely defined local matters ("all matters of a legislative character not locally inapplicable"), including the power to modify and repeal any laws then in existence in Puerto Rico. The Assembly would consist of two chambers: an Executive Council, invested with legislative and executive functions (a clear departure from the American principle of separation of powers), and a House of Delegates.

The U.S. Congress retained the power to annul the acts of the Puerto Rican legislature. The law vested the judicial power in the courts and tribunals already established by the military governors. The members of the House of Delegates would be elected by qualified voters residing in the island, but the governor, the members of the Executive Council, and the justices of the Supreme Court of Puerto Rico were to be appointed by the president of the United States. Only 5 of the 11 members of the Executive Council had to be native inhabitants of Puerto Rico.

Until 1946 all governors appointed by U.S. presidents were Americans. This fact was the source of many frictions and conflicts between the governors and the local legislature, always controlled by Puerto Ricans of the various political parties that gradually came into life under the new regime. The Organic Act of 1900 also extended to Puerto Rico all statutory laws of the United States "not locally inapplicable." It specifically exempted Puerto Rico from the application of U.S. internal

---

[1] *See* Dooley v. United States, 182 U.S. 222 (1901); Santiago v. Nogueras, 214 U.S. 260 (1909).

[2] Foraker Act, ch. 190, 31 Stat. 77 (1900).

[3] In the American legal tradition, an Organic Act is a statute that provides for the basic structure of a territorial government.

revenue laws. Special provisions were made for the collection of duties on merchandise entering and leaving Puerto Rican ports. Puerto Ricans were declared to be citizens of Puerto Rico.

The Foraker Act was perceived as a colonial statute by many disillusioned political leaders in Puerto Rico, who initially had called for the integration of the island into the United States as another state. That disappointment, together with the adverse reaction produced by the economic displacement of Puerto Rican *hacendados* and smaller farmers by the American sugar corporations, was to result in important cleavages in the political programs of the Puerto Rican elites. Although some would still favor integration, others would seek a greater degree of autonomy, and still others complete independence from the United States. To this day the "status" question has revolved around these three political projects.

In 1917 Congress passed the Jones Act.[4] This second Organic Law conferred U.S. citizenship on Puerto Ricans. However, Puerto Ricans residing in the island would not be eligible to vote for the president of the United States or elect representatives to the U.S. Congress. The Jones Act also had provisions bearing on the internal structure of the government of the island. It abolished the legislative functions of the Executive Council and established a bicameral legislature to be elected by popular vote. It also provided for a bill of rights. The Jones Act, however, did not alter the basic political and constitutional relationship with the United States.

In a series of cases spanning from 1901 to 1922, the U.S. Supreme Court decided that neither the Foraker nor the Jones Acts had constitutionally "incorporated" Puerto Rico into the United States. According to the Court, this meant that Puerto Rico should be considered as belonging to, but not being a part of, the latter. One practical effect of those decisions was to recognize the full authority of the U.S. Congress to legislate over Puerto Rico. That power would be restricted only by what the Court termed "fundamental rights" guaranteed by the federal Constitution to persons under the jurisdiction of the United States.[5]

It was not until 1946 that the president appointed the first Puerto Rican to hold the position of governor of the island. In 1947 Congress authorized Puerto Rico to elect its own governor for the first time. The following year the Puerto Rican electorate voted for the first Puerto Rican elected governor in the history of the country.

A resurgence of the nationalist movement in the island and the international pressure resulting, in part, from the post-World War II decolonization wave drove Congress and the ruling Popular Democratic Party to look for ways to defuse pro-independence support and seek a new international legitimacy for the regime. In 1950 Congress approved legislation to allow the Puerto Rican population to adopt its own constitution, subject to certain limitations.[6] Drafted by a Puerto Rican Constitutional Convention (with the abstention of the independence movement), the new constitution was submitted to the Puerto Rican electorate, which approved it. The approved charter was amended by the U.S. Congress before its final adoption in 1952.

The new constitution provided for the internal structure of the government of Puerto Rico and for a bill of rights. Although some have advanced arguments to the

---

[4] Jones Act, ch. 190, 39 Stat. 951 (1917) (codified at 48 U.S.C. § 731 (1987)).
[5] These cases will be analyzed in full detail *infra* in Part II.
[6] Pub. L. No. 600, 64 Stat. 319 (1950).

contrary, this bill of rights is generally regarded to limit only the actions of the Puerto Rican government and not those of the government of the United States. Constitutional protection of individual rights against the actions of the "federal" government has been held by U.S. courts to be grounded on the fundamental provisions of the Bill of Rights of the U.S. Constitution.

After adoption of the new constitution, Puerto Rico became officially known as the *Estado Libre Asociado de Puerto Rico*, or the Commonwealth of Puerto Rico, in its English-language version. Despite the new official name, the legislative history of the entire process clearly reveals that the U.S. Congress never intended to alter the basic legal and political relationship between the two countries.[7] In fact, the provisions of the Foraker and Jones Acts pertaining not to the internal government structure of Puerto Rico, but to its relationship with the United States, were left unmodified and were codified in a new Federal Relations Act.[8]

Continued allegations about the colonial nature of the arrangement led the Puerto Rican government to hold a plebiscite in 1967 in which the electorate was asked to express its preference for one of the three traditional alternatives: statehood (meaning becoming a state of the Union), Commonwealth, or independence. In the election the Commonwealth formula obtained slightly more than 60% of the votes. But the plebiscite was boycotted by most of the independence movement and part of the pro-statehood movement. Electoral participation turned out to be much lower than had been usual in general elections.[9] Moreover, the United States had not made any commitment to honor the results of the plebiscite. These and other factors led to the general understanding that the outcome was inconclusive.

All attempts by the pro-Commonwealth faction to "enhance" that status by gaining concessions for more autonomy—both before and after the 1967 plebiscite —had met with indifference or outright rejection by the U.S. Congress.[10] New international pressures, especially within the Decolonization Committee of the United Nations, as well as the turn of economic and political events in Puerto Rico and the United States, moved the Bush administration and the U.S. Senate in 1989 to set out a process, in conjunction with the three main political parties in the island, designed to culminate in a plebiscite to be held in 1991. This effort occupied much of the political energies of the political parties and other groups in Puerto Rico for nearly two years. It came to an end without producing the expected plebiscite. But it revealed many interesting and complex questions about the relationship between the

---

[7] *See* ARNOLD H. LEIBOWITZ, DEFINING STATUS: A COMPREHENSIVE ANALYSIS OF UNITED STATES TERRITORIAL RELATIONS 165–78 (1989); ANTONIO FERNÓS ISERN, ESTADO LIBRE ASOCIADO DE PUERTO RICO: ANTECEDENTES, CREACIÓN Y DESARROLLO HASTA LA ÉPOCA PRESENTE 81–197 (1974); 3 JOSÉ TRÍAS MONGE, HISTORIA CONSTITUCIONAL DE PUERTO RICO 274–310 (1982); *El informe Johnston, in* 1 JUAN M. GARCÍA PASSALACQUA & CARLOS RIVERA LUGO, PUERTO RICO Y LOS ESTADOS UNIDOS: EL PROCESO DE CONSULTA Y NEGOCIACIÓN DE 1989 Y 1990 94–95 (1990). This interpretation was recently adopted by the U.S. House of Representatives in the "Findings" incorporated into H.R. 856, known as the Puerto Rico Self-Determination Act, which was passed by a vote of 209 to 208 on March 4, 1998.

[8] *See* Public Law 600, § 4, 64 Stat. 319 (1950).

[9] *See* FERNANDO BAYRÓN TORO, ELECCIONES Y PARTIDOS POLÍTICOS DE PUERTO RICO 245–46 (1989).

[10] For a detailed history of those attempts, see JOSÉ TRÍAS MONGE, PUERTO RICO: THE TRIALS OF THE OLDEST COLONY IN THE WORLD (1997).

two countries and the attitudes of diverse segments of the U.S. political elites and the Puerto Rican population.

In 1993 the newly elected pro-statehood governor and the Legislative Assembly controlled by his New Progressive Party held another local plebiscite. This time the results were 48.4% for Commonwealth, 46.2% for statehood, and 4.4% for independence. The Commonwealth option defined in the ballot called for "improvements" in the Commonwealth status. But the pro-statehood government, as expected, did not take any steps to persuade Congress to legislate in that direction, arguing that it was up to the victors, that is, the opposition Popular Democratic Party, to make the appropriate moves.

In March 1996, Representative Don Young, Republican from Alaska, introduced legislation to provide for a federally backed plebiscite in Puerto Rico on the status question.[11] The Young Bill generated much controversy. The pro-Commonwealth faction charged that the proposed legislation was slanted in favor of statehood and threatened to boycott the process if the bill was approved in its original version. Both the pro-statehood New Progressive Party and the Puerto Rican Independence Party supported the measure. Other smaller, but vocal, sectors of the independence movement opposed the bill as presented. The Young Bill was withdrawn from the relevant House Committee in 1996 but was reintroduced in 1997.[12] After several hearings and a good number of revisions made in the appropriate committees, the Young Bill was finally put to a vote in the House in 1998 and approved with a margin of one vote,[13] with most Democrats voting in favor and most Republicans against the measure. The Clinton administration supported the legislation.

As approved by the House, the Young Bill called for a plebiscite to be held in Puerto Rico during 1998 on three alternatives: statehood; Commonwealth (defined as a territorial status); and separate sovereignty, an option that, in turn, included two possibilities—full independence or some sort of free association with the United States based on the recognition of Puerto Rico's sovereign status. The Senate failed to produce the corresponding legislation, and the prospects for a federally sanctioned plebiscite in 1998 fizzled.

Frustrated by congressional failure to deliver on the status issue, the New Progressive Party government organized still another local referendum on the question. The ballot contained five options: Commonwealth or *Estado Libre Asociado* (defined as a territory of the United States), free association, statehood, independence, and a fifth "None of the above" column included to satisfy the requirements of Puerto Rican constitutional case law on the matter. This was the first time that the free association alternative appeared on the ballot in a plebiscite over status in Puerto Rico. It was defined as a sovereign status leading to a special treaty of association with the United States. A small group of Popular Democratic Party members publicly supported this option.

The Popular Democratic Party, for its part, had objected vigorously to the definition of Commonwealth placed on the ballot. Finally, it decided to call on its followers to vote in the "None of the above" column as a way of expressing their rejection of the process. Many other individuals and groups who objected to the

---

[11] H.R. 3024, 104th Cong., 2nd Sess. (1996).
[12] H.R. 856, 105th Cong., 1st Sess. (1997).
[13] H.R. 856, 105th Cong., 2nd Sess. (1998) (enacted).

plebiscite for various reasons or who were disaffected with the policies and governing style of the New Progressive Party governor also found the "fifth column," as it came to be known, an attractive vehicle for venting their dissatisfaction.

The plebiscite was held in December 1998. The result stunned its organizers. The "None of the above" column won with 50.3% of the votes, statehood obtained 46.5%, independence 2.5%, the "territorial" Commonwealth .01%, and free association 0.3%. Following some public wrangling over the matter, the results were finally interpreted as a defeat for the statehood movement. After the referendum, Congress gave clear indications that it would not take up the matter again in the immediate future. The next move would depend on the outcome of the Puerto Rican general elections of November 2000.

As occurred with the plebiscite process that took place between 1989 and 1991, the intense public discussion surrounding Representative Young's initiative also brought to the fore significant issues concerning the resolution of Puerto Rico's status and the future of its relationship to the United States. The central aspects of both processes are directly relevant to the concerns of this book and will be discussed in some detail in the chapters that follow.

Economic and Social Transformations

The American occupation of Puerto Rico set in motion a series of profound economic and social transformations that would eventually change the character of Puerto Rican society. The first set of transformations took place during the initial three decades of the 20th century. The central process of the period was the definitive entrenchment of wage labor as the dominant mode of production in the island. The old world of the *haciendas* started to give way to the relations that emerged from the American sugar plantation and, to a lesser extent, from a growing manufacturing sector in the cities and towns. The result was an increasing proletarianization of the working classes, whose ranks were joined by displaced artisans, independent small farmers, *agregados*, and others. Sugar replaced coffee as the main crop due to several factors, including the economic policies of the new colonial administration, which tended to favor American investors. As many of its members became impoverished, the local landowning class linked to the coffee and tobacco economy was eventually displaced from its position of relative economic predominance.

Land began to be concentrated in the hands of the foreign sugar barons, whose influence on the political process became stronger and more evident with time. By 1930 American corporations owned 60% of the island's sugar industry, 80% of the tobacco industry, and 60% of banking investments and public utilities.[14] Between 1898 and 1930 some $120 million flowed to the island in the form of private capital.[15] Puerto Rico became an export enclave dependent on a single crop: sugar.[16] Simultaneously, its dependence on imported goods for domestic consumption increased. By 1910, 85% of Puerto Rican trade was with the United States. And by 1940 the

---

[14]DAVID HEALEY, DRIVE TO HEGEMONY: THE UNITED STATES IN THE CARIBBEAN, 1898–1917 267 (1988).

[15]*Id.*

[16]JAMES L. DIETZ, HISTORICA ECONOMICA DE PUERTO RICO (1989).

island, in spite of its small size and dire poverty, was already the ninth largest consumer of United States goods in the world and the second largest in the whole of Latin America. It was also the 10th largest source of supplies in the world for the American market and third largest in Latin America.[17]

The colonial administration undertook the task of improving part of the infrastructure (roads, sanitary facilities, sewage, etc.) and providing better health and educational services. But despite the evident growth in economic activity and the relative degree of modernization that resulted from improvements of the basic infrastructure, social conditions for most of the population remained dismal. In 1930 a commission of experts from the Brookings Institution in Washington, DC, reported that the conditions of the population at large were "deplorable"; that consumer prices were high because of the reliance on imports from the United States, while the average daily wage was only 70 cents of a U.S. dollar; that rural schooling was still poor; and that 74% of the rural population was still illiterate. The commission report concluded that "while it cannot be denied that the influx of capital has increased the efficiency of production and promoted general economic development, it does not follow that the benefits of this have accrued to the working people of the Island."[18] It was evident that the main beneficiaries of the process had been the American investors and some fractions of the Puerto Rican socially dominant class.

Political struggles would be related in many ways to these social transformations. Many *hacendados* who felt displaced by the new economic conditions, and their organic intellectuals, would return to the demand for autonomy, and even independence, while those closely linked to the American sugar industry would generally favor statehood. The workers, on the other hand, developed their own economic and political organizations to confront the sugar barons and the local landowner and capitalist class.

Partly due to the oppressiveness of the former Spanish regime, the party of the workers, the Socialist Party, who shared many of the views prevalent among the liberal elite at the beginning of the century about the progressive nature of American society, adopted a pro-American stance and favored statehood for the island. That position, buttressed by a gradual weakening of the economic base of the working class as a result of several factors, led the Socialist Party, at the end of the period, to forge the strangest of alliances with the local Republicans, who represented the interests of American capital and its intermediaries. Eventually the Socialist Party lost much of its support among the exploited rural and urban proletariat.

The 1930s witnessed an economic and political crisis, partly as a result of the Great Depression. Workers' strikes multiplied, and the nationalist movement became more militant. The Nationalist Party, founded in 1922, was violently suppressed and its leadership incarcerated. The crisis led to efforts to restructure the colonial regime and improve social conditions, partly as a way to ensure the stability of a colonial enclave whose strategic importance had become more evident during World War II. The restructuring process was made possible by three important developments: (a) the extension to Puerto Rico of President Franklin D. Roosevelt's New Deal policies,

---

[17] JUAN R. TORRUELLA, THE SUPREME COURT AND PUERTO RICO: THE DOCTRINE OF SEPARATE AND UNEQUAL 238 (1985).

[18] HEALEY, *supra* note 14, at 267; DIETZ, *supra* note 16, at 145–48.

(b) the newfound prosperity ensuing from the war, and (c) a rearticulation of the political process and class alliances in Puerto Rico.

In 1938 a group of Puerto Rican professionals and intellectuals broke from the existing Liberal Party and founded a new movement that led to the formation of the Popular Democratic Party. The movement was able to attract enough support from the landless peasants and the rural and urban proletariat to become the dominant political party for several decades. With backing from Washington, in the final years of the 1940s the Popular Democratic Party, in firm control of the local government, launched a new drive for development.

Initially, the Popular Democratic Party government experimented with an economic strategy based on direct government creation and administration of economic enterprises.[19] This approach was soon abandoned. Thereafter, the Puerto Rican government adopted a policy of "industrialization by invitation," which had profound effects on Puerto Rican society.[20] The main strategy consisted in providing extraordinary tax and other incentives to foreign investors. In its first phase, Operation Bootstrap was able to attract a large number of labor-intensive enterprises that required very little technology and paid very low salaries. The garment industry was a typical example. Fueled by these and related policies, the 1950s and 1960s witnessed a very rapid process of industrialization and urbanization that transformed the predominantly rural agrarian Puerto Rican social formation into a relatively modern, industrial, urban society.

As wages rose in Puerto Rico, other Latin American and Asian countries were able to offer more profitable opportunities for capital accumulation, and the labor-intensive, low-paying American enterprises began to resettle in some of those countries. The Puerto Rican government then decided to offer incentives to capital-intensive industries with the hope that these would trigger a process of linkages in the chain of supply and distribution of goods that would stimulate the emergence of local enterprise.[21] It was assumed that scores of local businesses would provide the goods and services needed by foreign enterprises to manufacture and market their products. The capital-intensive industries came (petrochemicals, pharmaceuticals, and others), but the new local businesses did not materialize.

The structural problems of the economy—such as its disproportionate dependence on foreign investment—were not solved. In fact, because of the very nature of the development program, many of Puerto Rico's most basic problems have intensified. As economic historian James L. Dietz correctly pointed out, Puerto Rico remained an export enclave (this time of manufactured goods), extremely reliant on foreign capital and, largely because agriculture had been marginalized, very dependent on imports for the satisfaction of the needs of its population. Local capital was either displaced or subordinated, most of the productive wealth of the country remained under external control, and Puerto Rico developed a very high unemployment rate from which it still suffers, all characteristic of developing economies.[22] Addi-

---

[19] Economic historian James L. Dietz has characterized this strategy as "state capitalism." *See* DIETZ, *supra* note 16, at 201–12.

[20] For an excellent comprehensive discussion of the subject see DIETZ, *supra* note 16. The brief description that follows draws heavily from his analysis.

[21] *Id.* at chap. 5.

[22] According to Puerto Rican economist Francisco Catalá, the high rates of unemployment in Puerto

tionally, disparities in income have remained significant. Around 50% of the population lives below the poverty level.

Certainly the standard of living came to be higher in Puerto Rico than in many Latin American and Caribbean countries (although substantially lower than in the continental United States). But this increase was not the product of a relatively self-sustained productive economy. To raise the standard of living the system had to depend on four mechanisms. The first was recourse to the government as a source of employment. For many years, the Puerto Rican government has been the largest employer in Puerto Rico.

Second, the economy has relied heavily on the transfer of monies from the U.S. government to the Puerto Rican government and to individuals. These transfers take several forms. Some are grants to the central and municipal governments for specific projects, such as infrastructure or housing development. Others are allotted to individuals by federal or local agencies through programs like the Nutritional Assistance Program (popularly known as "food stamps"), Medicaid, student grants and loans, Social Security benefits, and unemployment compensation. In 1980 "federal" transfers to Puerto Rico amounted to 30% of personal income and to 27% of the recurring revenues of the Puerto Rican government. In 1982 those transfers represented 28.1% of Puerto Rico's gross national product.[23] In 1993 federal aid rose to close to $9 billion, amounting to 50% of personal income in the island,[24] and by 1997 federal funds remitted to Puerto Rico totaled $10.77 billion.[25] This extraordinary dependence on federal monies has not decreased, despite the steps being taken in the United States to curtail the welfare state and shrink federal spending on social programs. A third mechanism, used to achieve greater consumption capacity, was a substantial increase of the public debt.

The fourth element of the strategy to deal with the economic situation has been the stimulation of migration to the continental United States as an "escape valve" for the country's social and economic problems. Between 1950 and 1970 net migration to the United States from Puerto Rico amounted to more than 600,000 people, that is, the equivalent of 27.4% of the population in 1950.[26] There are presently more than 2 million Puerto Ricans living in the United States. Many of those who migrated encountered very harsh conditions and various forms of discrimination in their new environment.[27] In the 1960s the median income of Puerto Ricans in the United States was much lower than those of White Americans and African Americans.[28] By that time, "more than 50 percent of Puerto Ricans in New York were incorporated as

---

Rico are due to four factors: (a) the collapse of agriculture as a source of jobs, (b) the reduction of job opportunities in the diminished labor-intensive manufacturing sector, (c) the relatively few jobs created by capital-intensive industries, and (d) the lack of development, for several complex reasons, of more aggressive local entrepreneurial initiatives (personal communication, September 7, 2000).

[23] Dietz, *supra* note 16, at 317, 319.

[24] TRÍAS MONGE, *supra* note 10, at 2.

[25] A. W. Maldonado, *A Message to Congress on the Eve of the Centennial*, THE SAN JUAN STAR (July 23, 1998), at 53.

[26] DIETZ, *supra* note 16, at 306.

[27] For references to the "racialization" and ethnic subordination of Puerto Ricans in the United States, see PUERTO RICAN JAM: ESSAYS ON CULTURE AND POLITICS 19–23 (Frances Negrón-Muntaner & Ramón Grosfoguel Eds. 1997) (PUERTO RICAN JAM).

[28] FRANCISCO A. SCARANO, PUERTO RICO: CINCO SIGLOS DE HISTORIA 762 (1993).

low-wage labor" in the manufacturing sector.[29] The rate of increase in income between 1960 and 1970 was lower among Puerto Ricans (13%) than among African
Americans (24%).[30] In 1970 more than 35% of Puerto Ricans in New York were
living below the poverty line.[31] Figures in education were similarly grim, with Puerto
Ricans falling well behind African Americans in terms of access to high school
education during the 1960s and 1970s.[32]

The deindustrialization of cities, like New York, with large concentrations of
Puerto Ricans has pushed the poorest among them to adopt survival strategies that
include living off welfare payments, working in the so-called informal or "underground" economy, and taking risks in the violent world of drug trafficking at the
lowest echelons of that business.[33]

Although the Puerto Rican population experiences many pressing social and
economic problems, for many years Puerto Rico has been a haven for foreign investment and a very profitable market for American products. According to Dietz,
in 1978, 34.1% of American direct investment in Latin America went to Puerto Rico,
while 42.4% of the profits accruing to U.S. corporations from the region came from
the island.[34] U.S. corporations operating in Puerto Rico, exempted from the payment
of federal taxes under a special provision of the U.S. Internal Revenue Code,[35] enjoyed rates of return of up to 98.6% over their invested capital. For the pharmaceu-
tical industry the rate was higher, going up to 246% over invested capital. In fact,
according to Dietz, at a given point almost 50% of world profits in this industry
were generated in Puerto Rico.[36] In 1999, U.S. goods exported to Puerto Rico
amounted to nearly $16 billion,[37] exceeded only by U.S. exports to Canada, Mexico,
Japan, United Kingdom, Germany, Republic of Korea, Netherlands, France, Taiwan
and Singapore.[38]

In the capital-intensive industries promoted by the government, only 25% of
income is distributed to the workers. In the chemical industry, the percentage is as
low as 16%.[39] In the overall economy (including government) in Puerto Rico, em-

---

[29] PUERTO RICAN JAM, *supra* note 27, at 22.

[30] SCARANO, *supra* note 28, at 762.

[31] *Id.*

[32] *Id.*

[33] *See id.* at 760–63; PUERTO RICAN JAM, *supra* note 27, at 22.

[34] DIETZ,, *supra* note 16, at 282.

[35] 26 USCA 936 (1986) (Supp. 1998).

[36] Dietz, *supra* note 16, at 322, 275. It is difficult to obtain more recent comprehensive statistics on
the profits made by 936 corporations operating in Puerto Rico. The U.S. Department of the Treasury
rendered its last report on the activities of these corporations in 1989. *See* U.S. DEPARTMENT OF THE
TREASURY, THE OPERATION AND EFFECT OF THE POSSESSIONS CORPORATION SYSTEM OF TAXATION:
SIXTH REPORT (1989). However, according to expert opinion on the matter, the rates of return of those
corporations still operating in Puerto Rico should remain very high because the basic conditions that
made them possible have not changed significantly. For example, elimination of the tax breaks under
section 936 of the Internal Revenue Code (IRC), see *infra* note 43, has not been completed yet and
many enterprises affected by changes in that provision have obtained tax exemptions under section 901
of the IRC that covers corporations operating in foreign countries (Francisco Catalá, personal communication, September 7, 2000).

[37] Information provided by the Planning Board of Puerto Rico, Sub-Program for Economic Analysis.

[38] http://www.bea.doc.gov/table2.htm

[39] Dietz, *supra* note 16, at 272.

ployees receive 40% of net income.[40] In the United States, more than 70% of income is distributed to employees in salaries and other benefits.[41] These figures reveal the extraordinary benefits that U.S. corporations obtain from investment in the island. As a market, Puerto Rico has also been very profitable for American corporations. In 1976–1977, Puerto Rico was the fifth largest market in the world for products produced in the United States. In 1978 it was the seventh largest market and the largest per capita importer of American commodities in the world.[42]

The fiscal crunch experienced in the United States in the 1980s and the repeated bipartisan calls to balance the federal budget focused the attention of congressional leaders on the special tax breaks granted to American corporations in Puerto Rico. With a substantial degree of compliance on the part of the pro-statehood local government, which viewed the special tax breaks as a political shot in the arm for the Commonwealth formula, the U.S. Congress approved legislation in 1996 eliminating Section 936 of the Internal Revenue Code and providing for a 10-year phasing-out period for the tax exemption program contained in that provision. The phasing-out period expires on January 1, 2006.[43]

With federal tax incentives reduced, there has been a substantial amount of concern about the future of the manufacturing sector in the island and the prospect for the creation of badly needed jobs. The new global economy and the series of free-trade agreements in the making in the American hemisphere are posing new challenges to the Puerto Rican economy. The pro-statehood government that came into power in 1993 placed its hopes for the economic future of Puerto Rico in the possibility of transforming it into a high-tech service-oriented economy, linked to the free-trade systems put in place by the United States, and on receiving substantial additional stimulus from the benefits expected from the island becoming another state of the Union. Whether all this will come to pass is still a very open question.

Strategic Importance

From the very beginning the U.S. military viewed Puerto Rico as an important strategic site. As a result, throughout the past century an ongoing process of militarization has permeated all aspects of Puerto Rican life. As Jorge Rodríguez Beruff, one of the foremost experts on the military history of Puerto Rico, perceptively noted, the American military presence in Puerto Rico must not be viewed merely in terms of the location of military bases on its territory, but as a multidimensional, integral phenomenon that penetrates all spheres of political, social, and economic life in Puerto Rico. "Colonial society is also a militarized society."[44] Rodríguez Beruff offered as examples the considerable level of military spending in Puerto Rico, the

---

[40] JUNTA DE PLANIFICACIÓN, INFORME ECONÓMICO AL GOBERNADOR, 1999, APÉNDICE ESTADÍSTICO, TABLA II.

[41] PAUL SAMUELSON & WILLIAM NORDHAUS, ECONOMÍA 216 (1999).

[42] Dietz, *supra* note 16, at 310 n.109.

[43] Small Business Job Protection Act of 1996, Pub. L. No. 104–188, 110 Stat. 1755, 26 U.S.C.A. 1601A (1996).

[44] Jorge Rodríguez Beruff, *La cuestión estratégico-militar y la libre determinación de Puerto Rico: el debate plebiscitario (1989–1993)*, in EL CARIBE EN LA POST-GUERRA FRÍA, ESTUDIO ESTRATÉGICO DE AMÉRICA LATINA (1992–1993) 98 (1994).

meddling of U.S. military officers in Puerto Rican politics, the high number of Puerto Rican government officers formally linked to the U.S. armed forces, and the official portrayal of U.S. military presence in Puerto Rico as essential to a stable relationship.[45] This theme cannot be pursued here, but it has to be noted.

Puerto Rico's strategic importance for the United States was recently summarized succinctly in an official report of the U.S. General Accounting Office to the Committee on Energy and Natural Resources of the U.S. Senate as part of the 1989–1991 plebiscite process:

> The island's central location is considered valuable as a communications and control center as well as an intermediate staging area for military operations elsewhere. Also, the island provides the potential for expanded military operations if necessary, and it affirms American presence in the Caribbean—a region considered vitally important to the United States.[46]

The United States operates an extensive network of bases and military installations in Puerto Rico. The most important complex is the Roosevelt Roads Naval Station on Puerto Rico's eastern coast. It is the largest U.S. naval base in the world and the most important training site for American military personnel in the Atlantic. It is used, besides, as a training facility for the navies of NATO members and Latin American countries. In 1999 the U.S. Army Southern Command was moved to Puerto Rico from Panama. The Southern Command has an operations range of 32 countries and 14 territories in the region.[47] The military facilities in the islands constituting the territory of Puerto Rico have also been an important component of the nuclear weaponry infrastructure of the United States.[48]

Puerto Rico has been a source of military personnel for the U.S. armed forces. More than 200,000 Puerto Ricans have served in those forces throughout this century. Puerto Ricans have participated in all major armed conflicts in which the United States has been involved since World War I, at a very high cost in terms of human lives and suffering.[49]

Despite hopes to the contrary expressed by some analysts and political leaders, the end of the Cold War may not have seen an end to the perception of the American military regarding Puerto Rico's strategic importance. In recent years the functions of the U.S. military have been reformulated to focus on the "War on Drugs," the control of illegal immigration, the protection of American markets, and international

---

[45] *Id.* at 102–104. For detailed analysis of the relationship between the military and political, social, and economic processes in Puerto Rico, *see also* MARÍA EUGENIA ESTADES FONT, LA PRESENCIA MILITAR DE ESTADOS UNIDOS EN PUERTO RICO 1898–1918 (1988); Jorge Rodríguez Beruff, *Puerto Rico and the Caribbean in the U.S.: Strategic Debate on the Eve of the Second World War,* 2 REV. MEXICANA DEL CARIBE 55 (1996); Humberto García Muñiz, *U.S. Military Installations in Puerto Rico: An Essay on Their Role and Purpose,* 24 CARIBBEAN STUDIES 79 (1991).

[46] U.S. GENERAL ACCOUNTING OFFICE, PUERTO RICO: INFORMATION FOR STATUS DELIBERATIONS 9d-7 to 9d-8 (1989) (GAO).

[47] Juanita Colombani, *Bastión militar Puerto Rico para EE.UU.,* EL NUEVO DÍA, Aug. 11, 1999, at 6.

[48] *See, generally,* BAR ASSOCIATION OF PUERTO RICO, REPORT OF THE SPECIAL COMMISSION ON NUCLEAR WEAPONS AND THE TREATY FOR THE PROSCRIPTION OF NUCLEAR WEAPONS IN LATIN AMERICA (1984).

[49] Rodríguez, *La cuestión estratégico-militar, supra* note 44, at 102; Manny Suárez, *260 Reservists Called Up: Assignments Not Yet Known for 3 P.R. Units,* THE SAN JUAN STAR, Sept. 27, 1990, at 1.

police force operations aimed particularly at checking "troublesome" regimes, especially in the "Third World." In each of those respects, Latin America and the Caribbean feature as priority areas in the strategic thinking of the U.S. military and political establishment. It should not seem strange then that, as in the past, Puerto Rico is considered one of the most fitting locations to serve as a support base for those new political and military objectives.[50]

In the past few years the United States has been expanding its police and military presence and activity in Puerto Rico, particularly in relation to efforts to stem illegal drug trafficking in the region.[51] The Drug Enforcement Administration, the Federal Bureau of Investigation, and the U.S. Coast Guard have increased their personnel in the island. Puerto Rico is again becoming a training center for Latin American and Caribbean police forces. Public controversies have surged about announced plans by the military to install additional electronic surveillance facilities in Puerto Rican territory.[52] Following its recent move, the U.S. Army Southern Command has begun operations in the islands.

These developments, along with comments made over the years after the collapse of the Soviet Union by key military officers of the United States, indicate that, far from diminishing, the strategic importance of Puerto Rico may have augmented. In October 1990 the commander of the U.S. Naval Marine Air Force in the Caribbean stated that the Persian Gulf conflict had enhanced the Caribbean's strategic importance for the United States and called the U.S. Navy in Puerto Rico "a sentinel for sea lanes . . . through which more than 50 percent of all oil and other materials are imported into the United States." Additionally, it was announced, the Roosevelt Roads Naval Base had served as a place to train fleet ships and squadrons heading for the Arabian Gulf.[53] In preparations for the plebiscite proposed for 1991, the U.S. Defense Department took the position that even if Puerto Ricans chose to convert their country into an independent republic, the United States must keep its military bases in Puerto Rico and have guaranteed access to its territory for defense-related activities.[54]

---

[50] *See* Carmen Gautier Mayoral, *The Effect of the New U.S. National Security Doctrine—the War on Drugs—on the Process of Self-Determination in the Subsidized Colonies of the Caribbean*, 53 REV. COL. AB. P. R. 31 (1992); Efrén Rivera Ramos, *Colonialism and Integration in the Contemporary Caribbean, in* 20 BEYOND LAW 189 (1998); I. Jaramillo Edwards, *La seguridad interamericana: Una problematización* (1992); Jorge Rodríguez Beruff & Humberto García Muñiz, *El debate estratégico en Estados Unidos y la revisión de la política militar hacia América Latina y el Caribe* 9 SOCIOLÓGICA (1994); R. Matos, *Drug Interdiction Center Opens*, THE SAN JUAN STAR, July 15, 1992, at 3; J. McKim, *National Guard Training for Low Intensity Warfare: Drug Warriors Hit the Trail in Southern P.R.*, THE SAN JUAN STAR, July 7, 1992, at 2.

[51] *See* FRONTERAS EN CONFLICTO: GUERRA CONTRA LAS DROGAS, MILITARIZACIÓN Y DEMOCRACIA EN EL CARIBE, PUERTO RICO Y VIEQUES (Humberto García Muñiz & Jorge Rodríguez Beruff Eds. 1999); Rivera Ramos, *supra* note 50.

[52] Rivera Ramos, *supra* note 50, at 200; FRONTERAS EN CONFLICTO, *supra* note 51.

[53] *P.R.'s Strategic Position Said Enhanced*, THE SAN JUAN STAR, Oct. 2, 1990, at 5.

[54] *See* Prepared Statement of Brigadier General M. J. Byron, Acting Deputy Assistant Secretary of Defense (Inter-American Affairs), in 1 *Political Status of Puerto Rico: Hearings on S. 710, S. 711, and S. 712 before the Senate Committee on Energy and Natural Resources*, 101st Cong., 1st Sess., at 134 (1989). For a succinct journalistic account of the influence of the American military establishment on decisions regarding the political status of Puerto Rico, see J. M. García Passalacqua, *100 Years of Secrets about P.R. Must End*, THE SAN JUAN STAR, July 26, 1998, at 85.

As this book was being prepared for publication, a resounding controversy exploded about the need for the U.S. Navy to continue its control of Vieques, an island that is part of the Puerto Rican territory. The Navy owns two-thirds of this populated island, where it conducts frequent training exercises with live ammunition. The Vieques facilities form part of the Roosevelt Roads complex. The dispute arose after a Puerto Rican civilian who worked as a guard for the U.S. Navy was accidentally killed on April 19, 1999 during air-to-ground bombardment exercises. The incident provoked an unprecedented consensus among political, religious, and civic forces in Puerto Rico, demanding that the Navy leave Vieques. On June 25, 1999, a special commission, appointed by Puerto Rico's Governor Pedro Rosselló, reported that Navy activities caused environmental, economic, social, physical, and emotional damage in Vieques, and posed a serious risk to the lives and safety of its population. The commission recommended immediate and permanent cessation of military activities in the island and the swift and orderly return of lands under military control to Vieques and Puerto Rico, respectively.[55] Meanwhile, dozens of people belonging to political, religious, labor, and other groups installed civil disobedience encampments inside Navy occupied land in Vieques. Puerto Rican Senator Rubén Berríos, president of the Puerto Rican Independence Party, was among them.

On December 3, 1999, the government of Puerto Rico announced that President Clinton had agreed to reduce military exercises and suspend live-fire bombardments for a period of 3 years, seek congressional approval to extend $40 million in aid to Vieques and to transfer certain lands to Puerto Rico, and to hold a referendum among Vieques residents to decide whether the Navy should remain indefinitely, eventually resuming live fire bombings, or leave after a period of 3 years, during which the Navy could conduct inert fire exercises. The president promised an additional $50 million if residents voted for the Navy to stay permanently.

There was substantial opposition to the agreement. On February 21, 2000, religious leaders of all denominations led a massive demonstration against the accord in San Juan. The civil disobedience campaign intensified. On May 4, 2000, more than a year after protesters had halted military maneuvers by camping inside the Vieques firing range, U.S. Marshals and FBI agents evicted them and dismantled their camps. But hundreds more crossed again into Navy land. As of this writing, federal authorities had arrested and charged more than 320 people for trespassing. Several Puerto Rican Independence Party Leaders, including two legislators, waited in prison for their trial for over a month. Meanwhile, the Navy began a public relations campaign to win popular support, insisting on its need to keep Vieques to maintain combat-ready forces.

Cultural Transformation and Resistance

In a broad sense, all aspects of Puerto Rican reality have a cultural dimension, for constitutional, political, economic, and military processes involve conceptions of the

---

[55] 1 COMISIÓN ESPECIAL DE VIEQUES, INFORME AL GOBERNADOR DE PUERTO RICO HON. PEDRO ROSSELLÓ 186–193 (1999).

world and values from which they cannot be extricated. Cultural transformations and resistance have been imbricated in all the structural and institutional changes described so far. However, it is worth noting certain specific aspects of Puerto Rican culture that have been of pivotal concern in the discussion on colonialism in Puerto Rico.

The first is the language question. The American colonial project, from its very early stages, entailed an effort at "Americanization," which had as one of its principal components the imposition of English as the language of communication in Puerto Rico.[56] With varying degrees of emphasis, English was used as the language of instruction in Puerto Rican private and public schools until the policy was abandoned (in public schools) as late as 1948. The change in policy was due to the strong resistance of many sectors of the Puerto Rican people.

Today, most Puerto Ricans residing in Puerto Rico speak Spanish as their native language. Although the number of those who read, write, and speak English with relative ease has increased, in 1981, according to government reports, a majority could not be considered bilingual.[57] In 1991 the Puerto Rican legislature passed a law making Spanish the official language of Puerto Rico.[58] The measure, which garnered applause overseas,[59] generated substantial controversy internally. In 1993, after winning the 1992 general elections by a considerable margin of votes, the pro-statehood New Progressive Party managed to pass another "language law" that established Spanish and English as the official languages of Puerto Rico.[60] This action also produced a strong reaction, this time from sectors identified with the independence movement and the pro-Commonwealth Popular Democratic Party.[61] The language issue became a principal bone of contention during the congressional initiatives, such as the Young Bill, to authorize a plebiscite on the future political status of Puerto Rico.[62]

Other aspects of the cultural interrelationship between U.S. society and the Puerto Rican people exhibit a greater degree of complexity. Certainly, a century of American influence has left an imprint on Puerto Rican society. The signs of that presence are everywhere. But they are particularly entrenched in the country's institutional framework and processes. In many ways the metropolitan society has become an "exemplary center" for Puerto Rican social life.[63] Economic practices,

---

[56] For a comprehensive study, see AIDA NEGRÓN DE MONTILLA, AMERICANIZATION, PUERTO RICO AND THE PUBLIC SCHOOL SYSTEM, 1900–1930 (1975).

[57] GAO, *supra* note 46, at 9c-2.

[58] Pub. Law No. 4 (1991) (Puerto Rico), P.R. LAWS ANN. tit. 1, § 51 (1991).

[59] As a result of the passage of the Official Language Act, the people of Puerto Rico, represented by Governor Rafael Hernández Colón, of the Popular Democratic Party, were granted the prestigious Prince of Asturias award by the Spanish government for their "defense of the Spanish language."

[60] Pub. Law No. 1 (1993) (Puerto Rico).

[61] For a commentary highly critical of both sides of the controversy, see Frances Negrón-Muntaner, *English Only Jamás but Spanish Only Cuidado: Language and Nationalism in Contemporary Puerto Rico, in* PUERTO RICAN JAM, *supra* note 27, at 257–85.

[62] *See* José Julián Álvarez González, *Law, Language and Statehood: The Role of English in the Great State of Puerto Rico*, 17 LAW & INEQ. J. 359 (1999). For another study on the relationship between language and colonialism in Puerto Rico, *see* PEDRO JUAN RÚA, LA ENCRUCIJADA DEL IDIOMA: ENSAYO EN TORNO AL INGLÉS OFICIAL, LA DEFENSA DEL ESPAÑOL CRIOLLO Y LA DESCOLONIZACIÓN PUERTORRIQUEÑA (1992).

[63] The concept is taken from CLIFFORD GEERTZ, NEGARA: THE THEATER STATE IN NINETEENTH

political processes, legal forms, educational policies, communication techniques, knowledge systems (including specific ways of problematizing reality and providing solutions to social and personal conflicts) and, to a certain degree, the very style of life of the metropolitan society have become paradigms generally adopted in the colonial society. The reproduction of American ways of living and acting has been especially, although not exclusively, prevalent among the Puerto Rican middle and upper classes. The process has led to a gradual incorporation and acceptance of some of the fundamental premises and values that underlie the institutional framework and life processes of the dominant society.[64]

Despite this undeniable influence, however, Puerto Ricans tend to view themselves as a distinct people. This fact came out forcefully in the most empirically grounded study conducted in the island recently on the question of cultural identity.[65] After carrying out numerous individual and group interviews ("focus groups") with people of all ideological persuasions, the author concluded that respondents "unequivocally identified themselves as Puerto Rican, believed that Puerto Rico was a uniquely recognizable entity, and felt positively toward that entity."[66] Often respondents said that "Puerto Ricanness was the product of a mixture of characteristic elements such as customs, traditions, history, and language."[67] They seemed to share a "sense of belonging" to that entity called Puerto Rico, and "many expressed a clear sense of Puerto Rico as having a defined culture, distinguishable from others by specific traits."[68]

There are many indications that a strong popular nationalism runs throughout Puerto Rican society. This is evident in the media, commercial advertisements, cultural festivities, youth gatherings, and the public discourse of all political sectors, including those who favor statehood. The country's rich artistic, literary, and musical traditions share many elements of the diverse Caribbean and Latin American cultures. There is a vibrant national popular culture that incorporates the European and African past as well as the many experiences and influences accruing inevitably from so many decades of American presence and contact. The synthesis is notably Puerto Rican, not Anglo-American.

The Legal System

The legal system has been one of the areas of Puerto Rican institutional life most directly influenced by American culture. One of the first tasks of the American military governors was to initiate a transformation of some of the major legal institutions existing in Puerto Rico before the occupation. Eventually, many provisions of the

---

CENTURY BALI (1980). Geertz describes the *exemplary center* as a center of power that becomes a standard of civilization for surrounding communities. *Id.* at 15. Drawing on this definition, I use the term to mean a community that exerts great influence over another by becoming its model.

[64] *See* a more elaborate analysis in Efrén Rivera Ramos, *Self-Determination and Decolonisation in the Society of the Modern Colonial Welfare State, in* ISSUES OF SELF-DETERMINATION (William Twining Ed. 1991).

[65] NANCY MORRIS, PUERTO RICO: CULTURE, POLITICS AND IDENTITY (1995).

[66] *Id.* at 78.

[67] *Id.* at 80.

[68] *Id.* at 95–97.

Civil Code were amended, and the Penal Code, the Political Code, and the Codes of Civil and Criminal procedure were replaced with analogous bodies of legislation taken from the states of Montana, California, and Idaho. New corporation and labor laws were adopted following North American models. In later years many of these codes and statutes would undergo revision by the Puerto Rican Legislative Assembly, but the influence of American legal principles and methods would remain evident.

A constant source of controversy has been the presence in Puerto Rico of a U.S. federal court with judges appointed by the president of the United States. Originally, all justices were Americans. But currently the court is integrated entirely by Puerto Rican lawyers appointed to the bench by the U.S. president. Proceedings of the court are conducted in English. In practice, it operates like any other court in the American federal judiciary. Its decisions are reviewed by the U.S. Court of Appeals for the First Circuit, located in Boston.

Also, from the earliest part of the century, presidential appointees to the Puerto Rican Supreme Court undertook to "Americanize" the judicial system and Puerto Rican substantive law.[69] Gradually, the Puerto Rican Supreme Court abandoned the civil law judicial tradition and came to resemble more and more a common-law court, and more specifically, an American court. This process was furthered by later Puerto Rican appointees. As I have stated elsewhere,

> Even during the period of highest influence of the heirs to the political tradition of self-government—the years of [Popular Democratic Party] absolute control of governmental institutions—when the Court was clearly the turf of the elite liberal professionals, this tendency [to Americanize the legal system] continued. In fact, during that time the tendency was reaffirmed and carried to its logical conclusion. The precedential value of the Court's decisions and the faculty to invalidate legislative and executive acts were firmly established. Inevitably, constitutional argument followed closely the tenets of American constitutional law.[70]

Many Puerto Rican justices (as well as many law school professors) have been trained in the leading American law schools, where they have imbibed the prevalent legal culture. This was the case even before the Constitution of 1952, which adopted a judicial structure, still in place, that closely follows the American tradition. The development of Puerto Rican legal culture has also implied changes in the structure and practices of the legal profession and in legal education. Those changes, however, cannot be attributed entirely to the Americanization of the legal system. They have been conditioned also by the processes that have transformed Puerto Rico from a chiefly rural, agrarian social formation into a predominantly urban, industrialized, capitalist (dependent) society, with an increasingly service-oriented economy and a relatively modern, technocratic, colonial welfare state.

---

[69] For a review of the process, see JOSÉ TRÍAS MONGE, LA CRISIS DEL DERECHO EN PUERTO RICO (1979), particularly at 14–22.

[70] Efrén Rivera Ramos, *The Supreme Court of Puerto Rico and the Separation of Powers Doctrine: Notes on Constitutional Argument and Social Conflict* 40–41 (footnote omitted) (1981).

Part II

The Judicial Construction
of Colonialism

Chapter 4
THE LEGAL DOCTRINE OF THE *INSULAR CASES*

Until the acquisition of new territories as a result of the Spanish American War, the policy in the law and tradition of the United States had been to eventually admit new territories as states of the Union.[1] The pattern was contained in the provisions of the Northwest Ordinance of 1787, a statute governing the vast territory that lay to the northwest of the original 13 states of the federation. As Leibowitz pointed out, "the Northwest Ordinance was either implicitly accepted as the governing statute for the newly acquired territories by the courts or was followed as the model in other governing legislation."[2]

The model provided for several stages, including investment of total government authority in an appointed governor, later establishment of an elected legislature and local courts, and final admission into statehood.[3] Leibowitz argued that the broad powers accorded Congress to deal with the territories was premised on the notion that territorial status was to be transitory and statehood would be the eventual result.[4] The legal basis for the exercise of broad congressional authority over the territories (as opposed to the states of the Union) was construed to lie in what is known as the Territorial Clause of the Constitution[5] and in the "inherent powers of a national sovereign government."[6]

The acquisition of overseas territories as a result of the Spanish American War and other events opened up an intense debate regarding the future of the new possessions. The polemic took place in Congress, academic journals, the press, and other public forums.[7] The starting point for much of the controversy was the allegation that these territories were different. They were far away geographically, not contiguous to the continent, densely populated, unamenable to colonization by settlement

---

[1] ARNOLD H. LEIBOWITZ, DEFINING STATUS: A COMPREHENSIVE ANALYSIS OF UNITED STATES TERRITORIAL RELATIONS 6 (1989); RAÚL SERRANO GEYLS (Demetrio Fernández Quiñones & Efrén Rivera Ramos, contributors) DERECHO CONSTITUCIONAL DE ESTADOS UNIDOS Y PUERTO RICO: DOCUMENTOS–JURISPRUDENCIA–ANOTACIONES–PREGUNTAS 449 (1986).

[2] LEIBOWITZ, *supra* note 1, at 6.

[3] *Id.* The term *statehood* is used here to refer to the status or condition of each one of the "states" that constitute the American federation. To avoid confusing it with the sense in which it is commonly used in international law, instead of "statehood" I use "independence" to refer to the condition enjoyed by sovereign states in the international community in connection with the debate regarding the status options of the American territorial possessions.

[4] *Id.* at 8.

[5] U.S. CONST. ART IV, § 3, cl. 2. The Territorial Clause reads, "The Congress shall have power to dispose of and make all needful Rules and Regulations respecting the Territory or other Property belonging to the United States; and nothing in this Constitution shall be so construed as to Prejudice any Claims of the United States, or of any particular State."

[6] LEIBOWITZ, *supra* note 1, at 10–16.

[7] For summaries of the different positions expounded during the discussions in Congress, the press, and the courts, *see,* among others, JUAN R. TORRUELLA, THE SUPREME COURT AND PUERTO RICO: THE DOCTRINE OF SEPARATE AND UNEQUAL chaps. 2, 3 (1985); SERRANO, *supra* note 1, at 449–50; AMERICAN IMPERIALISM IN 1898 chaps. 7–10 (T. P. Greene Ed. 1955).

on the part of Anglo-Americans and, above all, inhabited by alien peoples untrained in the arts of representative government.

Some had argued that because the peoples of those territories would never be assimilated into American culture, the territories should be relinquished. This was one strand of the so-called anti-imperialist movement. Another strand of the movement stood for the proposition that the United States could not constitutionally acquire territories and govern them as colonies. Others, within the "imperialist" camp, defended the power of the federal government not only to acquire territories but also to hold them as permanent dependencies, much in the manner in which the European powers governed their possessions. Still others argued that the territories should be retained but eventually granted equal rights with the other states.[8]

During the debates leading to the approval of the Foraker Act in 1900, which replaced the military government with a civilian administration in Puerto Rico,[9] the imperialist position prevailed. The Foraker Act was premised on the view that the United States could constitutionally acquire territories, free of constitutional restrictions, and govern them indefinitely as dependencies without steering them toward statehood.[10]

The legal community joined the debate, centering on the constitutional questions. Numerous articles appeared in many law journals, including the most prestigious ones, addressing the various issues involved as construed by the American legal establishment.[11] Eventually the U.S. Supreme Court would be called to pass upon those issues. By the time it did, however, acquisition was already an accomplished fact, the Foraker Act had come into effect, and President William McKinley, siding with the imperialists, had won a presidential campaign in which the matter of the new territorial acquisitions had been a central issue.

These developments, nonetheless, did not diminish the importance of the Court's intervention. The centrality of the Supreme Court of the United States in the resolution of important public matters invested its adjudication of the issues with a special significance. It finally put to rest the allegations that the American colonial venture was unconstitutional and, for all practical purposes, closed the debate within the American intellectual and governing elites. The doctrine of incorporation adopted in the *Insular Cases* helped to achieve that result.

The Doctrine of Territorial Incorporation

The name *Insular Cases* is normally given to a series of nine decisions rendered in 1901.[12] Seven of those cases arose from Puerto Rico, one from Hawaii, and one

---

[8] *See* chapter 1 for a fuller account of the debate between "imperialists" and "anti-imperialists."

[9] *See* chapter 3 for the details.

[10] SERRANO, *supra* note 1, at 450; Torruella, *supra* note 7, at 32–39; MARÍA EUGENIA ESTADES FONT, LA PRESENCIA MILITAR DE ESTADOS UNIDOS EN PUERTO RICO 1898–1918: INTERESES ESTRATÉGICOS Y DOMINACIÓN COLONIAL 105–129 (1988).

[11] Scores of articles were published in well-known American law journals concerning the legal and constitutional problems raised by the acquisition of the new territories. *See* chapter 1 n.59.

[12] De Lima v. Bidwell, 182 U.S. 1 (1901); Goetze v. United States, 182 U.S. 221 (1901); Grossman v. United States, 182 U.S. 221 (1901); Dooley v. United States, 182 U.S. 222 (1901) (hereinafter *Dooley I*); Armstrong v. United States, 182 U.S. 243 (1901); Downes v. Bidwell, 182 U.S. 244 (1901); Huus v.

from the Philippine Islands. However, some authors have extended the name to another set of cases decided from 1903 to 1914 dealing with the same or related questions[13] and others to a decision handed down in 1922 as well.[14] Of the 13 cases belonging to the second group, five originated in actions relating to Puerto Rico, six referred to the Philippines, one to Hawaii, and another to Alaska. The 1922 case dealt with the status of Puerto Rico. I will refer to all of them as the *Insular Cases:* All the issues were related, the second group of cases rested on the decisions made in 1901, and the 1922 case, *Balzac v. Porto Rico,* must be read as the culmination of the series because it reaffirmed and extended the doctrine of incorporation in light of new circumstances, such as the granting of U.S. citizenship to Puerto Ricans.

The academic debate in the law journals about the status of the territories and the rights of their inhabitants contained three general propositions. One group of writers held that the U.S. Constitution extended to the territories *ex proprio vigore.* That is to say, the Constitution imposed limitations that restrained the actions of Congress and the executive branch in the newly acquired lands. These limitations became operative by the mere fact of acquisition.[15] Another group of commentators argued that Congress enjoyed plenary powers over the territories and could act entirely as it saw fit, without constitutional limitations.[16] Finally, a third position suggested that although Congress had greater power over these territories, which were deemed not to have been "incorporated" into the Union, than over the territories subject to previous acquisitions, that power was limited by the "fundamental" provisions of the Constitution.[17] These arguments would figure prominently in the various decisions subscribed by the justices (both in the majority and the minority) in the *Insular Cases.*

In terms of past judicial pronouncements, two of the most frequently cited in the debate, especially by those who opposed holding territory with no intention of letting it become a state, were the opinions of Chief Justice Marshall in *Loughborough v. Blake*[18] and Chief Justice Taney in *Dred Scott v. Sandford.*[19] In the former, Marshall had defined the United States as including both states and territories, equally subject to the provisions of the Constitution. In the *Dred Scott* case the Court had held that a slave owner could not be deprived of his right to "property" over his

---

New York and Porto Rico Steamship Company, 182 U.S. 392 (1901); Dooley v. United States, 183 U.S. 151 (1901) (hereinafter *Dooley II*); and Fourteen Diamond Rings v. United States, 183 U.S. 176 (1901).

[13] Hawaii v. Mankichi, 190 U.S. 197 (1903); González v. Williams, 192 U.S. 1 (1904); Kepner v. United States, 195 U.S. 100 (1904); Dorr v. United States, 195 U.S. 138 (1904); Mendozana v. United States, 195 U.S. 158 (1904); Rasmussen v. United States, 197 U.S. 516 (1905); Trono v. United States, 199 U.S. 521 (1905); Grafton v. United States, 206 U.S. 333 (1907); Kent v. Porto Rico, 207 U.S. 113 (1907); Kopel v. Bingham, 211 U.S. 468 (1909); Dowdell v. United States, 221 U.S. 325 (1911); Ochoa v. Hernández, 230 U.S. 139 (1913); Ocampo v. United States, 234 U.S. 91 (1914).

[14] Balzac v. Porto Rico, 258 U.S. 298 (1922).

[15] *See, e.g.,* Carman F. Randolf, *Constitutional Aspects of Annexation,* 12 HARV. L. REV. 291 (1898); Simeon E. Baldwin, *The Constitutional Questions Incident to the Acquisition and Government by the United States of Island Territory,* 12 HARV. L. REV. 393 (1899).

[16] *E.g.,* Charles C. Langdell, *Status of Our New Territories,* 12 HARV. L. REV. 365 (1899); James Bradley Thayer, *Our New Possessions,* 12 HARV. L. REV. 464 (1899).

[17] *E.g.,* Abbot Lawrence Lowell, *Status of Our New Possessions—A Third View,* 13 HARV. L. REV. 155 (1899).

[18] Loughborough v. Blake, 18 U.S. (5 Wheat.) 317 (1820).

[19] Dred Scott v. Sandford, 60 U.S. (19 How.) 393 (1856).

slaves just by the fact that he brought his "property" into a particular "territory" of the United States. In his opinion, Chief Justice Taney made the following statement:

> There is certainly no power given by the Constitution to the Federal Government to establish or maintain colonies bordering on the United States or at a distance, to be ruled and governed at its own pleasure; nor to enlarge its territorial limits in any way, except by the admission of new States.... No power is given to acquire a Territory to be held and governed permanently in that character.
>
> ... The power to expand the territory of the United States by the admission of new States is plainly given; and in the construction of this power by all the departments of the Government, it has been held to authorize the acquisition of territory, not fit for admission at the time, but to be admitted as soon as its population and situation would entitle it to admission. It is acquired to become a State, and not to be held as a colony and governed by Congress with absolute authority.[20]

As formulated finally by the Court, the issues in the *Insular Cases* could be summarized in the following questions: What was the status of the new territories? How much power did Congress enjoy in their governance? And what were the rights of their inhabitants?

The Court rendered its decision on seven of the first group of nine cases on the same day: May 27, 1901. Despite this circumstance, in important respects they do not form a consistent set of decisions, especially because Justice Henry Billings Brown, who wrote the majority opinion in *De Lima v. Bidwell* and in the first *Dooley v. United States*, joined the judges who had formed the minority in those cases to constitute a new majority in *Downes v. Bidwell*. Eventually *Downes* became the most important case of the group.

The following discussion examines briefly the development of the legal doctrine the Court adopted. The reasoning of the Court will be analyzed in more detail in the following chapters.

De Lima

The first case, *De Lima*, was an appeal from the Circuit Court of the United States for the Southern District of New York involving an action originally instituted by the firm D. A. de Lima and Co. against the collector of the Port of New York. The claimant sought to recover duties exacted under protest on certain importations of sugar from San Juan, Puerto Rico, during the autumn of 1899. That is, the action had taken place subsequent to the cession of Puerto Rico to the United States but before passage of the Foraker Act. The petitioner argued that the U.S. Tariff Act of 1897, under which the exactions had been made, did not apply to Puerto Rico because the latter was not a foreign country as defined by the act. Puerto Rico, the argument went, had become a part of the United States by virtue of the Treaty of Paris. Therefore, any imposition of taxes and excises not applicable to other parts of the United States violated the Uniformity Clause of the U.S. Constitution.[21]

---

[20] *Id.* at 446–47.

[21] U.S. CONST. art. I, § 8, cl. 1: "The Congress shall have power to lay and collect taxes, duties, imposts and excises, to pay the debts and provide for the common defence and general welfare of the United States; but all duties, imposts and excises *shall be uniform throughout the United States*" (emphasis added).

The U.S. attorney general replied that the Uniformity Clause applied to the states and not to territories.[22] The solicitor general, in turn, in an extended argument covering many aspects of the question, argued essentially that (a) the act of cession did not make the territory, ipso facto, a part of the United States, but merely a possession; (b) newly acquired territory becomes a part of the United States only if Congress so determines; (c) the power of Congress over territories that have not become a part of the United States is "plenary," "absolute," and "full and complete," subject only to fundamental limitations imposed by the Constitution, as defined by the courts.[23]

The Supreme Court divided itself over the issue, with five justices holding against the validity of the tariff and four supporting the government's position.[24] Justice Brown wrote the majority opinion. He framed the issue narrowly: whether territory acquired by cession from a foreign power remained a "foreign country" within the meaning of the tariff laws. He concluded that at the time the duties were levied (after the cession had taken place), Puerto Rico was not a foreign country within the meaning of those statutes, but a territory of the United States. Therefore, the duties were illegally exacted. His argument hinged basically upon the definition of *foreign country*: "one exclusively within the sovereignty of a foreign nation and without the sovereignty of the United States."[25] In his opinion, the judicial, executive, and legislative precedents (including the Foraker Act) had established the principle that the mere cession and possession had the effect of changing the status of the territory for revenue purposes from foreign to domestic.[26] An act of Congress was not needed to make the territory domestic after cession.[27]

He added that the right to acquire territory—which he did not question—involved the right to govern and dispose of it[28] and that Congress had complete authority over the people of the territories. Quoting Chief Justice White in *National Bank v. County of Yankton*,[29] Brown stated that Congress "may do for the Territories what the people, under the Constitution, may do for the States."[30] That authority rises "not necessarily from the territorial clause, but from the necessities of the case."[31] Once acquired by treaty, the territory belongs to the United States and is subject to the disposition of Congress. The Court could not acquiesce in the assumption, he concluded, that a territory may be at the same time both domestic and foreign.[32] Justice Brown's opinion does not address the issue of whether there is a distinction between *belonging to* and *being a part of* the United States.

Justice Gray dissented very briefly on the grounds that the Court's decision was

---

[22] *De Lima*, 182 U.S. at 94–124.

[23] *Id.* at 124–74.

[24] The judges constituting the majority were Justices Henry Billings Brown, Rufus Wheeler Peckham, John Marshall Harlan, David Josiah Brewer, and Chief Justice Melville Weston Fuller. In the minority were Justices Joseph McKenna, George Shiras, Jr., Edward Douglas White, and Horace Gray.

[25] *De Lima*, 182 U.S. at 180, citing The Eliza, 8 F. Cas. 455 (Cir. D. Mass. 1813) (No. 4,346); Taber v. United States, 23 F. Cas. 611 (Cir. D. Mass. 1839) (No. 13,722); The Adventure, 1 F. Cas. 202 (Cir. D. Va. 1812) (No. 93).

[26] *Id.* at 181–94.

[27] *Id.* at 197.

[28] *Id.* at 196.

[29] National Bank v. County of Yankton, 101 U.S. 129 (1879).

[30] *De Lima*, 182 U.S. at 196.

[31] *Id.*

[32] *Id.* at 197.

incompatible with the Court's unanimous opinion in a previous case, *Fleming v. Page*,[33] and with the majority's opinion in *Downes,* decided that very day.[34] Justice McKenna filed a longer dissenting opinion, joined by Justices Shiras and White.[35] The gist of his argument involved a frontal rejection of what he obviously considered Justice Brown's excessive reliance on a definition (what is a "foreign country" or a "domestic territory"?). Between those "extremes" there are "other relations," argued McKenna, and Puerto Rico occupied one of them. Arguing that the administration of government entails more complexity than the administration of a piece of real estate and that the issues were more complicated than a "mere definition," Justice McKenna called attention to what he believed were the "practicalities" of the situation and the "great public interests involved." The Court's position that the mere cession of territory by a foreign power converts the former into a part of the United States would have the effect of reducing the flexibility accorded the nation's government by the treaty-making power enshrined in the Constitution. The consequences of the rigid interpretation rendered by the majority, he believed, would have the effect of crippling the nation as a power among nations. It would not be able to behave like them, to acquire territory—whether or not as an incident of war—and to make whatever provisions it saw fit in the appropriate treaties. The nation's representatives would enter into any negotiation bound beforehand and with their options limited.[36]

In *Goetze v. United States* and *Grossman v. United States,* decided together, the Court followed *De Lima* and reversed an administrative decision to collect duties on merchandise imported from Puerto Rico and Hawaii into the United States. These territories were not foreign countries within the meaning of the tariff laws, the Court held.[37]

Dooley I

Dooley v. United States (*Dooley I*) presented the same issue, but in a reverse factual situation. This time the question hinged on the legality of imports from the United States into Puerto Rico. The Court again followed *De Lima*, with opinions divided among the same two groups of judges. Once more, Justice Brown wrote the majority opinion. The majority held that duties collected under the authority of the military commander of the occupying forces and of the president of the United States as commander in chief during the period from the time of actual occupation to ratification of the Treaty of Paris had been legally exacted under the war powers of the executive. They had been imposed according to "the law of arms and the right of conquest" and the "general principles in respect to war and peace between

---

[33] In Fleming v. Page, 50 U.S. (9 How.) 603 (1850), the Court had validated the collection of duties upon merchandise imported from Tampico, Mexico, while under military occupation by the United States. It held that, although subjected to American military occupation, Tampico had not ceased to be foreign territory. In a previous case, United States v. Rice, 17 U.S. (4 Wheat.) 246 (1819), however, the Court had held that a region of the later state of Maine had been converted into a foreign territory by virtue of its temporary military occupation by the British during the War of 1812.

[34] *De Lima*, 182 U.S. at 220.

[35] *Id.* at 200–20.

[36] *Id.* at 218–20.

[37] *Goetze*, 182 U.S. at 221–22.

nations."[38] But the duties exacted after ratification of the treaty had been illegally seized, because Puerto Rico had ceased to be a foreign country. Brown offered as further justification a consideration of the "disastrous" consequences of a contrary decision for the economy of Puerto Rico. The country would be "foreign" for both Spain and the United States, becoming practically isolated in terms of trade, in detriment to "the business and finances" of the island.[39]

Justice White's dissent, joined by Justices Gray, Shiras, and McKenna, emphasized the impracticality of the theory of immediate incorporation by cession. It would deny Congress the flexibility necessary to make the required practical adjustments for the incorporation of the territory. The result in *Dooley I* was followed in *Armstrong v. United States*, which also involved duties upon goods imported into San Juan before and after ratification of the Treaty of Paris.

Downes

The next case was *Downes*.[40] Again the controversy involved duties on imports from Puerto Rico into the United States. But this time the collection had occurred after passage of the Foraker Act, which, as has been explained, established a civilian government in the island and expressly levied the tax in question in the case. The issue, therefore, involved the constitutionality of the pertinent provision of the Foraker Act.

The case produced a new majority in the Court. Justice Brown joined the four dissenting judges in *De Lima* to uphold the validity of the tax. However, the justices filed five separate opinions. Justice Brown delivered the conclusion and judgment of the Court. Justice White concurred in the judgment but rendered his own opinion—joined by Shiras and McKenna—expounding the reasons for his conclusion. Justice Gray, concurring also, stated that he agreed in substance with White but had decided to "sum up the reasons" for his concurrence separately. Chief Justice Fuller wrote a dissenting opinion, adhered to by Justices Harlan, Brewer, and Peckham. But Harlan, "in view . . . of the importance of the questions" involved and of the "consequences" that would follow from the Court's decision, saw fit to "add some observations"[41] in a vigorous dissent that was to become the first in a series of protestations against the course that the Court would follow thereafter regarding the territorial question.

The principal conclusion of Justice Brown's opinion was that the Uniformity Clause of the Constitution did not apply to Puerto Rico because Puerto Rico was "a territory *appurtenant* and *belonging to* the United States, but not a *part* of the United States within the revenue clauses of the Constitution."[42] The Foraker Act was constitutional so far as it imposed duties on imports from the island. The main practical, immediate effect of the decision was that the United States could now collect duties on imports from Puerto Rico, as authorized specifically by Congress. Prior to the Foraker Act, according to the *De Lima* case, such collection was not permitted under

---

[38] *Dooley I*, 182 U.S. at 230–31, quoting Justice Wayne in *Cross v. Harrison* (16 How.) 164 (1853).
[39] *Id.* at 236.
[40] *Downes*, 182 U.S. at 244.
[41] *Id.* at 376.
[42] *Id.* at 287 (emphasis added).

the general tariff laws, because Puerto Rico was not a foreign country. Of course, as will be discussed throughout this section, the larger effects were much broader than that.

The rationale of Justice Brown's conclusion included an appeal to what, to his mind, were the relevant legislative and judicial precedents and a consideration of what the consequences would be of a contrary holding. His conclusion included the view that Congress had plenary power over the territories, but subject to "fundamental limitations in favor of personal rights."[43] "The power to acquire territory by treaty," he affirmed, "implies the power to govern such territory, and to prescribe upon what terms the United States will receive its inhabitants and what their status shall be in what Chief Justice Marshall termed the 'American Empire.' "[44] In sum, the plenary power of Congress arose from the inherent right to acquire territory, from the Territorial Clause, from the treaty-making power, and from the power to declare and conduct war.[45] The Constitution applied to the territories only to the degree that it was extended to them by Congress. As to the probability of despotism resulting from such plenary power, the inhabitants of the new territories should not fear: "There are certain principles of natural justice inherent in the Anglo-Saxon character which need no expression in constitutions or statutes to give them effect or to secure dependencies against legislation manifestly hostile to their real interests."[46]

The significance of *Downes*, however, lies in Justice White's concurring opinion, in which he advanced his "incorporation" doctrine. The opinion obtained the total adherence of two of the justices, and a third agreed "in substance" with it. Eventually, Justice White's reasoning would become the unquestioned position of the Court.

White commenced by agreeing that Congress had plenary power over the territories:

> The Constitution has undoubtedly conferred on Congress . . . the right to create such municipal organizations as it may deem best for all the territories of the United States whether they have been incorporated or not, to give to the inhabitants as respects the local governments such degree of representation as may be conducive to the public well-being, to deprive such territory of representative government if it is considered just to do so, and to change such local governments at discretion.[47]

But, like Justice Brown, he believed that that power may be checked by "fundamental restrictions" that may not even be expressed in the Constitution:

> Whilst, therefore, there is no express or implied limitation on Congress in exercising its power to create local governments for any and all of the territories, by which that body is restrained from the widest latitude of discretion, it does not follow that there may not be inherent, although unexpressed, principles which are the basis of all free government which cannot be with impunity transcended.[48]

Regarding the applicability of the Constitution, White believed that the question

---

[43] *Id.* at 268.
[44] *Id.* at 279.
[45] *Id.* at 268.
[46] *Id.* at 280.
[47] *Id.* at 289–90.
[48] *Id.* at 290–91.

was not whether the Constitution was operative ("for that is self-evident"), but whether the provision Congress relied on to legislate for the territory was applicable.[49] In legislating for Puerto Rico (or the other territories) Congress was limited only by the "applicable" provisions of the Constitution. The particular provisions that would apply depended "on the situation of the territory and its relation to the United States."[50] The issue, then, whether the impugned tax violated the Uniformity Clause of the Constitution had to be resolved by answering the question whether Puerto Rico had been incorporated into the United States and had become an integral part of it. In formulating the issue in this way, White was constructing a new category in American constitutional jurisprudence: the unincorporated territory. Establishing a difference between incorporated and unincorporated territories was justified, according to him, by the "general principles of the law of nations," the Constitution itself, the Constitution "as illustrated by the history of the government," and the past decisions of the Court.

Sovereign nations, he argued, have an inherent right to acquire territory and to determine the relation of that territory to the new government, absent stipulations upon the subject between the old and the new masters.[51] He quoted Chief Justice John Marshall in *American Insurance Co. v. Canter*[52] to buttress his reading of international law and the U.S. Constitution. In that decision Justice Marshall stated,

> The Constitution confers absolutely on the government of the Union, the powers of making war, and of making treaties; consequently, that government possesses the power of acquiring territory, either by conquest or by treaty.[53] . . . If it [conquered territory] be ceded by treaty, the acquisition is confirmed, and the ceded territory becomes a part of the nation to which it is annexed, either on the terms stipulated in the treaty of cession, or *on such as its new master shall impose.*[54]

Justice White made an extensive review of the history of territorial acquisition in the United States, indicating the ways in which, in his view, Congress had expressed its intention of "incorporating" each and every one of the territories.[55] His final argument rested on what he perceived to be the consequences, or the "evil(s) of immediate incorporation." Among those "evils" he included the curtailment of the government's ability to terminate a successful war by acquiring territory through a treaty without immediately incorporating such territory into the United States or, in a nightmare scenario, the possibility of "millions of inhabitants of alien territory" being able, by their immediate incorporation into the United States by treaty, to overthrow "the whole structure of the government."[56]

The decision to incorporate implies a decision to divide with the "alien people" the "rights which peculiarly belong to the citizens of the United States."[57] Incorporation, therefore, was a political decision to be taken by the "people" of the United

---

[49] *Id.* at 292.

[50] *Id.* at 293.

[51] *Id.* at 300.

[52] 26 U.S. (1 Pet.) 511 (1828).

[53] *Downes*, 182 U.S. at 303.

[54] *Id.* at 302 (emphasis in original).

[55] *Id.* at 304–05, 320–29.

[56] *Id.* at 311, 313.

[57] *Id.* at 324.

States, represented in Congress, and not the automatic legal result of the acquisition of territory.[58] Incorporation could be effected either expressly or implicitly.[59] One indicator of the intent of Congress would be whether the inhabitants of the acquired territory had been granted U.S. citizenship and had been extended the rights and immunities of people residing in the Northwest Territory.[60]

Had Puerto Rico been incorporated into the United States by the provisions of either the Treaty of Paris or the Foraker Act? No, answered Justice White. Article IX of the treaty expressly provided that "the civil rights and political status of the native inhabitants of the territories hereby ceded to the United States shall be determined by Congress."[61] In other words, the treaty had left open the question of the status of the territory and the civil rights of Puerto Ricans, to be determined by further congressional action. On the other hand, Justice White concluded, the Foraker Act, "taken as a whole," showed the "manifest intention of Congress that for the present at least Porto Rico [sic] is not to be incorporated into the United States."[62] In arriving at that conclusion, White referred to the fact that the provision to confer U.S. citizenship on Puerto Ricans had been extricated from the bill before its enactment.[63] He concluded,

> The result of what has been said is that whilst in an international sense Porto Rico was not a foreign country, since it was subject to the sovereignty of and was owned by the United States, it was foreign to the United States in a domestic sense, because the island had not been incorporated into the United States, but was merely appurtenant thereto as a possession.[64]

Although the doctrine of incorporation was accepted by only four of the five justices constituting the majority in *Downes*,[65] all members of the majority agreed that Congress had plenary power over the territories acquired by conquest or treaty, subject to some still unspecified fundamental restrictions. In addition, they agreed, Puerto Rico was a possession belonging or appurtenant to the United States, but not a part of it, for the purposes of the revenue clauses of the Constitution.

Chief Justice Fuller's dissent advanced the proposition that the Constitution, being operative wherever the government acted, commanded uniformity in the imposition of taxes, as in other matters. This included commerce between the states and the territories. He argued that the *plenary power* of Congress referred to the determination of the political status of places over which it exercised exclusive jurisdiction, but not over rights, commerce, or other such activities affecting the life of the inhabitants of those places. Fuller criticized the concept of "incorporation," on which Justice White relied "as if [the term were] possessed of some occult meaning."[66] He denounced the view that the protection of the fundamental rights of

---

[58] *Id.* at 311–12.

[59] *Id.* at 339.

[60] *Id.* at 332–33.

[61] *Id.* at 339–40.

[62] *Id.* at 340. During the first decades of this century the Americans changed Puerto Rico's name to Porto Rico. The form used in the original will be retained in all quotations.

[63] *Id.* at 341.

[64] *Id.* at 341–42.

[65] I am including here Justice Gray's agreement "in substance" with Justice White's opinion.

[66] *Downes*, 182 U.S. at 373.

the peoples in the territories did not include guarantees against the differentiated assessment of impository measures.[67] He rejected the notion that

> if an organized and settled province of another sovereignty is acquired by the United States, Congress has the power to keep it, like a disembodied shade, in an intermediate state of ambiguous existence for an indefinite period; and more than that, that after it has been called from that limbo, commerce with it is absolutely subject to the will of Congress, irrespective of constitutional provisions.[68]

Justice Fuller added that the incorporation theory

> assumes that the Constitution created a government empowered to acquire countries throughout the world, to be governed by different rules than those obtaining in the original states and territories, and substitutes for the present system of republican government, a system of domination over distant provinces in the exercise of unrestricted power.[69]

In his dissent, Justice Harlan agreed with the chief justice that Puerto Rico had become a part of the United States within the meaning of the Uniformity Clause, at least after the ratification of the Treaty of Paris. He made two basic points in his argument: (a) that the Constitution applied to "all the peoples and all the territory" over which the United States could exercise jurisdiction or authority, whether within or without the states properly called, and (b) that the Constitution did not authorize Congress to institute a colonial regime anywhere in the world. Warning that the majority's decision could lead to "a radical and mischievous change" in the American system of government, passing from "the era of constitutional liberty" to an "era of legislative absolutism," he rejected the idea that the United States could embark on European-style colonialism:

> Monarchical and despotic governments, unrestrained by written constitutions, may do with newly acquired territories what this Government may not do consistently with our fundamental law. To say otherwise is to concede that Congress may, by action taken outside of the Constitution, engraft upon our republican institutions a colonial system such as exists under monarchical governments. . . .[70]
>
> The idea that this country may acquire territories anywhere upon the earth by conquest or treaty, and hold them as mere colonies or provinces—the people inhabiting them to enjoy only such rights as Congress chooses to accord them—is wholly inconsistent with the spirit and genius as well as with the words of the Constitution.[71]

Justice Harlan derided the notion that the inhabitants of the islands could rely for their protection on the supposed libertarian attitudes of their new masters. The founders of the nation themselves, he recalled, had been unwilling "to depend for their safety" on what Justice Brown had described as "certain principles of natural justice inherent in Anglo-Saxon character which need no expression in constitutions or statutes," for they "well remembered" the oppression visited on "Anglo-Saxons on this Continent" by "Anglo-Saxons across the ocean."[72]

---

[67] *Id.*
[68] *Id* at 372.
[69] *Id.* at 373.
[70] *Id.* at 381.
[71] *Id.* at 380.
[72] *Id.* at 381.

Harlan considered the notion of "incorporation" too imprecise. In any event, a domestic territory of the United States with an organized civil government established by Congress was, for all purposes, under the complete jurisdiction of the United States and, therefore, a part of, and incorporated into, the United States.[73] Puerto Rico, he argued, had been "incorporated" by the Treaty of Paris (specifically by the act of its ratification by the Senate), or by the appropriation of monies by Congress for the administration of the territory, or by the multiple provisions of the Foraker Act. To contend that it had not been incorporated was to rely solely on the fact that Congress had failed to use the word "incorporate" in the latter statute. "I am constrained to say," he commented, "that this idea of 'incorporation' has some occult meaning which my mind does not apprehend. It is enveloped in some mystery which I am unable to unravel."[74] Harlan recalled Justice Brown's assertion in the *De Lima* case that territory cannot be "domestic for one purpose and foreign for another."[75] "How Porto Rico can be a domestic territory of the United States, as distinctly held in *De Lima v. Bidwell*, and yet, as is now held, not embraced by the words 'throughout the United States', is more than I can understand," Justice Harlan concluded.[76]

Harlan's rejection of the incorporation doctrine continued until his death in 1911. In *Rasmussen v. United States*, a 1905 case, the Court decided that the constitutional requirement of a trial by jury of 12 applied to the territory of Alaska, because the latter had been incorporated into the nation. Harlan concurred in the judgment, not because there was evidence of Congress's intent to incorporate Alaska, as Justice White argued in the principal opinion, but because of his belief that the Constitution applies immediately upon acquisition.[77] He stated,

> The proposition that a people subject to the full authority of the United States for purposes of government may, under any circumstances, or for any period of time, long or short, be governed, as Congress pleases to ordain, without regard to the Constitution, is, in my judgement, inconsistent with the whole theory of our institutions.[78]

In that same case Justice Brown also rejected the incorporation doctrine as "confusing" and "of no practical value."[79] There were several difficulties with the doctrine, Brown indicated: May incorporation be direct or indirect? What is the difference between an "organized" and an "incorporated" territory? What language must Congress use to effect the result?[80] He adhered, rather, to the "extension" doctrine: Congress may deal as it pleases with a territory until it decides to extend to it the Constitution[81] "formally or by implication,"[82] with the constraint that there are some "natural rights" that could not be infringed upon. According to him this test was

---

[73] *Id.* at 389.
[74] *Id.* at 391.
[75] *Id.* at 385.
[76] *Id.* at 386.
[77] *Rasmussen*, 197 U.S. at 528–31.
[78] *Id.* at 530.
[79] *Id.* at 535.
[80] *Id.* at 533–34.
[81] *Id.* at 536.
[82] *Id.* at 532.

more easily and less confusingly applied. (It is evident, however, that his test entailed the same or similar problems of interpretation, especially when the intention to extend the Constitution was to be implied from congressional action.)

Huus, Dooley II, and *Fourteen Diamond Rings*

One further case decided on May 27, 1901, and another decided later that year on December 2 reaffirmed the conclusion arrived at in the *De Lima* case: that Puerto Rico was not a foreign country, but domestic territory. In *Huus v. New York and Porto Rico Steamship Company*, a unanimous Court held that vessels involved in trade between Puerto Rico and ports of the United States were engaged in coasting trade in the sense in which those words were used in the New York pilotage statutes (which meant "domestic," not "foreign" trade) and that the steam vessels taking part in such trade were to be regarded as coastwise steam vessels (therefore engaged in domestic trade) under certain federal laws. The decision was based on the language of Section 9 of the Foraker Act. That section provided for the "nationalization of all vessels" owned by inhabitants of Puerto Rico and for the admission of the same to all the benefits of the coasting trade of the United States and stated that "the coasting trade between Puerto Rico and the United States [should] be regulated in accordance with the provisions of law applicable to such trade between any two great coasting districts of the United States."[83]

In the second *Dooley v. United States (Dooley II)*, the Court, in an opinion written by Justice Brown, upheld the constitutionality of the Foraker Act insofar as it fixed the duties to be paid on merchandise imported into Puerto Rico from the United States (in this case, from New York). It had been argued that such provision violated Article 1, Section 9 of the Constitution, which provides that "no tax or duty shall be laid on articles exported from any state." Justice Brown reasoned that that constitutional provision referred to articles exported to foreign countries. Puerto Rico was not a foreign country, according to *De Lima*. Congress was exercising here wide powers conferred by Article I, Section 8 of the Constitution, which authorized it to "lay and collect taxes, duties, imposts and excises."[84] He envisaged no problems arising from the Uniformity Clause. "There is a wide difference," he argued, "between the full and paramount power of Congress in legislating for a territory in the condition of Porto Rico and its power with respect to the States, which is merely incidental to its right to regulate interstate commerce."[85]

Justice White, who had joined Justice McKenna's dissenting opinion in *De Lima* (maintaining that Puerto Rico was not either foreign or domestic, but somewhere in between), and who had concluded in *Downes* that Puerto Rico had not been incorporated into the United States, concurred in the judgment in *Dooley II*. He argued that Puerto Rico was not a foreign country, citing *De Lima* and *Dooley I* and referring to the fact that in *Downes* all members of the Court had agreed that Puerto Rico had either become a part of the United States or had come under its jurisdiction.[86]

Chief Justice Fuller dissented again, joined by Justices Harlan, Brewer, and Peck-

---

[83] *Huus*, 182 U.S. at 396.
[84] *Dooley II*, 183 U.S. at 155.
[85] *Id.* at 157.
[86] *Id.* at 163–64.

ham (the majority in *De Lima*, minus Justice Brown). He argued, in short, that the Constitution prohibited Congress to levy duties on exports and that the duties in question were, precisely, duties on exports. He added that the decision now made would enable Congress, under the guise of taxation, to exclude the products of Puerto Rico from the states and vice versa, notwithstanding what had been decided in *De Lima* (that since Puerto Rico had ceased to be foreign and had become domestic territory, it was not covered by the tariff laws of the United States).[87] Thus, both the majority and the minority opinions in this case relied on the rationale of *De Lima* to justify their differing conclusions. The disparate results in these cases (especially those decided on May 27, 1901) led one commentator to exclaim that "thus, amazingly, in one day, the Court held Puerto Rico to be in and/or out of the United States in three different ways!"[88]

In *Fourteen Diamond Rings v. United States* (decided the same day as *Dooley II*), the Court held that some diamond rings imported from the Philippines after ratification of the Treaty of Paris were not subject to duties as imports from a foreign country. Chief Justice Fuller, writing for the majority, cited *De Lima*. The Philippines were in the same situation as Puerto Rico, he concluded. Justice Brown concurred. The minority in *De Lima* dissented again.

Mankichi

There was no discussion of the incorporation doctrine in *Huus, Dooley II,* or *Fourteen Diamond Rings*. However, the doctrine continued to gather strength. In *Hawaii v. Mankichi*, decided in 1903, the question arose whether the Sixth and Ninth Amendments to the U.S. Constitution required that criminal convictions in the territory of Hawaii be secured only by indictment found by a grand jury and by a verdict rendered unanimously by a petty jury. The Republic of Hawaii had been annexed by virtue of a joint resolution (known as the Newlands Resolution) adopted by Congress on July 7, 1898.[89] The resolution provided for annexation of the Hawaiian Islands "as a part of the territory of the United States." It further dictated that "The municipal legislation of the Hawaiian Islands . . . not inconsistent with this joint resolution *nor contrary to the Constitution of the United States* . . . shall remain in force until the Congress of the United States shall otherwise determine."[90]

Formal transfer of the islands did not occur until August 12, 1898, and it was not until June 14, 1900, that Congress provided for the formal incorporation of the republic under the name of the "Territory of Hawaii," with special provisions regarding the empaneling of grand juries and for unanimous verdicts of petty juries.[91] No such provisions existed in the municipal legislation of the republic prior to that date. The conviction in question in the case occurred before June 14, 1900. The attorney general of the territory argued that mere annexation did not have the effect of incorporating Hawaii. He cited *Downes*. The appellee contended that Congress had incorporated Hawaii by virtue of the Newlands Resolution and, therefore, the

---

[87] *Id.* at 175–76.

[88] Torruella, *supra* note 7, at 61.

[89] The Newlands Resolution, 30 Stat. 750 (1898).

[90] *Id.*

[91] *Mankichi*, 190 U.S. at 210–11.

referenced provisions of the Constitution applied since the date the resolution came into effect. The doctrine of incorporation had not yet been adopted by a majority of the Court.

Justice Brown delivered the opinion of the Court, which held that the Newlands Resolution did not automatically abolish the criminal procedure theretofore in existence in Hawaii and, therefore, grand jury indictments and unanimous verdicts were not required. He was joined by two new justices, Oliver Wendell Holmes and William R. Day, appointed to the Court by President Roosevelt in 1902 and 1903 to replace Justices Gray and Shiras, respectively. Justices White and McKenna concurred but in a separate opinion they argued that Hawaii had not been incorporated into the union by the Newlands Resolution. The islands had only been annexed, not absolutely, but merely "as part of the territory of the United States" and simply declared to be subject to its sovereignty.[92] The proviso about the Constitution in the Newlands Resolution "clearly referred only to [those] provisions . . . which were applicable and not those which were inapplicable," that is, those fundamental provisions that were "by their own force applicable to the territory with which Congress was dealing."[93] The latter did not include indictment by grand jury or unanimous verdicts, according to White.

In their separate dissents, Chief Justice Fuller and Justice Harlan maintained that the history of the treaty of annexation, including the Newlands Resolution, unambiguously showed the intention of Congress to "incorporate" the islands into the United States.

Dorr

The doctrine of incorporation was finally embraced by a majority of the Court in 1904. The case was *Dorr v. United States*. The specific holding of the Court was similar to that in *Mankichi*: The constitutional right to trial by jury did not extend to the Philippines unless so provided by Congress. Eight justices adhered to the conclusion. Only Justice Harlan dissented. Justice Day delivered the opinion of the Court. He claimed that the 1901 *Insular Cases* had settled the question of the power of Congress to govern newly acquired territories:

> The recent consideration of this Court and the full discussion had in the opinions delivered in the so-called "Insular Cases," renders superfluous any attempt to reconsider the constitutional relation of the powers of the government to territory acquired by a treaty cession to the United States. *De Lima v. Bidwell*, 182 U.S. 1; *Downes v. Bidwell*, 182 U.S. 244.[94]

He then proceeded to adopt the doctrine of incorporation as had been expounded by Justice White in his concurrence in *Downes*:

> The limitations which are to be applied in any given case involving territorial government must depend upon the relation of the particular territory to the United States, concerning which Congress is exercising the power conferred by the Constitution.

---

[92] *Id.* at 219.
[93] *Id.* at 221.
[94] *Dorr*, 195 U.S. at 139.

> That the United States may have territory, which is not *incorporated* into the United
> States as a body politic, we think was recognized by the framers of the Constitution
> in enacting the article already considered, giving power over the territories, and is
> sanctioned by the opinions of the justices concurring in the judgment in *Downes v.
> Bidwell*. . . .
>
> Until Congress shall see fit to *incorporate* territory ceded by treaty into the United
> States, we regard it as settled by that decision that the territory is to be governed
> under the power existing in Congress to make laws for such territories and subject to
> such constitutional restrictions upon the powers of that body as are applicable to the
> situation.[95]

Regarding the specific question at hand, Justice Day determined the following:

> We conclude that the power to govern territory, implied in the right to acquire it, and
> given to Congress in the Constitution in Article IV, § 3, to whatever other limitations
> it may be subject, the extent of which must be decided as questions arise, does not
> require that body to enact for ceded territory, not made a part of the United States by
> Congressional action, a system of laws which shall include the right of trial by jury,
> and that the Constitution does not, without legislation and of its own force, carry such
> right to territory so situated.[96]

In a concurrent opinion, joined by Justices Fuller and Brewer, Justice Peckham
clarified that he voted with the majority because the specific point about trial by jury
had been decided in *Mankichi*, but he rejected that *Downes* be regarded as authority
for the case at hand because the various opinions rendered on that occasion were
"plainly not binding."[97] He was manifestly unwilling to adhere to the incorporation
theory. However, there were no other concurrent opinions, and only Justice Harlan
dissented. That meant that five justices of the majority of eight, including Justice
Brown, were technically adhering to the opinion delivered by Justice Day. Despite
the disparity of opinions in the 1901 cases, the justices chose to read those decisions
as supporting the view first expounded by Justice White in his concurrence in
Downes. That reading meant that the doctrine of incorporation was now the position
of a majority of the Court. The fact was noted unambiguously one year later by
Justice White himself, writing for the majority in *Rasmussen*. Stating correctly that
in *Dorr* the majority had adopted the doctrine of incorporation, Justice White relied
on its rationale to hold that Alaska had been incorporated into the Union. Chief
Justice Taft made a similar statement about the import of Dorr in the *Balzac* case in
1922.

Conclusion of the Debate

By mid-1904, therefore, the doctrine of the differentiated status of the newly acquired
territories and of the plenary power of Congress to govern them had been established.
The colonial condition of the territories and their peoples—totally subordinated and
subject to the mercy of Congress and, in many ways, of the federal executive—had

---

[95] *Id.* at 142–43 (emphasis added).
[96] *Id.* at 149.
[97] *Id.* at 154.

been given legal sanction by the highest court of the land. *Rasmussen*, decided in 1905, represented the final playing out of the debate in the highest judicial forum of the new imperial power. It was, however, a postmortem ritual. As if in a didactic summing up, the case brought into sharp focus the three contending positions, eloquently expounded by the principal characters themselves. Justice White, as was fit, explained and applied his incorporation doctrine with the new authority invested on his pronouncements by the concurring vote of a substantial majority. Justice Brown, in a minority of one, reiterated his extension doctrine, while Justice Harlan insisted on his belief that the Constitution applied to the territories immediately upon acquisition. The irony was that their differing analyses led to the same conclusion in the specific situation at hand. All of them agreed that the constitutional requirement of a trial by jury of 12 was extensive to Alaska. Of course, there were other ironies. The fate of the Caribbean and Pacific territories (with the exception of Hawaii), at least as far as the judicial sanction of colonialism was concerned, was consummated in the very case that clearly demonstrated one of the fundamental reasons for their differential treatment. After all, Alaska was sparsely populated and subject to control by white American settlers, conditions perceived to guarantee a relatively easy governance and assimilation.[98]

After 1905 there were no dissents in the Court in cases dealing with territorial matters, until 1911, when Justice Harlan filed a last dissent, without opinion, in *Dowdell v. United States*. There, among other holdings, the Court reaffirmed *Dorr* regarding the extension of trial by jury to the Philippines. After that decision there were no dissents from what had clearly become the doctrine of the Court. *Ocampo v. United States,* decided in 1914, also related to the extension of constitutional guarantees in the criminal process in the Philippines, and the Court rendered a unanimous decision reaffirming earlier cases and quoting *Mankichi, Dorr,* and *Dowdell.*

The test to determine what constitutional provisions and rights applied to the territories was now whether the territory had been incorporated into the Union. This raised the question of the criteria to be used in ascertaining whether incorporation had occurred. In *Downes*, Justice White had mentioned the granting of U.S. citizenship to the people of the territory as a clear indicator.[99] In *Rasmussen* he listed additional factors: (a) the intention of Congress as expressed in the treaties of acquisition,[100] (b) the character of the rights conferred by the treaty,[101] and (c) the nature of the legislation adopted by Congress concerning the territory (for example, the extension of laws concerning internal revenue taxation, customs, commerce and navigation, etc.).[102]

Justice White also considered relevant whether Section 1891 of the Revised Statutes of 1878 was made applicable to the territory.[103] That provision reads, "The Constitution and all laws of the United States which are not locally inapplicable shall have the same force and effect within all the organized territories, and in every

---

[98] See Chief Justice Taft's comments to that effect in *Balzac*, 258 U.S. at 309.

[99] *Downes*, 182 U.S. at 332.

[100] *Rasmussen*, 197 U.S. at 520.

[101] *Id.* at 523. In *Downes*, for example, White considered that conferring on the people of the new territories the rights and immunities enjoyed by people in the Northwest Territory would suggest the intention of Congress to incorporate. *Downes*, 182 U.S. at 333.

[102] *Rasmussen*, 197 U.S. at 523.

[103] *Id.* at 521–22.

territory hereafter organized as elsewhere within the United States."[104] This provision presented a stumbling block for the majority of the Court. Even if it was considered that the Constitution did not extend *ex proprio vigore* to the territories, through Section 1891 Congress had made the Constitution's provisions applicable to all "organized" territories of the United States, unless otherwise indicated by Congress itself.[105] It could be argued that the extension of the Constitution to a territory—which of course meant the full extension of rights as enjoyed by people in the states—was a clear indication of the intent to incorporate. By the mere act of "organizing" a territory, therefore, unless otherwise indicated, Congress would be declaring its will to incorporate that territory.

In the case of the Philippines, in fact, Congress had expressly provided that Section 1891 would be inapplicable to the islands.[106] The Court in *Dorr* took this declaration of Congress as one indicator that Congress had not wished to incorporate the Philippines. Congress, however, has never made the same declaration respecting Puerto Rico. If Puerto Rico was an organized territory, then Section 1891 would apply. As one critic of the *Insular Cases* has correctly argued, the Court never dealt satisfactorily with the issue of whether Section 1891 applied when deciding the status of Puerto Rico as a territory.[107]

In *Kopel v. Bingham*, decided on January 4, 1909, the Court in fact held that Puerto Rico was an organized territory of the United States. There the question was whether Puerto Rico was a "territory" for extradition purposes as defined in the relevant federal statute.[108] In an opinion delivered by Chief Justice Fuller with no dissents, the Court held that Puerto Rico, although not a territory incorporated into the United States, was a completely organized territory.[109] To explain what was meant by an "organized" territory, the Court resorted to the language used in a federal district court case and in a previous Supreme Court decision to define the term "territory" as contained in two different federal statutes. The Court quoted the following part of the definition of territory adopted by the district court for the Western District of Arkansas in *Ex parte Morgan*[110]:

> a portion of the country not included within the limits of any State, and not yet admitted as a State into the Union, but organized under the laws with a separate legislature under a territorial governor and other officers appointed by the President of the United States.[111]

---

[104] Revised Statutes of 1878 § 1891.

[105] As has been pointed out, according to the text, the "not locally inapplicable" proviso refers only to "laws" and not to the Constitution. TORRUELLA, *supra* note 7, at 108–09.

[106] Act of July 1, 1902, ch. 1369, Pub. L. No. 235, § 1, 32 Stat. 692 (1902).

[107] TORRUELLA, *supra* note 7, at 108–09.

[108] The governor of Puerto Rico had sought the extradition of an indicted person from the state of New York. The plaintiff argued that Puerto Rico was not a territory of the United States for purposes of the extradition act.

[109] *Kopel*, 211 U.S. at 476. The main rationale of the decision was that it was "impossible to hold that Porto Rico was not intended to have power to reclaim fugitives from its justice, and that it was intended to be created an asylum for fugitives from the United States." *Id.* at 474. In this case Chief Justice Fuller, a notorious dissenter in *Downes* and other previous cases, adopted the language of the doctrine of incorporation in his analysis.

[110] *Ex parte* Morgan, 20 F. 298 (D.C. Ark., Oct. 1883).

[111] *Id.* at 305; *Kopel*, 211 U.S. at 475. The full definition given in *Ex parte Morgan* was: "A territory, under the constitution and laws of the United States, is an *inchoate state*—a portion of the country not

In *In re Lane*,[112] the Supreme Court had referred to

> that system of organized government, long existing within the United States, by which certain regions of the country have been erected into civil governments. These governments have an executive, a legislative and a judicial system. They have the powers which all these departments of government have exercised, which are conferred upon them by act of Congress, and their legislative acts are subject to the disapproval of the Congress of the United States. They are not in any sense independent governments; they have no Senators in Congress and no Representatives in the lower house of that body except what are called delegates, with limited functions. Yet they exercise nearly all the powers of government, under what are generally called organic acts passed by Congress conferring such powers on them.[113]

Puerto Rico, the Court concluded, had been completely organized by the Foraker Act.[114]

After *Kopel*, then, the new doctrine regarding territories had completely crystallized. Territories can be either incorporated or unincorporated, organized or unorganized. The determination of their status depends on the will of Congress. A territory could be unorganized, yet incorporated. In fact, that had been the case of Alaska for some time, according to the *Rasmussen* case. By the same token, a territory could be fully organized, yet unincorporated. That, in the Court's opinion, was the situation of Puerto Rico. The description made in *In re Lane*, adopted fully in *Kopel*, fitted the Puerto Rican situation perfectly. With some modifications, it still does.

The Question of "Applicable" Rights

As the Court's doctrine developed, it was obvious that the determination of what constitutional rights could be claimed by the inhabitants of the newly acquired territories would be left to the judiciary. Most of the cases decided after 1901 dealt with this issue. In territories held not to have been incorporated by an act of Congress (after the doctrine was accepted by a majority), the determination hinged on whether the right in question was considered fundamental. But even before that, a majority of the Court had already accepted the fundamental/nonfundamental distinction as a basis for deciding the question.

In *Mankichi* the Court held that the rights to be indicted by grand jury only and to be convicted solely on a unanimous verdict were not extensive to Hawaii prior to its incorporation, because they were not fundamental rights but mere methods of procedure. Justices Fuller, Harlan, Brewer, and Peckham rejected the notion. Fuller

---

included within the limits of any State, and not yet admitted as a State into the Union, but organized under the laws with a separate legislature under a territorial governor and other officers appointed by the President of the United States." *Ex parte Morgan*, 20 F. at 305 (emphasis added). In his quotation, Justice Fuller excised the term *inchoate state*, which implies that a territory is a state in formation.

[112] *In re* Lane, 135 U.S. 443 (1890).

[113] *Id.* at 447; *Kopel*, 211 U.S. at 475–76. Fuller did not discuss the fact that in some of the previous cases the Court seemed to be using the term *organized* in the same or similar sense as the Court would later use the term *incorporated*.

[114] *Kopel*, 211 U.S. at 474, 476.

not only refused to accept the distinction, but argued that, in any event, the rights in question were "fundamental" enough:

> This is not a question of natural rights, on the one hand, and artificial rights on the other, but of the fundamental rights of every person living under the sovereignty of the United States in respect of that Government. And among those rights is the right to be free from prosecution for crime unless after indictment by a grand jury and the right to be acquitted unless found guilty by the unanimous verdict of a petit jury of twelve.[115]

Harlan referred to those guarantees as part of "Anglo-Saxon liberty."[116]

In *Dorr* and *Dowdell* the Court reached the same result—excluding the rights to indictment by grand jury and conviction by unanimous verdict—in regard to the Philippines.[117] To justify its position, the Court in *Dorr* appealed to a perceived need to respect the customs and traditions of the people in the territories. Justice Day also referred to the instructions transmitted by the U.S. president to the Philippine Commission charged with organizing a civil government in the new possession. Although the instructions provided for the extension of many guarantees analogous to those contained in the Bill of Rights of the U.S. Constitution, the right to trial by jury was carefully excepted. This exception was "doubtless due to the fact," Justice Day concluded, "that the civilized portion of the islands had a system of jurisprudence founded upon the civil law, and the uncivilized parts of the archipelago were wholly unfitted to exercise the right of trial by jury."[118]

The Court's thinking in the *Dorr* case contrasted with Justice Day's own opinion in *Kepner v. United States,* decided the same day. In the latter case the question was whether the guarantee against "double jeopardy," extended to the Philippines by presidential declaration and by an act of Congress, had to be interpreted as that expression was used in the Constitution, from which it was taken. The attorney general for the Philippines and the solicitor general of the United States had argued that the guarantee was not a fundamental right, but a question of method of procedure, and that respect for the institutions of the civil law prevalent in the Philippines demanded an interpretation of the guarantee as understood by Spanish law. Justice Day responded that it was the evident intention of Congress to "carry some at least of the essential principles of American constitutional jurisprudence" to those islands and to "engraft them upon the law of this people." He quoted the president's view that this must be done for "the sake of [the Filipinos'] liberty and happiness, however much [those principles] may conflict with the customs or laws of procedure with which they are familiar." He further quoted the president as being confident "that the most enlightened thought of the Philippine Islands fully appreciates the importance of these principles and rules, and they will inevitably within a short time command universal assent."[119]

The difference in rhetoric, however, does not make the decisions in *Dorr* and

---

[115] *Mankichi*, 190 U.S. at 225.

[116] *Id.* at 244.

[117] As has been noted above, in *Rasmussen* the Court decided that because Alaska had been incorporated by the terms of the treaty with Russia, a trial by jury of 12 was required as a matter of constitutional law.

[118] *Dorr*, 195 U.S. at 145.

[119] *Kepner*, 195 U.S. at 122–23.

Kepner irreconcilable. In the end, the latter hinged upon an interpretation of an act of Congress that provided for the extension of a guarantee against double jeopardy. In *Dorr* no such provision was present. The decision in *Kepner* does not question the power of Congress, it only interprets what Congress intended to do. Taken together, the decisions ultimately underline the fact that Congress has plenary power to govern the territories as it sees fit.[120]

Ocampo reaffirmed the rules established in *Kepner, Trono v. United States, Dowdell, Mankichi,* and *Dorr*. It reasserted the doctrine that the Constitution does not apply to the Philippine Islands of its own force. The case is also of some importance because it allowed the Supreme Court of the Philippines to retain some of the powers of the old Spanish *Audiencia*,[121] a body that had been abolished by an act of Congress. Thus, for example, the Philippine Court was allowed to find criminal defendants, upon their appeal, guilty of a higher offense or to increase their penalties. It was held also that that Court's appellate jurisdiction in criminal cases was not confined to a review of mere errors of law, but was extended to a review of the whole case. The effect was to strengthen the powers of the territorial government, under American control, to deal with violations of the new legal order.

Ochoa v. Hernández, decided in 1913, presented a different matter. In a unanimous opinion the Court declared invalid an order by General Guy V. Henry during his tenure as military governor of Puerto Rico shortening retroactively the period for acquisition of property by prescription. The general's action, the Court decreed, exceeded his presidentially delegated powers. The order was tantamount to a deprivation of property without due process of law, a violation that offended "fundamental principles" of the American political order. Because it relied on this rationale, the Court did not feel obligated to discuss whether the military governor's action constituted an infringement of a constitutional right.

In 1904 the Court, unanimously again, determined that citizens of Puerto Rico were not "aliens" within the meaning of the U.S. Immigration Act of March 3, 1891.[122] The case, *González v. Williams,* involved Isabella González, the Puerto Rican woman detained in the port of New York as an alien, whose story is told in the introduction to this book. The Court did not find it necessary to adjudge whether Puerto Ricans had acquired U.S. citizenship with the Foraker Act, as had been argued by the then resident commissioner of Puerto Rico, Federico Degetau (appearing as an amicus curiae).[123] The relevant test, rather, was alienage, the Court resolved.

Chief Justice Fuller, who authored the Court's opinion, reasoned that the Treaty of Paris had transferred the allegiance of the "native inhabitants" of Puerto Rico to the United States and that nothing in the Foraker Act indicated that Congress intended Puerto Ricans to be considered aliens and to be denied the right of access to the United

---

[120] In a companion case, decided the same day, Mendozana v. United States, 195 U.S. 158 (1904), the Court briefly disposed of a similar question following *Kepner*'s rationale. In Trono v. United States, 199 U.S. 521 (1905), the Court divided itself regarding the interpretation of the same "double jeopardy" clause. There the majority held that it was not a violation of the guarantee for the Supreme Court of the Philippines to find guilty of a greater offense a defendant who appeals his conviction of a lesser crime.

[121] The *Audiencia* had judicial and administrative functions and served as an appellate court in civil and criminal matters.

[122] U.S. Immigration Act, March 3, 1891, 26 Stat. 1084 (1891).

[123] *González*, 192 U.S. at 3–4, 12.

States.[124] In sum, the Chief Justice surmised, Puerto Ricans owed allegiance to the United States, they lived in the "peace of the dominion" of the latter, and their Organic Law (the Foraker Act) had been enacted by the United States and was enforced by officials sworn to support the U.S. Constitution—all of these circumstances indicated that they were not to be considered "aliens" for purposes of entry into the mainland.[125] Furthermore, González was not a passenger from a "foreign port."[126]

Fuller referred extensively to the opinion rendered in 1902 by the U.S. attorney general in the case of Adolfo Marín Molinas.[127] In it, the attorney general had advised the secretary of the treasury that Marín Molinas, a Puerto Rican artist temporarily living in France and there on the date of proclamation of the Treaty of Paris, should be considered a citizen of Puerto Rico under Section 7 of the Foraker Act. As such, he should also be considered an American artist for purposes of the exemptions contained in U.S. tariff laws. Relying on the ruling in *De Lima*, the attorney general had concluded that Marín Molinas came from a place that had ceased to be "foreign" within the meaning of the tariff laws and was now "fully organized" as a country [sic] of the United States by the Foraker Act.[128]

The judgment in *González* reflected well the legal situation of Puerto Rico and the other new territories as fashioned by the decisions of the Supreme Court in the *Insular Cases*. Both the territory and its people came to inhabit an intermediate status, a sort of juridical limbo. Puerto Rico belonged to, but was not a part of, the United States; Puerto Ricans were not citizens of the United States, but were not aliens either. At the same time outside and within the Constitution,[129] they could claim the protection only of some, but not all, the rights that the American legal system formally sanctioned.

Balzac: Citizenship and Incorporation

In 1917 Congress conferred U.S. citizenship on Puerto Ricans by virtue of the Jones Act.[130] From a legal point of view this act raised the question of whether Puerto Rico had finally been "incorporated" into the United States. As noted above, the bestowal of citizenship had been mentioned by Justice White as one of the indicators of

---

[124] *Id.* at 12.

[125] *Id.* at 13.

[126] *Id.* at 16.

[127] 24 Op. Att'y Gen. 40 (1902). The opinion refers to Marín Molinas by his second surname, Molinas. (In Spanish it is customary to use two surnames, in which case the convention is to refer to both; if one is dropped, it is usually the second one.)

[128] *González*, 192 U.S. at 15. It is interesting to note the contrast between the government's positions as expressed in the attorney general's opinion regarding Mr. Molinas, the artist, and in the solicitor general's argument in the González case. Perhaps a relevant clue to deciphering the difference is to be found in the fact that Ms. González was detained under the authority of a clause of the Immigration Act calling for the exclusion of persons "likely to become a public charge." As the solicitor general argued, "the attitude of the United States simply is that dangerous or feeble defectives among our island inhabitants are not to be admitted to the country as if they were citizens." *Id.* at 7. Did this reflect a desire to stem an influx of poor people from the new territories?

[129] WINFRED LEE THOMPSON, THE INTRODUCTION OF AMERICAN LAW IN THE PHILIPPINES AND PUERTO RICO: 1898–1905 213 (1989).

[130] *See* chapter 3.

congressional intent to incorporate. The Supreme Court resolved the issue in 1922 in *Balzac*. By this time there had been a substantial change in the Court's composition. Of the original participants in the 1901 cases, only Justice McKenna remained. Some of the judges who intervened in the second group of territorial-related decisions were still sitting on the Court, such as Justices Day, Holmes, Mahlon Pitney, Willis Van Devanter, and James Clark McReynolds. But there were three new justices: Louis D. Brandeis, John H. Clarke, and the new chief justice, former U.S. president William Howard Taft.

Balzac, editor of a Spanish-language daily newspaper in Puerto Rico, had been condemned to serve a 4-month and another 5-month jail sentence, with payment of costs in each case, for certain comments about the American governor of the island that the government considered libelous. The defendant had requested a trial by jury, although the code of criminal procedure of Puerto Rico granted a jury trial only in felony cases and not in misdemeanors. He alleged that he was entitled to a jury under the Sixth Amendment to the Constitution. The Supreme Court rejected his claim.

Chief Justice Taft wrote the opinion of the Court. Quoting the *Mankichi* and *Dorr* cases, he began by stating that it was "clearly settled" that the right to trial by jury does not apply to territories of the United States that have not been incorporated into the union.[131] It was "further settled," according to *Downes* and *Dorr*, that neither the Philippines nor Puerto Rico had been incorporated by the statutes providing for their provisional governments (in the case of Puerto Rico, the Foraker Act).[132] He then considered whether the Jones Act had the effect of "incorporating" Puerto Rico into the United States.

The chief justice noted that the 1917 act did not indicate by its title that it had the purpose of incorporating the island, nor did it contain any clause that declared such purpose or effect:[133]

> Had Congress intended to take the important step of changing the treaty status of Porto Rico by incorporating it into the Union, it is reasonable to suppose that it would have done so by the *plain declaration*, and would not have left it to mere inference.[134]

Probably aware that he was now requiring an express declaration of congressional intention, contrary to previous expressions of the Court that incorporation could be inferred from relevant indicia (and also presumably conscious that the doctrine of incorporation itself was no more than a recent judicial invention), Taft added,

> Before the question became acute at the close of the Spanish War, the distinction between acquisition and incorporation was not regarded as important, or at least it was not fully understood and had not aroused great controversy. Before that, the purpose of Congress might well be a matter of mere inference from various legislative acts; but in these latter days, incorporation is not to be assumed without express declaration, or an implication so strong as to exclude any other view.[135]

The chief justice also took as an indication of Congress's lack of intention to

---

[131] *Balzac*, 258 U.S. at 304.
[132] *Id*. at 305.
[133] *Id*. at 306.
[134] *Id*. (emphasis added).
[135] *Id*.

incorporate the fact that the Jones Act included a "bill of rights." Incorporation would have made the Constitution's bill of rights applicable *ex proprio vigore*, Taft reasoned, and therefore a statutory bill of rights would have been needless. This, to him, was a "conclusive" argument.[136]

But what about the extension of U.S. citizenship? Conferring citizenship, Taft explained, was "entirely consistent" with nonincorporation. The granting of citizenship to the inhabitants of Puerto Rico had only the following purposes: (a) "to put them as individuals on an exact equality with citizens from the American homeland"; (b) to extend to them the protection of the new sovereign against the world; and (c) to allow Puerto Ricans to move into the continental United States and, becoming citizens of any state, there to enjoy every right of any other citizen of the nation, without the need of naturalization.[137] Nothing further could be inferred from that act, he believed.

While residing in Puerto Rico, the Puerto Rican could not insist on a federal constitutional right to a trial by jury. For "it is locality that is determinative of the application of the Constitution, in such matters as judicial procedure, and not the status of the people who live in it."[138] And Puerto Rico was not the kind of territory to which the Constitution fully applied.

The chief justice was aware that his reasoning was at odds with the import of the Court's decision in *Rasmussen*. There the Court had considered as sufficient grounds to infer an intention to incorporate the fact that in the treaty of acquisition Congress had declared its desire to confer political and civil rights on the inhabitants of the Alaskan territory as American citizens:

> But Alaska was a different case from that of Porto Rico. It was an enormous territory, very sparsely settled and offering opportunity for immigration and settlement by American citizens. It was on the American continent and within easy reach of the then United States.[139] It involved none of the difficulties which incorporation of the Philippines and Porto Rico presents, and one of them is in the very matter of trial by jury.[140]

He expounded on what he considered those "difficulties" to be:

> The jury system needs citizens trained to the exercise of the responsibilities of jurors. In common-law countries centuries of tradition have prepared a conception of the impartial attitude jurors must assume.[141] The jury system postulates a conscious duty of participation in the machinery of justice which it is hard for people not brought up in fundamentally popular government at once to acquire. . . . Congress has thought that a people like the Filipinos or the Porto Ricans [sic], trained to a complete judicial system which knows no juries, living in compact and ancient communities, with def-

---

[136] *Id.* at 306–07.

[137] *Id.* at 308, 311.

[138] *Id.* at 309.

[139] Whether Alaska was within easier reach than Puerto Rico is doubtful. And, of course, distance or difficulty of access was not a factor considered relevant in the case of Hawaii, which was also "incorporated" into the Union.

[140] *Balzac*, 258 U.S. at 309.

[141] Of course, no mention is made of the treatment that African Americans and other minorities had experienced at the hand of "impartial" White jurors "trained" to the "exercise of the[ir] responsibilities" in the common-law system of the United States.

initely formed customs and political conceptions, should be permitted themselves to determine how far they wish to adopt this institution of Anglo-Saxon origin, and when. Hence the care with which . . . the United States has been liberal in granting to the Islands acquired by the Treaty of Paris most of the American constitutional guarantees, but has been sedulous to avoid forcing a jury system on a Spanish and civil-law country until it desired it.[142]

Taft again addressed the issue of the advisability of inferring an intention to incorporate from the act of granting citizenship status:

We need not dwell on another consideration which requires us not lightly to infer, from acts thus easily explained on other grounds, an intention to incorporate in the Union these distant ocean communities of a different origin and language from those of our continental people. Incorporation has always been a step, and an important one, leading to statehood. Without, in the slightest degree, intimating an opinion as to the wisdom of such a policy, for that is not our province, it is reasonable to assume that when such a step is taken it will be begun and taken by Congress deliberately and with a clear declaration of purpose, and not left a matter of mere inference or construction.[143]

The Court rejected Balzac's argument that Puerto Rico had also been incorporated by the effect of the numerous congressional statutes providing for the organization of a U.S. district court in the island, the review by the federal judiciary of the Puerto Rican Supreme Court in cases in which the Constitution of the United States was involved, the entry of Puerto Rican youths into the American military academies, the sale of U.S. stamps in the island, and the extension to Puerto Rico, in one way or another, of revenue, navigation, immigration, national banking, bankruptcy, federal employers' liability, safety appliance, extradition, and census laws. "None of these nor all of them put together," Justice Taft pronounced, "furnish ground for the conclusion pressed on us."[144]

Concluding that "on the whole" there were "no features" in the Jones Act from which to infer the purpose of Congress to incorporate Puerto Rico into the Union "with the consequences which would follow," Taft added that, in any event, substantially the same question had been disposed of by the Court in a very brief *per curiam* decision rendered in 1918 without full-length discussion of the issues. The decision had involved two cases: *Porto Rico v. Tapia* and *Porto Rico v. Muratti*.[145] In the first case the issue was whether a defendant charged with a felony some 12 days after passage of the Jones Act could be brought to trial without indictment by a grand jury as required by the Fifth Amendment to the U.S. Constitution. In the other case the felony charged was alleged to have been committed before passage of the 1917 Act, but prosecution was begun afterward. The U.S. District Court for Puerto Rico and the Puerto Rican Supreme Court, respectively, had held that indictment by grand jury was required after the Jones Act came into effect. The U.S. Supreme Court summarily reversed both, citing *Downes*, *Mankichi*, and *Dorr*. This

---

[142] *Balzac*, 258 U.S. at 310–11.

[143] *Id.* at 311.

[144] *Id.* at 311–12.

[145] Porto Rico v. Tapia, 245 U.S. 639 (1918); Porto Rico v. Muratti, 245 U.S. 639 (1918).

reversal, the Court declared in *Balzac*, amounted necessarily to holding that the Jones Act had not incorporated Puerto Rico.[146]

In *Balzac* Chief Justice Taft summarized the import of the *Insular Cases* thus:

> The Constitution of the United States is in force in Porto Rico as it is wherever and whenever the sovereign power of that government is exerted. This has not only been admitted but emphasized by this court in all its authoritative expressions upon the issues arising in the *Insular Cases*. . . . The Constitution, however, contains grants of power and limitations which in the nature of things are not always and everywhere applicable, and the real issue in the *Insular Cases* was not whether the Constitution extended to the Philippines or Porto Rico when we went there, but which of its provisions were applicable by way of limitation upon the exercise of executive and legislative power in dealing with new conditions and requirements.[147]

Within the logic of the discourse adopted by the Court in this and some of the previous cases, some of Chief Justice Taft's statements are certainly problematic. It is important to address them briefly to enrich the context of the discussion in the following chapters of this part of the book.

First, according to Taft the "real issue" in the *Insular Cases* was not whether the Constitution extended to the Philippines or Puerto Rico, but which of its provisions were applicable. A perusal of the debate within the Court indicates that the applicability of the Constitution *ex proprio vigore* was a central issue. "Whether the Constitution follows the flag" was the popular formulation of the controversy. Justice Brown's extension doctrine was a straight negative answer to the question. It was only as a result of the decisions in the cases, with the development of the incorporation doctrine, that the issue became *which* constitutional clauses applied. The Court created a doctrine to allow Congress and the executive to deal with the "new conditions and requirements" to which Taft so candidly referred—the acquisition of overseas territories inhabited by peoples of different races and cultures and not yet subject to the control of White American settlers. The issue had been whether the United States could constitutionally subject those peoples to a condition of permanent subordination. The majority in the previous cases had answered the question in the affirmative, elaborating a doctrine that provided the legal justification for the new expansionist venture.

Second, that "locality" and not the status of the people became the determinative criterion regarding the applicability of constitutional guarantees in matters of judicial procedure was the product of a kind of circular reasoning, operating at two different levels, resulting from the development of the cases as a whole. The status of the territories as "localities" had been determined initially with reference to the characteristics of the peoples inhabiting them. Those characteristics—racial and cultural differences, different legal and political traditions, and so forth—justified, in the Court's mind, the creation of a distinct new category, the unincorporated territory. Moreover, before *Balzac*, the nature of the rights conferred on the people was considered indicative of the will to incorporate. In other words, incorporation—that is, the status of the territory—flowed, among other things, from the nature of rights extended. Now, *Balzac*'s rationale, coming full circle, made determination of the

---

[146] *Balzac*, 258 U.S. at 313.
[147] *Id.* at 312–13.

status of the territory dispositive of the question of the nature of the rights to be enjoyed by the inhabitants.

Third, the reasons given by Taft for the conferral of citizenship to Puerto Ricans do not convincingly refute the argument that the action implied incorporation and, therefore, the full extension of constitutional rights. It does not make much sense to assert, as Taft did, that congressional intention not to extend the protections of the Sixth Amendment regarding trial by jury can be inferred from the desire of Congress to put Puerto Ricans "on an exact equality with citizens from the American homeland." As to mobility to the continent, the Court itself had held in *González* that it was not necessary for Puerto Ricans to be U.S. citizens to enjoy the right of free access to the states proper. His argument also implies that there is a need to move to one of the states for a U.S. citizen to "complete" his or her citizenship, that is, to have full access to the enjoyment of political and other rights. American constitutional doctrine, however, had long rejected the notion that a person has to be a citizen of one of the states to be a citizen of the United States.[148] What the Court's position entails is the inevitable conclusion that what Puerto Ricans were getting was a "second-class" citizenship, as so many critics have pointed out.[149] Last, historical research has demonstrated that there were probably other reasons for granting citizenship.[150] But this point will be taken up in chapter 7.

Finally, there is the question of the reasons for refusing to extend to Puerto Ricans the right to trial by jury. The argument that it was out of respect for local legal customs and traditions is hardly convincing. After all, from the very first days of the occupation, the military regime and later Congress had engaged in a massive effort to overhaul the legal system in effect in Puerto Rico since Spanish times, especially regarding criminal and procedural matters.[151] Impositions of an even more profound nature were also attempted, as in the matters of language,[152] political institutions, and education. Furthermore, jury trials were already in effect for felonies in Puerto Rican courts as provided by the Code of Criminal Procedure, a product of one of the many legal reforms carried out under the American regime. A probable explanation for this refusal to grant trial by jury the status of a constitutional right will be offered in chapter 6.

The flaws in Taft's reasoning do not necessarily mean that he and the other justices had misread the intention of congressional and executive policy makers. The explanation more probably lay in the fact that, for reasons that have been suggested already and should become more apparent further below, both the Court and the so-

---

[148] *The Slaughter House Cases*, 83 U.S. (16 Wall.) 36, 74 (1873).

[149] *E.g.*, TORRUELLA, *supra* note 7; ROGERS M. SMITH, CIVIC IDEALS: CONFLICTING VISIONS OF CITIZENSHIP IN U.S. HISTORY 433 (1997).

[150] *See* SERRANO, *supra* note 1, at 478; ESTADES, *supra* note 10, at 165–215; TORRUELLA, *supra* note 7, at 85–93; SMITH, *supra* note 149, at 433; José Cabranes, *Citizenship and the American Empire*, 127 U. PA. L. REV. 391 (1978); Ana Sagardía de Alvarado, *Puerto Rico en la encrucijada del '98: Impacto del cambio de soberanía en la ciudadanía de los puertorriqueños*, 11 CULTURA 14 (1997).

[151] For an analysis of the legal reforms carried out in the Philippines, with less-extensive reference to the situation in Puerto Rico, see THOMPSON, *supra* note 129. For analogous processes in Puerto Rico see CARMELO DELGADO CINTRÓN, DERECHO Y COLONIALISMO: LA TRAYECTORIA HISTÓRICA DEL DERECHO PUERTORRIQUEÑO 55–72 (1988); JOSÉ TRÍAS MONGE, EL SISTEMA JUDICIAL DE PUERTO RICO 67–69 (1978); Eulalio A. Torres, *The Puerto Rico Penal Code of 1902–1975: A Case Study of American Legal Imperialism*, 45 REV. JUR. U.P.R. 1–83 (1976).

[152] *See* chapter 3.

called political branches of the government were pursuing a policy of differential treatment regarding the former Spanish possessions that was difficult to square with past (and contemporaneous) practice, traditions, and principles.

In summary, the Court in *Balzac* took the doctrine of incorporation one step further to require an express declaration of Congress, in so many words, of its intention to incorporate a territory. It also put to rest the allegation that granting citizenship to its people alters the status of a territory. It made revealingly clear the considerations that both the Court and Congress had in mind when treating these territories differently. And it "settled" for many years to come the question of the status of the countries acquired by the United States as a result of the Spanish American War.[153]

---

[153] The social, cultural, and political effects of the extension of American citizenship to Puerto Ricans will be examined in chapter 7.

Chapter 5
THE LEGAL THEORY AND IDEOLOGY OF THE *INSULAR CASES*

In the process of developing the doctrine of territorial incorporation and determining the juridical status of the new territories, the members of the Supreme Court of the United States applied explicit or implicit conceptions of law, theories of interpretation and adjudication, notions about the nature of rights, and assumptions about the function of the judicial process and the Court itself. It is to this "applied jurisprudence" or "practical" legal theory that I now turn my attention.[1] For the applied jurisprudence of each legal operator is an ingredient in the social process involved in the act of making legal decisions; it is part of the exercise of justification and, therefore, of the process of legitimation of social and political relations. Moreover, the legal discourse[2] elaborated in the justices' lengthy discussions in the *Insular Cases* was permeated by wider conceptions and values whose analysis is necessary to understand properly the import of the legal doctrine their decisions established:[3] It is in this sense that the term *ideology* is used in this chapter. The first part examines the legal theory of the *Insular Cases,* and the second focuses on the ideology permeating the decisions.

Legal Theory of the *Insular Cases*

I will examine three aspects of the legal theory of these cases: (a) the justices' general conceptions of law and their theories of interpretation and adjudication, (b) their views of the judicial function, and (c) their assumptions about the nature of rights.

---

[1] By *"applied jurisprudence,"* I mean those theories or general views about law explicitly or implicitly present in the actual practice of legal operators.

[2] The term *discourse* is used here in a limited sense to refer to a specific set of linguistic phenomena. There is a wider meaning of *discourse,* as used in contemporary philosophical and sociological literature, that includes both speech acts and their corresponding social practices. *See, e.g.,* MICHEL FOUCAULT, LA VERDAD Y LAS FORMAS JURÍDICAS 162–63 (Enrique Lynch trans., 3rd ed. 1988).

[3] This analysis rests on the proposition that law has a *cognitive/axiological* dimension. That is, it incorporates categories of perception and evaluation of reality that can be related to the prevailing "common sense" at a given moment and place within a certain community. That law itself may be a constitutive element of that "common sense" does not preclude that law may, at the same time, be constituted through a process of incorporation of categories of perception and evaluation formed primarily within other "discourses" or other dimensions of social life. This reciprocal conditionality of law and other dimensions of the social world is a basic assumption adopted in this book.

Of course, that social phenomenon we call modern law cannot be reduced to this cognitive/axiological dimension. For modern law's specificity consists of the complex articulation of several elements. One of them is law's *normative* character: the fact that legal processes and practices are conducted and justified in reference to a structure of norms. Another salient ingredient is that law is a type of discourse that is generally cast in the language of justification. Additionally, law is one of the principal sites for the exercise of power in contemporary societies.

Conceptions of Law and Theories of Interpretation and Adjudication

Formalism Versus Pragmatic Instrumentalism

A striking feature of the jurisprudential implications of the *Insular Cases* is the tension and interplay between, and attempts to accommodate, formalist and instrumentalist views of law and of the process of legal interpretation. By *formalism* I mean the conception of law as a system of concepts, rules, and principles that must be logically and coherently applied to every situation, to a large extent irrespective of immediate social or practical consequences. Of course, there are varieties and degrees of formalism. But this is its fundamental proposition for the purpose at hand.[4]

By *pragmatic instrumentalism* I refer to a mode of reasoning predicated on the proposition that law, laws, and the legal process serve identifiable goals, purposes, and policies and that the adjudicator must take into consideration the social and political consequences of his or her decisions.[5] Again, there are several versions of instrumentalism. In the cases at hand instrumentalism takes fundamentally the form of a central preoccupation with the consequences of the decision made or the doctrine adopted.

A more or less distinct pattern of interaction between these two views of law emerges from the decisions. In general, the members of the majority responsible for the development of the incorporation doctrine in the 1901 cases adopted a strongly instrumentalist stance, while the dissenters, Harlan especially, argued for what amounts to a "principled" approach that is generally formalist, although not crudely so.[6] After 1904, when the doctrine had already been established, the majority swung to a generally formalist approach, relying heavily on the precedential value of the 1901 cases and "logically" deducting the applicable rules from them. In 1922, in the *Balzac* case, Chief Justice Taft grounded his decision on the "precedents" established by the previous cases but added a heavily consequentialist, and in that sense pragmatic, analysis to confront the "new situation" created by the Jones Act of 1917,

---

[4] Discussions of formalism abound in legal literature. *See, e.g.*, ROBERTO MANGABEIRA UNGER, LAW IN MODERN SOCIETY: TOWARD A CRITICISM OF SOCIAL THEORY 48–58 (1976); THE CRITICAL LEGAL STUDIES MOVEMENT 1–2, 8–11 (1986); MAX WEBER, ECONOMY AND SOCIETY (G. Roth & C. Wittich Eds. 1978); Duncan Kennedy, *Legal Formality*, 2 J. LEGAL STUD. 351 (1973); MORTON J. HORWITZ, THE TRANSFORMATION OF AMERICAN LAW: 1780–1860 chap. 8 (1977).

[5] I take the term *pragmatic instrumentalism* from Robert S. Summers, *Pragmatic Instrumentalism in Twentieth Century American Legal Thought—A Synthesis and Critique of Our Dominant General Theory about Law and Its Use*, 66 CORNELL L. REV. 861 (1981). In the sense it is used here "instrumentalism" must be distinguished from the meaning given to it in discussions of Marxist legal theory to designate the position taken by those who view law essentially as an instrument of the ruling classes. *See, e.g.*, Bob Jessop, *On Recent Marxist Theories of Law, the State and Juridico-Political Ideology*, 8 INT'L J. SOC. LAW 339 (1980); THE POLITICAL ECONOMY OF LAW: A THIRD WORLD READER 3–10 (Y. Ghai et al. Eds. 1987). For detailed analyses of instrumentalism as a theory of legal interpretation in the sense used by Summers, *see also* Summers, *supra*, at 861; LORD LLOYD OF HAMPSTEAD AND MICHAEL D. A. FREEMAN, LLOYD'S INTRODUCTION TO JURISPRUDENCE 695–98 (5th ed. 1985); HORWITZ, *supra* note 4.

[6] By a principled approach, I mean a mode of argumentation based on the notion that courts should apply rules and principles and enforce rights, rather than advance policies and implement goals. *See, generally* RONALD DWORKIN, TAKING RIGHTS SERIOUSLY (1977).

which conferred U.S. citizenship on Puerto Ricans.[7] A brief examination of some examples will be useful.

In his dissenting opinion in the first case decided, *De Lima*,[8] Justice McKenna, joined by Justices Shiras and White, decried the excessively "definitional" approach the majority took, through Justice Brown's opinion, to conclude that Puerto Rico was not a foreign country. Justices McKenna and Shiras, it must be remembered, were the first to adhere to Justice White's theory of incorporation. In *De Lima* Brown's reasoning had been founded on his interpretation of the relevant precedents and on logical deduction from the provisions of the Constitution, and he expressly refused to take account of the resulting "inconvenience" of the Court's holding. McKenna's principal argument was consequentialist. The interpretation of the Constitution the Court adopted would "cripple" the United States as a power among nations, for it would not be able to behave like them, with the ability to acquire territories and govern them as best fitted its interests as a nation. He advised consideration of the "practicalities" of the situation and attention to the "great public interests" involved. The Constitution, he believed, was to be viewed as an instrument, rather than a limitation, of power for the nation.

The argument must have had an impact on Justice Brown, for in *Dooley I* he adopted the consequentialist approach of his adversaries to arrive at the same conclusion as in *De Lima*. His opinion makes constant references to the "necessities" of the case and the practical requirements of the administration of the territory.[9] He detailed the "disastrous" consequences for the economy of Puerto Rico to hold that it remained a foreign country after ratification of the Treaty of Paris.[10] The dissenters, Justices White, Gray, Shiras, and McKenna, countered his arguments with equally consequentialist considerations that demonstrated, to their mind, the "impracticality" of the theory of immediate incorporation by cession. Immediate incorporation, they argued, would deprive Congress of the necessary time to put a machinery in place for the collection of duties and other incidents of administration before the territory could be considered a part of the United States.[11]

In *Downes*, Justice Brown joined the previous dissenters to hold that Puerto Rico belonged to but was not a part of the United States.[12] Brown timidly attempted to

---

[7] The consequentialist nature of the Court's reasoning in the first group of cases has been noted in Marcos A. Ramírez, *Los Casos Insulares*, 16 REV. JUR. U.P.R. 121 (1946). The Ramírez article, however, does not consider fully the extent to which formalism and consequentialism interact in the opinions of the Court. Moreover, because the author analyzes only the cases decided until 1904, he is unable to discuss the shifts in interpretative techniques adopted by the Court from 1904 to 1922.

[8] Full citations of all the *Insular Cases* appear in Chapter 4, nn.12–14. For purposes of economy, in this and the following chapter I will use the shorter citation form. Likewise, only the justices' last names will be used throughout these two chapters, because their full names were provided in chapter 4.

[9] *Dooley I*, 182 U.S. at 232–33.

[10] *Id.* at 235–36.

[11] *Id.* at 242.

[12] The switch in Justice Brown's position from *De Lima* to *Downes* has puzzled more than one commentator. *See* JUAN R. TORRUELLA, THE SUPREME COURT AND PUERTO RICO: THE DOCTRINE OF SEPARATE AND UNEQUAL 53 (1985). I believe that Brown was especially impressed by the fact that the action questioned in the first case was a purely administrative decision taken before Congress had legislated specifically for Puerto Rico. After Congress had expressed its will to impose a duty on imports from the island, Brown simply followed suit. Of the three positions the justices took in the cases, Brown's extension doctrine provided for the widest congressional discretion.

make a principled decision by examining at length what he thought were the relevant legislative and judicial precedents.[13] He even tried to distinguish the *Dred Scott* case. But by now totally converted to instrumentalism, his main argument consisted in warning of the "extremely serious consequences" of the proposition made by the new dissenters, notably Harlan and Fuller, that the Constitution applied immediately upon acquisition of the new territory:

> Indeed it is doubtful if Congress would ever assent to the annexation of territory upon the condition that its inhabitants, however foreign they may be to our habits, traditions and modes of life, shall become at once citizens of the United States.[14]

The new majority feared that any other interpretation would curtail the flexibility of the United States to act. Brown envisioned another set of consequences if the theory of the immediate application of the Constitution were upheld. He warned that the extension of the general revenue laws of the United States could upset the economy of the territories, inviting "violations of law so innumerable as to make prosecutions impossible," and almost certainly "alienat[ing] and destroy[ing] the friendship and good will of that people for the United States."[15] This latter argument could be interpreted as merely a rationalization that played to the concerns of Puerto Ricans, particularly the business and commercial elites. But it also shows a perceptive preoccupation with, on the one hand, problems of law and order relating to the governance of the colony and, on the other, the necessity to procure a degree of consent to colonial rule.

Justice White's famous concurrence in *Downes*—the judicial source spring of the theory of incorporation—also drew substantially on consequentialist reasoning for its conclusions. He listed what he considered the "evils of immediate incorporation" and alluded to the "dangers" to the American people of such a result.[16] Referring to the necessities arising out of a war successfully fought by the United States and leading to the acquisition of territory, he commented,

> It being true that incorporation must necessarily follow the retention of the territory, it would result that the United States must abandon all hope of recouping itself for the loss suffered by the unjust war, and, hence, the whole burden would be entailed upon the people of the United States. This would be a necessary consequence, because if the United States did not hold the territory as security for the needed indemnity it could not collect such indemnity, and on the other hand if incorporation must follow from holding the territory the uniformity provision of the Constitution would prevent the assessment of the cost of the war solely upon the newly acquired country.[17]

Adroitly choosing his examples, perhaps with a certain audience in mind (Captain Alfred Thayer Mahan, Vice President Theodore Roosevelt, and the promoters of naval expansion?),[18] White elaborated:

---

[13] A failed attempt at "integrity" in the Dworkinian sense? *See* RONALD DWORKIN, LAW'S EMPIRE (1986).

[14] *Downes*, 182 U.S. at 279–80.

[15] *Id.* at 284.

[16] *Id.* at 308.

[17] *Id.*

[18] *See* chapter 1.

> Suppose the necessity of acquiring a naval station or a coaling station on an island inhabited with people utterly unfit for American citizenship and totally incapable of bearing their proportionate burden of the national expense. Could such an island, under the rule which is now insisted upon, be taken? Suppose again the acquisition of territory for an interoceanic canal, where an inhabited strip of land on either side is essential to the United States for the preservation of the work. Can it be denied that, if the requirements of the Constitution as to taxation are to immediately control, it might be impossible by treaty to accomplish the desired result?[19]

In discussing the applicability of the grand jury and unanimous verdict guarantees to the "unincorporated" territory of Hawaii in the *Mankichi* case, Justice Brown argued that to ascertain the intention of a legislative body (Congress in this case), the adjudicator must look at the consequences or results of a "literal" interpretation of the legislative enactment. If the consequences are "disastrous" one must infer that the result was not intended. In *Mankichi*, he pointed out, holding that the constitutional guarantees applied ipso facto by virtue of the act of annexation of Hawaii[20] would have as a consequence that "every criminal convicted of a felony" between the annexation (1898) and the Organic Act of 1900 would have to be released and every verdict in civil cases by a less than unanimous jury would have to be nullified.[21] The "law of necessity" prescribed a different result.[22]

The instrumentalist stance of the new majority composed by Justices Brown, White, Shiras, McKenna, and Gray in the early stages of the development of the doctrine regarding the territories was most frontally rejected by Chief Justice Fuller and Justice Harlan in several of the opinions. Dissenting in *Downes,* Fuller called for a "textual" reading of the Constitution:

> Some argument was made as to general consequences apprehended to flow from this result [the invalidation of the tariff provisions of the Foraker Act], but the language of the Constitution is too plain and unambiguous to permit its meaning to be thus influenced. There is nothing "in the literal construction so obviously absurd, or mischievous, or repugnant to the general spirit of the instrument as to justify those who expound the Constitution" in giving it a construction not warranted by its words.[23]

He likewise refused to accept as valid the arguments made by representatives of "certain industries" that filed briefs supporting the power to impose tariffs on the new territories to "diminish competition." If producers in the states believed the Constitution should be amended to achieve that result, the amendment procedure should be followed.[24] Nor was it true, Justice Brown contended, that absolute power was essential to the acquisition of vast and distant territories.[25] But after all, he concluded, these were merely political arguments that had not "the requisite certainty to afford rules of judicial interpretation."[26] And he called for the application of "well

---

[19] *Downes*, 182 U.S. at 311.

[20] The Newlands Resolution, 30 Stat. 750 (1898).

[21] *Mankichi*, 190 U.S. at 216.

[22] *Id.*

[23] *Downes*, 182 U.S. at 374.

[24] *Id.*

[25] *Id.*

[26] *Id.* at 375.

settled rules which govern the interpretation of fundamental law, unaffected by the theoretical [political, it is to be presumed] opinions of individuals."[27]

In his dissent in *Mankichi*, Fuller again referred to the "plain and unambiguous" language of the Newlands Resolution, which had the effect of incorporating Hawaii and precluding any legislation contrary to the Constitution. Resort to construction or interpretation, he felt, was absolutely uncalled for.[28] Moreover, arguments "ab inconvenienti" were "unsafe" guides. To depart from the "plain meaning" of the statute was to "usurp legislative functions."[29] Fuller also thought it proper to scrutinize the "intention" of the legislator. But his procedure was to examine the words of the statutes and treaties, including the preambles, to search for their "meaning," disregarding the possible "inconvenience" of the practical consequences of the Court's decision.

Justice Harlan took a similar stance in that same case. He advocated interpreting the law "as it is written," rejecting arguments based on policy or convenience and leaving the "consequences for the lawmaking power."[30] His position, however, was somewhat more complex, as demonstrated by his arguments in *Downes*. At one point he derided the imprecise nature of White's incorporation theory. It seems to be endowed, Harlan commented caustically, with some "occult meaning" that must be deciphered. Moreover, Justice White seemed to be requiring an express inclusion of the word "incorporation" in the legislation enacted by Congress while, Harlan believed, the Court must look at the effects of the action taken by Congress. He reviewed the provisions of the Foraker Act to describe those effects.[31] This line of argument can be read as an attack on an extreme variety of formalism—conceptualism—to which Harlan believed Justice White's theory paradoxically led.

In other passages Justice Harlan adopted his own variety of formalism. He argued that the Constitution is not to be obeyed or disobeyed "as the circumstances of a particular crisis" in history may suggest,[32] that its operation "cannot be stayed by any branch of the Government in order to meet what some may suppose to be extraordinary emergencies,"[33] and that its "meaning" cannot depend "upon accidental circumstances."[34] "We cannot violate the Constitution in order to serve particular interests in our own or in foreign lands," he proclaimed.[35]

An interesting case was presented by Justice Holmes, who became notorious for his pragmatism and his famous assertion that experience rather than logic is the life of the law.[36] In *Kepner*, a Philippines case, he filed his only dissent in these cases,

---

[27] *Id.*

[28] *Mankichi*, 190 U.S. at 233.

[29] *Id.*

[30] *Id.* at 247–48.

[31] *Downes*, 182 U.S. at 389. Justice Harlan is referring to the juridical effects of the legislation, as inferred from its provisions, and not to its social effects or consequences.

[32] *Id.* at 384.

[33] *Id.* at 385.

[34] *Id.*

[35] *Id.* One of Harlan's typical statements regarding the matter is "Indeed it has been announced by some statesmen that the Constitution should be interpreted to mean not what its words naturally, or usually, or even plainly, import, but what the apparent necessities of the hour, or the apparent majority of the people, at a particular time, demand at the hands of the judiciary. I cannot assent to any such view of the Constitution." *Mankichi*, 190 U.S. at 241.

[36] OLIVER WENDELL HOLMES, THE COMMON LAW 1 (1881).

at odds with the interpretation of the double jeopardy guarantee adopted by the majority. In what probably should be taken as tongue-in-cheek argumentation, he declared that the Court's decision (in favor of the defendant) would have serious consequences.[37] Yet, he added, he would not stop to examine them, "as such considerations are not supposed to be entertained by judges except as inclining them to one of two interpretations, or as a tacit last resort in case of doubt."[38] He preferred, in this case, to have recourse to "logic and rationality."[39] The result, of course, would be a stricter interpretation of the provision in question.

The shift to a more formalistic approach on the part of the entire Court was evident after the first group of cases was decided, and especially after 1903. A good example is *González*,[40] which addressed the controversy over whether Puerto Ricans were aliens for the purposes of the immigration acts. The reasoning of the Court hinged largely on a definition: "What is an alien?"

As a whole, however, the most important opinions, those that proved to be the foundation of the doctrine of incorporation and of the plenary power of Congress, were decidedly, even explicitly, instrumental in tone. Perhaps it is not coincidence that this instrumental approach was pressed upon the Court straightforwardly by the government. The closing paragraph of the solicitor general's argument before the Court as reported in the published decision of the *De Lima* case contains an exemplary formulation of a purposive interpretation of the Constitution:

> Is the Constitution a stumbling block, or a trap, caught in which we shall excite the pity of our friends and the derision of our foes? I refuse to believe so. The Constitution is no mere declaration of denials. It created a nation. . . . When it conferred power, it took care not to cripple action. It still remains the most perfect instrument ever struck off at a given time by the brain and purpose of man, under which we are armed for every emergency and able to cope with every condition.[41]

Contextualism

Not surprisingly, the justices who advocated the instrumentalist approach also promoted a contextualized reading of the relevant judicial precedents and past government practice. Two good examples are Justice McKenna's dissent in *De Lima* and White's concurrent opinion in *Downes*. McKenna's argument suggests a view of interpretation as a collective process involving those who drafted the Constitution and those who have been called subsequently to apply it. Hence the need to take into account the interpreter's contemporary context as well.

The method includes consideration of the institutional context in which interpretation takes place—the functions of each branch of government, for McKenna, and the "nature of the government," for White. In a turn of the argument that would sound curious in light of later jurisprudential debates, the rigid formalism attributed to Justices Harlan and Fuller, and to Justice Brown in *De Lima*, is equated by Mc-

---

[37] "At the present time in this country there is more danger that criminals will escape justice than that they will be subjected to tyranny." *Kepner*, 195 U.S. at 134.

[38] *Id.*

[39] *Id.*

[40] 192 U.S. at 1.

[41] *De Lima*, 182 U.S. at 173–74.

Kenna and White with a usurpation of the "political" functions of the legislature by depriving it of the required flexibility to act. The highly contextualized instrumentalist approach they adopted, to their mind, permitted respect for the will of the political branches. That will was read as denying immediate "incorporation" to the new territories.

Chief Justice Taft further developed this contextualized methodology in *Balzac*.[42] The shift from the doctrine of "implied" to "express" incorporation that his opinion practically signifies was mandated, he stated, by the needs of "these latter days." A change in the historical situation required a modification of the legal test, according to Taft. His opinion provided several concrete examples of contextualized readings of past and recent government decisions, such as his discussion of the differences between Alaska and the situations of Puerto Rico and the Philippines. Equally suggestive of attention to contemporary events is his speculation about the reasons that prompted Congress to confer U.S. citizenship on Puerto Ricans, such as the need to afford them protection "against the world." Related to an action taken by Congress in 1917, this argument resonates with subtextual allusions to the presence of German submarines in the Caribbean. Of course, this "contextualized" reading of everything from the debates in the Constitutional Convention and the decisions in the *Fleming, Rice*, and *Scott* cases to the various treaties and acts annexing other territories allowed the Court to create a new doctrine fitted to what the Court, Congress, and the executive understood were the "new conditions" attendant to these most recent acquisitions.

Instrumental Eclecticism

The alternation from a predominantly instrumentalist and contextualized interpretative technique in the 1901 decisions to a largely formalist approach in the second group of cases and back to instrumentalism and contextualism in *Balzac* provides a picture of a strategy of interpretation[43] that is, ultimately, profoundly instrumentalist. In effect, this strategy of contextual selection of interpretative techniques—evident in those shifts as well as in the intermingling of approaches within some of the opinions themselves—can best be described as *instrumental eclecticism*. The techniques and modes of reasoning the justices used were heavily influenced by the results that they were likely to produce. Thus, the explicit instrumentalism of the first group of decisions allowed the new doctrine to develop, the formalism of the second group had the effect of confirming and settling the theory of incorporation, and Taft's contextualized approach in *Balzac* was able to take account of the "new conditions" and of the legal challenge that the granting of citizenship implied to reaffirm the earlier rulings and leave the status of Puerto Rico as a territory unchanged.

This instrumental eclecticism was evident also in the combination of arguments from natural law—the references to "higher principles," "natural rights," "inherent, although unexpressed principles," and so forth—and consequentialist considerations

---

[42] 258 U.S. 298 (1922).

[43] For the usefulness of the concept of "*strategy*" to explain behavior in anthropological and sociological studies, *see* PIERRE BOURDIEU, IN OTHER WORDS: ESSAYS TOWARD A REFLEXIVE SOCIOLOGY (1990).

of policy.[44] Similarly, the arguments oscillate between modes of logical reasoning[45] and the use of multiple sources of criteria for constitutional and statutory interpretation: text, general principles, precedent, "opinion of contemporaries," history, traditions, consequences, context, "nature of government," and so on.[46]

From the point of view of American legal history, this feature of the cases is highly revealing. It is generally believed that the end of the 19th and the beginning of the 20th centuries were a period of heightened formalism in American legal thought and judicial practice.[47] How can this view be reconciled with the explicit instrumentalism the majority of the Court adopted in 1901 in the *Insular Cases*? A probable answer is the following: Formalism and instrumentalism as methodologies of interpretation always coexist to a certain degree in the legal system. Whether one predominates at a given moment is always the result of the convergence of internal and external factors that must be analyzed in their specific articulation.[48] In general formalism tends to surface in two types of situations: situations of relative stability in the legal and political system, when struggles about legal meanings have already been settled (however provisionally), or controversial situations in which, due to the particular conjunctural balance of forces, conflicts are being resolved through the reaffirmation of principles previously adopted. Instrumentalism tends to prevail, however, when the legal system is confronted with new challenges—as was the case during the period of New Deal legislation in the United States—or when there is a fundamental shift in policy (or in the conditions for the pursuit of an established policy) that requires new legitimation.

Thus, the formalism of the latter part of the 19th century was adequate for domestic issues. As Horwitz has argued, by that time the business elite had already established its hegemony, and the basic principles of American "private" law had been settled.[49] But at the end of the century the United States was entering a new stage in international relations: the imperialist–expansive stage. New situations relating to the results of the imperialist drive called for flexibility in the application of law and the development of legal doctrine, such as the definition of the legal status of the newly acquired possessions. The judiciary thus required recourse to the instrumental eclecticism apparent in the cases under discussion. For a time, then, for-

---

[44] *See, e.g.*, Justice Brown's opinion in *Downes*, 182 U.S. at 282, and Justice White's concurrence in *id.* at 290–91.

[45] *See* White's explicit assertion that he would rely both on deductive and inductive reasoning to arrive at his result, *Downes*, 182 U.S. at 300.

[46] *See* particularly the opinions of Justices Brown and White in *Downes*; Ramírez, *supra* note 7, at 135.

[47] HORWITZ, *supra* note 4; Summers, *supra* note 5; MICHAEL D. A. FREEMAN, LLOYD'S INTRODUCTION TO JURISPRUDENCE 655 (6th ed. 1994). An awareness of the prevailing formalism of the times is evident in the solicitor general's argument in the *Insular Cases*, in which he rhetorically presses his consequentialist reasoning almost reluctantly, apologetically even. *De Lima*, 182 U.S. at 137.

[48] Horwitz, for example, has argued that during the post-Revolutionary period in the United States, instrumentalism in "private law" coexisted with formalism in the adjudication of issues of "public law." According to him the instrumentalist approach in private law allowed for shifts in power to the merchant and entrepreneurial groups that were then vying for a hegemonic position, while formalism in public law prevented redistributionary efforts that would be detrimental to the interests of those same groups. HORWITZ, *supra* note 4, at 254–56. Only after the 1840s would there be a convergence leading to a heightened kind of formalism both in private and public law. *Id.* at 258.

[49] *Id.* at 254–59.

malism in domestic legal issues would cohabit with instrumentalism in legal matters relating to the territories, until the legal principles best suited for the "new situation" (from the metropolitan point of view) became settled.

A second conclusion from the analysis of the *Insular Cases* is relevant to today's theoretical debates. There has been a tendency to equate formalism with "conservative" views, with the legitimation of existing power structures, and "progressive" approaches with consequentialist reasoning and contextualized methodologies for the determination of "meaning." The lesson that may be drawn from the *Insular Cases* is that contextualism must be contextualized. After all, the determination of the relevant "context" in the course of interpretation is ideologically informed. What counts as pertinent contextual data, whether historical or contemporary, is to a great extent conditioned by the views of those making the selection and by their own biographical and social contexts. Indeed, all theories of interpretation, including contextualism, need to be analyzed in the context of their genesis, development, and application. In other words, there must be a sociology of theories of interpretation.

We have seen how, following an instrumental, contextualized approach to legal interpretation, the Supreme Court in effect legitimated colonialism. In the process of determining the relevant history and the consequences of its decisions, the Court was continually engaging in acts of ideological selection and thematization.[50] Determining the history that counts and the consequences that matter is as much a site for struggle in the conflicts over meaning as selecting the pertinent legal data and the adequate interpretative techniques.

Judicial Function

There was not much rhetorical disagreement between the different majorities and minorities in the *Insular Cases* about the need for the Court to exercise "judicial restraint" in their resolution of the important matters under discussion. What they disagreed on was who was actually displaying the required self-control. Thus Justice McKenna, in his dissent in *De Lima,* advised engaging in judicial moderation. The Court, he believed, was casting unnecessary legal fetters on Congress and the executive by denying them the needed flexibility to deal with the new territories. On the other hand, Justice Harlan, arguing for quite different results, more than once urged the Court not to "amend" judicially the Constitution by extending Congress and the executive a power not sanctioned by the latter instrument.[51]

The Nature of Rights

The edifice of the incorporation doctrine—not less than the "extension" doctrine advocated by Justice Brown—is mounted upon a hierarchical conception of rights that draws distinctions in terms of the importance and degree of protection among the various claims that subjects can make to a legal system. Thus, at various points, the Court's opinions elaborate a discourse based on the differences between "natural" and "artificial" rights (Brown in *Downes*), between "fundamental" and "non-

---

[50] *See* Jürgen Habermas, Legitimation Crisis 60 (1988).
[51] *See, e.g., Dorr,* 195 U.S. at 155.

fundamental" rights (Brown in *Downes* and *Mankichi*), and between "fundamental rights" and "questions of procedure" (*Mankichi*, *Dorr*, and *Kepner*).

Of course, the distinction between "natural" and "artificial" rights is part of the longstanding polemic between positivists and natural law theorists within the liberal tradition. In Brown's opinion the difference was posited as one between those rights that are "indispensable to a free government," which he called "natural rights" (he listed among them freedoms of religion, speech, and press; personal liberty and individual property; due process of law; free access to courts of justice; equal protection of the laws; and immunities from unreasonable searches and seizures and from cruel and unusual punishment), and those rights "peculiar to Anglo-Saxon jurisprudence," which he termed "artificial or remedial rights" (including "rights to citizenship, to suffrage, and to the particular methods of procedure pointed out in the Constitution").[52]

The opposition between fundamental and nonfundamental rights is played out in the cases as part of two different approaches to constitutional interpretation. The majority in *Downes*, *Mankichi*, and similar cases held that even if Congress possessed plenary power over the territories, the Constitution imposed certain fundamental limitations wherever Congress exerted its power. Those limitations concerned the inhabitants' "personal" rights as opposed to political rights. Furthermore, even personal rights, particularly in the context of criminal law, could be classified into those that were "fundamental" and those that referred to mere "questions of method or procedure." These distinctions were rejected or questioned expressly by Justices Harlan and Fuller. The Constitution, they believed, did not make such classifications, especially regarding "personal" rights.

Ideology of the *Insular Cases*

In chapter 1, I analyzed notions of history, society, order, and progress and of the relations among people that served as justifications for and provided impetus to the expansionist drive of the United States at the end of the 19th century. In this part I will connect the doctrine and the legal theory of the *Insular Cases* to those conceptions. I will also explore how the doctrine of incorporation was related to prevailing notions about "property," "democracy," the different versions of imperialism promoted by diverse groups, and finally the important concept of self-determination.

Ideology of Expansion

The discourse of the *Insular Cases* incorporated many of the beliefs and attitudes that constituted what I have termed the "ideology of expansion."[53] First of all, it was overtly racist. A few quotations will illustrate this point. It is fitting to start with the arguments pressed upon the Court by the government's representative. The solicitor general of the United States, referring to the effect of the Treaty of Paris respecting the Philippines, argued,

---

[52] *Downes*, 182 U.S. at 282–83.

[53] *See* chapter 1 for a full discussion of the topic.

Certainly the treaty never intended to make these tropical islands, with their savage and half-civilized people, a part of the United States in the constitutional sense, and just as certainly did make them a part of the United States in the international sense.[54]

In *Downes,* Justice Brown expressed the following:

It is obvious that in the annexation of outlying and distant possessions grave questions will arise from differences of race, habits, laws and customs of the people, and from differences of soil, climate and production, which may require action on the part of Congress that would be quite unnecessary in the annexation of contiguous territory inhabited only by people of the same race, or by scattered bodies of native Indians. . . .[55]

A false step at this time might be fatal to the development of what Chief Justice Marshall called the American Empire. Choice in some cases, the natural gravitation of small bodies toward large ones in others, the result of a successful war in still others, may bring about conditions which would render the annexation of distant possessions desirable. If those possessions are inhabited by alien races, differing from us in religion, customs, laws, methods of taxation and modes of thought, the administration of government and justice, according to Anglo-Saxon principles, may for a time be impossible, and the question at once arises whether large concessions ought not to be made for a time that ultimately our own theories may be carried out, and the blessings of a free government under the Constitution extended to them.[56]

Chief Justice Taft in *Balzac* crowned the series of decisions with the following statement:

We need not dwell on another consideration which requires us not lightly to infer . . . an intention to incorporate in the Union these distant ocean communities of a different origin and language from those of our continental people.[57]

Justice Harlan rebutted Justice Brown's racial argument thus:

Whether a particular race will or will not assimilate with our people, and whether they can or cannot with safety to our institutions be brought within the operation of the Constitution, is a matter to be thought of when it is proposed to acquire their territory by treaty. A mistake in the acquisition of territory, although such acquisition seemed at the time to be necessary, cannot be made the ground for violating the Constitution.[58]

In *Dorr,* Harlan lamented the Court's refusal to extend the constitutional right to a trial by jury to the Philippines, commenting,

Guaranties for the protection of life, liberty and property, as embodied in the Constitution, are for the benefit of all, of whatever race or nativity, in the States composing the Union, or in any territory, however acquired, over the inhabitants of which the Government of the United States may exercise the powers conferred upon it by the Constitution.[59]

---

[54] *De Lima,* 182 U.S. at 138.
[55] *Downes,* 182 U.S. at 282.
[56] *Id.* at 286–87.
[57] *Balzac,* 258 U.S. at 311.
[58] *Downes,* 182 U.S. at 384.
[59] *Dorr,* 195 U.S. at 154.

The obvious racism of the Court's expressions was consistent with the adherence by some members to the tenets of Manifest Destiny and Social Darwinism, which were part of the ideological framework of the dominant circles in the United States. Permeating the decisions is the notion that the peoples of the new territories were incapable of self-government. Moreover, they were considered unfit to become full-fledged members of the American polity with a right to participate in its government. The majority opinions, especially, reflect in many fundamental ways the principal features of the ideology of expansion discussed in detail in chapter 1.

Another, related discourse stresses the separateness between the conquering people and the conquered. Again, it is a discourse constructed around binary categories that privilege one pole of the equation. Justice White referred to "alien and hostile peoples."[60] Those peoples are the "others," constructed as such, as Justice Harlan perceptively noted, by labeling them "dependent peoples" or "subjects" inhabiting territories that are named "dependencies" or "outlying possessions."[61] From the imperial perspective, the "other" is inferior, less capable, predestined to be governed, to be held in tutelage, to be "civilized" or "protected," to be brought within the ideological world of the dominating power, but sufficiently at a distance so as not to confuse the respective communities they inhabit. In short (in the "constitution-alized" world of American political life), this "other" was to be kept at the same time "within and without"[62] the Constitution.

Ideologically, imperialism is ultimately based on this imaginary construction of the other as inferior.[63] This is the symbolic basis of the doctrine of incorporation. Keeping the "other" as a "separate," and subordinate, identity and entity justified governing it without the restraints imposed by membership in the political community of the imperial power. At the same time, constructing the "other" as inferior, as incapable, justified not treating the group as an equal in the community of sovereign nations, therefore justifying again its subordination as a colonial territory. Even the formal equality that had come to be accepted as desirable by Western liberal political theory could be flouted in its two prevailing senses: equality of status within the domestic political community and equality of respect within the international community.

"Territories" as Property

The strategy of interpretation adopted by the Court's majority in *Downes* and its progeny rested in a very central way in the decision to treat the newly acquired territories and their peoples as property. Of course, treating people as property was part of the American political and legal heritage. It was part of the ideological justification of slavery and of the subjugation of women. Treating other peoples as property was also a key feature of the various waves of European colonialism.

The relatively recent history of the United States, however, prevented the simple declaration that the new peoples were "chattels" of the federal government. The

---

[60] *Downes*, 182 U.S. at 308.

[61] *See Mankichi*, 190 U.S. at 240 (Harlan, J., dissenting).

[62] WINFRED LEE THOMPSON, THE INTRODUCTION OF AMERICAN LAW IN THE PHILIPPINES AND PUERTO RICO: 1898–1905 213 (1989).

[63] Peter Fitzpatrick, *Imperial Deviations* (1989).

reasoning expressed in the decisions was somewhat more sophisticated. It consisted, first, in addressing the matter of the status of the territory as a question of defining the legal characterization of a "locality" and then transferring to its people the characteristics of the place. But, as has been noted, the definition of the "locality" itself was performed in reference to the supposed deficiencies of its people. This continuous conflation between "people" and "locality"—the "locality" was ultimately privileged as the conceptually determining category—allowed the Court's members to formulate the question as one relating to the power to "dispose" of the "territory."

The textual basis for the analysis was provided by the Territorial Clause of the Constitution, which empowers Congress "to dispose of and make all needful rules and regulations respecting the Territory or other property belonging to the United States."[64] The reasoning also involved equating the terms *territory* and *property* used in the cited provision. In the resulting discourse, the "territory"—denoting the locality, but including its people—could be described as "belonging to" but not "a part of" the United States. Its inhabitants became derivatively "subjects" to be ruled and "disposed of."

Thus, the attorney general of the United States could argue that

> We must not forget that "*territory* belonging to the United States" is the common *property* of the United States and is to be administered at the common expense and for the common benefit of the States united, who jointly, as a governing entity, *own* it.
>
> Porto Rico and the Philippines were not won by arms and taken over by treaty through the efforts or influence or at the expense of the inhabitants, but through the might of the United States, upon their demand and upon their contribution of $20,000,000 to Spain, and upon the assumption by treaty of solemn national obligations which the United States, not the *islands* or their *inhabitants*, are bound to observe and keep.
>
> The *inhabitants* of the islands *are not joint partners* with the States in their transaction.
>
> The *islands* are "*territory belonging to the United States,*" not a part of the United States. The islands were the things acquired by the treaty; the United States were the party who acquired them, and to whom they belong. The *owner and the thing owned* are *not the same.*[65]

It is within the framework of this type of discourse that Justice White found it necessary to argue, quoting writers in international law, that a sovereign nation has the right to acquire "territory" and to determine its relation to the new government by "any of the recognized modes by which private property is acquired by individuals."[66]

Kelman called this process *substantive reification*: the construction of a value-laden general category under which the most diverse realities are subsumed, allowing them to be treated in a similar fashion.[67] Thus "private property" is turned into a "thing." Categorizing something as "property" then permits discussion of different actions (e.g., plant closures, expelling someone from one's home, etc.) as instances

---

[64] U.S. CONST. art. IV, § 3, cl. 2.

[65] *De Lima*, 182 U.S. at 102 (emphasis added).

[66] *Downes*, 182 U.S. at 300–04.

[67] *See* MARK KELMAN, A GUIDE TO CRITICAL LEGAL STUDIES 270–71 (1987).

of the exercise of the right of private property.[68] In this case, classifying the countries recently annexed as "property" allowed treating them as objects at the disposal of their "owner," the United States of America. This is part of the process of legitimation of colonization.[69]

This was not a necessary result. That is, it was not the inevitable product of the "correct" application of some legal principle that mandated that the territories be treated as property. The contingency of the event is suggested, if not by anything else, at least by the fact that some members of the Court were willing to rely on other categories, referring to the acquired territories as "countries" or "provinces" and to their inhabitants as "peoples."[70]

Vision of Democracy

The *Insular Cases* reflect a certain vision of democracy. One of the fundamental tenets of this vision was the conception of political participation as a privilege, not a right. Access to the privilege was restricted to those capable of exercising it, and determination of this capability involved various degrees of manifest or subjacent racial overtones. One of the crudest formulations of this conception had been provided by John W. Burgess, the prominent constitutional theorist of the times, who seems to have had substantial influence on many statesmen and legal scholars of the day: "The Teutonic nations can never regard the exercise of political power as a right of man; such a right must be based on political capacity of which the Teutonic nations are the only qualified judges."[71]

This vision implied that democracy—in the sense of a prerogative to take part in the decisions affecting the political community—was not intended for the colonies. The solicitor general in his argument put it quite succinctly: "Now, notwithstanding this expansive outlook," referring to the view of the founders that the United States was bound to expand beyond the seas, "it does not appear that the fathers of the Constitution worried themselves about 'the consent of the governed' outside of the States they lived in, which alone were to participate in political power."[72]

In the same vein Justice White asserted that the principle of "no taxation without representation"—so central in the political discourse of the American revolutionaries of the 18th century—did not apply to the territories.[73] He also argued that the rights of the conquered people were to be determined by the conqueror; in other words, this determination was not subject to democratic theory.[74]

It is one thing to acquire territory; to incorporate that territory into the nation is

---

[68] The examples are Kelman's, *id.*

[69] A commentator has noted that "half a century after the United States proclaimed the inadmissibility of the ownership of persons, [the Court] affirmed its acceptance of the contemporaneous European concept of the ownership of peoples." José Cabranes, *Citizenship and the American Empire*, 127 U. PA. L. REV. 391, 487 (1978).

[70] *See Downes*, 182 U.S. at 373 (Fuller, C. J., dissenting).

[71] *Quoted in* ROBIN F. WESTON, RACISM IN U.S. IMPERIALISM: THE INFLUENCE OF RACIAL ASSUMPTIONS ON AMERICAN FOREIGN POLICY 1893–1946 at 16 (1972).

[72] *De Lima*, 182 U.S. at 142.

[73] *Downes*, 182 U.S. at 299.

[74] *Id.* at 303–04.

quite another, Justice White's theory asserted. To incorporate implies a decision to share with the alien people "the rights which peculiarly belong to the citizens of the United States."[75] Incorporation, then, means bringing the "other" into the political community that was designed for the "we." He considered it a step not to be taken lightly, and certainly not with everyone. Again, democracy was viewed as a matter not of right, but of worthiness to belong to the political community. This was part of the rationale behind excluding African Americans, Native Americans, Asians, Mexican Americans, women, and the poor from the political process throughout American history.

Justice White and the other members of the majority in *Downes* and related cases were careful to establish that "plenary power" did not mean "arbitrary power." Thus, they fashioned the corollary doctrine of "fundamental rights" as a means of recognizing certain claims relating to the personal protection of individuals and their property, irrespective of the status of the territory. This was to be a colonial project, indeed, but one worthy of an "enlightened" colonialism.

Ultimately, this view was compatible with the old distinction between classical liberalism and democracy that went back to the European political struggles of the 17th and 18th centuries. Regarding the discourse of "rights," liberalism can be viewed as more a matter of carving out for the individual an autonomous zone that is to be free from government intervention, whereas democratic claims have more to do with collective aspirations to participate in community processes. In other words, the discourse of the judges revealed a tension between negative and positive conceptions of liberty.[76] Hence the recurrence of notions of "higher principles" and "natural rights"—referred to always as "negative liberty," in an all-too-familiar liberal discourse—while at the same time the Court insistently negated any implication that those "natural" or "fundamental rights" included the claim to become part of the American political community or to participate in decision making in (even when subject to the authority of) the American state.

Justice White himself expressed it very clearly:

> There is in reason then no room in this case to contend that Congress can destroy the liberties of the people of Porto Rico by exercising in their regard powers against freedom and justice which the Constitution has absolutely denied. There can also be no controversy as to the right of Congress to locally govern the island of Porto Rico as its wisdom may decide and in so doing to accord only such degree of representative government as may be determined on by that body.[77]

Reason is taken as the guide to the definition of freedom and justice. The justificatory rhetoric of this brand of colonialism was definitely shaped by the ideology of the Enlightenment, as much as liberalism had been.[78] However, by 1901, just slightly more than 100 years after the Declaration of Independence, democracy was not to be derived from reason, but from convention, from the will of a particular

---

[75] *Id.* at 324.

[76] For the distinction between "negative" and "positive" conceptions of liberty, see SIR ISAIAH BERLIN, FOUR ESSAYS ON LIBERTY 118–172 (1969).

[77] *Downes*, 182 U.S. at 298–99.

[78] For the historical connection between European imperialism and the Enlightenment, see Fitzpatrick, *supra* note 63; J. D. NEDERVEEN PIETERSE, EMPIRE AND EMANCIPATION: POWER AND LIBERATION ON A WORLD SCALE (1990).

community. From this perspective, other less capable, less enlightened communities that through the operation of the inevitable forces of social evolution came to be wards of their more advanced counterparts had to content themselves with the "blessings" bestowed on them by a liberal Constitution that guaranteed the protection of some claims, as defined by the superior polity, while being denied the right to govern their own destinies.

A related distinction elaborated by the cases is that between the "civil rights" of the inhabitants and the "political status" of the territory. This conceptual differentiation—already present in the language of the Treaty of Paris—has been a key ingredient in the development of a political framework that has facilitated American hegemony in Puerto Rico. It has allowed for the establishment of a partial democracy and of an internal regime based on the rule of law that nevertheless preserves the fundamental political subordination of the country to the metropolitan state.[79]

This vision of democracy as applied to the peoples of the newly acquired possessions entailed both discontinuity and continuity with previous history. It departed from the standard policy regarding territories acquired in the past and from the legal trend toward formal inclusion established by the post-Civil War amendments to the Constitution. At the same time, it was consistent with the practices of exclusion—both formal and material—that were still prevalent in American political, social, and economic life at the turn of the century.

Two Versions of Imperialism

The conflict between the majority (best represented by Justices White and McKenna in the early stages, and later by Justices Day and Taft) and the minority (especially Justices Fuller and Harlan) in the *Insular Cases* embodied a tension between two versions of imperialism. The majority view, which eventually became that of the entire Court, sanctioned the realization of the expansionist project through formal colonialism, that is, through the direct political subordination and control of overseas territories and peoples that were not considered part of the nation. The minority position rejected this form of colonialism, but was not necessarily opposed to overseas expansion and the annexation of other countries and peoples, even through conquest. It only had different conceptions about the formal political and legal consequences of such ventures.

Thus, Chief Justice Fuller would argue that while the founders did not exclude expansion, it had to be carried out within the framework of the Constitution.[80] This meant that if overseas territories were annexed, they had to be incorporated into the union and their inhabitants accorded full civil rights. Whether that meant also being immediately accorded political rights is not made clear. But according to past practice it probably implied eventual admission as states. Justice Harlan took a similar outlook. Furthermore, he seemed to believe that the United States could exert its "authority" and "influence" in the world through other means.[81] This stance was shared by many in the "anti-imperialist" group, which had opposed colonial acquisitions since the middle of the 19th century while favoring the extension of American

---

[79] This theme will be developed further in chapter 8.
[80] *Downes*, 182 U.S. at 374–75.
[81] *Id.* at 386.

hegemony through commercial activity (an anticipation of what in modern times has come to be known as the "Coca Cola Empire").

The controversy was not about the legitimacy of expansion through acquisition of territory, but about the consequences of such acquisition. Nor was there any disagreement as to the need to accord Congress and the executive a wider latitude in dealing with the territories. It was the extent of that latitude that bothered the minority. Justice Harlan's position is best clarified through an analysis of *Grafton*,[82] a case rarely cited in discussions about the *Insular Cases*. In this case the Court held unanimously that an American soldier who had been acquitted by a military court, under the authority of the United States, of a crime allegedly committed in the Philippines could not be tried subsequently for the same offense in a civil court exercising authority in the territory. The Court's rationale, in an opinion written by Justice Harlan, was based on the notion that both courts existed and operated by virtue of the authority of the same government—that of the United States.[83] In developing his argument Justice Harlan explained that the relation between the Philippines and the United States was not the same as that between a state and the U.S. government. The government of a state does not derive its powers from the United States, whereas the government of a territory owes its existence wholly to the United States: "The jurisdiction and authority of the United States over that territory and its inhabitants, for all legitimate purposes of government is paramount."[84]

Puerto Rico, of course, was in the same condition. This reasoning meant, then, that a distinction had to be drawn between the question of whether the Constitution applied *ex proprio vigore,* as Harlan had so strenuously argued throughout the cases, and the question of the relationship between the territory and the government of the United States. Even if the Constitution applied of its own force and immediately upon acquisition, Congress had absolute—in the sense of exclusive—power to govern the territory. It could exert over the territory power that it could not exercise over the states.

Justice Harlan's concern throughout his various dissents was the limitation of that power of governance in the classical liberal tradition. Hence his opposition to the "fundamental rights" corollary of the incorporation theory. He saw the overtly colonial scheme sanctioned by the Court as an abdication of liberal constitutionalism. The implications of this conception are important from the point of view of the distinction between liberal and democratic conceptions of governance. The "paramount" power that Congress could exercise over the peoples of the territories—even according to Harlan—was not the result in any sense of the consent of the governed, as in democratic theory, but of the act of conquest that brought those peoples into the dominion of the United States. This was, of course, a decidedly imperialistic conception of right.

This conflict of visions echoed the debate that had taken place and was still current in academic, journalistic, and other political forums. It must be remembered that one strand of the anti-imperialist position rejected annexation because it would provide the "alien people" of the possessions a basis to claim a right to participate in the government of the nation.[85] Once the acquisition of territories was an accom-

---

[82] Grafton v. United States, 206 U.S. 333 (1907).

[83] *Id.* at 335.

[84] *Id.* at 354.

[85] *See* chapter 1.

plished fact, some "anti-imperialists" argued, the Constitution mandated the full incorporation of those peoples into the country's constitutional framework. In sum, the position taken by Justices White, McKenna, and Day and the others would result in the total subordination of the peoples of the territories, whereas, notwithstanding their denunciation of colonialism and domination, that espoused by Justices Harlan and Fuller implied the immediate full annexation and, presumably, accelerated Americanization of those peoples.

Self-Determination

The conceptual scheme of the *Insular Cases* is entirely incompatible with any notion of self-determination. Despite the competing conceptions that have been advanced in the struggles to provide it with specific content, at a minimum the concept of *collective self-determination,* from a normative point of view, implies the legal or moral right of a people or group (however it is defined) to determine its status and associations with other peoples or groups and to fashion the organizing principles of its social existence.[86]

The logic of the Court's discourse, however, presupposes the plenary power of the United States to determine the political condition and the civil and political rights of the people of the acquired territory. In *Downes* Justice White explicitly proclaimed that it was the prerogative of the conqueror to decide the destiny of the conquered.[87] Of course, this principle already underlay the transaction involved in the Treaty of Paris. And both Congress and the executive had proceeded under its fundamental premise. This normative theory of heterodetermination cannot be separated from the other elements of the ideology permeating the cases.[88]

It is not anachronistic to level this critique against the Court's political rationale, for many reasons. First of all, by the end of the 19th and beginning of the 20th centuries, the concept of collective and, specifically, national self-determination was already current in international political debates, particularly in Europe.[89] Second,

---

[86] For detailed discussions of the various conceptions of self-determination in a variety of contexts, *see* ISSUES IN SELF-DETERMINATION (William Twining Ed. 1991); SELF-DETERMINATION: NATIONAL, REGIONAL AND GLOBAL DIMENSIONS (Y. Alexander & R. Friedlander Eds. 1980); J. A. DE OBIETA CHALBAUD, EL DERECHO HUMANO DE LA AUTODETERMINACIÓN DE LOS PUEBLOS (1985); D. RONEN, THE QUEST FOR SELF-DETERMINATION (1979); M. Pomerance, *The United States and Self-Determination: Perspectives on the Wilsonian Conception,* 70 AM. J. INT'L L. 1 (1976) [hereinafter Pomerance, *United States and Self-Determination*]; M. Pomerance, *Self-Determination Today: The Metamorphosis of an Ideal,* 19 ISRAEL L. REV. 310 (1984); Mihailo Markovic, *The Principle of Self-Determination as a Basis for Jurisprudence,* 13 ARCHIV FÜR RECHTS-UND SOZIALPHILOSOPHIE (BEIHEFT NEUE FOLGE) 181 (1980).

[87] *Downes,* 182 U.S. at 303–04.

[88] European colonialists also entertained the notion that colonial subjects should not be recognized a right to self-determination. Peter Fitzpatrick quoted John Westlake as asserting that " 'the African' may 'have had a right to law' but not 'a right to self-determination . . . because the African had not yet found a self to determine.' " According to Westlake, "of uncivilized natives international law takes no account. This . . . does not mean that all rights are denied to such natives, but that the appreciation of their rights is left to the conscience of the state within whose recognized territorial sovereignty they are comprised." PETER FITZPATRICK, THE MYTHOLOGY OF MODERN LAW 109 (1992).

[89] See Pomerance, *United States and Self-Determination, supra* note 86; Efrén Rivera Ramos, *Self-Determination and Decolonisation in the Society of the Modern Colonial Welfare State,* in ISSUES OF SELF-DETERMINATION, *supra* note 86.

the principle of "consent of the governed" had been part of American political discourse since the Revolution. Third, the political debate in the United States contemporaneous to the *Insular Cases* had produced explicit affirmations of the right of the peoples of the territories to be consulted regarding their future.[90]

Fourth, some members of the Court made references to the fact that the Court's position entailed establishing a "system of domination"[91] "not as the Constitution requires, nor as the people governed may wish."[92] (It must be added, however, that although this revealed an awareness of the colonial nature of the project, it is not clear whether Justices Harlan and Fuller believed that some sort of consultation with the people of the territories was required before annexation. The rest of their analyses suggests, on the contrary, that they shared the belief that the United States could acquire territory as it desired, irrespective of the wish of its inhabitants.) Fifth, by the time the *Balzac* case was decided in 1922, President Woodrow Wilson had explicitly espoused the principle of self-determination as a fundamental principle in international relations.[93] Finally, some prominent Puerto Ricans had been promoting the idea of a plebiscite to determine the political condition of the country. One of them was Eugenio María de Hostos, a noted intellectual and advocate of independence for the island who at one point had integrated a commission that met with President William McKinley to discuss the Puerto Rican problem.[94] These observations clearly indicate that there were contemporaneous alternative visions upon which to found a policy to deal with the peoples of the territories in accordance with principles of self-determination.

---

[90] For example, Senator William E. Mason, Republican of Illinois, presented the following resolution to express the sense of the Senate: "Wheras all just powers of government are derived from the consent of the governed: Therefore be it RESOLVED BY THE SENATE OF THE UNITED STATES, That the Government of the United States of America will not attempt to govern the people of any other country in the world without the consent of the people themselves, or subject them by force to our dominion against their will." *Quoted* in THOMPSON, *supra* note 62, at 43. For other examples *see id.* at 43–46.

[91] *Downes*, 182 U.S. at 373 (Fuller, C. J., dissenting).

[92] *Mankichi*, 190 U.S. at 240 (Harlan, J., dissenting).

[93] Pomerance, *United States and Self-Determination*, *supra* note 86; Rivera Ramos, *supra* note 89. Of course, for Wilson the principle was applicable only to European peoples. The peoples of Latin America, the Caribbean, and other "less civilized" regions were thought to be incapable of determining their own destinies. WESTON, *supra* note 71, at 19.

[94] EUGENIO MARÍA DE HOSTOS, AMÉRICA: LA LUCHA POR LA LIBERTAD 240 (Manuel Maldonado Denis Ed. 1988); Carmelo Delgado Cintrón, *Hostos ante el 1898*, EL NUEVO DÍA, Jan. 11, 1992, at 51.

Chapter 6
THE CONSTITUTIVE EFFECTS OF THE *INSULAR CASES*

What effects did the *Insular Cases* have on the configuration of the imperial and colonial experience being created? To answer the question is to reveal important aspects of the constitutive power of law. After this exploration, I will provide an explanation of the sociohistorical factors that combined to produce the results embodied in the cases, drawing on the analysis in chapter 1 of the main forces and tensions surrounding the expansionist drive of the United States. These cases were an important part of a historic compromise among the dominant groups in the United States that allowed the colonial project to unfold.

Effects of the Court's Actions

Justification of Power and Legitimation of the Colonial Project

The doctrine developed in the *Insular Cases* provided an explicit justification of the use of power in the new American colonial project. It produced an authoritative rationale for the claim that Congress could exercise almost unrestricted power over the peoples of the territories, maintaining their subordination. In this sense the cases legitimated through discursively validated claims[1] a particular power relationship.

Processes of legitimation in the modern world cannot be understood unless they are seen as the result of a complex articulation of elements that converge to produce a generalized acceptance of existing power relations. A theory of legitimation must include an examination of those various forces and ingredients. At a minimum, four elements should be analyzed. The first may be called *explicit justification,* that is, the political, moral, and legal arguments overtly offered to justify power relations and social practices. Second, one must look at the material conditions and practices through which interpreted needs and aspirations are meant to be satisfied in a given community. Third, account should be taken of the structures designed to channel—or exclude—the input of members of a particular community in the process of defining its needs and elaborating strategies for their satisfaction. Finally, one should identify the worldviews within which the interpretation of needs takes place.[2] A social

---

[1] JÜRGEN HABERMAS, LEGITIMATION CRISIS (1988).

[2] This formulation attempts a synthesis of the legitimation theories propounded by Max Weber and Jürgen Habermas. In essence, Weber maintained that in societies where what he called "legal domination" prevails, the legitimation of political authority rests with the existence of a system of abstract, general, rationally formal rules that prescribe not only the powers that can be exercised in accordance with those rules, but also the procedures and institutions by which the rules may be established or modified. Legitimation, therefore, is derived from law. MAX WEBER, ECONOMY AND SOCIETY 212 *ff* (G. Roth & C. Wittich Eds. 1978). *See also* Roger Cotterrell, *Legality and Political Legitimacy in the Sociology of Max Weber, in* LEGALITY, IDEOLOGY AND THE STATE 70–71 (David Sugarman Ed. 1983); ROGER COTTERRELL, THE SOCIOLOGY OF LAW 152–57 (2nd ed. 1992). Habermas, on the other hand,

theory of law calls for an examination of the ways in which law and legal ideologies and processes become imbricated in these four aspects of the legitimation process. In this chapter I focus my attention on explicit justification as an element of legitimation. The other elements are examined in chapters 7 and 8.

Constitutionalism has been central as an ideology for the justification or critique of the exercise of power in American political and social life, and law has had an equally central role in the processes of explicit justification as an ingredient of legitimation. Through developments known to those familiar with U.S. constitutional history, the Supreme Court of the United States became entrusted with the task of being a final arbiter in struggles about constitutional meaning. Within this context, in the 19th and early 20th centuries the United States, perhaps more than any other industrial capitalist society, experienced an accelerated process of "institutionalization of general practical discourse"[3] through the judiciary, epitomized in the functions of the Supreme Court. Law became objectified morality, given with an authoritative voice by judges throughout the land, with the ultimate sanction of the body of brethren who sat in Washington.

As I have noted above, any system of legitimation in modern societies must, in some degree or other, combine explicit justification, by reference to a discursively validated rationality, with the production of a perception that the system somehow is effective in satisfying interpreted and articulated needs. One probable explanation for the particular effectiveness of the judicially based system for producing legitimation in the United States is the fact that, since the early days of the republic, the Supreme Court has been able to elucidate and "settle" important questions of state and social life in the course of adjudicating highly particularized disputes. The pronouncements of the Supreme Court are never made in response to abstract questions, but in the context of resolving practical problems that are perceived as important by the litigants for their immediate consequences and by jurists, academics, politicians, interest groups, the media, and others for their longer-range implications.

In the *Insular Cases* the larger questions of the nature of the U.S. government and the degree to which the Constitution sanctioned a system of colonial domination were always answered in the process of adjudicating specific conflicts among concrete agents promoting their interests in the context of the new conditions and relationships whose legitimacy was now being questioned through the judicial apparatus. This continual movement from the experience of power as it is felt in very

---

tied legitimation to the capacity of the economic and political systems to satisfy needs. Yet he established a link between legitimation and normative structures to the extent that those structures contribute to the definition of needs and expectations. *See generally* HABERMAS, *supra* note 1. A synthesis of both theoretical approaches leads to the proposition that neither bare rationality nor the pure and simple satisfaction of needs, by itself, is sufficient to guarantee legitimation. Therefore, while a given rationality, however defined, must be linked to the satisfaction of needs and aspirations, the latter must occur within a process somehow conceived to be "rational," that is, responding to a conception of justice that may be "discursively validated." Without discussing either Weber or Habermas, Pierre Bourdieu arrived at a similar conclusion when he asserted that the efficacy of law as symbol depends on its association to "real needs and interests." Pierre Bourdieu, *The Force of Law: Toward a Sociology of the Juridical Field*, 38 HASTINGS L. J. 805, 840 (1987). *See also* Efrén Rivera Ramos, *Self-Determination and Decolonisation in the Society of the Modern Colonial Welfare State, in* ISSUES OF SELF-DETERMINATION (William Twining Ed. 1991).

[3] HABERMAS, *supra* note 1, at 16.

concrete situations to the elucidation of the more general, "political" questions not only serves an important ideological function,[4] but is itself a source of legitimation for the authority of the Court.

The pronouncements of the Court, invested with that practically legitimated authority, have a force lacking in the proclamations of other agents. After all, "in the case of the social world, speaking with authority is as good as doing."[5] This explains in part the need felt by the American governing elites (discussed in chapter 1) to have the new colonial project explicitly justified by the highest tribunal in the land.

Explicit justification as an incident of legitimation always raises the question of audience. Whom was the Court addressing? First of all, to the litigants, it is obvious, and all those similarly situated. This allowed for the authoritative settling of many of the localized conflicts and disputes that the new situation promoted. Such disputes included those among sectors of the American agricultural, manufacturing, and commercial establishments, whose immediate interests clashed or became threatened by the economic activity of others in the territories or by the practices of the metropolitan state.

But in a wider sense, there were two principal audiences regarding the question of the legitimacy of the colonial order. To the Puerto Rican political elites, the rulings of the Court generally came as an unwelcome, imposed reaffirmation of the policies Congress and the executive had already established. In this sense the exercise was not strictly one of justification, but might be considered rather an example of what Bourdieu would call *symbolic violence,* which he defined as the imposition of "principles of division," that is, of the categories created for the unequal distribution of power.[6]

However, the explicit justification of the exercise of colonial power was probably most directly addressed to the intellectual and political elites of the United States. The material and symbolic stratification of society provides a context for the differentiation of needs for justification.[7] Social consciousness is not homogenous, even among members of the same social group. There are many "common senses" (in Gramscian terminology[8]) that must be satisfied by those exercising power. The intense debate that had accompanied the process of acquisition of new territories had to be settled for the process to continue its course. There was a need to develop a truly *common* sense among the organic intellectuals of the metropolitan state.[9]

---

[4] As Cotterell observed, "What may be much more central to law, understood primarily but not exclusively as state law, is the production of ideologically and technically important doctrine by courts and other state controlled dispute institutions on the occasion of dispute processing, rather than the processing itself, which concerns only a small minority of disputes arising in society." Roger B. M. Cotterrell, *The Sociological Concept of Law*, in Lord Lloyd of Hampstead & Michael D. A. Freeman, Lloyd's Introduction to Jurisprudence 677 (5th ed. 1985).

[5] Pierre Bourdieu, In Other Words: Essays toward a Reflexive Sociology 53 (1990).

[6] *Id.*; Richard Terdiman, *Translator's Introduction* to Bourdieu, *supra* note 2, at 805–13.

[7] Chambliss and Seidman, for example, have argued that in capitalist societies the rule of law governs the lives only of the middle class. Legal–rational legitimacy, they contend, is used as a way of disciplining dissident elements of the ruling class, while the working class is subjected to other methods. W. Chambliss & Robert B. Seidman, Law, Order and Power 315 (2nd ed. 1982). Whether the example would hold true in all situations, all historical periods, and all capitalist social formations is open to question, but the argument does suggest that not all legitimation strategies, methods, or techniques are equally effective in all sectors of a given society.

[8] *See* Antonio Gramsci, Selections from the Prison Notebooks (Q. Hoare & G. N. Smith Eds. & Trans. 1971).

[9] The concept of *organic intellectual* is taken from Gramsci. For Gramsci, an organic intellectual

The decisions of the *Insular Cases* had precisely that effect. We have seen how by 1904 the doctrine of incorporation had already been established. Gradually the doctrine came to be accepted by the dissenting justices (except Harlan), by the academic community, and by politicians. The legal "truths" that Puerto Rico and the Philippines were "unincorporated territories," that Congress had plenary power over them, that their inhabitants could claim only limited protection from the Constitution, and so forth came to be part of the social understanding of the policy makers, part of the way in which the political reality of the new territories came to be perceived. In this sense the doctrine became part of the "reality" of the colonial project. When the decision in *Balzac* was delivered in 1922, there was hardly any discussion of its implications.[10] The colonial venture had been justified at the representational level of law.

Constitution of the Legal and Political Subject

The force of law as constitutive of society consists in a very fundamental way in its capacity to create a legal subject: that is, an agent or entity endowed with entitlements and obligations. In the social understanding that is part of the ideological basis of law's effectivity, this agent or entity is considered capable of making juridically recognizable claims. At the same time, the agent or entity becomes an object over which power may be legitimately exercised. The "subject" is constructed, then, both as an agent, (relatively) capable of willing and acting (someone endowed with "subjectivity"), and as a body submitted to authority (someone "subjected" to a given power).[11] Law, especially constitutional law, also creates political subjects in the sense that it legitimates the status of political actors—that is, agents endowed with the legal capacity to make certain claims in the political field—while simultaneously legitimating the exercise of state power over those subjects. The *Insular Cases* created both legal and political subjects in the senses described above. The subjects were defined as the inhabitants of unincorporated territory.

The process by which a subject is created through law has several dimensions and involves several "capacities" of the law as a constitutive discourse. Let us examine several that operated in the *Insular Cases*.

Reification

Creating a subject involves a process of *reification:* that is, construction of a category that acquires the quality of an object. The category substitutes the physical referents. The particularities of the realities that the category is intended to represent fade away

---

is one who emerges from a particular social group, shares the group's basic conceptions, and conducts thinking and organizing functions closely related to the process whereby the group seeks to establish or reproduce its hegemony over other groups. *See id.* at 5–14.

[10] JUAN R. TORRUELLA, THE SUPREME COURT AND PUERTO RICO: THE DOCTRINE OF SEPARATE AND UNEQUAL 100 n.347 (1985).

[11] It is perhaps this double operation of the law in the process of creating a subject that gives it its ambiguous quality in relation to experiences of emancipation and oppression. For at one level it provides a discourse of right, fueling aspirational drives, while at another it is felt as a constraint, as a submission to power.

as they are subsumed in the universal quality of the category. In a sense, the particular realities exist no more. The category, treated as a reality, becomes the truly real, distinct from other "realities." Or, as Bourdieu would express it, reality is reduced to the "useful fiction we term its juridical definition."[12]

In the *Insular Cases* the "reality" created was that of the "unincorporated territory." The unincorporated territory did not have any existence before the cases were decided. But the authoritative pronouncement of the Court brought it into existence "in reality, in other words, first and foremost, in people's minds (in the form of categories of perception)."[13]

Those "unincorporated territories" were inhabited by individuals, who, in their relationship to the new colonial power, now became subjects in both the legal and political senses.

Categorizing, of course, has consequences.[14] It involves the creation of a status from which rights emerge or by virtue of which they are denied. Puerto Rico was converted—through categorization—into an "unincorporated territory." And that justified subsequent exercises of power over its people. Not being included in a certain category also has implications. Certain effects would have followed, for example, from a declaration by the Court that Puerto Rico was an "incorporated territory," or that it was not a "territory" at all, or that it should be treated as a "nation" in the sense that the concept was then understood.

Legal struggles are often struggles to define the subject. All the cases under discussion were part of that process. But the sense of a struggle over this construction of the subject becomes very evident in a case like *González v. Williams*. In this regard the central questions in that case were the following: What is a Puerto Rican? To whom does he or she owe allegiance? (Allegiance, of course, is fundamentally a matter of having certain obligations.) Is a citizen the same as a subject? The case ultimately defined Puerto Ricans not as a nation, but as inhabitants of an island that had become a possession of the United States.[15]

The choice of categories was crucial. The concept of "inhabitant" has a neutral quality, deprived as it is of any reference to culture, history, language, or other elements constituent of a national identity. Moreover, the term connotes a certain atomization, an ultimately individualist reduction, that avoids the consequences of any notion of collective right.

This process of creation of the subject started from the very moment of acquisition. It was part of the process of negotiation of the Treaty of Paris. Congress and the executive had uttered their own authoritative word in the Foraker Act. In Section 7 of that act the political entity known as the "people of Porto Rico" was defined as the "inhabitants" of Puerto Rico, which included former Spanish nationals who had not sworn allegiance to Spain after a certain date and continued to reside in the island, as well as U.S. citizens residing there.

---

[12] Bourdieu, *supra* note 2, at 835.

[13] BOURDIEU, *supra* note 5, at 54.

[14] MARK KELMAN, A GUIDE TO CRITICAL LEGAL STUDIES 271 (1987).

[15] The Court quoted approvingly from the attorney general's opinion in the *Molinas* case, 24 Op. Att'y Gen. 40 (1902), in which the attorney general referred to the Puerto Rican artist stranded in Paris as "one of those turned over to the United States by Article IX of the treaty [of Paris]," adding that he was "also clearly a Porto Rican; that is to say, a permanent inhabitant of that island." *González*, 192 U.S. at 15. *See* chapter 4, nn.122–29 and accompanying text.

The category "people of Porto Rico" was a legal construct imposed by the
United States—another act of symbolic violence. (The altered spelling is symbolically significant, for it signified both the identity of the definer of the identity and
the fact that it involved an act of "misidentification.") This legal subject consisted
of the "inhabitants" of a place, categorized in a certain way. It was not a nation, a
historical community that defined itself with reference to a common language, culture, experience, or other such criterion. Those facts were relevant only insofar as
they were construed as defining an inferior people in need of tutelage. The *Insular
Cases*, then, were part of a process of construction of a new identity and of the
constitution of a new legal and political subject.

The "Power of Naming"

The creation of the subject through processes of reification is an instance of the
performative power of law,[16] or the power to constitute by naming, that is, to "create
the things named."[17] As Bourdieu pointed out, law's power consists in "confer[ring]
upon the reality which arises from its classificatory operations the maximum permanence that any social entity has the power to confer upon another, the permanence
which we attribute to objects."[18] It involves an "ontological slippage" that "leads
from the existence of the name to the existence of the thing named."[19] The effectivity
of the performative utterance resides in the authority of the speaker.[20] It does not
matter, of course, what the source of that authority may be; as in this case, it could
even be an act of conquest.

In the *Insular Cases* the Supreme Court was exercising its "power of naming."
It named the "others" in order to constitute them. Labeling the newly acquired lands
"unincorporated territories" was to constitute them as such. The process of constituting the "others" by naming them was, in turn, informed by the worldview that
was part of the ideology of the cases described in the previous chapter and was
predicated upon the type of binary reasoning discussed in chapter 1.

Conflating the Descriptive and the Normative

Creation of the subject as bearer of entitlements and as an object of the exercise of
power also involves a process of conflation of the descriptive and the normative.[21]
This entails another type of slippage in two mutually reinforcing directions. The
prescribed becomes the described,[22] but also the described—or the thing constituted
through naming—acquires a moral quality.

In this case the status of "unincorporated territory" was the result of a normative
conclusion. The Court concluded that there were lands that should be treated as

---

[16] Bourdieu, *supra* note 2; BOURDIEU, *supra* note 5; JEAN FRANCOIS LYOTARD, THE POSTMODERN
CONDITION: A REPORT ON KNOWLEDGE (1984).

[17] Bourdieu, *supra* note 2, at 838.

[18] *Id.*

[19] BOURDIEU, *supra* note 5, at 55.

[20] LYOTARD, *supra* note 16, at 9.

[21] KELMAN, *supra* note 14, at 291, 294.

[22] *Id.* at 294–95.

things called "unincorporated territories." The normative conclusion was presented as the discovery of a truth: that there are such things as unincorporated territories. That entity, normatively created, became a "thing" that had its own existence. From then on, the United States possessed lands that were unincorporated territories.

At the same time a reverse slippage occurred, especially when dealing with specific territories. The Court spoke a legal "truth," that is, it described a legal reality. The denotative statement was: Puerto Rico *is* an unincorporated territory. From that description flowed a normative conclusion: Puerto Rico *should be treated as* an unincorporated territory.

Of course, the linkage between the authority to declare the truth and the authority to declare what is just is part of all processes of legitimation.[23] The cognitive and the evaluative cannot be separated in the discourses of power. Their fusion is one element that contributes to the specificity of law. Bourdieu perceptively noted that the force of law hinges in part on the fact that it operates at the intersection of the discourse of politics and the discourse of science.[24]

Creation of a Discursive Universe

A third effect of the *Insular Cases* was the creation of a discursive universe within which further discussion of the colonial problem would be conducted. Taking as its point of departure the categories of perception and valuation produced by Congress, the executive, and others engaged in the academic and public debate, the Supreme Court elaborated, and to a great extent crystallized, the parameters of future legal and political discussions regarding the territories. It constructed the framework for the production of further discourse. In so doing it determined what would be a legitimate argument and what would not.

This is a very powerful attribute of courts. It involves a process of thematization and selection, that is, a determination of what categories, arguments, interests, values, themes, claims, and aspirations will be granted access to the discourse of law.[25] In the Anglo-American legal tradition, the rule of precedent provides this power with an internally legitimated basis and an added force. One effect of the rule of precedent is to allow for the discussion and application of the legal doctrine established by a series of cases without reference to the ideological presuppositions that underlie the "holdings" of the Court. This feature accounts to a great extent for the perception of fixity of legal doctrine, masking its usually contingent character.

The way in which further discussion of legal issues was to be affected by the *Insular Cases* is evident in a number of cases decided after *Balzac* and until the present. This is not the place to discuss them in detail. Suffice it to say that those decisions have been part of a process of piecemeal judicial decision making regarding the applicability of constitutional provisions to Puerto Rico and the constitutional guarantees that its "inhabitants" may claim.[26]

---

[23] LYOTARD, *supra* note 16, at 9.

[24] Bourdieu, *supra* note 2.

[25] As Cotterrell has noted, one of the vital forms of power is the power to set the agenda of debate or decision. Cotterrell, *supra* note 4, at 678.

[26] *See, e.g.*, Bianchi v. Morales, 262 U.S. 170 (1923); Calero Toledo v. Pearson Yacht Leasing Co., 416 U.S. 663 (1974) (due process of law); Examining Board v. Flores de Otero, 426 U.S. 572 (1976)

After the process that led to the creation of the Commonwealth in 1952, there has been much theoretical discussion about whether Puerto Rico ceased to be a "territory" of the United States. Three general positions have been adopted. One asserts that a new status emerged in 1952. Another holds that, although it introduced some changes, Commonwealth is just another type of unincorporated territory. And a third affirms that nothing was fundamentally changed by the "creation" of the Commonwealth.[27] Federal and Puerto Rican courts have dealt with the issue in conflicting and largely ambiguous language.[28] In practice, however, Congress, the executive, and the Supreme Court have proceeded under the assumption that Congress has plenary power to govern the country in the fashion authorized by the holdings of the *Insular Cases*. In 1978 and 1980, more than three-quarters of a century after the first group of cases was decided, the Court relied on their language and rationale to hold that, pursuant to its powers under the Territorial Clause of the Constitution, Congress can discriminate against residents of Puerto Rico when legislating on social and welfare matters.[29]

The conceptual categories the *Insular Cases* created have also provided a framework for political discussion outside the judicial sphere. In this respect the opinions and decisions of the Court constituted one of the first attempts to bring the discussion of the problem of the acquired lands and their peoples under the discursive universe of the imperial power. For example, the term "colony"—so common in the debates of the day—would eventually disappear. The United States, from very early on, refused to admit that it had "colonies." It had only overseas "territories." The Court has legitimated this political use of language by always treating the question as one of distinguishing between incorporated and unincorporated "territories."

The weight of this force in the realm of political discourse was evident during the 1989–1991 process regarding the proposal to hold a plebiscite to decide the political future of Puerto Rico.[30] The congressional reports and background materials produced by legislative committees had to adopt as their working premise the doctrine that had been established by the Court between 1901 and 1922.[31] Much of the

---

(equal protection of the laws); Segurola v. United States, 275 U.S. 106 (1927); Torres v. Puerto Rico, 442 U.S. 475 (1979) (search and seizure clause of the Fourth Amendment); Califano v. Torres, 435 U.S. 1 (1978) (right to travel).

[27] U.S. GENERAL ACCOUNTING OFFICE, PUERTO RICO: INFORMATION FOR STATUS DELIBERATIONS 4–6 (1989) [GAO].

[28] For discussions of the relevant judicial decisions, *see id.* at 4–6 to 4–28; RAÚL SERRANO GEYLS (Demetrio Fernández Quiñones & Efrén Rivera Ramos, contributors) DERECHO CONSTITUCIONAL DE ESTADOS UNIDOS Y PUERTO RICO: DOCUMENTOS–JURISPRUDENCIA–ANOTACIONES–PREGUNTAS 496–561 (1986); ARNOLD H. LEIBOWITZ, DEFINING STATUS: A COMPREHENSIVE ANALYSIS OF UNITED STATES TERRITORIAL RELATIONS 47–53, 178–185 (1989).

[29] *See* Califano v. Torres, 435 U.S. 1 (1978) (Congress may constitutionally exclude Puerto Rico from applicability of Supplemental Security Income Program, which provides for aid to qualified aged, blind, and disabled persons in the United States); Harris v. Rosario, 446 U.S. 651 (1980) (Congress can determine that Puerto Rico will receive less financial assistance than the states to provide aid to families with needy dependent children).

[30] *See* S. 710, 711, 712, 101st Cong., 1st Sess. (1989); H.R. No. 4765, 101st Cong., 2nd Sess. (1990).

[31] *See, e.g.*, GAO, *supra* note 27; U.S. CONGRESSIONAL RESEARCH SERVICE (CRS), DISCRETION OF CONGRESS RESPECTING CITIZENSHIP STATUS OF PUERTO RICO (1989); U.S. CONGRESS, HOUSE COMMITTEE ON INTERIOR AND INSULAR AFFAIRS, REPORT TOGETHER WITH ADDITIONAL VIEWS ON PUERTO RICO SELF-DETERMINATION ACT, H.R. 4765, 101st Cong., 2nd Sess. (1990).

public debate reflected both the constraints imposed by the discursive universe the Court created and attempts to break away from those parameters.

The public conflicts and struggles about meaning that are always a central feature of political debate hinged around questions such as the following: Was this a "decolonization" process, or an exercise of the discretionary power of Congress to "dispose of the territory"? Was this an instance of a people's drive for "self-determination," subject to the rules and principles of international law, or was it merely the resolution of a "domestic" problem of the United States regarding the future of several million U.S. citizens? (Here surfaced the problem of how and by whom an identity is constructed.) Was Congress willing to relinquish its "powers" under the Territorial Clause?

One of the final strokes that eventually produced the death of the plebiscite legislation was the testimony, in February 1991, of Attorney General of the United States Richard Thornburgh on behalf of the Department of Justice before a Senate committee considering the bill. In essence Thornburgh declared that Puerto Rico was subject to the sovereignty of the United States by virtue of the Territorial Clause, that there was serious doubt whether Congress would ever limit its powers under that clause as long as Puerto Rico did not become either an independent republic or a state of the union, and that, because the United States exercised sovereignty over Puerto Rico, the principles of international law regarding self-determination and decolonization were not applicable. This is, clearly, the framework of analysis sanctioned by the Supreme Court in the *Insular Cases*.[32]

That conceptual framework dominated, with added force, the political discussion generated in 1996 with the filing of a bill by Representative Don Young, Republican from Alaska, to provide for a federally sanctioned vote in Puerto Rico on the status question. The United States–Puerto Rico Political Status Act, finally approved by the House of Representatives on March 4, 1998, as a result of that process, unmistakably adopted the doctrine of the *Insular Cases* as the controlling legal parameter with which to gauge the current relationship between the United States and Puerto Rico. In a list of "findings" incorporated into the enacted bill, the House explicitly claimed that the authority exercised by the U.S. Congress over Puerto Rico rested on the Territorial Clause of the Constitution as interpreted by the U.S. Supreme Court. Puerto Rico, this piece of legislation asserted, still remained an unincorporated territory of the United States, subject to the full authority of Congress under the Territorial Clause. Regarding the adoption of Commonwealth in 1952, House Bill 856 stated that

---

[32] *See, generally,* GAO, *supra* note 27; HOUSE COMMITTEE ON INTERIOR AND INSULAR AFFAIRS, *supra* note 31; 1 JUAN M. GARCÍA PASSALACQUA & C. RIVERA LUGO, PUERTO RICO Y LOS ESTADOS UNIDOS: EL PROCESO DE CONSULTA Y NEGOCIACIÓN DE 1989 Y 1990 (1990); Harry Turner, *The Odyssey of Puerto Rico's Plebiscite: 1988–1990,* THE SAN JUAN STAR, Dec. 23, 1990, at 1, 24; U.S. Congress, *Political Status of Puerto Rico: Hearings on S. 710, S. 711, and S. 712 before the Senate Committee on Energy and Natural Resources,* 101st Cong, 1st Sess. (Vol. 1) 163, 122, 148 (1989) [*Hearings*]) (statements of Rafael Hernández Colón, governor of the Commonwealth of Puerto Rico; Carlos Romero Barceló, former governor of the Commonwealth of Puerto Rico; and Rubén Berríos Martínez, president of the Puerto Rican Independence Party); Raúl Serrano Geyls, *Memorandum to the Senate Committee on Energy and Natural Resources,* July 7, 1989; Carlos Gallisá, *Ha muerto el plebiscito,* CLARIDAD, Feb. 22 to 28, 1991, at 12, 29; Juan Mari Bras, *La cláusula territorial,* CLARIDAD, Dec. 7 to 13, 1990, at 30; Juan M. García Passalacqua, *La evolución del nuevo E.L.A,* EL NUEVO DÍA, Dec. 20, 1990, at 81.

the approved constitution established the structure for constitutional government in respect of internal affairs without altering Puerto Rico's fundamental political, social, and economic relationship with the United States and without restricting the authority of Congress under the Territorial Clause to determine the applicability of Federal law to Puerto Rico.[33]

"The Commonwealth," the relevant "finding" added, "remains an unincorporated territory and does not have the status of 'free association' with the United States as that status is defined under United States law or international practice."[34] According to the bill, the ruling of the Supreme Court in the 1980 case *Harris v. Rosario*[35] confirmed that Congress continues to exercise authority over Puerto Rico as territory belonging to the United States pursuant to the Territorial Clause of the United States Constitution, "a judicial interpretation of Puerto Rico's status which is in accordance with the clear intent of Congress that establishment of local constitutional government in 1952 did not alter Puerto Rico's fundamental status."[36]

The full U.S. Senate did not act on equivalent legislation pending before that body. However, hearings conducted on the issue by the relevant committee clearly revealed that the senators' understanding of the legal situation was similar to that expressed by the House of Representatives.[37] On the other hand, the cochair of the White House Puerto Rico Working Group, in charge of voicing the administration's policy on Puerto Rico political status legislation, was reported as holding an analogous position. He was quoted as stating that although Commonwealth had been an "important step in the development of Puerto Rico's self-government," the U.S. federal government still had final authority over the island under the Territorial Clause. In his opinion, Commonwealth "did not change the island's fundamental relationship with the U.S."[38] The consensus generated by the *Insular Cases* among the governing groups of the United States regarding the powers of the federal government over so-called "unincorporated territories" was alive and in good health almost a century after the production of the legal doctrine of incorporation.

---

[33] H.R. 856, 105th Cong., 2nd Sess. § 2(4) (1998) (enacted).

[34] *Id. Free association* refers to the relationship emerging from a freely entered agreement of political association between two sovereign countries. The status of free association was recognized by the United Nations as a legitimate solution to a colonial relationship provided several conditions are met. The decision to associate must be free and voluntary and the peoples of the territory concerned should retain the rights to determine their internal constitution without outside interference and to freely terminate the relationship. G.A. Res. 1541 (XV), 15 December 1960. *See* ADOLFO MIAJA DE LA MUELA, LA EMANCIPACIÓN DE LOS PUEBLOS COLONIALES Y EL DERECHO INTERNACIONAL 119–122 (1968); ANTONIO CASSESE, SELF DETERMINATION OF PEOPLES: A LEGAL REAPPRAISAL 73 (1995); *Declaración del Colegio de Abogados de Puerto Rico sobre la situación actual del proceso de descolonización de Puerto Rico ante el Comité de Descolonización de la Organización de Naciones Unidas (1979)*, 47 REV. COL. ABOG. P.R. 265 (1986).

[35] 446 U.S. 651 (1980). *See supra* note 29.

[36] H.R. 856, 105th Cong., 2nd Sess. § 7 (1998) (enacted). *See also* H.R. 3024, 104th Cong., 2nd Sess. (1996); U.S. CONGRESS, HOUSE COMMITTEE ON RESOURCES, REPORT TOGETHER WITH DISSENTING AND ADDITIONAL VIEWS TO ACCOMPANY H.R. 3024, 104th Cong., 2nd Sess. (1996); H.R. 856, 105th Cong., 1st Sess. (1997).

[37] *See* Robert Friedman, *Senate Status Hearings End in Stalemate*, THE SAN JUAN STAR, July 17, 1998, at 7.

[38] *Id.*

Construction of a Context for Action

The *Insular Cases* provided a normative justification for the exercise of power that became part of the context for future action both on the part of the different organs of the metropolitan state and on the part of the Puerto Rican elites and the Puerto Rican people. Creating a context for action is one of the ways in which law becomes part of social reality. The Court's doctrine authorized certain practices that, when realized, reproduced both the conditions for existence of the colonial project and the framework for discourse and action that the doctrine had generated.

The Court's doctrine provided constraints on as well as opportunities for action. The opportunities were of a wider latitude for Congress and the federal executive, while the constraints were to weigh more heavily on the people of the territories. I have referred already to the later cases decided by the Court authorizing Congress to discriminate against the "residents" of Puerto Rico when legislating on social and welfare matters. As discussed in fuller detail below, in the section titled *Ensuring Flexibility*, the *Insular Cases* illustrate the facilitative power of law. They provided the metropolitan state with the needed flexibility to govern the newly acquired lands at its own discretion and to shape gradually the policies that the new stage of overseas expansion required.

The Wider Process of Legitimation

The doctrine the Supreme Court established in the *Insular Cases* necessarily and by itself did not determine future events in Puerto Rico. One must avoid the legal determinism implicit in the analysis of at least one critic of the cases, who saw the Supreme Court as the ultimate culprit for the perpetuation of the colonial condition of Puerto Rico. That author has attributed to the doctrine established by the cases everything from the emergence of the proindependence movement to the "politico-legal schizophrenia" that, according to him, underlies the adoption of Commonwealth status, the extreme economic dependence of Puerto Rico, the inadequacies and politicization of the educational system, and the serious social ills brought about by the dislocation of the population and the processes of mass migration to the United States.[39]

Torruella's position fails to take into account Congress's role in perpetuating the colonial condition by declining to incorporate Puerto Rico expressly and make it an offer of statehood or, in the alternative, provide for its eventual independence. In fact, all the evidence shows that the Court has always acted in accordance with congressional policy. More fundamentally still, the *Insular Cases*, by themselves, do not bear sole responsibility for the lack of a stronger and more effective movement for independence within Puerto Rico that would have forced Congress and the American executive to end the colonial situation.

The full explanation has to take account of multiple factors that include, but are not limited to, legal processes, events, and ideologies. Views like the one Torruella expressed turn legal phenomena into the ultimate determinants of political, social,

---

[39] TORRUELLA, *supra* note 10, at 117–265.

and economic conditions. Judicial decisions, however, have not been the ultimate determinants of the reproduction of the colonial condition.

Yet those decisions (and their rationales) have produced the four important consequences examined above: an explicit justification of the exercise of power, a legal and political subject, a discursive universe, and a context for action. These legal consequences have become intertwined with the entire social, economic, and political life of Puerto Rico. Through their ramifications the doctrine established by the *Insular Cases* became a constitutive part of the colonial project and of Puerto Rican reality.

All of those effects were part of a wider process of legitimation. The doctrine of the unincorporated territory, the plenary power of Congress, and the distinction between fundamental and nonfundamental constitutional rights (as the criterion for determining which claims could legitimately be made by Puerto Ricans and the peoples of the other territories) would not only serve as an explicit justification of colonial subordination. They would also affect the material conditions and the practices designed to satisfy interpreted needs, as will be partially analyzed in chapter 7. They would also shape the mechanisms devised to channel claims and input into the process of definition of needs and the ideological framework within which those needs would have to be defined. These two aspects will be touched upon in chapter 8.

One further comment is apposite about the wider implications of the *Insular Cases*. A certain paradox haunted the different positions within the Court. As has been noted, the view taken by Justices White, Day and the other members of the eventual majority would result in the total subordination of the peoples of the territories; whereas the position espoused by Justices Harlan and Fuller would have led to the immediate full incorporation and unabated Americanization of those peoples. The paradox is that despite their denunciation of colonialism and domination, if Harlan's and Fuller's had been the winning argument, the possibility of independence for Puerto Rico might have been foreclosed. The most overtly colonialist position —that taken by the majority—was the one that, at the same time, left open the doors to the independence movement.[40] Thus, the Court, in justifying the crudest form of colonialism, sowed the seeds of its critique, and by legitimating the exercise of colonial power, the Court created the basis of the delegitimation of that power.

Sociohistorical Factors

Several sociohistorical factors converged to produce the doctrine the Court adopted in the *Insular Cases*. Evidence of those factors can be found both in the text and in the context of the opinions. That context includes the set of forces identified in chapter 1 as the "determinants" of expansion in the United States during the late 19th century and the ideological currents and debates among the American ruling elites. Attention must be given also to the composition of the Court and to its relationship to the so-called "political" branches of government, particularly in the field of foreign policy and international activity. Furthermore, when the effects of the

---

[40] José Cabranes, *Citizenship and the American Empire*, 127 U. PA. L. REV. 391, 441 (1978).

cases can be reasonably related both to the text and the context, they provide important clues to the doctrine's development that cannot be overlooked.

Determinants and Ideology of Expansion and the Political Debates of the Day

The following discussion carries forward the analysis in Part I and chapter 5 of the forces driving the U.S. expansionist drive. The influence of those forces on the court highlights the significance of the doctrine of incorporation in that period of U.S. history and helps us to understand the historic compromise among the American ruling elites the *Insular Cases* brought about.

I have already analyzed in some detail the ideology that permeates the cases related to the notions and values prevalent among the American elites during the latter part of the 19th century. This ideology—as a "power in the domain of consciousness"[41]—must be regarded as one of the factors converging in the production of the doctrine of territorial incorporation after the acquisition of the territories from Spain.

Moreover, there are abundant clues in the texts of the opinions that the justices were perfectly aware of the economic, strategic, and international forces shaping the imperial adventure of the United States at the turn of the century. Three fundamental drives served as powerful undercurrents in the expansionist movement: the search for new markets, strategic considerations, and the felt need to compete with other imperial powers for the control of routes, markets, and advantageous military locations.[42] The justifications provided by the majority of the Court and the protestations of the minority in the *Insular Cases* reflected an understanding of these forces and of the debate over the long-term interests of the United States as interpreted by the dominant groups. The dissents filed by Justices Harlan and Fuller, especially, articulated this awareness with great clarity. That awareness reveals that most of the justices actively sought to produce the consequences discussed in this chapter and confirms the instrumental character of their decisions.[43]

Search for New Markets

In general, the opinions of Harlan and Fuller disclosed the perception that the Court was engaging in an explicit justification of colonialism and that it was developing the doctrines as an instrument of the colonial project, under the guise of attending to "suppose[d] extraordinary emergencies."[44] Justice Harlan's famous dissent in the *Mankichi* case is worth quoting at length for the revealing summary it contains of the forces he discerned at work in the arguments and decisions of the Court:

> It would mean that the will of Congress, not the Constitution, is the supreme law of the land only for certain peoples and territories under our jurisdiction. It would mean

---

[41] KARL MARX, PARIS MANUSCRIPTS, *quoted in* DAVID MCLELLAN, MARX BEFORE MARXISM 181 (2nd ed. 1980).

[42] *See* chapter 1 for a full discussion of these drives.

[43] *See* the discussion in Chapter 5.

[44] *Downes*, 182 U.S. at 385 (Harlan, J., dissenting).

that the United States may acquire territory by cession, conquest or treaty, and that Congress may exercise sovereign dominion over it, outside of and in violation of the Constitution, and under regulations that could not be applied to the organized Territories of the United States and their inhabitants. It would mean that, under the *influence and guidance of commercialism and the supposed necessities of trade*, this country had left the old ways of the fathers as defined by a written Constitution, and *entered upon a new way*, in following which the American people will lose sight of or become indifferent to principles which had been supposed to be essential to real liberty. It would mean that, if the principles now announced should become firmly established, the time may not be far distant when, under the exactions of *trade and commerce*, and to gratify an *ambition to become the dominant political power in all the earth*, the United States will acquire territories in *every direction*, which are inhabited by human beings, over which territories, to be called *"dependencies"* or *"outlying possessions,"* we will exercise *absolute dominion*, and whose inhabitants will be regarded as *"subjects"* or *"dependent peoples,"* to be controlled as Congress may see fit, not as the Constitution requires, *nor as the people governed may wish*. Thus will be engrafted upon our republican institutions, controlled by the supreme law of a written Constitution, a *colonial system* entirely foreign to the genius of our Government and abhorrent to the principles that underlie and pervade the Constitution. It will then come about that we will have *two* governments over the peoples subject to the jurisdiction of the United States, one, existing under a written Constitution, creating a government with authority to exercise only powers expressly granted and such as are necessary and appropriate to carry into effect those so granted; the other, existing outside of the written Constitution, in virtue of an unwritten law to be declared from time to time by Congress, which is itself only a creature of that instrument.[45]

The implications of this quotation are several. First, Harlan realized that the United States was entering a new phase. This recognition of a new situation was also apparent in Chief Justice Taft's reference in the *Balzac* case to the demands placed by "these latter days" on the policies adopted by Congress and the executive and the decisions of the Court.[46]

Second, Harlan's reference to "commercialism" and the "necessities of trade" clearly suggests that the new doctrine was being elaborated in response to the perceived needs of the new stage of capitalist expansionism that expressed itself in the active search for new markets. Of course, apart from this general economic drive, the cases illustrate the conflicts that emerged among specific economic interests. The search for new markets and colonial enclaves had created a new contradiction: the possibility of competition from products coming from the newly acquired territories. There were frequent allusions in the arguments put before the Court about the fear of opening up the United States market to those products.[47] In the *Downes* case, Chief Justice Fuller referred to "certain industries" that wanted to "diminish or remove competition."[48] To a great extent it was this immediate conflict that gave rise to the first group of cases.

It was a complex situation. While some producers in the United States feared competition from the territories, the U.S. importers of those products and some of the exporters from the colonies were also American businesses. In a way, the Court

---

[45] *Mankichi*, 190 U.S. at 239–40 (emphasis added).
[46] *Balzac*, 258 U.S. at 306.
[47] *See* the arguments of the petitioner and the solicitor general in *De Lima*, 182 U.S. at 90, 137.
[48] *Downes*, 182 U.S. at 374.

was confronted with the conflict between protecting some of those specific interests and providing a legal justification for the grander expansionist project. Some of the concrete results of the cases were contradictory from the point of view of the immediate question of the restriction of trade with the territories. Thus, in *De Lima*, the result favored free trade, while in *Downes*, the specific outcome resulted in its restriction. The difference may be explained by the fact that in the former case Congress had not yet expressed its view specifically on the matter (the case involved the application of the general tariff laws of the United States) while, in the latter, the Court was reviewing a statute (the Foraker Act) especially adopted to regulate the situation regarding one of the territories (Puerto Rico).

In the end the Court opted for allowing Congress the maximum degree of flexibility. It justified the latter's exercise of plenary power and the subordination of the new territories to the absolute will of the federal government. This flexibility left open the possibility of protecting or not the local producers through the imposition of tariffs and duties, as Congress saw fit according to the circumstances. In many cases, the court was able both to afford protection to the U.S. producers and to justify the acquisition of the new territories.

Strategic Concerns

Relating the doctrine of the *Insular Cases* to the strategic concerns of the United States is more difficult to do by merely examining the text of the opinions. However, there are some indications that the members of the Court appreciated the importance of their decisions in this regard. Harlan's reference to the ambition of the country's leaders to turn the United States into the "dominant political power of the earth" manifests his grasp of the nature of the expansionist drive of the American bureaucratic elite. That drive was perceived to depend on the implementation of a program for naval expansion, whose contours had already been elaborated by the end of the 1890s.[49] But more revealing in this respect are Justice White's comments, in his seminal concurrence in the *Downes* case, linking the advisability of the adoption of the incorporation doctrine to the known military and foreign policy objectives of the United States, including a specific reference to the need to acquire naval stations and territory to build an interoceanic canal.[50]

The most important link between the cases and the strategic concerns of the United States, however, emerges from the effects of the doctrine itself. While stating that Puerto Rico was not *a part of* the United States, the Court held that the islands *belonged to* the United States. This formulation allowed Congress and the executive to dispose of the territory at will for military purposes, including segregating land to establish bases and other military installations, using the islands for military exercises and, eventually, recruiting Puerto Ricans to the ranks of U.S. military forces.

---

[49] By the end of the 1890s, public discussion and political and bureaucratic planning had given shape to a relatively coherent project for expansion. It included the enlargement of the U.S. Navy, the acquisition of colonies, the establishment of bases and coaling stations in the Caribbean and the Pacific, and the construction of an interoceanic canal in the Central American isthmus. See the discussion of the strategic program of the United States at the time in chapter 1.

[50] *Downes*, 182 U.S. at 311 (White, J., concurring). *See* chapter 5 n.19 and accompanying quotation.

This military presence in Puerto Rico was crucial in the establishment and reproduction of American dominion in the Caribbean and the wider Atlantic region.[51]

Competition With Other Powers

The arguments of both the majority and the minority in the *Insular Cases* reflected
concern about the role of the United States in the new scramble for colonies that
had erupted among European and other powers. There were constant allusions to the
need to grant Congress and the executive the required powers to contend advanta-
geously with other nations and not to be "left behind" in the international competition for power. Apparently, such was the force of this argument that it obligated
Justice Harlan to meet it with the following comment:

> It was said that the United States is to become what is called a "world power," and
> that if this Government intends to keep abreast of the times and be equal to the great
> destiny that awaits the American people, it *must* be allowed to exert all the power
> that other nations are accustomed to exercise. My answer is, that the fathers never
> intended that the authority and influence of this nation should be exerted otherwise
> than in accordance with the Constitution.[52]

Contemporary Political Debates

The Court's language bears a striking similarity with the discourse that permeated
the political debates regarding the territories. In fact, if in any group of legal texts
there is an almost complete blurring of the alleged difference between legal and
political discourse, it is in the cases under study. This fact in itself provides evidence
of the degree to which the decisions of the Court were influenced by those debates.[53]

It is no coincidence, for example, that arguing for the ratification of the Treaty
of Paris, Senator Joseph B. Foraker of Ohio, who later was to sponsor the act bearing
his name that established a civil government for the Philippines and Puerto Rico,
would assert the following:

---

[51] *See* related analysis in chapter 3. For detailed discussions of the strategic importance of Puerto
Rico for the United States during the course of the 20th century, see MARÍA EUGENIA ESTADES FONT,
LA PRESENCIA MILITAR DE ESTADOS UNIDOS EN PUERTO RICO 1898–1918: INTERESES ESTRATÉGICOS
Y DOMINACIÓN COLONIAL (1988); FRONTERAS EN CONFLICTO: GUERRA CONTRA LAS DROGAS, MILI-
TARIZACIÓN Y DEMOCRACIA EN EL CARIBE, PUERTO RICO Y VIEQUES (Humberto García Muñiz & Jorge
Rodríguez Beruff Eds. 1999); Jorge Rodríguez Beruff, *Puerto Rico and the Caribbean in the U.S.
Strategic Debate on the Eve of the Second World War*, 2 REV. MEXICANA DEL CARIBE 55 (1996);
Humberto García Muñiz, *U.S. Military Installations in Puerto Rico: An Essay on Their Role and Purpose*,
24 CARIBBEAN STUDIES 79 (1991); BAR ASSOCIATION OF PUERTO RICO, REPORT OF THE SPECIAL COM-
MISSION ON NUCLEAR WEAPONS AND THE TREATY FOR THE PROSCRIPTION OF NUCLEAR WEAPONS IN
LATIN AMERICA (1984); Prepared Statement of Brigadier General M. J. Byron, Acting Deputy Assistant
Secretary of Defense (Inter-American Affairs), *in 3 Hearings, supra* note 32, at 134; GAO, *supra* note
27, at 9d.7–8.

For an analysis of how the military importance of Puerto Rico further enhanced the power that
Congress and the executive may exercise over its affairs, in accordance with American constitutional
doctrine, *see* Leibowitz, *supra* note 28, at 16.

[52] *Downes*, 182 U.S. at 386.

[53] For an account of the Senate debates, see WINFRED LEE THOMPSON, THE INTRODUCTION OF
AMERICAN LAW IN THE PHILIPPINES AND PUERTO RICO: 1898–1905 at 35–48 (1989).

> We find in this instrument [the Constitution] a grant of power to the United States Government to make war, a grant of power to make treaties, each and both carrying along with it and with them the power also to acquire territory and, as a result of that, the power to govern territory.[54]

Territory could be acquired through a variety of means and for a diversity of purposes, including establishing coaling stations or as an indemnity after war. Because these were constitutional purposes, "no consent of the people is necessary."[55] Foraker further alleged that the Constitution did not extend to the territories of its own force.[56] In that same debate Senator Henry Cabot Lodge argued that "the power of the United States in any territory or possession outside the limits of the States themselves is absolute, with the single exception of the limitation placed upon such outside possessions by the thirteenth amendment [the prohibition against slavery]."[57] These and numerous other examples led Thompson to conclude that

> Although the arguments were not generally as finely crafted nor the complexities of the issues as carefully weighed, the fundamental constitutional issues had been framed [during the political debates in the Senate] along lines that are readily recognizable in the later decisions of the Supreme Court in the *Insular Cases*.[58]

Officers linked to the executive and the military had produced similar arguments to those of Senators Foraker and Lodge. Thus, the Schurman Commission, appointed by President William McKinley to advise the administration on the exertion of authority and the implementation of policies in the Philippines,[59] had taken the view as early as 1899 that the power of Congress to define the relationship of the territory to the United States was virtually unlimited.[60] According to the Commission,

> The Constitution gives Congress authority to make rules and regulations for the domain beyond the limits of the States. But the restrictions which the Constitution imposes upon Congressional power when operating within the States do not adhere to it when operating outside the States; that is, in the Territories.[61]

As an example, the commissioners argued that there was no constitutional requirement to establish uniform duties or excises throughout the territories in the same fashion as in the states. To them, this was a matter that rested totally on the discretion

---

[54] *Quoted in id.* at 44.

[55] *Id.* at 45.

[56] *Id.*

[57] *Id.* at 46–47.

[58] *Id.* at 47. An analogous point has been made by Cabranes, "The doctrine of territorial incorporation developed by the Court in the *Insular Cases* and the cases following was based on precisely the *same considerations* that determined the nature of the 1900 legislation for Puerto Rico: an apprehension that the peoples of the new insular territories were aliens and a belief that the United States ought not to deal with them as though they were Americans." Cabranes, *supra* note 40, at 440 (footnote omitted)(emphasis added).

[59] The Commission was composed by its chairman, Jacob G. Shurman, president of Cornell University, and Charles Denby, a former minister to China; Dean C Worcester, a scientist with prior experience in the Philippines; Rear Admiral George Dewey, of the U.S. Navy; and Army Major General Elwell S. Otis, then commander of the American troops in Manila. THOMPSON, *supra* note 53, at 52.

[60] *Id.* at 57.

[61] *Id.*

of Congress.[62] Again, this position substantially prefigured the outcome of the *Insular Cases.*

Ensuring Flexibility

The most important underlying rationale of the *Insular Cases*—and, therefore, an indispensable element in any attempt to explain the reasons for the doctrine they established—is the majority view that the Court must allow Congress and the executive the widest latitude and flexibility in shaping the policies toward the peoples of the newly acquired lands. Both the text of the opinions and the effects of the decisions substantiate this conclusion.

The awareness of this "need" for flexibility was already present in Justice McKenna's dissent in *De Lima,* the first of the cases decided.[63] It was further displayed in Justice Brown's opinion in the *Downes* case,[64] where he explicitly stated that "a false step at this time might be fatal to the development of . . . the American Empire."[65] In the *Dorr* case, Justice Day, writing for the majority, stressed the fact that the framers of the Treaty of Paris intended to reserve to Congress "a free hand" in dealing with the newly acquired possessions.[66] Chief Justice Taft, speaking on behalf of a unanimous Court, expressed his view that the real issue of the *Insular Cases* had been the extent of the power of Congress to deal with these "new conditions and requirements."[67]

The doctrine the Court adopted, in effect, would provide this flexibility for this new phase in the expansionist drive of the American Empire. In fact, the doctrine heightened not only congressional and executive, but also judicial, discretion in matters relating to the territories.[68] The piecemeal application of constitutional provisions —overseen by the Court itself—resulting from the fundamental rights corollary of the incorporation doctrine provides an excellent example. Although at times expressed as responding to a concern for the territories, this process of gradual extension of rights was based ultimately on a preoccupation with the viability of the colonial project.

The doctrine allowed for flexibility and adaptability in several areas. For example, it permitted Congress to protect American producers, when it was convenient to do so, by imposing tariffs and duties on trade between the states and the territories.

---

[62] *Id.* at 57–58.

[63] *De Lima,* 182 U.S. at 218–20.

[64] *Downes,* 182 U.S. at 279.

[65] *Id.* at 286; Marcos A. Ramírez, *Los Casos Insulares,* 16 REV. JUR. U.P.R. 121, 140 (1946).

[66] *Dorr,* 195 U.S. at 143. Cabranes quoted Frederick R. Coudert, a lawyer prominently involved in the litigation of the *Insular Cases,* who, referring to a conversation with Justice White, regarding their outcome, stated, "It is evident that he was much preoccupied by the danger of racial and social questions of a very perplexing character and that he was quite as desirous as Mr. Justice Brown that Congress should have a *very free hand* in dealing with the new subject populations." Cabranes, *supra* note 40, at 441; *also quoted in* Ramírez, *supra* note 65, at 141 n.33 (emphasis added). *See also* Jaime B. Fuster, *The Origins of the Doctrine of Territorial Incorporation and Its Implications Regarding the Power of the Commonwealth of Puerto Rico to Regulate Interstate Commerce,* 43 REV. JUR. U.P.R. 259, 293 (1974).

[67] *Balzac,* 258 U.S. at 312.

[68] LEIBOWITZ, *supra* note 28, at 29; Ramírez, *supra* note 65, at 141.

Congress and the executive, through their control of the territorial governments, enjoyed a freer hand to deal with questions of law and order. The reform of criminal law and criminal procedure in the territories and the withholding of important rights —such as the right to trial by jury or the right to bear arms—have to be understood in the context of the need to ensure the governability of foreign peoples now under the jurisdiction of the United States and not always acquiescent to its rule. This was a crucial matter, especially in the Philippines, where an armed insurrection against the American regime had been waged for several years.

Additionally, Congress was left to adopt policies for the colonies unhindered by the need to provide political participatory rights to their inhabitants. As has already been noted, in the years to come the doctrine would serve also to justify discriminatory treatment in the extension of social and welfare entitlements and benefits (which, incidentally, resulted in lowering the costs of maintaining the colonial regime). Finally, both Congress and the executive would have greater latitude to dispose of the lands, the resources, and the peoples of the territories for military purposes. In sum, the doctrine of incorporation authorized the U.S. government to exert direct rule over other lands and other peoples without the difficulties inherent in dealing with formally sovereign states and unencumbered by the complications of admitting these distant and different peoples into the American federation.

Composition of the Court

The composition of the Supreme Court during the period under study is another factor contributing to the development of the doctrine of territorial incorporation. Many of its members came from the ranks of, or had been linked to, the bureaucratic and military elite, the "neoaristocratic" element,[69] and the group of professionals and intellectuals who had been central in promoting the expansionist drive at the turn of the century.[70] Some had performed specific functions and played important roles in either the elaboration or the implementation of the policies and practices of the U.S. government in the territories.

Justice William R. Day, who wrote the majority opinion in the *Dorr* case, was appointed to the Court in 1903 by President Theodore Roosevelt, an avowed expansionist. He had been assistant secretary of state and had been involved in the negotiations with Spain just before the Spanish American War. Despite initially expressing anti-annexationist views, Day, a fervent admirer and loyal follower of President McKinley, finally complied with the president's wishes and presided over the negotiations and eventual signing of the Treaty of Paris.[71]

Justice Henry Moody also had been closely connected to the military establishment and the expansionist project. Appointed to the Court by President Theodore

---

[69] I am using the term in the sense used in GEORGE LISKA, CAREER OF EMPIRE: AMERICA AND IMPERIAL EXPANSION OVER LAND AND SEA 175, 179, 183 (1978). *See* the description given in chapter 1 of this book at nn.29–33 and accompanying text.

[70] *See* chapter 1.

[71] THE JUSTICES OF THE UNITED STATES SUPREME COURT 1789–1969: THEIR LIVES AND MAJOR OPINIONS 1781 (Leon Friedman & Fred L. Israel Eds. 1969); [JUSTICES OF THE SUPREME COURT]; TORRUELLA, *supra* note 10, at 65–66, n.237. *See also* JULIUS W. PRATT, EXPANSIONISTS OF 1898: THE ACQUISITION OF HAWAII AND THE SPANISH ISLANDS 327–60 (1936).

Roosevelt in 1906, he had served as the latter's secretary of the navy from 1902 to 1904 and supported the president's expansionist views. As a congressman, he led a mission to Cuba that resulted in the acquisition of Guantánamo and incorporation of the Platt Amendment to the Cuban Constitution authorizing U.S. intervention in Cuba under certain circumstances.[72] He had been instrumental in the establishment of a naval base in the Philippines and had acted as cochairman, with Alfred Thayer Mahan, of a committee that proposed a complete restructuring of the Navy.[73]

After acceding to the presidency in 1908, William Howard Taft appointed four new justices (Lurton, Hughes, Lamar, and Devanter) and successfully nominated Justice White (the author of the incorporation doctrine) to the post of chief justice. In 1921 Taft himself became chief justice of the Supreme Court and wrote the opinion in the *Balzac* case. During his political career, Taft had been a key figure in the development of the colonial policy of the United States. Despite an effort to substitute dollar for gunboat diplomacy in Central America and the Caribbean, as president, Taft had overseen an American armed intervention in Nicaragua and the near occupation of the Dominican Republic in 1912.[74] In 1909 he intervened directly in a critical conflict between the American governor of Puerto Rico and the local legislature, overriding an action of the latter. He had been governor of the Philippines; secretary of the War Department, with direct jurisdiction over matters affecting the Philippines, Puerto Rico, and the Panama Canal; and provisional governor of Cuba under the provisions of the Platt Amendment.[75]

Insular Cases as Compromise

The doctrine of incorporation the Court developed can be read as a compromise between the contending political forces of the moment: that is, between the imperialist and anti-imperialist positions. The latter included two groups: those who, on racist grounds, opposed the acquisition of territory, for it meant the incorporation of inferior peoples into the American polity, and those who argued that, having obtained the territories, the full protection of the Constitution must be accorded to their peoples.

The Court's decisions sanctioned the colonial project of the imperialists, recognizing the right of the United States to acquire territory through conquest or otherwise and to govern it at discretion. The "fundamental rights" corollary of the doctrine may be regarded as a gesture to those anti-imperialists who favored full extension of the Constitution, while the other faction of the movement, the most overtly racist one, had grounds for relief in the aspect of the incorporation doc-

---

[72] The Platt Amendment, proposed by Senator Orville H. Platt of Connecticut, was a rider added to the U.S. Army Appropriations Bill of March 1901 providing, among other things, for the U.S. acquisition of a naval base in Guantánamo Bay, Cuba, and U.S. intervention in that country whenever it was deemed necessary "for the preservation of Cuban independence." Act of Mar. 2, 1901, ch. 803, 31 Stat. 897. The terms of the Platt Amendment were enacted into the Cuban Constitution to encourage withdrawal of U.S. troops after the Spanish American War.

[73] JUSTICES OF THE SUPREME COURT, *supra* note 71, at 1778–81; TORRUELLA, *supra* note 10, at 77 n.270.

[74] DAVID HEALEY, DRIVE TO HEGEMONY: THE UNITED STATES IN THE CARIBBEAN 1898–1917 at 145–63 (1988).

[75] TORRUELLA, *supra* note 10, at 95 n.332.

trine—that the territories were not "part of the United States"—that effectively excluded the colonials from the American political community.

If read in this light, the cases illustrate how law is often an arena for the provisional resolution of political conflict and how legal doctrine serves to crystallize the compromises among feuding political camps. It must be noted, however, that in this instance, the conflicting views were largely those of members of the American elites. And the compromise was scarcely related to the desires of those most directly subjected to the rigors of its consequences. In the end, the compromise had more to do with the viability of the colonial project than with the possibility of an alternative resolution of the power relationship.

Concluding Remarks

Confronted with the question of the legitimacy of the U.S. colonial enterprise at the turn of the century, the Supreme Court fashioned a legal doctrine that provided an explicit justification for the exercise of almost unrestricted power over peoples and lands acquired as the result of the Spanish American War. Establishing a hitherto nonexistent difference between "incorporated" and "unincorporated" territories, the Court in effect allowed Congress and the executive the maximum leeway possible to develop and implement the policies that the new phase of overseas expansionism required.

To fashion the doctrine, the majority of the Court adopted a strategy of interpretation characterized by a pronounced contextualism and an instrumental eclecticism that allowed it to shift from overtly instrumental to strictly formalist approaches to adjudication as the circumstances required. The Court's discourse, moreover, was permeated by an ideological outlook that incorporated many of the beliefs of the times: Manifest Destiny, Social Darwinism, the idea of the inequality of peoples, and a racially grounded theory of democracy that viewed it as a privilege of the "Anglo-Saxon race" rather than as a right of those subjected to rule. Treating the new lands as mere property, the Court precluded any conception of governance that would require the consent of the governed.

The doctrine of the *Insular Cases* became a constituent part of the American colonial project—a dimension of the realities of power in the new American colonies. In this sense, the cases clearly exemplify the performative power of law: its capacity to create the realities that it names. The Court constructed a world populated by inhabitants of so-called unincorporated territories: a world that, by virtue of being so categorized, could be legitimately ruled over with almost unrestricted discretion by the functionaries of the imperial state. The cases also created a discursive universe that provided the parameters for any future discussion of the destiny of the inhabitants of that legally (politically) constructed world. Both the legal fiction and the discursive universe so constructed would be part of the practical context—of the opportunities for and constraints on action—in the new colonial societies.

In the elaboration and adoption of the doctrine of territorial incorporation a complex articulation of factors converged to drive the capitalist, industrial, partially democratic republic to its new phase of imperial expansionism. Such factors included the search for new markets, military expansion overseas, and the felt need of its ruling classes to compete favorably with the new imperial powers of Europe and

Asia. The Court's composition—many members were closely linked with the groups that favored expansionism—and the interclass transactions of the ruling elites of the American state were additional factors at work in the production of the doctrine. Moreover, the centrality of the Supreme Court in the resolution of important political disputes in the United States made almost inevitable its intervention in one of the great controversies of the times and provided its pronouncements with an extraordinary force whose consequences are being felt to this day. The *Insular Cases* cannot be read as the ultimate determinants of the colonial condition of Puerto Rico, yet they constitute a very important and dramatic example of legal events that have shaped the colonial experience of the Puerto Rican nation throughout this century.

Part III

The Production of Hegemony in Puerto Rican Society

Chapter 7
HEGEMONY THROUGH CITIZENSHIP

The extension of American citizenship to Puerto Ricans in 1917 has proved to be one of the most important legal events in the history of the relationship between the United States and Puerto Rico. This chapter analyzes the long-term effects of that event.

U.S. citizenship has become a crucial element in the reproduction of American hegemony among the Puerto Rican population. It has produced significant consequences in the realm of experience and ideology. In particular, (a) it created a context for social practice and action; (b) it constituted new political subjects—Puerto Ricans as American citizens; (c) it has affected the process of the formation of the "self" among Puerto Ricans; (d) it constructed a new juridicopolitical "reality" that has placed significant constraints on the metropolitan state itself; and, finally, (e) it has been a salient factor in the multidimensional process involved in the reproduction of consent to the continued association with the United States.

Background

Before the Spanish American War, the acquisition of new territory by the United States had always led at some point to the extension of citizenship to the inhabitants of the territory as part of the process of eventual admission to the union. The territories acquired in 1898, however, opened up a new debate. Should their inhabitants be granted citizenship? And if so, what would the consequences be of such action? Underlying the debate was the fear—at times expressed very explicitly—of incorporating into the union peoples deemed to be different, even inferior.

As a leading scholar on this issue has argued convincingly, many congressmen and decision makers in Washington made a distinction between the Philippines and Puerto Rico.[1] The peoples of the Philippines were considered more "alien" than the Puerto Ricans. Those who favored extending citizenship to Puerto Ricans were prone to stress that the latter's European roots were more substantial than those of the Filipinos. Moreover, the fact that the American occupation of the Philippines had been met by armed resistance from sectors of the local population and that hostilities were still raging cast doubts regarding the governability of the new territory. Cabranes argued that the delay in considering a bill granting citizenship to Puerto Ricans was due mainly to the desire to avoid setting a precedent for the Philippines.[2]

---

[1] José Cabranes, *Citizenship and the American Empire*, 127 U. Pa. L. Rev. 391 (1978).

[2] Extended discussions about the background to the citizenship bill can be found in José Trías Monge, 1 Historia constitucional de Puerto Rico 70–110 (1981); Raúl Serrano Geyls (Demetrio Fernández Quiñones & Efrén Rivera Ramos, contributors), Derecho constitucional de Estados Unidos y Puerto Rico: Documentos–jurisprudencia–anotaciones–preguntas 467–70 (1986); Cabranes, *supra* note 1, at 435–71.

From 1901 until the passage of the Jones Act[3] in 1917, 21 bills were presented in Congress with the purpose of making Puerto Ricans American citizens.[4] The decision was finally made during the 64th Congress of the United States.[5]

Section 5 of the Jones Act declared as citizens of the United States all "citizens" of Puerto Rico, as defined by Section 7 of the Foraker Act,[6] and all "natives" of the island who were absent temporarily from their country at the date of proclamation of the Treaty of Paris, who had since returned and established residence in Puerto Rico, and who did not hold the citizenship of any other country. It further provided that any person who did not wish to become a U.S. citizen could so declare before a court of law within six months of the act's taking effect. Furthermore, the act made provision for certain persons born to an "alien" parent in Puerto Rico and residing permanently in the island to acquire U.S. citizenship by making a sworn declaration of allegiance to the United States before the U.S. District Court for Puerto Rico.

The citizenship provision of the Jones Act amounted to a collective naturalization of Puerto Ricans. However, people born thereafter in Puerto Rico would not acquire citizenship automatically, although they could do so derivatively, in accordance with the relevant statutes then in force.[7] Subsequent enactments produced the current legal situation whereby all Puerto Ricans become U.S. citizens at birth.[8] For the purposes of this book, the fundamental consideration is the basic decision to grant citizenship to Puerto Ricans. It was that political decision, implemented through law in a process that began with the passage of the Jones Act in 1917, that has had the important consequences examined in this chapter.

---

[3] Jones Act, ch. 190, 39 Stat. 951 (1917) (codified at 48 U.S.C. § 731 (1987)).

[4] JUAN R. TORRUELLA, THE SUPREME COURT AND PUERTO RICO: THE DOCTRINE OF SEPARATE AND UNEQUAL 85 (1985); *see also* Cabranes, *supra* note 1.

[5] The bill was presented as H.R. 9533 on January 20, 1916, by Representative William A. Jones of Ohio. The House approved it on May 13, 1916. On December 5 of the same year, President Woodrow Wilson urged Congress to pass the bill, which was voted on favorably by the Senate on February 20, 1917. After a legislative conference to iron out differences, the House and Senate passed the bill on February 24 and 26, respectively. President Wilson signed it into law on March 2, 1917. *See* TORRUELLA, *supra* note 4, at 90–91.

[6] Foraker Act, ch. 90, 31 Stat. 77 (1900) (codified at 48 U.S.C. 731). See chapter 3 for a brief description of the provisions of the Foraker Act.

[7] José Julián Álvarez González, *The Empire Strikes Out: Congressional Ruminations on the Citizenship Status of Puerto Ricans*, 27 HARV. J. LEGIS. 309, 325 (1990).

[8] The key statutory provisions are sections 201(a) and 202 of the Nationality Act of 1940, 54 Stat. 1137, 1139 (1940), which became effective on January 13, 1941, and section 302 of the Immigration and Nationality Act of 1952, 66 Stat. 236 (1952) (codified at 8 U.S.C. 1402). The Nationality Act of 1940 provided that "a person born in the United States, and subject to the jurisdiction thereof" was a citizen of the United States at birth. It included Puerto Rico in the definition of "United States." Apparently to cover the situation of all those born prior to its effective date, Section 202 of the act provided that all persons born in Puerto Rico on or after April 11, 1899, and still subject to the jurisdiction of the United States were declared to be citizens of the United States. The Immigration and Nationality Act of 1952, which is considered to have merely restated the provisions of the 1940 act (*See* Álvarez, *supra* note 7, at 325), declared that all persons born in Puerto Rico on or after April 11, 1899, and prior to January 13, 1941, subject to the jurisdiction of the United States but not yet citizens thereof, should be regarded as American citizens as of January 13, 1941. It further provided that "all persons born in Puerto Rico on or after January 13, 1941, and subject to the jurisdiction of the United States, are citizens of the United States at birth" 8 U.S.C. § 1402 (1988). See the discussion in Álvarez, *supra* note 7, at 325–26.

The Question of Motives

Why did the United States grant American citizenship to Puerto Ricans?[9] The question has been debated at some length by leading historians and constitutional scholars in Puerto Rico and the United States.[10] Early interpretations tended to attribute the decision to the need to recruit Puerto Ricans for the armed forces.[11] But Cabranes has convincingly refuted this argument,[12] pointing out that American citizenship is not a prerequisite to conscription. In fact, he argued, aliens were made subject to the draft during the Civil War, the Spanish American War, and World War I. His research has established that even the men among those few Puerto Ricans who chose not to become American citizens after the Jones Act were considered by the American authorities to be subject to military conscription under existing American law.[13] Moreover, as the U.S. Supreme Court correctly noted in *González v. Williams* in 1904, by virtue of the Army Appropriation Act of March 2, 1903,[14] the "citizens" of Puerto Rico were already eligible for enlistment in the regular army of the United States.[15]

The preceding facts and arguments, however, do not warrant Cabranes's conclusion that "nothing in the annals of Congress would suggest that the collective naturalization of the Puerto Ricans was a matter concerned in any way with military concerns."[16] If not conscription, certainly wider strategic preoccupations figured principally among the considerations borne in mind by American decision makers.

The most important and best researched scholarship on this issue[17] seems to agree that the decision to extend American citizenship to Puerto Ricans was predicated on the will to retain Puerto Rico as a permanent possession of the United

---

[9]The problem of ascertaining the "motives" or "intentions" of a legislative body is complex. Moreover, the "purpose" of a legislative enactment and its effects must be distinguished. (For a discussion of the distinction between the concepts of "function" and "purpose" in law, see ROGER COTTERRELL, THE SOCIOLOGY OF LAW: AN INTRODUCTION 72–73 (1992)). Although this book is concerned mostly with the effects of law, the theoretical framework it adopts calls for attention to the "motives" and "intentions" of social actors. Moreover, the very concept of hegemony, so central to the basic argument of the book, suggests the need to focus on questions of social strategy, that is, on the purposive dimension of social action. Finally, as my argument will hopefully demonstrate, in the particular case under discussion there has been a remarkable connection between the "motives" of Congress and other American decision makers and the "effects" of the citizenship provision of the Jones Act.

[10]See Cabranes, *supra* note 1; ARNOLD H. LEIBOWITZ, DEFINING STATUS: A COMPREHENSIVE ANALYSIS OF UNITED STATES TERRITORIAL RELATIONS (1989); MARÍA EUGENIA ESTADES FONT, LA PRESENCIA MILITAR DE ESTADOS UNIDOS EN PUERTO RICO 1898–1918: INTERESES ESTRATÉGICOS Y DOMINACIÓN COLONIAL (1988); TORRUELLA, *supra* note 4; JOSÉ TRÍAS MONGE, 2 HISTORIA CONSTITUCIONAL DE PUERTO RICO (1981); Raúl Serrano Geyls, *El misterio de la ciudadanía*, 40 REV. COL. AB. P.R. 437 (1979); Ana Sagardía de Alvarado, *Puerto Rico en la encrucijada del '98: Impacto del cambio de soberanía en la ciudadanía de los puertorriqueños*, 11 CULTURA 14 (1997).

[11]*See, e.g.*, MANUEL MALDONADO DENIS, PUERTO RICO: A SOCIO-HISTORIC INTERPRETATION 108 (1972).

[12]Cabranes, *supra* note 1.

[13]*Id.* at 407–08.

[14]32 Stat. 927, 934 (1903).

[15]González v. Williams, 192 U.S. 1, 6 (1904).

[16]Cabranes, *supra* note 1, at 408.

[17]*See* Cabranes, *supra* note 1; LEIBOWITZ, *supra* note 10; ESTADES, *supra* note 10; Serrano, *supra* note 10; JOSÉ TRÍAS MONGE, PUERTO RICO: THE TRIALS OF THE OLDEST COLONY IN THE WORLD (1997).

States. Leibowitz reported that then Secretary of War Henry Stinson considered the granting of citizenship "as a step toward full self-government following the Canadian model with citizenship *assuring a continuing bond between Puerto Rico and the United States.*" Some congressional figures, Leibowitz added, "viewed citizenship as *assuring permanent association.*"[18]

Cabranes concluded expressly that the citizenship provision responded to the "widely shared assumption that Puerto Rico was permanently to remain under the American flag."[19] He quoted the author of the bill, Representative Jones, as saying that "the purpose of the United States seems clearly to be to retain Puerto Rico permanently."[20] He also quoted the American governor of Puerto Rico, Arthur Yager, who stated that

> Puerto Rico . . . will always be a part of the United States, and the fact that we now, after these years, make them citizens of the United States simply means, to my mind, that we have determined practically that the American flag will never be lowered in Porto Rico and it is for their good, and for ours, that the American flag remains permanently in Porto Rico.[21]

Within this larger objective, according to Cabranes, the citizenship provision was envisioned as a way to defuse the growing independence sentiment among the population by reinforcing in them a sense of "belonging" to the United States.[22]

Historian María Eugenia Estades Font[23] concluded that the underlying motive for extending citizenship was to consolidate American hegemony in Puerto Rico. The need for such a step arose because of two internal factors, according to Estades: (a) the growth of the independence movement (in this she coincided with Cabranes and Sagardía) and (b) the emergence of a strong labor movement that was showing an increasing tendency to participate in Puerto Rican political life. Although generally pro-American, the labor movement had a radical proindependence wing. The extension of American citizenship was viewed as a means to promote loyalty to the American regime and to confront the growing wave of social and political agitation. With the imposition of citizenship, she argues, the U.S. government was making patent its will to retain Puerto Rico permanently.[24]

It is also evident from the research conducted by these and other scholars that strategic considerations were central to the decision. The United States was becoming increasingly involved in World War I and was plunging itself headlong into international affairs. Even within the political and military establishment, many had come

---

[18] LEIBOWITZ, *supra* note 10, at 146 (emphasis added).

[19] Cabranes, *supra* note 1, at 443–44.

[20] *Id.* at 473.

[21] *Id.* Representative Austin of Tennessee made a similar comment: "I think it is a waste of time about this independence of Porto Rico. . . . They are not going to have independence, but are going to stay under the flag, not only this year, but for all years to come." *Quoted in id.* at 475.

[22] *Id.* at 466, 442. *In accord* Sagardía, *supra* note 10.

[23] ESTADES, *supra* note 10.

[24] *See id.* at 202–15. Estades quoted U.S. Army Colonel George Colton, military governor of Puerto Rico, who on November 15, 1911, recommended granting citizenship to Puerto Ricans to placate criticism within the United States and in Latin America regarding American colonial policy and to counter emerging proindependence sentiment in Puerto Rico. *Id.* at 208. The Bureau of Insular Affairs, the agency charged with the supervision of territorial matters, had expressed that Puerto Rico had become a "permanent part" of the United States and that it was "wise" to strengthen that bond. *Id.* at 209.

to view the fact that the United States had colonies as a blight that could backfire during the country's struggle to consolidate and expand the space newly won or about to be gained in the world arena. At the same time, there was perceived need to consolidate control of the island for its strategic value.

President Woodrow Wilson had been foremost among those expressing these concerns. In his third Annual Message to Congress in December 1915, he urged the nation's lawmakers to deal with the Philippine and Puerto Rican questions, which he considered intimately related to the country's national security and preparations for its defense. He asked Congress to take action regarding the pending bills on the matter, so that the United States would be free to assume its new "duties" on the world scene.[25] Congressional leaders expressed their views on the subject very clearly. According to Leibowitz, for some of them citizenship would guarantee not only "permanent association," but also "the long-term benefits" of "Puerto Rico's strategic military placement."[26] Both Cabranes and Torruella quoted Representative Cooper of Wisconsin, who during the final debate on the Jones Act in 1917 expressed the following:

> We are never to give up Porto Rico for, now that we have completed the Panama Canal, the retention of the island becomes very important to the safety of the canal, and in that way to the safety of the Nation itself. It helps to make the Gulf of Mexico an American lake. I again express my pleasure that this bill grants these people citizenship.[27]

Other members of Congress made similar expressions regarding the importance of Puerto Rico for the defense of the Panama Canal during the congressional debate on the bill.[28]

After a brief examination of the historical context in which the citizenship provision was approved, constitutional scholar Raúl Serrano Geyls correctly concluded that Cabranes's assertion that military considerations were not related at all to the extension of citizenship cannot hold. According to Serrano, given that the island was strategically important for the United States, that the latter was already immersed in World War I by the time the bill was approved, and that the citizenship measure was viewed as the principal means to contain and weaken the strong proindependence feeling among Puerto Ricans, the conclusion is inevitable that the war situation was a precipitating factor in Congress's decision in 1917 to take action on the citizenship proposal, which had been under its consideration since 1900:[29]

> To conclude otherwise would be to think that while they were discussing the Puerto Rican case, the American lawmakers were totally oblivious of the war situation in which their country was involved and of the vital strategic importance of the island, and that they failed to see the intimate relationship between both matters. That position seems to me frankly indefensible.[30]

---

[25] *Quoted in id.* at 202.

[26] LEIBOWITZ, *supra* note 10, at 146.

[27] Cabranes, *supra* note 1, at 485 n.459; TORRUELLA, *supra* note 4, at 86 n.290.

[28] *See* Serrano, *supra* note 10, at 444–45.

[29] *Id.* at 446–47.

[30] Id. at 447 (translation supplied). The original Spanish text reads "Lo contrario nos llevaría a pensar que mientras discutían el caso de Puerto Rico, los legisladores norteamericanos estaban totalmente

Thus, the consensus is that citizenship was granted to further American hegemony in Puerto Rico at a time when the United States was confronting an international crisis (World War I) and when social and political agitation was growing in its strategically important colony. One of the leading experts on the history of U.S. citizenship laws has expressed a similar view. In a recent book Rogers M. Smith stated that the initial reluctance to extend American citizenship to Puerto Ricans began to give way during World War I, "when a disgruntled Caribbean colony seemed a dangerous liability." Consequently, he added, "in 1917 Congress grudgingly granted Puerto Ricans U.S. citizenship."[31]

The decision must be seen also in the context of persistent American efforts to expand its control of the Caribbean region at the time. For example, while the Puerto Rican citizenship provision was passing through Congress, the United States was in the process of acquiring the Virgin Islands from Denmark. The relevant convention was signed on August 4, 1916, and proclaimed by the president on January 25, 1917.[32] Congress acted to provide for a temporary (military) government for the Virgin Islands on March 3, 1917,[33] the day after President Wilson signed the Jones Act for Puerto Rico. Other actions by President Wilson's administration in the region at the time included (a) the invasion of Haiti in June 1915 and the establishment of a "protectorate" that lasted until 1934; (b) the invasion of the Dominican Republic in May 1916, initiating an occupation that lasted eight years, during which U.S. admirals and generals ruled the country directly; (c) a treaty with Nicaragua in 1916 virtually establishing a protectorate over the Central American nation; and (d) the dispatch of American troops to Cuba in 1917 with the declared intention of training the year round, but that amounted to an effective military and political intervention.[34]

Some members of Congress and other parties had expressed objections and reservations about extending citizenship to Puerto Ricans.[35] However, when the final decision was made, there seems to have been a consensus among the various dominant sectors of U.S. society that such a course of action was desirable.[36] As occurred

---

ajenos a la situación de guerra en que se encontraba su país y a la vital importancia estratégica de la isla, y que no alcanzaban a ver la íntima relación entre ambos asuntos. Esa postura me parece francamente indefendible."

[31] ROGERS M. SMITH, CIVIC IDEALS: CONFLICTING VISIONS OF CITIZENSHIP IN U.S. HISTORY 433 (1997). In Balzac v. Porto Rico, 258 U.S. 298 (1922), Chief Justice Taft concluded that the decision to grant citizenship to Puerto Ricans was to be explained by the "desire to put them as individuals on an exact equality with citizens from the American homeland, to secure them more certain protection against the world, and to give them an opportunity, should they desire, to move into the United States proper and there without naturalization to enjoy all political and other rights." *Id.* at 298. In light of the research discussed in the text, Chief Justice Taft's explanation of the intentions of Congress seems more like an exercise in judicial rationalization than a plausible interpretation of the historical record. It must be noted, however, that the "opportunity . . . to move into the United States" was one of those perhaps unintended effects of the citizenship provision that has had an appreciable impact on the history of the Puerto Rican people.

[32] 39 U.S. Stat. 1706 (1916).

[33] Act of March 3, 1917, 39 U.S. Stat. 1132 (1917).

[34] DAVID HEALEY, DRIVE TO HEGEMONY: THE UNITED STATES IN THE CARIBBEAN, 1898–1917 at 180–99 (1988).

[35] Some of the objections had to do with fears that Puerto Ricans were not ready for citizenship and that extending it to them "would contribute to the 'mongrelization' of America." SMITH, *supra* note 31, at 433.

[36] I have quoted expressions from leading spokespersons from Congress and the executive, including

over the course of the decisions in the *Insular Cases* establishing a special constitutional regime for the newly acquired territories, the determination to extend U.S. citizenship to Puerto Ricans seemed to result from a new common sense among the dominant sectors of the metropolitan state about the tenor of the relationship being constructed with the territories and populations compounding the expanded, and still growing, American Empire.

Was Citizenship Imposed on Puerto Ricans?

The Puerto Rican proindependence movement has always maintained that American citizenship was imposed on Puerto Ricans. Other sectors have disagreed. A study by Cabranes,[37] one of the most important studies on the question, concluded that Congress did not impose citizenship on the Puerto Rican population. The author argued that the grant of citizenship involved "no element of compulsion," as it "was generally believed to conform to the wishes of the people of Puerto Rico."[38] He added that any opposition to the measure was isolated or expressed in equivocal terms.[39] But Serrano[40] has countered persuasively Cabranes's arguments using the very data of the latter's study.[41]

Certainly, in the early days of the American occupation there had been unanimous support among the Puerto Rican political parties for the granting of citizenship.[42] However, the situation started to change around 1912.[43] Important sectors of the Puerto Rican elite had become increasingly disillusioned with the American regime. Not only were the new American sugar barons displacing many of them economically, but the American political establishment had consistently denied substantial political reforms and had refused outright to make any promise to incorporate Puerto Rico as a state of the union.[44] Since the adoption of the Foraker Act of 1900

---

the military establishment. Important endorsements were consigned also from organizations representing commercial interests and the American labor movement. Thus, in 1909, support for the citizenship provision came from the National Board of Trade and the American Federation of Labor. TORRUELLA, *supra* note 4, at 88 n.300. In 1908 both national political parties had promised American citizenship to Puerto Ricans. *Id.*

[37] The study by Cabranes was first published as *Citizenship and the American Empire: Notes on the Legislative History of the United States Citizenship of Puerto Ricans*, 127 U. PA. L. REV. 391 (1978). It appeared one year later in book form, with the same title, published by Yale University Press, New Haven. Quotations in this book are from the *University of Pennsylvania Law Review* article. José A. Cabranes is a prominent Puerto Rican attorney and scholar who served as general counsel to Yale University and currently holds a judgeship in the U.S. federal judiciary. He was mentioned as a possible nominee to the U.S. Supreme Court in replacement of retiring Associate Justice Byron White.

[38] Cabranes, *supra* note 1, at 487.

[39] *Id.*

[40] Professor Raúl Serrano Geyls is a former associate justice of the Supreme Court of Puerto Rico, a retired professor of constitutional law of the University of Puerto Rico School of Law, and distinguished professor at the School of Law of the Interamerican University of Puerto Rico. He is the author of the leading textbook on United States and Puerto Rican constitutional law.

[41] See Serrano, *supra* note 10.

[42] See ESTADES, *supra* note 10, at 202–15; Cabranes, *supra* note 1 *passim*.

[43] ESTADES, *supra* note 10.

[44] For a more detailed explanation of the economic and social transformations Puerto Rico was undergoing at the time, see chapter 3.

—perceived clearly as a colonial statute—and the blessing bestowed by the Supreme Court in the *Insular Cases* on the colonial policy pursued by Congress and the executive, those disenchanted sectors began to lean appreciably toward a proindependence or pro-autonomy stance.

In 1913 the Union Party, which held an effective electoral majority among enfranchised Puerto Ricans, adopted independence as its "supreme ideal."[45] In 1914 Puerto Rico's House of Delegates, the only elected body in the island at the time, expressed its opposition to U.S. citizenship, and the declaration was transmitted to Congress.[46] That same year, then resident commissioner for Puerto Rico in Washington, Luis Muñoz Rivera, the foremost leader of the Union Party, expressed his reservations about a citizenship bill pending in Congress on the grounds that it would compromise Puerto Rico's possibility of becoming independent in the future.[47] In 1916, during the debate on the Jones Bill, Muñoz Rivera reaffirmed his opposition and called for a plebiscite on the matter among the Puerto Rican population.[48] Congress paid no heed to the plebiscite proposition.

As Serrano observed, the only declarations in the *Congressional Record* from official representatives of Puerto Rico from 1914 to 1916 were in opposition to the citizenship provision of the Jones Act.[49] Furthermore, the president of the Bar Association of Puerto Rico, representing his own and several other professional, civic, and cultural organizations, testified before a congressional committee against the citizenship proposal, arguing, as Muñoz Rivera had done, that it would constitute an obstacle to Puerto Rican independence.[50] Resident Commissioner Muñoz Rivera died on November 15, 1916, during the congressional recess and before the Jones Act was passed.

Cabranes made much of the fact that, after the resident commissioner's death, a bipartisan commission from Puerto Rico, headed by the politician who was to become Muñoz Rivera's successor, testified before the relevant Senate committee in support of the Jones Bill.[51] He took this as a definitive indication that opposition to the citizenship provision had waned in the island. The argument, however, is riddled with problems. First of all, the group's opinion did not represent the position of any official political body or functionary from Puerto Rico. Second, the event took place during the transition within the Union Party following the loss of its principal leader and spokesperson. Third, it is not clear to what extent the leaders of the Puerto Rican political parties viewed their position as a pragmatic stance before what they considered an inevitable development. After all, as Cabranes himself recognized, the commission appeared before the Senate committee shortly after President Wilson urged Congress to take favorable action on the pending Jones Bill, characterizing the matter as of "capital importance."[52] In addition, besides extending citizenship, the bill provided for reforms in the colonial government, some of which could have been perceived as potentially increasing the influence of the Puerto Rican political

---

[45] Serrano, *supra* note 10, at 441.

[46] *Id.*; Cabranes, *supra* note 1, at 468; TORRUELLA, *supra* note 4, at 90.

[47] Cabranes, *supra* note 1, at 464–70.

[48] Id. at 479; Serrano, *supra* note 10, at 441.

[49] Serrano, *supra* note 10, at 441–43.

[50] Cabranes, *supra* note 1, at 474–75.

[51] *Id.* at 482–84.

[52] *Id.* at 482–83.

elites in the affairs of government. Finally, as drafted, the bill would deprive any person who rejected U.S. citizenship of substantial political rights, including the right to hold important offices in the government of the United States or Puerto Rico. According to Puerto Rican historian Ana Sagardía de Alvarado, this latter fact may explain the Union Party's final acceptance of U.S. citizenship, lest its leadership become disenfranchised and excluded from the legal political process.[53]

Whether the majority of the population favored or opposed citizenship is unclear.[54] Serious research must be conducted on the many questions remaining unanswered. To what extent did the political elites actually represent the views and interests of the majority? Was the citizenship issue of importance only to the elites at the time of its extension to Puerto Ricans? The question of citizenship has become an important element in the popular imagination with the passing of time. But has this been an effect of the accomplished fact of the extension of citizenship in 1917? In any event, there is no evidence that Congress made any effort to ascertain the wishes of the population at large at the time. As noted above, the proposal by Puerto Rico's official representative to Congress to hold a plebiscite on the matter was disregarded.

The most important fact sustaining the imposition thesis was the mode in which the acquisition of citizenship was to be acquired. Congress decreed that residents of Puerto Rico would become U.S. citizens unless they declared affirmatively their wish not to become so, before a court of law, within six months of the passage of the act. The requirements for rejection must have been quite burdensome to a population that was largely illiterate at the time and unaccustomed, even culturally resistant, to participating in legal proceedings.[55] Moreover, the Jones Act placed significant restrictions and political penalties on those who rejected citizenship. Non-U.S. citizens would not be able to vote or hold important public office in Puerto Rico. In effect they would be proscribed from the "official" political life of the country. Later prohibitions restricted the capacity to engage in certain professions.[56] Under the circumstances, it is understandable that "only 288 persons took the legal steps necessary to decline United States citizenship."[57] The result might have been different if Congress had determined that people had to take affirmative steps to acquire U.S. citizenship and had resolved to preserve the political rights of those who chose to remain "citizens of Porto Rico." As Serrano Geyls concluded,

---

[53] Sagardía, *supra* note 10, at 18.

[54] But see one author's assessment that "the evidence, moreover, clearly pointed to the Puerto Rican people's deep regard for its association with the United States, irrespective of the constant shower of humiliating charges that they were unfit for self-government. American citizenship was to be received gratefully, no matter what." TRÍAS MONGE, *supra* note 17, at 76. The author does not cite any relevant evidence contemporary to the act of extending citizenship in 1917 to support his rather conclusory opinion. It has become clear with the passage of time, however, that the Puerto Rican people would come to value American citizenship, as the remainder of this chapter demonstrates. Whether that was the generalized situation in 1917 is not clear from the available historical data and, at best, is still to be ascertained by detailed historical research.

[55] Puerto Rican *campesinos*, who constituted the majority of the population, tended to pride themselves on not having ever had to appear before a court of law. For a poetic expression of this feeling, see the poem "*El desahucio*" ("The eviction") by Puerto Rican poet Lorenzo Coballes Gandía.

[56] Raúl Serrano Geyls, *The Territorial Status of Puerto Rico and Its Effects on the Political Future of the Island*, 11 REV. JUR. U.I. 385, 411 (1977); Serrano, *supra* note 10, at 443.

[57] Cabranes, *supra* note 1, at 488.

This was obviously an imposed citizenship, because those who did not accept it would become outcasts in their own land, and because that option, repugnant as it was, was offered only to those who were adults at the time. Minors and the millions of Puerto Ricans born afterwards did not even have that opportunity.[58]

Legal Effects of the Citizenship Provision

Legal consequences are largely a matter of social understandings. Of course, it is the understanding of legal actors with authority that accounts ultimately for the "legal effect" of a juridical proposition. Reading "meaning" into a legal text is one of the fundamental activities of legal operators. But the effective fixation of meaning in legal texts is a function of power. Moreover, it is a characteristic of liberal legal systems that the distribution of power to read meaning into texts is asymmetrical and, more specifically, hierarchical.[59]

To ask the question, What legal effects did the citizenship provision of the Jones Act have on the legal and political status of Puerto Rico? is to ask, What was the understanding, among legal decision makers with authority in the United States, of the normative consequences of the grant of citizenship? In other words, how did they interpret that the metropolitan state became bound by such a decision regarding its position vis-à-vis the Puerto Rican community?

Of course, one could also ask the following: What was the understanding among Puerto Ricans of the normative consequences that should follow from the act that had forced them, for all practical purposes, to become U.S. citizens? Answering that question would not be a simple matter. For Puerto Rico at that time was not, and has never been, a homogenous society, as some political discourses, including the nationalist, would suggest. Taking due regard of the class, racial, gender, and other social cleavages then existing in the Puerto Rican community would most probably condition the results of the inquiry. The historical record indicates that, at least among some within the Puerto Rican elites, particularly those favoring statehood for the island, the hope was kindled that citizenship implied "incorporation" into the United States, as that term was then understood within the dominant legal and political

---

[58] Serrano, *supra* note 10, at 443. The text in Spanish reads "Esta era obviamente una ciudadanía impuesta, porque los que no la aceptaran se convertirían en parias dentro de su propia tierra, y porque esa opción, aún deleznable como era, se ofreció sólo a los que entonces eran adultos. Los menores de entonces y los millones de puertorriqueños nacidos después, ni tan siquiera tuvieron esa oportunidad." Cabranes himself stated, "The bill made any ... decision to decline American citizenship an effective waiver of participation in the public life of the island" and "the intended exclusion of noncitizens of the United States from the public life of the island ... clearly gave Puerto Ricans little real choice in the matter." Cabranes, *supra* note 1, at 484, 459. A more generously worded description of the process has been offered by José Trías Monge: "Official Washington did not care about the appearance of coercion that permeated the whole process, for the collective naturalization method was imposed when individual naturalization, together with a larger measure of self-government, was acceptable to the Union [Party]." TRÍAS MONGE, *supra* note 17, at 97. In any event, Trías added, "American citizenship was granted under the worst possible light." *Id.*

[59] Concerning the broader question of the relationship among meaning, power, and structures of domination, Giddens has stated, "The reproduction of structures of domination, one must emphasize, expresses asymmetries in the forms of meaning and morality that are made to 'count' in interaction, thus tying them in to divisions of interest that serve to orient struggles over divergent interpretations of frames of meaning and moral norms." ANTHONY GIDDENS, NEW RULES OF SOCIOLOGICAL METHOD 157 (1976).

circles of American society.[60] However, the extension of citizenship had not been a negotiated event. It had not been the product of an exercise in codetermination, not to say self-determination, on the part of the Puerto Rican people. It was not the social understanding within the dominated society that counted, but rather the meaning that the decision makers in the highest echelons of the dominant state would be willing to read into their unilateral action. The asymmetry of the power relationship was evident.

Legal actors endowed with some authority in the lower ranks of the hierarchy of power in the colonial apparatus—including judges of Puerto Rican origin—had come to the conclusion that the grant of citizenship implied a decision to make Puerto Rico not merely a possession, but part of the United States. Thus, shortly after the passage of the Jones Act, the Supreme Court of Puerto Rico, in a decision written by Justice Adolph J. Wolf,[61] determined that by virtue of that statute Congress had in effect incorporated the island into the United States.[62] The U.S. District Court for Puerto Rico took a similar stance.[63]

The Supreme Court would settle the matter in due course. In 1917 it reversed summarily both the Supreme Court of Puerto Rico and the federal District Court on the question.[64] In 1922 the highest U.S. tribunal stated explicitly its grounds for holding that the legal consequences of the citizenship provision were negligible, as far as the political status of Puerto Rico was concerned.[65] After the extension of citizenship, said the Court, Puerto Rico continued to be an unincorporated territory of the United States.[66] The only juridical effect of the Jones Act, according to Chief Justice Taft, was that residents of Puerto Rico who were American citizens could move into the continental United States and there enjoy the "civil, social and political" rights of any other citizen of the nation.[67] Until then, citizenship had been

---

[60] See LEIBOWITZ, *supra* note 10, at 147; TRÍAS MONGE, *supra* note 17, at 76.

[61] Justice Wolf was appointed to the Supreme Court of Puerto Rico by President Theodore Roosevelt on May 15, 1904, and served until November 15, 1940. At the time the referenced decision was rendered, the Supreme Court was composed of three Puerto Ricans and two Americans.

[62] Muratti v. Foote, 25 D.P.R. 568 (1917).

[63] See Porto Rico v. Tapia, 245 U.S. 639 (1917).

[64] Porto Rico v. Muratti, 245 U.S. 639 (1917) and Porto Rico v. Tapia, 245 U.S. 639 (1917). For a critique of the position taken by both the Supreme Court of Puerto Rico and the U.S. District Court for what is characterized as their "absolute disconnection" with the political realities of the day, see JOSÉ TRÍAS MONGE, EL CHOQUE DE DOS CULTURAS JURÍDICAS EN PUERTO RICO 170–72 (1991). According to Trías, the results of the appeals to the U.S. Supreme Court were easily predictable.

[65] Balzac v. Porto Rico, 258 U.S. 298 (1922).

[66] The *Balzac* case is discussed in detail in chapter 4, dealing with the *Insular Cases*.

[67] *Balzac*, 258 U.S. at 308; *See also* Cabranes, *supra* note 1, at 442. Leibowitz has commented, "The significance to be accorded the grant of citizenship has never been resolved. The unilateral conferring of citizenship was regarded by both Puerto Rico and the United States as extremely important; in Puerto Rico as an act of *legal* consequence but in the United States Congress as primarily of *psychological* significance. Despite the grant of citizenship, Congress continued to treat United States citizens in Puerto Rico as aliens for a variety of purposes; and in the key areas of political and economic participation, citizenship was of no consequence at all. Puerto Rico in recent years, like other territorial areas, has sought to give effect more generally to the grant of citizenship, again without success." LEIBOWITZ, *supra* note 10, at 147–48 (emphasis added). One arguable effect, according to Leibowitz, has been to increase federal judicial control over the Puerto Rican government. He pointed to cases like Ortiz v. Hernández Colón, 475 F.2nd 135 (1st Cir., 1975), where a U.S. Court of Appeals, referring to the need to protect the "U.S. citizens resident in Puerto Rico," affirmed the decision of the U.S. District

generally considered an indication of incorporation into the United States.[68] But after the precedent-setting *Balzac* case, Congress would feel free to extend U.S. citizenship to the peoples of other American territories without the implication of incorporation or the promise of eventual statehood.[69]

Although some have criticized the *Balzac* Court for not deciding that citizenship meant incorporation,[70] the historical context indicates that the Supreme Court interpreted correctly the intentions of Congress and the executive branch. The interpretation was not exclusively the Court's. Those at the helm of all branches of the metropolitan government saw as fit that citizenship be granted for particular political, strategic reasons without effectuating a change in the political condition of the territory.[71] It was the social understanding of the legal and political actors located at the highest tiers of the metropolitan state that alien peoples of conquered or recently acquired territory could be made citizens of the United States while maintaining them in a subordinate political condition. As Smith stated,

> Everyone understood that Puerto Ricans were not being granted civic equality. They still had no right to vote for the federal office-holders who wielded veto powers over all their legislation. They also did not have the full protection of the Bill of Rights and other constitutional guarantees. Those denials were authoritatively upheld by a highly race-conscious Supreme Court.[72]

Citizenship did not efface colonialism. Under the circumstances, it was meant to consolidate it, to make it more palatable, and to make those subject to it more easily governable. As Sagardía noted, by extending citizenship, the U.S. Congress "strengthened, politically and legally, its position in Puerto Rico, without having to incorporate the Island. Now it was not governing the citizens of Puerto Rico, but the citizens of the United States in Puerto Rico."[73] Congress would still exercise governance while holding those new citizens of the metropolitan state in a situation of legal and political subordination.

If according to the understanding that prevailed among policy makers and the highest legal authorities in the United States, the Jones Act was not meant to have any significant legal effects regarding the constitutional status of Puerto Rico, the extension of citizenship did have other repercussions on the lives of the population of the territory. The most important ones have been cultural and sociopolitical, as will be demonstrated below.

Court for Puerto Rico to intervene in a matter relating to actions taken by the Puerto Rican government in the electoral field. *Id.* at 146.

[68] *See* chapter 4, The Legal Doctrine of the Insular Cases; *see also* Downes v. Bidwell, 182 U.S. 244, 332, 333 (1901).

[69] U.S. citizenship was extended to residents of the Virgin Islands in 1927, of the Pacific island of Guam in 1950, and of the Northern Mariana Islands, also in the Pacific, in 1976.

[70] *See, e.g.,* TORRUELLA, *supra* note 4.

[71] In seeming accord with this interpretation, see Cabranes, *supra* note 1, at 442; TRÍAS MONGE, *supra* note 64, at 171.

[72] SMITH, *supra* note 31, at 433.

[73] Sagardía, *supra* note 10, at 19.

Citizenship as a Representational Construct

The concept of citizenship has had a long and varied history in Western political thought and practice.[74] However, certain recurrent themes have been associated with the notion. As Heater has stated,

> Very early in its history the term already contained a cluster of meanings related to a defined legal or social status, a means of political identity, a focus of loyalty, a requirement of duties, an expectation of rights and a yardstick of good social behaviour.[75]

In a very basic sense *citizenship* has been used ordinarily to connote a certain relationship between individuals or groups of individuals and a body politic. That relationship implies both subjection and the notion that certain claims may be made reciprocally between the individuals and the political body involved. In other words, the meaning of citizenship flows from an understanding that a particular bond ties the individual and the political community. The bond is cemented through the exercise of power, either to protect or to demand, and through the feeling that emanates from the experience of being protected or somehow included in the group.

In more specific terms *citizenship* has been thought to imply the recognition of a defined legal status, as Heater stated. That status operates to equate members of a community, at least at an abstract, formal level, as well as to differentiate those within and without the community.[76] Thus, in many communities citizenship conjures powerful images of belonging and expectations of certain treatment. It is also an efficacious medium for the construction of barriers to exclude "others" not belonging to the community. It is in this sense that citizenship is often used in the context of immigration and naturalization. As Smith observed,

> Citizenship laws—laws designating the criteria for membership in a political community and the key prerogatives that constitute membership—are among the most fundamental of political creations. They distribute power, assign status, and define political purposes. They create the most recognized political identity of the individuals they embrace, one displayed on passports scrutinized at every contested border. They also assign negative identities to the "aliens" they fence out. Citizenship laws . . . literally constitute—they create with legal words—a collective civic identity. They proclaim the existence of a political "people" and designate who those persons are as a people, in ways that often become integral to individuals' senses of personal identity as well.[77]

Especially in modern societies, the reciprocal claims that citizenship is considered to justify are formulated in terms of rights asserted or obligations imposed. The main obligation on the part of the individual is usually thought to be the display of loyalty, both symbolically and materially, as in the actual offering of the citizen's

---

[74] For a comprehensive study of the concept from Greek antiquity to the present, see DEREK HEATER, CITIZENSHIP: THE CIVIC IDEAL IN WORLD HISTORY, POLITICS AND EDUCATION (1990).

[75] *Id.* at 163.

[76] *See* CITIZENSHIP 9 (G. Andrews Ed. 1991).

[77] SMITH, *supra* note 31, at 30–31.

body and time for the defense of the political community through military service.[78] The main claims or "rights" associated with the concept are "minimally the right to a civic identity and to civic participation."[79] "Citizenship is political identity par excellence," asserted Heater,[80] adding that "a citizen's identity is an awareness of his relationship to his state and to his fellow citizens."[81]

Traditionally, citizenship rights were confined to so-called civil and political rights. However, during the course of the 20th century, some have extended the notion of citizenship rights to include claims for social, economic, and cultural entitlements. Thus, Plant argued that

> the idea of citizenship is not just concerned with civil and political rights, vitally important though these are. The left also has to articulate and defend a concept of social citizenship, and this has two broad aspects. The first is that citizenship as a status confers some rights to resources such as income, health care, social security and education. The second aspect is that citizens should be empowered more as consumers whether in the market or in the public sector. It also implies that as we have equal civil and political rights as citizens—that is, equality before the law—the distribution of the *social means* of citizenship should be as fair and as equal as can be attained without infringing the other rights of citizenship.[82]

Heater formulated the argument in the following manner:

> We need to be clear about what is meant by the term "social citizenship." It is the belief that, since all citizens are assumed to be fundamentally equal in status and dignity, none should be so depressed in economic or social condition as to mock this assumption. Therefore, in return for the loyalty and virtuous civic conduct displayed by the citizen, the state has an obligation to smooth out any gross inequalities by the guarantee of a basic standard of living in terms of income, shelter, food, health and education.[83]

Claims of citizenship status have been wielded as a weapon of "liberation," as in the struggles of the French revolutionaries against the *ancien régime*. But the extension of citizenship has also served the purpose of consolidating domination and reaffirming subjection. Empires have used the imagery of citizenship to allure potential subjects into their fold and to extend their control over territories and peoples without excessive recourse to force. Thus, *civitas*, which at first connoted a privileged status among Roman subjects, was used eventually as a tool of "Romanization" among the peoples conquered in the sweeping growth of the Roman empire and as a means to exact their loyalty.[84]

---

[78] Regarding the subjection of bodies in premodern and modern times, see generally MICHEL FOUCAULT, LA VERDAD Y LAS FORMAS JURÍDICAS (1988). For the association of the notion of citizenship with military duties throughout ancient, medieval, and modern history, see HEATER, *supra* note 74.

[79] P. SELZNICK, LAW, SOCIETY AND INDUSTRIAL JUSTICE 249 (1969); *see also* David Held, *Between State and Civil Society: Citizenship, in* CITIZENSHIP, *supra* note 76, at 20.

[80] HEATER, *supra* note 74, at 184.

[81] *Id.* at 183.

[82] Raymond Plant, *Social Rights and the Reconstruction of Welfare, in* CITIZENSHIP, *supra* note 76, at 56.

[83] HEATER, *supra* note 74, at 267.

[84] *See* 3 THE NEW ENCYCLOPAEDIA BRITANNICA (MICROPAEDIA) 341 (15th ed. 1991); *see also* HEATER, *supra* note 74, at 16–20. "The Romans annexed the loyalty as well as the territory of their defeated enemies, for the status of Roman citizenship became much prized." *Id.* at 16.

In recent years there has been a renewed interest in the concept of citizenship, especially in the most advanced industrialized countries. The debate has hinged principally on the need to demand enhanced participation in the affairs of the political community. This concern has been stimulated by the increasing awareness that, despite the recognition of formal equality, many groups and individuals hold only "second-class citizenship" because of racial, gender, class, and other differences.[85] That awareness has led to harsh critiques of the "ideal of universal citizenship," which is seen as a mask for group oppression and subordination.[86] In this context, some have called for a redefinition of citizenship that takes into account the social realities of difference.[87]

In the United States the meaning of citizenship has undergone several transformations in the course of the development of American political and constitutional discourse.[88] However, according to Smith, a constant feature in the construction of those meanings, at least until the early part of the 20th century, was the blending of liberal and republican rhetorical traditions with inegalitarian ascriptive doctrines of racial, gender, and cultural superiority that had effectively kept the poorer classes, the nonwhite races, and women in subordinated positions in American life.[89] Moreover, symbolic shifts in the construction of the notion of citizenship at different historical moments increased or diminished the bearing of the status of citizen on the enjoyment of rights.[90]

Cabranes pointed out that as the 19th century came to an end, "the exaltation of American citizenship—by imperialist and anti-imperialist alike—was a notable and not surprising characteristic of the expansive and optimistic period during which the United States embarked upon its colonial enterprise."[91] The touting of the privileges of citizenship became a way of reinforcing "a sense of permanent inclusion in the American political community, in a nonsubordinate condition, in contrast to the position of aliens, subjects or even nationals."[92] At this time the inhabitants of Puerto Rico came to be designated as "nationals" of the United States, although they were not citizens.[93] The elaboration of a new legal construct—that of "national" in opposition to "citizen"—would allow the United States to govern the peoples of the newly acquired territories while holding them in a position of political subordination.[94]

For strategic and political reasons, the United States decided to extend citizenship to Puerto Ricans. The consequences ascribed to that action, however, effectuated

---

[85] See HEATER, *supra* note 74, at 60, 99–104; Held, *supra* note 79, at 20; Iris Marion Young, *Polity and Group Difference: A Critique of the Ideal of Universal Citizenship*, 99 ETHICS 250 (1989).

[86] See Young, *supra* note 85.

[87] CITIZENSHIP, *supra* note 76, at 14; Young, *supra* note 85; Iris Marion Young, *Difference and Policy: Some Reflections in the Context of New Social Movements*, 56 CINCINNATI L. REV. 535 (1987); MARTHA MINOW, MAKING ALL THE DIFFERENCE: INCLUSION, EXCLUSION AND AMERICAN LAW (1990).

[88] For a comprehensive analysis of the differing meanings ascribed to the notion of citizenship in the United States from colonial times until the early years of the 20th century, *see* SMITH, *supra* note 31.

[89] *Id.*

[90] See Alexander M. Bickel, *Citizenship in the American Constitution*, 15 ARIZ. L. REV. 369 (1973).

[91] Cabranes, *supra* note 1, at 396 n.12.

[92] *Id.*

[93] *See, e.g.,* González v. Williams, 192 U.S. 1 (1904).

[94] Cabranes, *supra* note 1, at 396 n.12.

yet another change in the significance of the status of U.S. citizen. After the Jones
Act of 1917 and the *Balzac* case of 1922, the concept of citizenship was divested
again of any special, homogenous meaning denoting full membership in the political
community, a connotation that seems to have developed during the course of the
debate regarding the future of the new possessions. In the new "legal situation," to
be a full member of the political community a person had to be a citizen, but being
a citizen alone was not sufficient to become a full member of the political community,
especially if the person was a resident of one of the territories. As Senator Foraker,
the author of the first Organic Act for Puerto Rico, stated regarding the intended
effects of the Jones Act,

> In adopting the term "citizens" we did not understand, however, that we were giving
> to those people [Puerto Ricans] any rights that the American people do not want them
> to have. "Citizens" is a word that indicates, according to Story's work on the Con-
> stitution of the United States, allegiance on the one hand and protection on the other.[95]

Citizenship, according to the Senator, "conferred the right to vote or to participate
in the government upon no one."[96]

Smith found that by the end of this period in American history, as the United
States grappled with the political implications of its newly expanded empire, the
"collisions and coalitions among American ideologies and interests [had] produced
a four-part hierarchical structure of citizenship laws that characterized Progressive
Era civic orderings generally." According to Smith, this structure included

> first, the excluded status of people denied entry to and subject to expulsion from the
> U.S., generally owing to their ethnic or ideological traits; second, colonial subjectship,
> reserved chiefly for territorial inhabitants declared racially ineligible for citizenship;
> third, second class citizenship, usually understood as required by improvident grants
> of formal citizenship to races not capable of exercising it, and as the proper status for
> women; and fourth, full citizenship, including voting rights.[97]

He added that Congress decided that Filipinos, "somewhat like Chinese laborers,"
were in the first category. Guamanians, considered to be "more compliant, yet also
racially inferior," would fit in the second one (until 1950, when they were extended
U.S. citizenship, making their situation like that of Puerto Ricans). Puerto Ricans
were to be placed in the third category, enjoying "something like the second-class
citizenship of blacks and Native Americans, as well as women." Finally, the residents
of Hawaii and Alaska, "where there were enough nonaboriginal people," could be
regarded as "full citizens residing in a U.S. territory on its way to statehood."[98]

Detaching citizenship from the right of political participation, as in the case of
residents of Puerto Rico, Guam, and the Virgin Islands, has become a central feature

---

[95] *Quoted in id.* at 428.

[96] *Id.* at 428. Divesting the concept of citizenship from any automatic association with the right of
political participation has been a familiar device in Western political practice. Two salient examples have
been the Roman concept of *civitas sine suffragio* and the distinction between "active" and "passive"
citizens drawn by the Abbé Sieyes during the French Revolutionary period. *See* HEATER, *supra* note 74,
at 16, 49–50. A contemporary example of the establishment of formal categories of citizens with divergent legal consequences is found in the British Nationality Act of 1981. *See id.* at 104.

[97] SMITH, *supra* note 31, at 429.

[98] *Id.* at 429–30.

of the legal framework of the American colonial enterprise.[99] That has been one of the major effects at the representational level of the Jones Act and the *Balzac* case. This result was similar to that rendered by another conceptual separation brought about by the first group of the *Insular Cases*. There, the Court stressed the difference between fundamental human rights and nonfundamental, democratic rights (or rights of political participation). In *Downes v. Bidwell*, for example, Justice Brown established a distinction between "natural rights," such as freedom of speech, and "artificial rights," such as "the rights to citizenship, to suffrage," and to certain methods of procedure.[100] That disjunction would allow for the establishment of a regime of liberal rights within a colonial context. (This theme will be developed further in chapter 8.) The Jones Act and the *Balzac* case carried forward this conceptual cleavage within the category of what Justice Brown had called "artificial rights." In the new social understanding of the American governing elites, citizenship and the right of political participation parted company.

This recasting of citizenship in a fresh representational mold allowed for a new construction of the "other." The former "aliens" residing in the recently acquired territories, who later had become "nationals" of the United States (different from its "citizens"), now were transformed into "citizens," but still of a different kind. The prevailing perception and feeling that Puerto Ricans are "second-class citizens" and the debate regarding the "nature" of their citizenship (that is, whether it is invested with constitutional or merely statutory rank) may be understood as a manifestation, in the realm of experience, of that differentiated construction. Ultimately that construction can be viewed as an effect of the sustained tension between the perceived need to retain and exercise control over subordinated communities and the desire to legitimate the exercise of such power by pursuing what has been taken to be, at least by some within the governing organs of the metropolitan state, an "enlightened" territorial policy.

The Constitutive Social Effects of the Citizenship Provision

A New Context for Social Practice and Action

One of law's contributions to the constitution of social experience is the extent to which it creates a context for action. The extension of U.S. citizenship to Puerto

---

[99] The dilemmas confronted by the American colonizers regarding the extension of citizenship rights to the peoples of the territories was not unlike the predicament faced by European powers in their own colonies. Heater expressed the matter of European imperialism by saying, "The truth of the matter is that no modern imperial power solved the riddle of citizenship. There were two possible approaches: a unified imperial citizenship or local citizenship specific to individual colonies. The status presupposes some sense of community and common loyalty. Yet cultural heterogeneity rendered this extremely difficult for the great bulk of Asians and Africans, especially in an age when the mother countries were culturally homogenous. Secondly, citizenship as the right to a certain minimum of social welfare was impossible of extension to, say, the poverty-stricken millions of the Indian subcontinent. And thirdly, citizenship as equal political participation was impossibly dangerous for the imperial power to conceive, since the overseas electorate would in total submerge the domestic." HEATER, *supra* note 74, at 130–31. According to Heater, the alternative strategy adopted by the British and the French consisted in the introduction of political rights at the local level. *Id.* at 131.

[100] *Downes*, 182 U.S. at 282–83.

Ricans produced a new ensemble of social meanings within which certain practices in which Puerto Ricans engaged or would engage in the future would have to be conceptualized and evaluated. This new set of understandings would also stimulate practices that would significantly affect the relationship between the metropolitan state and the colonial society. This was to be the case with migration.

One of the principal effects of the citizenship provision was to facilitate the movement of Puerto Ricans from the island to the continental United States. It is clear that from a strictly "legal" point of view, U.S. citizenship was not necessary for that purpose. As early as 1904 the Supreme Court had decided that Puerto Ricans could move freely into the United States, although they were not U.S. citizens.[101] However, it is also obvious that citizenship made it easier for many Puerto Ricans to migrate.[102] Those bearing the condition of "citizens" would more readily entertain expectations of equal treatment once on the continent than those who fell into the lesser category of "nationals."

At the end of the first decade of the 20th century, net migration of Puerto Ricans to the United States amounted to a bare 2,000 persons. By 1919, two years after the Jones Act came into effect, the number had increased more than five-fold. By 1929 net migration had jumped to 42,000 people. The great mass movement to the United States, however, occurred after World War II. It is estimated that in the 1950s about 470,000 people left Puerto Rico for the continental United States.[103] Between 1950 and 1970 net migration from Puerto Rico amounted to 605,550 people, equivalent to 27.4% of the island's population in 1950.[104] While in 1910 there were only some 1,500 Puerto Ricans living in the United States, by 1970 there were close to a million and a half.[105] Presently there are more than 2 million people of Puerto Rican descent living in numerous states.

Of course, the grant of citizenship was not the cause of this mass movement of people. The "expulsion factors"[106] that accounted for this exodus included the dire poverty in Puerto Rico, especially before World War II, and later the sustained high unemployment rates characteristic of the Puerto Rican economy. There is evidence, also, that the governments of both Puerto Rico and the United States at various points actively fostered the migration of Puerto Ricans to U.S. cities and farms to relieve the "excess population" in the island[107] and to supply needed labor for the U.S. economy, especially during the economic boom following World War II.[108] But, although citizenship was not the cause, it was certainly a facilitative condition.

---

[101] González v. Williams, 192 U.S. 1 (1904).

[102] *See* Cabranes, *supra* note 1, at 400.

[103] The statistics quoted in the above sentences are taken from BLANCA G. SILVESTRINI & MARÍA D. LUQUE DE SÁNCHEZ, HISTORIA DE PUERTO RICO: TRAYECTORIA DE UN PUEBLO 582 (1987).

[104] JAMES L. DIETZ, HISTORIA ECONÓMICA DE PUERTO RICO 306 (1989) (Originally published as ECONOMIC HISTORY OF PUERTO RICO: INSTITUTIONAL CHANGE AND CAPITALIST DEVELOPMENT (1986)).

[105] FERNANDO PICÓ, HISTORIA GENERAL DE PUERTO RICO 256 (1986).

[106] Some of the sociological literature on migration designates as "expulsion factors" the various conditions prevailing in the country of origin that contribute to the decision to emigrate. The conditions that make the receiving country an attractive destination for migrants are referred to as "attraction factors." *See* Robert Pastor, *La migración en la cuenca caribeña*, 6 EL CARIBE CONTEMPORÁNEO 105, 121–22 (1982).

[107] DIETZ, *supra* note 104, at 301–08.

[108] *See* SILVESTRINI & LUQUE DE SÁNCHEZ, *supra* note 103, at 582–85; PICÓ, *supra* note 105, at 255–57.

The effects of this massive movement of people cannot be underestimated. Economically, it served as an escape valve that made easier the much-touted "economic miracle" that took place in the island after the 1950s. The economic growth made possible by a strategy of development that relied heavily on the exportation of excess human resources served to defuse social agitation and instability. Moreover, the possibility of migration presented itself as a ready "individual solution" to the problem of poverty, an alternative that acted as a disincentive to organized social struggle within Puerto Rico.

Mass migration has nourished the development of a complex demographic reality and extensive and intensive cultural contacts between Puerto Ricans and the dominant society. It has produced a social world divided demographically and culturally. Puerto Ricans in New York and other cities of the United States have been enmeshed in the cultural tension between the Anglo-American culture, in which they have had to struggle for subsistence, and a Puerto Rican identity that most of them cherish and fight to preserve. Puerto Ricans in Puerto Rico are linked to the United States by more than the formal political and legal relationships between the two countries and the economic and military presence of the United States in the island. They are connected to that society also through ties with relatives who live in American cities and towns throughout the entire nation; through lived experiences in those settings as students, workers, or unemployed migrants at some point in their lives; through shared cultural icons, such as Puerto Rican pop artists and athletes who have made their careers in the mainland while maintaining their attachment to Puerto Rico; and, not least importantly, through the ever-present possibility of having to migrate at some future date in an attempt to escape the harsh realities of the island.[109] There is a continuous flow of Puerto Ricans between the islands of Puerto Rico and the cities of the mainland. Such is the intensity of this exchange that some have spoken of Puerto Rico as a "translocal nation."[110]

The Constitution of the Political Subject: Puerto Ricans as American Citizens

The Foraker Act of 1900 and the judicial decisions in the *Insular Cases* created a legal and political subject, that is, a social actor endowed with the right to make certain claims while becoming subject to the authority of the metropolitan state. That legal and political subject had been defined as a "resident" or "inhabitant" of an unincorporated territory. By virtue of the Jones Act, that "resident" or "inhabitant" —until then legally considered a citizen of Puerto Rico and a "national" of the United States—now became an American citizen. In *Balzac* the latter category was interpreted to have little juridical import regarding the status of Puerto Rico. However, it did have significant political effects. One of the main political repercussions

---

[109] In a poll conducted by a professional polling firm for a local newspaper in Puerto Rico, nearly half of those interviewed (46%) indicated that they had lived in the continental United States, whereas 83% said that they had relatives living there. EL NUEVO DÍA, Aug. 12, 1997, at 6.

[110] *See, e.g.,* Agustín Lao, *Islands at the Crossroads: Puerto Ricanness Traveling between the Translocal Nation and the Global City, in* PUERTO RICAN JAM: ESSAYS ON CULTURE AND POLITICS (Frances Negrón-Muntaner & Ramón Grosfoguel Eds. 1997).

of citizenship has been its conversion into a discursive instrument for the formulation of reciprocal demands between the United States and Puerto Rican society.

Demands From the Metropolis: Loyalty and Military Services

The paramount demand the metropolitan state has made on Puerto Ricans as individuals and as a community during the eight decades that have followed the imposition of U.S. citizenship has been loyalty, at both the symbolic and material levels. Evidence of this loyalty has included military services.[111] The islands constituting the Puerto Rican territory have served as locations for important U.S. military installations; as platforms for military intelligence activities in the Caribbean; as training sites for the armed forces of the United States and its allies, including NATO forces; and as a source of personnel for the American Army, Navy, Air Force, and other military bodies. More than 200,000 Puerto Ricans served in the U.S. armed forces during the 20th century.[112] As indicated in chapter 3, to this day political and military services are required of the Puerto Rican territory and people through their active insertion in the military operations of the United States in the region, including the recent activities in connection with drug trafficking and illegal immigration.

Although U.S. citizenship was not a requirement for conscription, as in the case of migration, it facilitated the incorporation of Puerto Ricans into the U.S. military either for obligatory or voluntary service. After all, it seems more justifiable to require military loyalty from "citizens" than to force noncitizens to comply with an obligation that puts their lives at risk. Similarly, the withholding of substantial amounts of land and other resources for military purposes is more readily validated by recourse to the notion that the community affected is composed of citizens of the state to whose military forces such resources are allotted.

The massive incorporation of Puerto Ricans into U.S. military forces has fostered an intensive contact with one of the most ideologically oriented institutions any country can have. It is the function of the military to inculcate a sense of loyalty and a pronounced "patriotic" feeling among its ranks. In some Puerto Ricans negative experiences in the American armed forces have produced a heightened anti-Americanism, stronger antimilitary stances, a greater sense of their Puerto Rican identity, and a more pronounced willingness to engage in social struggles.[113] But the contrary effect has also been produced, perhaps to a greater degree. Because of their highly ideological role in the formation of American patriotic sentiments, the U.S. armed forces have been keenly instrumental in the process of creating an attitude of admiration and "loyalty" toward the United States among important sectors of the Puerto Rican population.[114]

Fernando Picó, a prominent Puerto Rican historian, has observed that the generation of World War II veterans exerted a modernizing influence in Puerto Rico. Benefits accruing to them because of their military service opened up access to

---

[111] Consult chapter 3 for a description of the military importance of Puerto Rico for the United States throughout the 20th century.

[112] Puerto Ricans had been eligible to enlist in the U.S. armed forces before 1917. But the granting of citizenship undoubtedly facilitated their conscription afterward.

[113] See PICÓ, supra note 105, at 252.

[114] See id.; see also ESTADES, supra note 10, at 18, 95–99, 141, 143, 222.

secondary or higher education, to funds for the construction of modern housing units, to relatively well-compensated employment in the federal government and other institutions, and to a variety of services and goods not available to other sectors of the population.[115] In Puerto Rico modernization has been generally associated with Americanization,[116] a fact that has often led either to a rejection of the institutions of modernity on nationalist grounds or to a blind adherence to anything American in the name of progress. It is understandable, then, that the modernizing influence of American military institutions has operated to consolidate the hegemonic position of the United States within significant sectors of Puerto Rican society. Citizenship, images of modernity, an admiration of American institutions, and loyalty to a powerful state have been conjoined in a formidable manner to produce an active acquiescence to American rule.

Demands From Puerto Ricans: Social and Economic Welfare and Political Participation

As American citizens, Puerto Ricans have been actively demanding subjects. In this sense, the construction of the meaning of citizenship within the Puerto Rican community has not been a unilateral process of impositions from above, although these have abounded. Once confronted with the fact that they had become U.S. citizens, many Puerto Ricans, individually, collectively, and through their internal representative political bodies, have deployed the notion of citizenship to discursively validate their demands before the metropolitan state. The citizenship rationale has served as a justification for several types of claims. The most important ones have been access to the social and economic programs administered by the U.S. government and, to a lesser degree, greater political participation.[117]

The Supreme Court has held that Congress may discriminate against Puerto Rico in the allotment of funds for social programs.[118] However, this has not prevented Puerto Rican political leaders belonging to the major political parties—including those who favor some form of autonomous status for the island—to levy claims for broader access to the federal government's social and welfare programs, justified with the political argument that Puerto Ricans are American citizens.[119] This discursive practice was initiated early in the century, when the American governors appointed by the president sought to validate their requests for funds for the island with the argument about citizenship. Thus, in 1930, then Governor Theodore Roosevelt, Jr., argued in the following terms:

> There are those who argue that as Puerto Rico does not pay her share of taxes to the Federal government she should not be included in these benefits [federal aid]. To my

---

[115] PICÓ, *supra* note 105, at 252.

[116] GORDON K. LEWIS, PUERTO RICO: FREEDOM AND POWER IN THE CARIBBEAN 316 (1963).

[117] See Efrén Rivera Ramos, *Self-Determination and Decolonisation in the Society of the Modern Colonial Welfare State*, in ISSUES OF SELF-DETERMINATION 120 (William Twining Ed. 1991); Cabranes, *supra* note 1, at 400–01; LEIBOWITZ, *supra* note 10, at 150.

[118] Califano v. Torres, 435 U.S. 1 (1978); Harris v. Rosario, 446 U.S. 651 (1980).

[119] For a typical mode of formulation of such demands, see Statement by the Governor of Puerto Rico, Rafael Hernández Colón, in 1 *Political Status of Puerto Rico: Hearings on S. 710, S. 711, and S. 712 before the Senate Committee on Energy and Natural Resources*, 101st Cong., 1st Sess. 170 (1989) [*Hearings*].

mind this is a false and short sighted position. The people of Puerto Rico are citizens of the United States. It is incumbent upon the United States, if the Declaration of Independence means more than empty words, to endeavor to provide all its citizens a fair opportunity in life. It is only by aid of the Federal government that this can be accomplished for our people in Puerto Rico.[120]

This justificatory discourse achieved new heights during the 1960s, when monetary transfers from the U.S. government to Puerto Rico registered impressive leaps. By 1980 such transfer payments to individuals amounted to 30% of personal income in Puerto Rico. That same year grants in aid from the federal government constituted 35% of recurrent revenues of the government of Puerto Rico.[121] In 1997, federal funds going to Puerto Rico totaled $10.77 billion, an increase of $4.6 billion over a period of 10 years.[122] This enormous dependence on U.S. federal monetary transfers both to the government and to individuals in Puerto Rico has become one of the characteristic features of what I have labeled the modern colonial welfare state.[123]

Of course, the widespread extension of economic assistance and social welfare programs cannot be understood exclusively as a response to demands from Puerto Ricans because they are American citizens. Those disbursements have served a key function in the preservation of social stability in a U.S. military bastion in the Caribbean. They have contributed also to produce a higher consumer capacity in a community that was offered to the region as an alternative model to the communist regime of Cuba during the ideological struggles of the Cold War. Nevertheless, the citizenship argument has acted as a powerful justification for those demands. To the extent that such a rationale has formed part of the social understanding prevalent within the Puerto Rican masses, it has become "a power in the domain of consciousness."[124]

The citizenship rationale has also served to advance arguments for broader political participation. An important claim justified on the basis of U.S. citizenship has been the request made by a significant sector of the population that Puerto Rico be admitted as the 51st state of the union. A paradigmatic formulation of the argument is to be found in a statement by one of the most outspoken civic leaders in favor of the statehood option:

> Statehood, no doubt, is the solution to the dilemma of second-class citizenship and the inferior second-class mentality for all Puerto Ricans, either living in the island or in the 50 states. It offers the equality, full dignity and the self-determination we have sought for over 500 years.[125]

---

[120] *Annual Report of the Governor of Puerto Rico, 1929–30*, at 15–16 (1930). *Quoted in* Trías Monge, *supra* note 17, at 85.

[121] Leibowitz, *supra* note 10, at 150.

[122] Alex W. Maldonado, *A Message to Congress on the Eve of the Centennial*, San Juan Star, July 23, 1998, at 53.

[123] *See* Rivera Ramos, *supra* note 117. For further analysis of the economic conditions of Puerto Rico under the American regime, *see* chapter 3.

[124] Karl Marx, Paris Manuscripts, *quoted in* David McLellan, Marx before Marxism 181 (1980).

[125] Miriam Ramírez de Ferrer, *Statehood Is Solution to 2nd Class Citizenship*, San Juan Star, May 1, 1998, at 55. *See also* Statement by Carlos Romero Barceló, former Governor of the Commonwealth of Puerto Rico, *in* 1 *Hearings*, *supra* note 119, at 113–31.

The prostatehood movement has grown steadily during the past three decades, although in recent years it has given some signs that it may have reached a peak, at least temporarily.[126] Demands for greater political participation in the decision-making process of the metropolitan state, on the other hand, have not been successful.[127] "Statehooders," nonetheless, continue relying on the discourse of citizenship to further their claims.[128] One of the most prominent leaders of the movement, Carlos

---

[126] A poll conducted in 1989 by a professional polling firm for EL NUEVO DÍA, a Spanish-language daily published in San Juan, revealed that for the first time in Puerto Rican history, preference for the statehood option among registered voters came out ahead of other status options: 41% of respondents chose statehood, 37% Commonwealth, and 4% independence; 12% were undecided, and 6% stated they would not vote (EL NUEVO DÍA, Oct. 2, 1989, at 4). Another poll conducted in July 1992 by a different polling firm for one of the major Puerto Rican broadcasting companies produced slightly different results, but the statehood option still led the list of alternatives (42% for statehood, 41% for Commonwealth status, 4% for independence, 2% for a new option, the associated republic, and 10% undecided). (Data furnished by Marilú Torres from the Statistics Office of the News Department of TV Channel 2, Telemundo; *see also* P. García, *Ligera ventaja de la estadidad sobre el ELA*, EL NUEVO DÍA, Aug. 6, 1992, at 11.)

In November 1992 the New Progressive Party (NPP), which advocates statehood, won the general elections by a wide margin. Not all those who voted for the NPP may be considered statehooders. Many may have cast a protest vote against the pro-Commonwealth incumbent or may have been unattracted by the Popular Democratic Party's new candidate for the governorship. However, the fact that a pro-statehood party was voted into office was not devoid of significance.

Stimulated by its victory, the NPP promoted a local plebiscite on the three traditional options of statehood, Commonwealth, and independence. The plebiscite was held in November 1993, exactly a year after the NPP's electoral victory in the general elections. Contrary to the ruling NPP's expectations, the Commonwealth formula won over statehood by slightly over 2% (48.4% to 46.2%). The NPP won again the general elections in 1996, this time by a much wider margin than in 1992. Subsequent polls conducted by professional pollsters for the local Puerto Rican press revealed either an advantage of several percentage points for the Commonwealth formula over the statehood option, with a slight decline of the latter (*see* EL NUEVO DÍA, Aug. 12, 1997, at 4), or a virtual tie between the two options (*see* SAN JUAN STAR, June 8, 1998, at 4). In December 1998, another local referendum on the status question resulted in a defeat for statehood (which obtained 46.5% of the votes) as the majority of the voters (50.3%) opted for a "None of the above" column endorsed by the pro-Commonwealth party. *See* chapter 3. For a good collection of documents that reflect the development of the annexationist ideology throughout the 20th century, preceded by a thoughtful commentary by the editor, see LAS IDEAS ANEXIONISTAS EN PUERTO RICO BAJO LA DOMINACIÓN NORTEAMERICANA (Aarón Ramos Ed. 1987).

[127] The most recent attempts to provide for a federally sanctioned plebiscite on the political status of Puerto Rico stalled in Congress during 1998. *See* the discussion in chapter 3. After the inconclusive results of the plebiscite held by the Puerto Rican government at the end of that year, the U.S. Congress seemed reluctant to initiate a new process in the near future. For a discussion of failed attempts at obtaining greater participation in federal decision making on the part of Puerto Rico, *see* TRÍAS MONGE, *supra* note 17.

[128] On July 19, 2000, Jaime Pieras, a U.S. Federal District Court Judge of Puerto Rican origin, held that not allowing Puerto Ricans residing in Puerto Rico to vote for president of the United States violated their constitutional rights as U.S. citizens. Igartúa de la Rosa v. United States, No. Civ. 00-1421(JP) (D. Puerto Rico). On August 29, 2000, the judge ordered the Commonwealth of Puerto Rico to create a mechanism "by which the U.S. citizens residing in Puerto Rico will vote in the upcoming and subsequent presidential elections and to provide for the appointment of presidential electors." *Id.*, "Final Judgement." The ruling was contrary to a previous decision by another judge of the same court affirmed by the First Circuit Court of Appeals, Igartúa de la Rosa v. the United States, 842 F. Supp. 607 (D. Puerto Rico), aff'd, 32 F.3rd 8 (Ist Cir. 1994), cert. denied, 514 U.S. 1049 (1995). Following Judge Pieras's decision, the Puerto Rican legislature passed and the governor signed legislation providing for Puerto Ricans to vote in U.S. presidential elections. The U.S. Department of Justice appealed Judge Pieras's decision to the First Circuit Court of Appeals and the Puerto Rican Independence Party and other groups

Romero Barceló, a former governor of Puerto Rico and, as of this writing, resident commissioner for Puerto Rico in Washington, has suggested that, in the long run, statehood will be the inevitable result of the extension of U.S. citizenship to Puerto Ricans in 1917. In response to a question about the possibility of statehood being discarded as an option, Romero Barceló stated,

> Statehood will not be pushed out of the picture. Who best saw this was an independence leader: José de Diego.[129] He was opposed to [the extension of] American citizenship precisely because once citizenship was granted the road to statehood would be irreversible. . . . It is irreversible. Because we are American citizens.[130]

Even the long-asserted right of the Puerto Rican people to self-determination has been promoted recently within a discursive strategy that takes as its basic premise the condition of Puerto Ricans as U.S. citizens. Thus, Puerto Rican prostatehood spokespersons and U.S. congressional leaders sympathetic to their cause have founded their calls to hold a federally sanctioned plebiscite on the political status of Puerto Rico on the "right to self-determination" of "U.S. citizens residing in Puerto Rico." This discursive tack was very evident during the 12-hour debate conducted on the floor of the U.S. House of Representatives in March 1998 concerning Representative Don Young's bill to provide for a plebiscite on the status issue.[131]

The discourse of U.S. citizenship has served additionally to make claims aimed at shielding the Puerto Rican community from the "excesses" of U.S. demands on Puerto Rico and Puerto Ricans based on that same citizenship. A clear example has been the opposition voiced by most Puerto Ricans to military exercises the U.S. Navy conducts in the Puerto Rican island of Vieques. Opposition to the Navy has been voiced from different perspectives. The Puerto Rican government, prostatehood politicians, sectors of the Puerto Rican press, and congressional allies have made it a point, however, to stress that their demands that the U.S. Navy pull out of Vieques are not based on an anti-American disposition. Rather, they assert, the claim is based on what they perceive as the rights of Vieques residents, as U.S. citizens, to be protected in their lives, peace, and security.[132] The Navy, on the other hand, alleging

---

challenged in Puerto Rican courts the constitutionality of the ensuing legislation. The latter cases were immediately removed to the Federal District Court. As of this writing, these court actions were pending.

[129] José de Diego (1866–1918) was an independence leader who became president of the House of Delegates and of the House of Representatives of Puerto Rico. He belonged to the Union Party. De Diego was the author of the memorandum addressed to the president and the Congress of the United States, approved by the Puerto Rican House of Delegates on March 1914, opposing the extension of U.S. citizenship to Puerto Rico. In 1917 he proposed holding a plebiscite so that Puerto Ricans could choose between statehood and independence for the island. JOSÉ DE DIEGO, II OBRAS COMPLETAS (PROSA. NUEVAS CAMPAÑAS. EL PLEBISCITO) 232, 465 (1966).

[130] Leonor Mulero, Carlos Romero Barceló: "Las memorias no son publicables en vida," EL NUEVO DÍA, Aug. 1, 1999, at 4, 6.

[131] See, e.g., U.S. CONGRESS, 144 CONG. REC. H772, 3, 10, 22 (daily ed. March 4, 1998) (statements by Reps. Young, Miller, and Kennedy).

[132] During a rally held in Washington in support of the Vieques cause, Rep. Charles Rangel, Democrat from New York, remarked that "things like this cause people to remember we're talking about American citizens, we're not just talking about a country in the Caribbean." Rep. Luis Gutiérrez, Democrat from Illinois, a Puerto Rican sympathetic to independence for the island, made similar comments, reminding those present that what happened in Vieques "happened to people who are U.S. citizens." Robert Friedman, Vieques Gains Ground on National Front, SAN JUAN STAR, Aug. 5, 1999, at 5; Leonor Mulero, Congresistas unidos por Vieques, EL NUEVO DÍA, Aug. 5, 1999, at 4.

that Vieques is essential to national security, has reminded its opponents that the U.S. Navy is also "Puerto Rico's Navy" and that its role in Vieques is to "protect" and "defend our country."[133] Once again, the discourse of citizenship is deployed as argument and counterargument to exact either protection or loyalty. In the process, the link of the Puerto Rican community to the United States is discursively reaffirmed.

Recent postnationalist critiques of Puerto Rican history and politics have also made U.S. citizenship a central element of academic analyses and political proposals. According to this view, U.S. citizenship provides a common ground for most Puerto Ricans to unite in search of a decolonization process that would not only maintain, but enhance, the benefits that have flowed to the Puerto Rican population from their legal status as U.S. citizens. The analysis is based on the fact that more than 90% of voters in Puerto Rico have expressed support for status alternatives that include the preservation of U.S. citizenship, including statehood, the present Commonwealth, and some form of free association with the United States. Beyond these differences in status preferences, there is the common value of U.S. citizenship, these critics argue. Rather than "national self-determination," they propose the "free determination of citizens." Aware of the territorial limitations of U.S. citizenship as applied to Puerto Rico, this group proposes that Puerto Ricans demand equality of democratic rights by claiming the right to vote for the president of the United States and to elect voting representatives to Congress. It does not matter whether these objectives are achieved by reforming the current Commonwealth status, by becoming an incorporated territory, or by acceding to statehood. In this sense, their position transcends the traditional struggles among supporters of fixed status formulas.

Moreover, they suggest, the meaning of citizenship should be expanded to include social, cultural, and ecological rights not yet recognized in American political and constitutional discourse. In their view, these claims could serve to build bridges across gender, racial, ethnic, and other divides between Puerto Ricans and other communities in the mainland United States.[134] The defense of U.S. citizenship that this radical "postmodern" critique of Puerto Rican nationalism puts forth is based on a close identification of the status of U.S. citizens with the rights that have accrued to Puerto Ricans as a result of the constitutional system developed under the American regime. It also rests on an assumption about the type of claims that such status is capable of justifying.[135]

The discussion in this section illustrates one of the operations of law in the social world. The Jones Act and the *Balzac* case created an "objective" legal subject, that is, a social actor endowed with certain rights and obligations defined by these

---

[133] Julio Ghigliotty, *Firmes en que no hay nada como la Isla Nena*, EL NUEVO DÍA, Aug. 4, 1999, at 5.

[134] See Juan Duchesne et al., *Algunas tesis democráticas ante el plebiscito de 1998*, DIÁLOGO, March 1999, at 38–39.

[135] The position these authors expressed rests on an interpretation of the value that Puerto Ricans place on U.S. citizenship that the argument developed in this book tends to share. However, one possible pitfall of their political proposal is its potential to "essentialize" citizenship, particularly U.S. citizenship, minimizing its historically contingent character. The shifts in meaning accorded to the notion of citizenship in U.S. history noted in a previous section of this chapter should warn against that danger. "Citizenship" and "nationality" are both cultural constructs. Naturalizing either involves similar risks for subaltern groups and communities.

authoritative legal texts.[136] Many Puerto Ricans have appropriated that category—
U.S. citizen—and perceive themselves as such. They act according to that perception. In this sense, they have become "subjective" legal subjects.[137] This is exemplified by Puerto Ricans' response to the possibility of migration after 1917, by their
incorporation into the U.S. armed forces, by their claims for access to the social and
economic programs of the metropolitan state, by their demands for broader political
participation and more extensive rights, and by their requests for protection against
the actions of agents of the federal government itself. Some have even impressed
the category with their own meaning, that is, they have ascribed to that legal status
their own imagined consequences.[138]

   This demonstrates how law's substance can be constructed from "below" as
well as from "above."[139] Puerto Ricans were made American citizens as an act of
imposition. The metropolitan policy makers meant that action to have a certain import. However, in their daily practices, in their demands, and in the rhetoric of their
claims, a substantial number of Puerto Ricans have negotiated their status as subjects
and have impressed new meanings, perhaps unintended ones, on the category constructed as an exercise of symbolic power[140] from the commanding heights of the
imperial state.[141]

Citizenship and the Formation of the "Self": The Question of Identity

As in any other community, the formation of identities in Puerto Rican society is a
very complex process involving multiple determinations. Individuals and groups develop self-perceptions and are defined by others with reference to factors such as
gender, race, skin color, social origin, age, place of birth, religious beliefs, modes of
sexuality, political affiliation, professional or occupational status, place of residence,

---

[136] The basic operation of law as a pragmatic discourse is the creation of legal subjects. This occurs
through a process of production of categories that define certain identities: the citizen, the debtor, the
husband or wife, and so forth. Each category specifies the rights, duties, prerogatives, and powers
attributed to the agents subsumed in the category. What I call the "objective" legal subject, for lack of
a better term, is the category defined in a given manner in legal texts. It is the category as interpreted
by authorized legal operators. That category "exists" in the normative world of law and can be analyzed
as a legal concept. The fact that there may be different interpretations of the meaning of the category
does not deny its existence as a concept in the legal world. In sum, the objective legal subject is the
citizen, the debtor, the husband or wife, as abstractly defined in the legal text. To a great extent, it exists
in the legal text independently of its effects in real subjects, that is, in individual and social agents.

   [137] The "subjective" legal subject is the individual (or collective) agent that views herself as invested
with the attributes with which the legal norm endows her or with which she thinks the norm should
endow her. It is the agent that considers himself or herself to be a citizen, a debtor, a husband or a wife.
In other words, it is the concrete agent who sees himself as a legal subject, because of the knowledge
or the belief that the law so recognizes him.

   [138] For example, strictly speaking, many of the rights enshrined in the U.S. Constitution are extensive
to all "persons" under the jurisdiction of the United States, regardless whether they are citizens or not.
Yet many people attribute the "enjoyment" of such rights to the legal fact of being U.S. citizens.

   [139] W. E. Forbath et al., *Introduction: Legal Histories from Below*, 1985 WISC. L. REV. 759 (1985).

   [140] Pierre Bourdieu, *The Force of Law: Toward a Sociology of the Juridical Field*, 38 HAST. L. J.
805 (1987) [*hereinafter* Bourdieu, *Force of Law*]; PIERRE BOURDIEU, IN OTHER WORDS: ESSAYS TO-
WARDS A REFLEXIVE SOCIOLOGY (1990) [*hereinafter* BOURDIEU, IN OTHER WORDS].

   [141] For the suggestion that "people vested with little or no power may nevertheless exercise control"
over their lives, see Martha Minow, *Identities*, 3 YALE J. L. & HUMAN. 97, 106 (1991).

personality traits and characteristics, and even musical and literary tastes. Ascription to legal categories that assign rights and obligations also contribute, at times only momentarily, others in a more durable fashion, to shape self-views and ways of naming oneself.

This complex articulation of shared experiences and categorical appropriations makes for the production of multiple identities. They are multiple in the sense that there may be significant differences among individuals and groups, but also in the sense that each individual's or group's self-perception is actually a composite of many identitary elements.[142] The relative weight of any of these factors and the manner in which they come together vary from case to case and are part of what confers uniqueness on every individual. Each person is thus someone akin to others in relation to a series of commonly shared experiences and characteristics and a unique personality that integrates those elements in a very particular way. The Puerto Rican community is no exception to this reality.

In the Introduction to this book I discussed how Puerto Ricans are generally believed to form a distinct national group, with a common heritage, common traditions, and centuries of intensely shared experiences. Most Puerto Ricans perceive themselves in this way. Ascription to a Puerto Rican national community has been an important part of the discourses on identity in Puerto Rican society.[143] Yet, the condition of U.S. citizen, with all its attendant images and material effects, is an identitary factor to which some Puerto Ricans also seem to relate. The legal category U.S. citizen provokes self-ascriptions that, in many people (strong empirical evidence about the extent of the phenomenon is still to be produced), conjoin with other factors to produce self-images in which being an American citizen is an important constituent element. In some cases the status of U.S. citizen has attenuated the relative weight of other historically significant factors like ethnicity, language, and culture in the process of identity formation. In others, the fact of being an American citizen is not seen as in any way detracting from those other factors, but merely as adding an additional element to the self-definition.

Thus, for example, in the study conducted for the Ateneo Puertorriqueño[144] cited in the Introduction, 97.3% of those interviewed answered that they regarded themselves as Puerto Ricans.[145] Yet a majority of the interviewees (58.4%) also considered themselves to be *estadounidenses*[146] (which in Spanish means "belonging or relative to the United States of America" or "a native of that country"[147]). Those responsible for the study, perceiving an apparent "confusion" in the answers, pointed to the fact that 80% of those who identified themselves as *estadounidenses* gave as their reason

---

[142] I am using the term *identitary* to mean *referring to identity*. Thus, an *identitary element* would be a factor contributing to a person's identity understood both as self-perception and as the result of attribution by others, such as gender, race, language, or occupation.

[143] *See* discussion and evidence cited in the Introduction, notes 11–17 and accompanying text.

[144] *Ateneo Puertorriqueño* is a cultural institution established in 1876 to promote science, literature, and the arts. Its declared objectives include "the study, defense, and diffusion of Puerto Rican values." ATENEO PUERTORRIQUEÑO, ESTATUTOS X, 1 (1995).

[145] HISPANIA RESEARCH CORPORATION, MEMORANDO ANALÍTICO SOBRE EL ESTUDIO DEL IDIOMA EN PUERTO RICO–SOMETIDO A ATENEO PUERTORRIQUEÑO 56 (1993).

[146] *Id.* at 59.

[147] 1 REAL ACADEMIA ESPAÑOLA, DICCIONARIO DE LA LENGUA ESPAÑOLA 601 (20th ed. 1984) (translation supplied).

the circumstance that they were American citizens.[148] That made the authors think that the "confusion" was due to the use of the term *estadounidense*, which for many may not convey the same meaning as *americano*, the Spanish word for "American," generally used in Puerto Rico with a stronger ethnic connotation. They concluded that the use of the chosen term may have led the interviewees to interpret that the question related to "citizenship" and not to national identity. As the authors of the study themselves commented, because the survey did not inquire into the meaning those interviewed accorded U.S. citizenship, it was not possible to ascertain with more precision the implications of their answer.[149] In any event, the results of the Ateneo study reveal that U.S. citizenship is regarded as an important identitary factor by a considerable number of Puerto Ricans, although the extent, depth, and cultural and psychological implications of this phenomenon require stronger empirical verification.

Informal, private conversation; public political and social discourse, and literary examinations of the question of identity do reflect, however, that many Puerto Ricans oscillate between the reaffirmation of their separate national identity, maybe as an act of cultural survival, and the proclamation of their American citizenship, perhaps as an act of political necessity. For some, U.S. citizenship may be a mere legal expedient.[150] Yet others seemingly have come to regard it as a desirable self-definitional focus.[151] Inside many, two distinct discourses appear to struggle or collaborate for their control as subjects: the discourse of American citizenship and the discourse of *la puertorriqueñidad* (the set of characteristics thought to define Puerto Rican identity). This has constituted an agonizing experience for many people, especially among intellectuals. Others seem to exhibit an astonishing capacity to dissolve, in their daily lives, any contradictions (or at least act as if there were none). An emblematic expression of this internal dynamic was made public recently by Rosario Ferré, a leading contemporary Puerto Rican writer, whose works of fiction have frequently addressed the issue of national identity. A member of one of the most prominent political families in the country, she used to be a public advocate for Puerto Rican independence but has converted to the cause of statehood. In an article published in the *New York Times*, Ferré manifested the following:

> As a Puerto Rican writer, I constantly face the problem of identity. When I travel to the States I feel as Latina as Chita Rivera. But in Latin America, I feel more American than John Wayne. To be Puerto Rican is to be a hybrid. Our two halves are inseparable; we cannot give up either without feeling maimed. . . . For many years, my concern was to keep my Hispanic self from being stifled. Now I discover it's my American self that's being threatened.[152]

---

[148] HISPANIA RESEARCH CORPORATION, *supra* note 145, at 59.

[149] This survey should be compared with the study in NANCY MORRIS, PUERTO RICO: CULTURE, POLITICS, AND IDENTITY (1995). Morris's study was based on group and individual interviews with politicians and young political activists. She reported that her interviewees and focus group participants generally agreed that they felt Puerto Rican and did not feel *estadounidense*. *Id.* at 113. There were a few exceptions, however, among statehood supporters. Two of them maintained "that there was no difference between being Puerto Rican and *estadounidense*." *Id.* at 108.

[150] *See id.* at 110. Morris cited a Commonwealth party focus group member as saying, "The passport is more like a legal element. It's a legal card that is not tied to sentiment." *Id.*

[151] *Id.* at 108, 112.

[152] Rosario Ferré, *Puerto Rico, U.S.A.*, NEW YORK TIMES, March 19, 1998, at A-23.

An important consequence of the "legal fact" that Puerto Ricans are considered American citizens has been the production of conflicting discourses regarding the question of self-determination. Throughout the 20th century, the concept of self-determination has been used in international legal and political discourse to refer, among other things, to the right of a "people" to determine their political status. Assertions of the right to self-determination have been most frequently, although not exclusively, made in the context of colonial situations. A basic theoretical and political problem has always been the question of defining the collective "self" to whom the right accrues. The problem usually involves disputes about who should be included within the group that is to exercise the right.

This version of the issue has been manifested in the Puerto Rican case in the form of an ongoing debate about the inclusion of stateside Puerto Ricans in any vote on political status choices.[153] However, in recent years, another related, but somewhat different, dimension of the matter has surfaced. Increasingly, especially among U.S. congressional leaders, the question of the definition of the political status of Puerto Rico has been described as providing an opportunity for the "U.S. citizens" of Puerto Rico to exercise their "right to self-determination."[154] This conception has been countered by the view that the relevant subject of the right to self-determination in this case is the "Puerto Rican people" or "Puerto Ricans" as constituting a distinct nationality defined by cultural, historical, and analogous factors.[155]

This clash of visions has significant psychological, sociological, cultural, and political implications. But, additionally, it could have important bearing, from the point of view of international law, American constitutional law, and Puerto Rican legislation, on such issues as what alternatives should be placed on the ballot, what substantive requirements the options should meet, who has the right to vote, who controls voting requirements, and so forth.[156] U.S. citizenship, the definition of a

---

[153] During discussion on H.R. 856, the Young Bill, Puerto Rican-born Rep. José Serrano, Democrat from New York, proposed an amendment that would have granted the right to vote in the projected plebiscite on the political status of Puerto Rico to persons born in Puerto Rico but residing in the United States. One of those opposing the proposal was prostatehood Resident Commissioner Carlos Romero Barceló. The amendment was defeated by an overwhelming majority. U.S. CONGRESS, 144 CONG. REC. H819, 177–178, 78 (daily ed. March 4, 1998) (statement by Res. Comm. Romero Barceló; recorded vote).

[154] See H.R. 856, 105th Cong., 2nd Sess. Findings Nos. 14, 15 (1998) (enacted); U.S. CONGRESS, 144 CONG. REC. H772, 3, 10, 22 (daily ed. March 4, 1998) (statements by Reps. Young, Miller, and Kennedy); U.S. CONGRESS, HOUSE COMMITTEE ON RESOURCES, REPORT TOGETHER WITH DISSENTING AND ADDITIONAL VIEWS TO ACCOMPANY H.R. 3024, ADDITIONAL VIEWS BY PATRICK J. KENNEDY at 44–47, 104th Cong., 2nd Sess. (1996).

[155] See, e.g., Manuel Rodriguez Orellana, Young, Craig Paved the Way for a Better Bill, SAN JUAN STAR, June 7, 1998, at 87. The author, a member of the Puerto Rican Independence Party, quoted the party's president, Puerto Rican Senator Rubén Berríos, as saying that "the problem of Puerto Rico is not . . . disenfranchisement of a minority or an issue of civil rights. . . . It is a problem of national rights; of the inalienable right of a nation, of a people, to govern themselves."

[156] A good example of an effort to define Puerto Rican identity in terms of American citizenship, rather than in reference to cultural or related characteristics, and its significance for political status legislation, can be found in a commentary made by U.S. Senator J. Bennet Johnston in San Juan to the effect that the status of being Puerto Rican is not a racial or ethnic question, but a matter of residency and citizenship. The senator was answering an inquiry regarding the demand of many Puerto Ricans living in the United States to participate in any plebiscite on political status held in Puerto Rico. (Notes taken by the author during the press conference held by Senator Johnston in San Juan on June 16, 1989.)

political "self," and the right to self-determination have thus become enmeshed in the conflicting visions and discourses that circulate in the Puerto Rican colonial context.

Aware of the effects that the granting of U.S. citizenship has had on the creation of identities and worldviews within the Puerto Rican community, including the possible repercussions on the determination of its political future, some independence followers have launched a direct attack on the status of U.S. citizenship imposed on Puerto Ricans in the early part of this century. The most salient recent case is that of Juan Mari Bras, a prominent lawyer and independence leader. Referring to his action as a "legal experiment," Mari Bras, a native of Puerto Rico, presented himself in July 1994 at the U.S. embassy in Venezuela and, following the prescribed procedures, renounced his U.S. citizenship. Eventually, the State Department issued him a "Certificate of Loss of Nationality of the United States." Upon relinquishing his U.S. citizenship, Mari Bras returned to Puerto Rico. His right to vote in Puerto Rican elections was challenged by a well-known statehood advocate,[157] who alleged that Puerto Rican law made it a voting requirement to be an American citizen.[158] Mari Bras, in turn, based his right to vote in Puerto Rican elections on the provisions of several instruments of international law and on his "natural right" to his own nationality. The Puerto Rican Superior Court, in a decision signed by a Puerto Rican judge, rejected the challenge and ruled for Mari Bras.[159] The Court determined that the latter was a "Puerto Rican citizen," according to Puerto Rican statutory law, and that to deprive him of his right to vote in Puerto Rican elections for not being a U.S. citizen would violate the Constitution of Puerto Rico.

The identity question was addressed squarely in the judge's opinion. He stated,

> no law can change the reality that a person born in Puerto Rico of Puerto Rican parents, and with established residency in Puerto Rico, is *by natural right*, one of the constituents of the "people of Puerto Rico," which created the [Puerto Rican] Constitution, and as such a member of the Puerto Rican political community with an inherent right to participate in its electoral processes. The Puerto Rican political community is defined better by the citizenship of Puerto Rico than by U. S. citizenship. That is "a fact not subject to historical rectifications" and "a reality which no law can change."[160]

"The idea," the judge added, "that we Puerto Ricans constitute a community with our own identity and culture has roots that go back several centuries. . . . We the members of that community define ourselves precisely as Puerto Ricans, with Puerto Rico as the center of our aspirations."[161] The Supreme Court of Puerto Rico, in a

---

But see H.R. 4765, a bill approved by the U.S. House of Representatives, titled "Puerto Rico Self-Determination Act," which, if it had finally become law, would have authorized the government of Puerto Rico to extend the right to vote in the plebiscite to Puerto Ricans not residing in Puerto Rico. Such persons were defined to include "those born in Puerto Rico or those who have at least one parent who was born in Puerto Rico" (H.R. 4765, 101st Cong., 2nd Sess., § 3, 1990; *see also* U.S. CONGRESS, HOUSE COMMITTEE ON INTERIOR AND INSULAR AFFAIRS, REPORT TOGETHER WITH ADDITIONAL VIEWS TO ACCOMPANY H.R. 4765, 101st Cong., 2nd Sess. at 15–16 (1990).

[157] Dr. Miriam Ramírez de Ferrer, to whom reference was made in *supra* note 125.

[158] *See* P.R. LAWS ANN. tit. 16, § 3053.

[159] Ramirez de Ferrer v. Mari Bras, Civ. Num. KAC 96-0856 (1996). The decision was rendered by Superior Court Judge Angel G. Hermida.

[160] *Id.* at 25 (emphasis in the original; translation supplied).

[161] *Id.* at 27, 29.

divided decision, affirmed, with a technical modification, the lower court's judgment.[162] Mari Bras's vote was cast in the 1996 general elections and eventually counted. His example was followed by others. But in their cases the U.S. State Department and U.S. consular offices have refused either to process their petitions or to emit the certificates of loss of citizenship.[163]

Finally, in June 1998, the U.S. State Department issued a letter to Mari Bras vacating the Certificate of Loss of Nationality that it had extended him in 1995. Among other things, the letter informed the Puerto Rican attorney that by refusing to register as an "alien" in Puerto Rico, he had failed to demonstrate that he in effect intended to relinquish his U.S. citizenship. The State Department added that it considered Mari Bras a U.S. citizen "by virtue of [his] birth in Puerto Rico."[164] Mari Bras maintains that because of his Puerto Rican nationality and Puerto Rican citizenship, he has an "inalienable right" to live in Puerto Rico.[165] "The identity of Puerto Ricans is the kernel of this debate," Mari Bras affirmed, and he announced that he planned to take his case to an international human rights forum.[166]

The citizenship provision of the Jones Act of 1917 can be interpreted as an attempt to impose an identity from above. The construction of this legal identity was not negotiated at the official normative level. However, it has been "negotiated" in the terrain of ordinary social practice.[167] Many Puerto Ricans have actively assumed the prescribed identity and have made it work to their individual advantage.[168] One would have to distinguish in this respect among social classes or groupings, for as Minow has observed, "each person is situated differently in relation to constraints. . . . The weight of one's own experiences and social position and the press of others' expectations and practices stack the negotiations over identity."[169]

In Puerto Rico different social groups may have responded differently to the situation. But throughout the entire society any observer can detect specific ways of managing the category of U.S. citizenship to produce an economic, political, social, or psychological benefit. Of course, the imposition has also met with resistance, from the most violent to the most subtle. However, the fact that many people in Puerto Rico "negotiate" in many ways their relationship to the concept of U.S. citizenship

---

[162] Ramírez de Ferrer v. Mari Bras, 97 J.T.S. 134 (1997).

[163] See Lozada Colón v. U.S. Department of State, 2 F. Supp. 2nd 43 (D.D.C. 1998), aff'd 170 F. 3rd 191 (D.C. Cir., 1999).

[164] Robert Friedman, *Renunciation Oath Set Aside in Case of U.S. Citizen Mari Bras*, SAN JUAN STAR, June 5, 1998, at 8.

[165] *Id.*; Robert Friedman, *Mari Bras Says Reversed Ruling Violates His Citizenship Rights*, SAN JUAN STAR, June 7, 1998, at 6.

[166] Rubén Berríos, president of the Puerto Rican Independence Party, which does not recommend the renunciation of U.S. citizenship as a political tactic, has been cited as stating that the Mari Bras case is a clear indication that Puerto Rico is a colony of the United States and that the only way to secure Puerto Rican citizenship is through political independence. In the same context, he was also quoted as expressing his belief that U.S. citizenship could be preserved under certain circumstances in an independent Puerto Rico. *Berríos: Decision on Mari Bras Shows P.R. Still a Colony*, SAN JUAN STAR, June 7, 1998, at 6.

[167] For an excellent analysis of the "negotiated quality of identities," see Minow, *supra* note 141. The author examines how people "negotiate their identities" in the course of their daily lives. See *id.* at 127.

[168] Minow has suggested that "people with little power may also find latitude for action by creating expectations in others or by remaking their own desires in line with others' expectations." *Id.* at 106.

[169] *Id.* at 110.

should not be taken as an indication that they are readily willing to forsake other important identitary factors. As Minow perceptively suggested,

> signs of assimilation by a group treated as less powerful than the majority deserve a second look because they may indicate subtle acts of resistance and accommodation by people seeking to retain an independent identity without risking conflict or further suppression.[170]

The theoretical conclusion must be that structures and discourses of domination are not constructed solely "from above." Those subjected to them many times participate actively in their production and have a capacity to affect their form and even their consequences. Very often this is the only kind of resistance possible (or considered possible) under the circumstances. One of the most dramatic historical examples of this phenomenon was the creolization of European culture throughout the Americas. In fact, Puerto Ricans had been the product of this complex process during the Spanish regime. Managing citizenship and the other elements of U.S. political culture has been a key feature of the process of recreation of a Puerto Rican identity during the 20th century.

Construction of a New Juridicopolitical Reality

The highest legal decision makers in the United States interpreted the provision granting U.S. citizenship to Puerto Ricans as an act of little juridical consequence as far as the constitutional and political condition of Puerto Rico was concerned. This does not mean, however, that citizenship has been devoid of legal implications. First, like any other legal event, it has contributed to create a normative context within which individual and collective action is to take place. Moreover, both as text and as performative speech act,[171] the provision operates within a broader normative universe, within a hermeneutic tradition (that is, a particular history of acts of interpretation), and within an aggregate of practices facilitated by the normative situation it created. That wider normative framework, that interpretative tradition, and that ensemble of practices condition any further acts of interpretation and can place restraints even upon the metropolitan state itself. This is one of the ways in which law becomes part of the social world.

The phenomenon became apparent in an extraordinary fashion in 1989 during the course of hearings held by the Committee on Energy and Natural Resources of the U.S. Senate on several bills proposing a plebiscite on the political status of Puerto Rico and during the intense public discussion they generated.[172] Each of the three

---

[170] *Id.* at 115.

[171] *See* JEAN FRANCOIS LYOTARD, THE POSTMODERN CONDITION: A REPORT ON KNOWLEDGE (1984); PETER GOODRICH, LEGAL DISCOURSE: STUDIES IN LINGUISTICS, RHETORIC AND LEGAL ANALYSIS (1987); Bourdieu, *Force of Law, supra* note 140.

[172] For detailed information on the entire process, see *Hearings, supra* note 119; U.S. CONGRESS, HOUSE COMMITTEE ON INTERIOR AND INSULAR AFFAIRS, *supra* note 156; U.S. GENERAL ACCOUNTING OFFICE, PUERTO RICO: INFORMATION FOR STATUS DELIBERATIONS (1989); 1 JUAN M. GARCÍA PASSALACQUA & C. RIVERA LUGO, PUERTO RICO Y LOS ESTADOS UNIDOS: EL PROCESO DE CONSULTA Y NEGOCIACIÓN DE 1989 Y 1990 (1990); Álvarez, *supra* note 7; Harry Turner, *The Odyssey of Puerto Rico's Plebiscite: 1988–1990*, SAN JUAN STAR, Dec. 23, 1990, at 1; J. Schmalz, *With Encouragement*

principal political parties in Puerto Rico—the Popular Democratic Party, which endorses the present *Estado Libre Asociado*; the New Progressive Party, which favors statehood; and the Puerto Rican Independence Party—were asked to submit drafts of the terms and conditions they wished to be included in the plebiscite bill regarding their respective status preferences. The proposals of the political parties became the subject matter of the hearings held by the Senate Committee.

During one of the public sessions, the committee chairman, Senator J. Bennett Johnston, a Democrat from Louisiana, announced that, at the committee's request, the Congressional Research Service (CRS) had conducted a study[173] that concluded that the American citizenship of most Puerto Ricans would not be constitutionally protected if Puerto Rico's residents opted for independence.[174] The rationale for the CRS study was based on a distinction established by the U.S. Supreme Court between what it has labeled "statutory citizenship" and the status of citizen acquired by virtue of the provisions of the first sentence of the Fourteenth Amendment to the Constitution, which declares that all persons born or naturalized in the United States are American citizens.[175] In *Afroyim v. Rusk*,[176] a 1967 decision, the Court had decided that a U.S. citizen may not be deprived of that citizenship against his or her will. However, in *Rogers* it had clarified that the principle applied only to Fourteenth Amendment, first sentence citizens and not to those who become citizens by virtue of a statute. The CRS memorandum argued that because, according to the decisions in *Downes v. Bidwell* and *Balzac v. Porto Rico*, Puerto Rico was not a part of the United States, people born there cannot be considered to have been born in the United States. Therefore, they are not Fourteenth Amendment, first sentence citizens. Accordingly, their citizenship, of statutory origin, can be revoked against their will.

The CRS memorandum caused an uproar in Puerto Rico. As a commentator correctly noted, "the potential political impact of the memorandum went far beyond the issue of independence."[177] For "if the Constitution does not constrain congressional discretion in decision making with regard to the citizenship status of Puerto Ricans, this is due to the legal structure defining Puerto Rico's *present* political status of commonwealth."[178] This explains why not only the Puerto Rican Independence Party, but also the Popular Democratic Party, the pro-Commonwealth party, objected vigorously to the conclusions drawn by the CRS. Both parties filed their responses with the Senate Committee.[179]

---

of U.S., *Puerto Rico Seeks an Identity*, NEW YORK TIMES, July 10, 1989, at A1; Beatriz De la Torre, *Plebiscite Born in Carter Era: Status Seen in Domain of Foreign Policy*, SAN JUAN STAR, July 1, 1989, at 1; Carlos Gallisá, *Ha muerto el plebiscito*, CLARIDAD, Feb. 22 to 28, 1991, at 12.

[173] U.S. CONGRESSIONAL RESEARCH SERVICE, DISCRETION OF CONGRESS RESPECTING CITIZENSHIP STATUS OF PUERTO RICO (1989) (CRS MEMO). A second memorandum followed addressing some of the criticisms leveled at the original one. Legal Memorandum of John H. Killian, Senior Specialist, American Constitutional Law, CRS, American Law Division, November 15, 1990.

[174] 1 *Hearings*, *supra* note 119, at 180.

[175] *See* Rogers v. Bellei, 401 U.S. 815 (1971).

[176] Afroyim v. Rusk, 387 U.S. 253 (1967).

[177] Álvarez, *supra* note 7, at 315.

[178] *Id.* (emphasis in the original).

[179] *See id.* at 315–16 n.23. For journalistic accounts and commentaries on the polemic *see, e.g.*, Maritza Díaz Alcaide, *Polémica por la permanencia de la ciudadanía*, EL MUNDO, June 11, 1989, at 6; *Independentistas insistirán en doble ciudadanía*, EL MUNDO, June 11, 1989, at 8; Benny Frankie Cerezo, *Sobre la ciudadanía*, EL MUNDO, June 11, 1989, at 42.

The Puerto Rican Independence Party submitted a position paper refuting the CRS opinion.[180] Its author, Professor José Julián Álvarez González, formulated a well-reasoned argument regarding the legal complications entailed by a unilateral decision to revoke citizenship, even in the case of independence. The paper accepted the premise that the citizenship most Puerto Ricans hold is of statutory character. In that sense, they would not be protected by the citizenship provision of the Fourteenth Amendment. However, the author argued, other constitutional provisions (like the due process clause, the equal protection guarantee, and the prohibition against bills of attainder) could be interpreted to preclude Congress from either depriving Puerto Ricans of their citizenship unilaterally or forcing them to choose between their U.S. citizenship and the citizenship of the new independent Puerto Rican nation.[181]

The Álvarez González paper also highlighted some of the "practical problems" that could effectively thwart any attempt by Congress to limit the recognition of dual citizenship only to those Puerto Ricans holding U.S. citizenship before the proclamation of independence.[182] Those problems include the difficulties that may be created for divided families with members living in both the United States and Puerto Rico who might want to reunite after independence. What would be the fate of Puerto Ricans living in the United States who might want to return to Puerto Rico and, once there, retain U.S. citizenship without remaining "foreigners in their own land"? What about those who renounce U.S. citizenship and some day want to rejoin their relatives in the United States? Álvarez asked whether Congress would "make it harder for Puerto Ricans than for any other nationality to apply for permanent residence and, eventually, for naturalization." And what would Congress do about the children of those who retain their U.S. citizenship but remain in Puerto Rico? Would Congress be willing to approve an amendment "tailored to exclude Puerto Ricans, and Puerto Ricans alone, from the *jus sanguinis* principles" established in the Immigration and Naturalization Act of 1952?[183]

The cited examples, according to Álvarez, demonstrate that the effects of the decision to grant citizenship cannot be easily undone.[184] He concluded with an endorsement of dual citizenship as the "only practical solution for an independent

---

[180] Preliminary Position Paper Submitted by the Puerto Rican Independence Party to the Committee on Energy and Natural Resources of the United States Senate Concerning the March 9, 1989, Memorandum of the Congressional Research Service on the Subject of the Citizenship Status of Puerto Ricans, 14 June 1989. The paper was written by José Julián Álvarez González, professor of constitutional law at the University of Puerto Rico School of Law. An expanded version was published later in the *Harvard Journal on Legislation* under the title *The Empire Strikes Out: Congressional Ruminations on the Citizenship Status of Puerto Ricans, see* Álvarez, *supra* note 7. Further references will be to the journal article.

[181] Álvarez, *supra* note 7, at 337–57. The American constitutional scholar Lawrence Tribe made analogous arguments on behalf of the Popular Democratic Party in a letter addressed to the Senate Committee. *See* 3 *Hearings, supra* note 119, at 60; Álvarez, *supra* note 7, at 315–16 n.23. See also the written statement submitted by the president of the House of Representatives of Puerto Rico, José R. Jarabo, *in* 2 *Hearings, supra* note 119, at 86.

[182] Álvarez, *supra* note 7, at 357–61.

[183] *Id.* at 357–58.

[184] *Id.* at 360. The author added the following comment: "There are human, historical, and political factors that need to be assessed. Most importantly, the cost of undoing the 1917 decision should not fall on the Republic of Puerto Rico or on Puerto Rican families." *Id.*

Puerto Rico."[185] Of course, as the author himself acknowledged, any argument about the resolution of the perceived constitutional and legal problems relating to the collective deprivation of citizenship ultimately involves an exercise on prediction regarding the course the U.S. Supreme Court may elect to take, if the problem ever arose.[186] The highest U.S. tribunal may eventually decide to sanction (or refuse to intervene in) whatever decision is made in this regard by Congress and the executive, as it did in the *Insular Cases*, and as it has done so often, especially concerning matters related to the foreign policy interests of the United States.[187] However, as Álvarez and others have suggested, it could not do so without having to confront, or choosing to ignore, fundamental issues arising from the American normative order and its constitutional discourse.

Developments surrounding consideration of the bill later introduced by Representative Don Young to provide for a plebiscite began to clarify the inclinations of a substantial number of members of Congress regarding the legal interpretations and policy solutions that could eventually be adopted to address the complex problems raised by the 1989 CRS memorandum and the discussion it precipitated. Thus, in a report rendered to accompany H.R. 3024, the original Young Bill, the Committee on Resources of the U.S. House of Representatives fully incorporated the CRS thesis about the statutory nature of Puerto Rican U.S. citizenship. It also stressed the wide latitude Congress enjoys when dealing with citizenship issues in the case of the territories. Citing the CRS memorandum, the report stated that it was "self-evident" that the "current U.S. citizenship of persons born in Puerto Rico during the territorial period is restricted and less-than-equal." It interpreted *Gonzalez v. Williams*,[188] one of the *Insular Cases* discussed in Part II, as establishing that Puerto Ricans have U.S. nationality, but that the specific citizenship of the population of the territory "is subject to the discretion of Congress under the Territorial Clause." In 1917, the report continued,

> Congress ended the limited territorial citizenship of Puerto Ricans, but the U.S. citizenship granted by statute since 1917 is limited, restricted and less-than-equal citizenship. Full equal citizenship, irrevocable in the same legal and political sense as citizenship due to birth in a state of the union, comes only with full integration of Puerto Rico into the union.[189]

---

[185] *Id.* at 365. This was the position held by the Puerto Rican Independence Party (PIP) throughout the remainder of the 1989–1991 process. More recently, the PIP has modified somewhat its position, admitting the possibility that U.S. citizenship be retained by those who already possess it, but that Congress could terminate statutory citizenship prospectively for those not yet born.

[186] *Id.* at 343–45. The author quite appropriately quoted Oliver Wendell Holmes. *Id.* at 343 n.141.

[187] *See* Mora v. McNamara, 389 U.S. 934 (1967); J. Newberry, *Constitutional Law: Political Question Doctrine and Conduct of Foreign Policy*, 25 HARV. INT'L. L. J. 433 (1984). For a Supreme Court decision partly based on the rationale of the *Insular Cases* sustaining actions of American federal law enforcement agents in Mexican territory, see United States v. Álvarez Macháin, 504 U.S. 655 (1992). For a federal district court decision refraining to judge on the merits a controversy relating to the U.S. State Department's refusal to issue a certificate of loss of nationality to a Puerto Rican-born person who had renounced his U.S. citizenship, see Lozada Colón v. State Department, *supra* note 163. The deciding judge ruled that the matter involved the "much debated political question as to the status of Puerto Rico and its nationals in relation to the United States" and recommended that the plaintiff seek "another, more appropriate forum" to air his views. *Id.* at 46.

[188] *González*, 192 U.S. 1 (1904)

[189] U.S. CONGRESS, HOUSE COMMITTEE ON RESOURCES, REPORT TOGETHER WITH DISSENTING AND ADDITIONAL VIEWS TO ACCOMPANY H.R. 3024, 104th Cong., 2nd Sess. at 33–34 (1996).

The report added that because the Constitution has been partially extended to Puerto Rico, including fundamental rights of due process and equal protection, Congress "obviously cannot exercise its discretion in an arbitrary and irrational way."[190] But election by the Puerto Rican people of a status that implies separate sovereignty would be a reason legitimate enough to alter or modify the statutory U.S. citizenship extended to them. Of course, the report acknowledged, Congress "must preserve the right of statutory citizenship for those who individually do not want to participate in the change of nationality along with the general population." But even in such a case, it concluded, such citizenship still would not be equal to that of those born in the United States, and Congress could take action to define its nature and prerogatives. In any event, retention of U.S. citizenship after Puerto Rican separate sovereignty is attained would be limited to the lifetime of those individuals so choosing. The report underscored the conclusion that the "statutory right of U. S. citizenship based on birth in Puerto Rico as it is today, and as it will be if the voters approve separate sovereignty, is not full Constitutionally-protected citizenship."[191]

H.R. 856, the bill finally approved by the House of Representatives on March 4, 1998, adhered to these views. It did not provide for any type of collective dual citizenship in a separately sovereign Puerto Rico. It prescribed that if the latter were the choice adopted, U.S. nationality and citizenship would be ended along with U.S. sovereignty. The bill specified that birth in Puerto Rico and relationship to persons with "statutory" U.S. citizenship by birth in the former territory would not be bases for U.S. nationality or citizenship. By way of exception, persons who had such citizenship would have a statutory (as opposed to a constitutional) right to retain U.S. nationality and citizenship for life, by entitlement or election, as provided by Congress, on condition of continued allegiance to the United States. The House bill further indicated that professing allegiance to any other sovereign nation (including the sovereign nation of Puerto Rico) would be grounds for forfeiting such statutory citizenship.[192]

These provisions were intended to address the claims that those who already possess U.S. citizenship have entitlements that merit some degree of protection, while foreclosing the possibility of creating a wholesale situation of dual citizenship in a sovereign Puerto Rico. A germane bill submitted to the U.S. Senate took a similar approach but was never voted on.[193] Because no legislation was finally approved, many of the questions raised still remain open. However, the positions taken by the slim majority that favored the Young Bill and by the congressional reports produced during the process will likely have significant bearing on future attempts at legislating on the matter.

What the entire discussion indicates is that the decision to impose U.S. citizenship on Puerto Ricans in 1917 has created a complex web of legal problems that have become part of the political reality within which any decision on the future political status of Puerto Rico will have to be made. In this sense, the citizenship

---

[190] *Id.* at 34. In this sense, the report seems to incorporate some of the legal warnings advanced by the position paper submitted by the Puerto Rican Independence Party during the previous Johnston hearings.

[191] U.S. CONGRESS, HOUSE COMMITTEE ON RESOURCES, *supra* note 189, at 34–35.

[192] H.R. 856, 105th Cong., 2nd Sess. § 4(a)(B)(4) (1998).

[193] S. 472, 105th Cong., 1st Sess. § 2 (d)(B)(4) (1997). It is far from settled that the solution proposed would effectively solve all the problems raised by the Puerto Rican Independence Party position paper.

provision, in combination with other fundamental norms and principles of the U.S. legal system, has become part of the normative context in which American colonialism operates in Puerto Rican society and with which any decolonization process would have to contend. As the cited House report acknowledged, sharing the view Álvarez expressed, the question of nationality and citizenship has become "one of the most difficult issues to address" in the self-determination process of the people of Puerto Rico, so that "untying the knot with regard to citizenship is going to be difficult."[194] This statement reveals an awareness that, despite the doctrine of the plenary powers of Congress over the territories, certain actions taken by Congress under such authority condition the possibilities or the form of further congressional intervention.

In other words, the exercise of power by the metropolitan state creates a context for its own future actions. Sometimes that context can have limiting effects, such as the legal and political problems that would be involved in revoking U.S. citizenship of Puerto Ricans who already possess it. The stumbling blocks to this action are legal, political, and cultural. From this perspective, the situation created by the citizenship provision can be considered a prime example of how those who construct a particular type of discourse in the exercise of power can become subject to the conditioning effects of their own discourse.

Citizenship and the Reproduction of Consent

One of the main arguments of this book is that, from its inception, the American colonial venture in Puerto Rico has been a hegemonic project in the Gramscian sense. In other words, the agents of that venture have sought to create mechanisms capable of inducing the active consent to—or a relatively generalized acceptance of—American domination among the Puerto Rican population.

The reproduction of consent to American rule, especially after the 1940s, has been the result of the complex articulation of multiple factors. Some of them relate to the material conditions of existence that have become part of the experience of several generations of Puerto Ricans, particularly after the social, economic, and political transformations the country underwent following World War II. Those material conditions include the relative economic growth of the country and an increase in the standard of living of significant sectors of the population, secured through their access to education, better sanitary conditions, higher paying jobs, a relatively modern infrastructure, and a variety of government social and economic programs. Other factors have to do with the set of representations—the ensemble of categories of perception and evaluation of reality[195]—that have constituted the dominant frameworks for the interpretation of experience. One such representation is the way Puerto Ricans explain to themselves how those material conditions have been achieved and what the connection is between those developments and the country's relationship to the United States. Other representations involve how Puerto Ricans construe their needs, what they consider legitimate or adequate means for satisfying them, and what they deem to be the range of the desirable and the possible.

---

[194] HOUSE COMMITTEE ON RESOURCES, *supra* note 189, at 31.

[195] BOURDIEU, IN OTHER WORDS, *supra* note 140.

U.S. citizenship has played a significant role in Puerto Ricans' ongoing consent to American rule. Citizenship has operated at the intersection of both the realm of experience and the domain of representation to help construct particular interpretations of the social world in the Puerto Rican community. In those interpretations, many people associate U.S. citizenship with tangible economic, political, social, and cultural benefits. From passports, to security, to rights, there is a wide spectrum of benefits that are seen as flowing directly from the condition of U.S. citizenship.[196] In other words, U.S. citizenship has been closely tied to the satisfaction of needs.[197] It has been appraised as making the desirable possible. The link to the United States, exemplified and cemented by the legal status of U.S. citizen, is thus regarded as one of the main circumstances, if not the principal one, that makes those gains come true. The bond is, therefore, positively valued. The conditions for its continuation are readily accepted. To that extent, the status of American citizen has been a prime factor in the reproduction of consent to American rule.

This consent is not necessarily based on a distorted vision of reality, amounting to some type of "false consciousness" that impedes the majority from seeing the "true light."[198] Rather, it is the product of a rational and emotional calculation, at different levels of consciousness, that places a premium on certain needs and makes a pragmatic choice.[199] The situation goes even further. U.S. citizenship has become an important value in both its material and its symbolic senses. Materially, it is seen as adding to the aggregation of goods individually and collectively enjoyed in the community. Symbolically, it is viewed as opening a cultural space that allows for the discursive validation of a variety of claims and for the realization of certain types of relationships. One of those claims has to do with greater political participation. One kind of relationship that that cultural space is thought to foster are legal relationships, that is, the configuration of a zone of interaction based on the notion of rights, particularly vis-à-vis the metropolitan state and the colonial government.[200] The value of U.S. citizenship is appreciated to the extreme that the mere possibility of its loss generates fears and anxieties. As the position on dual citizenship taken by the Puerto Rican Independence Party during the 1989–1991 plebiscite process clearly indicated, at that point even political independence was inconceivable to many without retention of the citizenship of the former colonial power. Important political

---

[196] See MORRIS, *supra* note 149, at 110, 112 (quoting participants in focus groups referring to passports, travel, and security as advantages bestowed by citizenship); Duchesne et al., *supra* note 134, at 39 (arguing that the benefits of U.S. citizenship include the "conquest" of democratic, civil, labor, and women's rights as well as access to the "social resources" of the United States).

[197] Habermas has convincingly explained the relationship between legitimation and the satisfaction of needs in late modern societies. *See* JÜRGEN HABERMAS, LEGITIMATION CRISIS (1988); *see also* chapter 6 of this book, n.2 and accompanying text; Bourdieu, *Force of Law*, *supra* note 140, at 805, 840 (the efficacy of law as symbol depends on its association to "real needs and interests"). For a previous work applying these notions to the case of Puerto Rico, including the question of citizenship, *see* Rivera Ramos, *supra* note 117.

[198] For a similar argument, see Ramón Grosfoguel, *The Divorce of Nationalist Discourses from the Puerto Rican People: A Sociohistorical Perspective, in* PUERTO RICAN JAM, *supra* note 110, at 57–58. Grosfoguel argued that Puerto Ricans know very well what their alternatives are and that the majority actively opt for various forms of close association with the United States and the preservation of their U.S. citizenship. *Id.* at 57–58, 67.

[199] *See id.* at 68.

[200] This notion will be developed further in chapter 8.

events that took place during the 1990s further corroborated the fact that U.S. citizenship has become internalized as a value by a substantial sector of Puerto Rican society. We will examine some of those events in this section.

The acceptance of American rule is not necessarily the result of "false consciousness," but that does not mean that the interpretations of a substantial number of Puerto Ricans about the meaning of citizenship and about the importance of the relationship with the United States has not been influenced by discourses expressly aimed at constructing the worldview of which those interpretations partake. It is true that the social construction of American citizenship as value has involved the complex interaction of the experiences and practices described above. But it is also the case that that construction has owed much to a particular official rhetoric that has emphasized the virtues of being an American citizen. Thus, for example, the Preamble to the Constitution of Puerto Rico, which came into effect in 1952, expressly proclaims that the people of Puerto Rico consider as "determining factors" in their lives the citizenship of the United States of America and the "aspiration continuously to enrich our democratic heritage in the individual and collective enjoyment of its rights and privileges." Another determining factor, according to the Preamble, is the people of Puerto Rico's "loyalty to the principles" of the U.S. Constitution. That rhetoric has been reproduced in the public discourse of the pro-Commonwealth and prostatehood political parties.[201] The events narrated in this section substantiate some of the repercussions of that discourse.

Measurement of the long-term effects of a particular legal provision is normally a very difficult matter. However, those interested in the social study of legal and political processes in Puerto Rico had a rare opportunity to confirm several important hypotheses in the public discussion that began in January 1989 with the proposal to hold a federally sanctioned plebiscite on political status and extended to December 1991, when the government of Puerto Rico held a referendum to ascertain the opinion and will of Puerto Rican voters on several political and cultural issues. The evidence generated in those processes included manifold official documents and statements (many of them already cited here), legislative and executive acts, news reports, public debates, journalistic and academic commentary, media surveys, publicity campaigns, and the result of the 1991 referendum itself, with its varied interpretations. Following is a succinct summary of the relevant features of that process regarding the specific question of citizenship.

The publication in early June 1989 of the CRS memorandum on the nature of the U.S. citizenship held by Puerto Ricans produced a very strong reaction in Puerto Rico. One of its implications, as pointed out above, was that the citizenship currently held by most Puerto Ricans was vulnerable to any action by the U.S. Congress if the latter wished to modify or even revoke it. The governing party, the Popular Democratic Party, objected to the CRS's conclusions. The Puerto Rican press re-

---

[201] In its 1980 party platform, the New Progressive Party solemnly declared as its duty to "strengthen continuously the rights inherent to our American citizenship and the bonds that tie us permanently to our fellow citizens of the 50 states." *Programa de Gobierno del Partido Nuevo Progresista para el cuatrienio 1981–84*, at 6 (1980). The 1988 Popular Democratic Party Platform, in turn, stated that "Puerto Rico values its relationship with the United States of America, whose citizenship it shares" and declared the "inviolability of the common American citizenship." *Partido Popular Democrático, Programa de Gobierno 1989–1992: Vamos por buen camino* 3, 38 (1988). Jointly both parties usually garner more than 90% of the votes in Puerto Rican elections.

corded the apprehensions of many Puerto Ricans over the prospect of losing their citizenship. The reaction was so vehement that Senators Johnston and McClure, the chairman and the ranking Republican member, respectively, of the U.S. Senate Committee on Energy and Natural Resources, felt the need to declare publicly in Puerto Rico that the U.S. citizenship of Puerto Ricans under either statehood or Commonwealth was deemed unrepealable by the U.S. Congress.[202] The CRS memorandum, Senator Johnston commented, referred only to the situation that would emerge in the event Puerto Ricans voted for the option of independence in the proposed plebiscite.[203] The "assurances" were given by the Senators the day that their committee was to commence hearings in San Juan on the pending plebiscite bills.

During the hearings, prominent leaders of the governing Popular Democratic Party made it a point to congratulate the Senators for their stance and to stress their view that even under Commonwealth the American citizenship of Puerto Ricans should be "guaranteed."[204] Probably due to their assessment of the complexities of the issue and the vigorous response registered in Puerto Rico, eventually both Senators Johnston and McClure would be won over to the idea that even in the case of independence Puerto Ricans should be able to retain their American citizenship. Thus, they subscribed the "dual citizenship" proposal of the Puerto Rican Independence Party.[205] Eventually the House of Representatives would abandon the idea of dual citizenship.[206] But the discussion brought forcefully to the public's mind in Puerto Rico and, to a certain degree, in Washington the strong attachment that many Puerto Ricans professed to their American citizenship as a value to be preserved.

The point would be brought home even more clearly in December 1991. After a 2-year process, the plebiscite bills died in the U.S. Congress due largely to differences in approach between the leadership of the House and the Senate. It suffered also from the reservations about, and in some cases outright opposition to, some of the bill's provisions expressed by influential members of Congress.[207] The failure of

---

[202] As has been noted above, this view has been modified by the official statements produced during the process initiated by the Young Bill, first H.R. 3024 (1996) and later H.R. 856 (1997).

[203] Notes taken by the author during the press conference held by Senators Johnston and McClure in San Juan, Puerto Rico, on June 16, 1989. *See also Johnston: Citizenship Safe*, SAN JUAN STAR, June 17, 1989, at 1; Maritza Díaz Alcaide, *Johnston lamenta "mal entendido*," EL MUNDO, June 17, 1989, at 3; J. Bennet Johnston, *Irrevocable la ciudadanía*, EL MUNDO, June 17, 1989, at 27 (an article published by the U.S. senator in one of the main Spanish-speaking newspapers in the island). *See also* 1 GARCÍA PASSALACQUA & RIVERA LUGO, *supra* note 172, at 13; 2 *Id.* at 39.

[204] 2 *Hearings*, *supra* note 119, at 41, 85.

[205] However, Edward S. G. Dennis, acting deputy attorney general of the United States, testifying before the committee at a later date "on behalf of the [Bush] Administration," voiced the latter's opposition to the dual citizenship concept because it would "obscure the reality of independence for the Puerto Rican voter" and it would be "fundamentally inconsistent with granting full independence to the Island." Statement of Edward S. G. Dennis, *in* 3 *Hearings*, *supra* note 119, at 27–28.

[206] H.R. 856, 105th Cong., 2nd Sess. (1998); HOUSE COMMITTEE ON RESOURCES, *supra* note 189.

[207] The Senate Energy and Natural Resources Committee reported favorably, on a close vote of 11 to 8, S. 712, which contained detailed provisions about each of the alternatives to be presented to the Puerto Rican electorate. The House of Representatives approved on a voice vote a much shorter bill, H.R. 4765, which did not specify the substantive content of each of the status options, providing only for the procedure to be followed. The chairman of the Senate committee refused to consider the House version, and the differences could not be reconciled in time to have a plebiscite law before the desired date.

During the course of the debates and discussions it became evident that some of the most important

Congress to provide for the plebiscite was interpreted by many as a blow to the statehood movement particularly.[208] With general elections due in Puerto Rico in November 1992, apparently the principal leaders of the Popular Democratic and the Puerto Rican Independence Parties felt the need to foreclose the possibility that a victory of the prostatehood New Progressive Party would give way to a plebiscite organized locally including only the statehood option (a plebiscite of the yes-or-no variety).

In this context, the leaders of the Popular Democratic Party and the Puerto Rican Independence Party sought to obtain a binding expression from the Puerto Rican electorate concerning several "principles" that would guide future attempts to solve the political status of the island. Originally they obtained the consent of the New Progressive Party leadership. But, partly as a result of an internal conflict within the latter's ranks and a subsequent change at the party's helm, the New Progressive Party withdrew from the project. The governing Popular Democratic Party and the legislative representation of the Puerto Rican Independence Party, against the protestations of the New Progressive Party, proceeded to approve a law providing for a referendum to be held in December 1991.[209] Billed as a "Referendum on Democratic Rights," the event was clearly an aftermath of the public discussion that had engaged much of the energy of government, parties, and people alike during consideration of the plebiscite bills.

The electorate would be asked to vote yes or no to a list of "democratic rights"

---

concerns in each chamber related to the statehood option. Some had objected to what they considered a bias toward that alternative in the bill reported originally out of Senator Johnston's committee. Others expressed reservations about the "cost" of statehood to the U.S. treasury (particularly by virtue of a projected increase in social welfare benefits for the residents of the new state). Still others opposed firmly any suggestion that the proposed plebiscite law be self-executing, that is, that the winning formula be implemented automatically, without further action to the effect on the part of the U.S. Congress. This latter provision was found problematic particularly regarding the statehood option. A fundamental concern that emerged with peculiar force in the final phases of the process had to do with the obvious cultural differences between Puerto Rico and the United States, a fact viewed by many as particularly problematic for, if not an insurmountable obstacle to, the statehood solution. *See, generally, Hearings, supra* note 119; GARCÍA PASSALACQUA & RIVERA LUGO, *supra* note 172.

The proposed plebiscite also encountered some opposition in Puerto Rico, especially from the more radical proindependence groups, from sectors of the academic community, and from organizations and individuals active in diverse social movements. The main criticisms referred to what was perceived as the excessive control of the process by the U.S. Congress; the almost exclusive role conferred to the political parties, to the detriment of other social movements, organizations, and sectors of Puerto Rican society; the reluctance of the U.S. Congress to admit expressly that it was dealing with a colonial problem and to recognize the applicability of international law and the need for the active participation of international organs, such as the United Nations; and the failure to incorporate into the discussions important social and economic problems faced by the Puerto Rican community, such as the need to guarantee environmental safeguards, human rights, and the demilitarization of Puerto Rico under all the formulas. For examples of the various positions, *see* Statement to the Senate Committee by Carlos Gallisá, secretary general of the Puerto Rican Socialist Party, *in* 2 *Hearings, supra* note 119, at 131–39; Statement to the Senate by Roberto Roldán Burgos, general coordinator of the Instituto Puertorriqueño de Derechos Civiles (Puerto Rican Civil Rights Institute), *id.* at 446–65; MOVIMIENTO SOCIALISTA DE TRABAJADORES, NUESTRA POSICIÓN SOBRE EL PLEBISCITO (1989); Ivonne Acosta, Afirmación Socialista Unitaria, *Plebiscito, estado y lucha popular* (1989); Carmen Gautier Mayoral, *Apathy over Plebiscite*, July/Aug. CARIBBEAN CONTACT 15 (1990); Wilfredo Mattos Cintrón, *The Puerto Rican Plebiscite* (1990).

[208] *See* GARCÍA PASSALACQUA & RIVERA LUGO, *supra* note 172, at 378; *see also supra* note 207.

[209] Pub. L. No. 85 (1991), also known as the "Guarantee of Democratic Rights Act."

that the U.S. and Puerto Rican governments should honor in case of any change of status. The yes vote would signal agreement with all the rights listed, while the no vote would mean a rejection of the entire list.[210] It was not possible to vote separately for each of the "guarantees" subject to vote. The six "rights" were contained in Article 2 of the act and were defined as (a) the inalienable right to determine freely and democratically the political status of Puerto Rico; (b) the right to choose a status of "full political dignity without colonial or territorial subordination to the plenary powers of Congress"; (c) the right to vote for the three recognized status alternatives —Commonwealth, statehood and independence—based on the sovereignty of the people of Puerto Rico; (d) the right to demand that the winning alternative in a status consultation obtain more than half the votes cast; (e) the right that any consultation on status shall guarantee, under any alternative, Puerto Rican culture, the Spanish language, and the country's identity, including its current independent participation in international sports events; and (f) the right that any consultation on status shall guarantee, under any option, "the American citizenship safeguarded by the Constitution of the United States of America." The inclusion of the provision on citizenship was a clear indication that the leadership of both the procommonwealth Popular Democratic Party and the Puerto Rican Independence Party considered that no change in status would be possible without guaranteeing the permanence of American citizenship.

The prostatehood New Progressive Party took a vehement stance against the list of "democratic rights" and organized a vigorous campaign in favor of the no option in the referendum. Despite the provision on citizenship (which the New Progressive Party characterized as a hoax, arguing that only statehood could provide an effective and permanent guarantee of U.S. citizenship), the prostatehood forces interpreted the referendum as an attempt to "separate" Puerto Rico from the United States. In fact, the gist of the campaign for the no vote consisted in asserting that a yes majority would be considered by the United States as a desire on the part of Puerto Ricans to follow a more independent course in the future. The New Progressive Party pointed to the clause in the referendum bill that sought to preserve Puerto Rico's culture, language, and identity as evidence of the alleged underlying purpose of the proponents of the yes vote. They argued further that a yes victory would jeopardize the many federally funded social and welfare programs to which Puerto Ricans have access currently. Ultimately, they underlined, such a victory would lead to the loss of U.S. citizenship.[211]

---

[210] Strictly speaking, the legal effect of a victory by the yes option would have been to mandate the Puerto Rican government to conduct another referendum to amend the Constitution of Puerto Rico in order to incorporate six "guarantees" regarding any future action on the status of Puerto Rico. Also, it would have constituted a petition to the U.S. government to honor such guarantees.

[211] In a much publicized and controversial lecture delivered at the University of Puerto Rico School of Public Communication on April 22, 1992, a public relations expert, Joe Franco, who worked on the referendum campaign on behalf of the New Progressive Party, explained how the "fear" campaign was designed and implemented. One of the principal features of the massive campaign, he stated, was to emphasize that a yes vote would put U.S. citizenship at high risk. Franco's candid remarks were the subject of intense controversy during the campaign leading to the general elections held in the island in November 1992. *See* Nilka Estrada Resto, *Rehúsa Victoria retirar la cuña del publicista Franco*, EL NUEVO DÍA, Aug. 15, 1992, at 24; Iván Cardona, *Joe Franco: ¿Qué hace en la Academia?*, DIÁLOGO, Oct. 1992, at 44.

The no option obtained significant support from at least one important Washington lawmaker.

The proponents of the yes vote, on the other hand, interpreted the exercise as an opportunity to affirm Puerto Rico's national identity. They also expended much effort trying to explain that U.S. citizenship was not at risk. In fact, they argued, the sixth clause of the list of claimed rights sought precisely to make that citizenship unassailable under any political status.[212] The argument, apparently, was not convincing enough.

Despite predictions by political pundits to the contrary, the result of the referendum was a resounding victory for the no option.[213] Given the background of the previous public discussions on the plebiscite bills of 1989–1991, the context of the referendum, the nature of the campaign, the arguments and interpretations put forth by all parties, and the opinions and commentaries of the general public recorded by the Puerto Rican written and electronic press, it must be concluded that a substantial number of those voting for the no option did so out of apprehension over the possible loss of benefits associated with the relationship with the United States, not least of which was the condition of U.S. citizen.[214] Clearly, the discourse of U.S. citizenship, that is, the set of perceptions of reality, values, and social practices that have emerged around that concept, has been a crucial element in the production either of an active loyalty to the metropolitan state or, at the very least, of a generalized acquiescence to American rule.[215]

Several days before the referendum was held, Rep. Robert J. Lagomarsino, a Republican from California and the ranking minority member of the House Insular and International Affairs Subcommittee, which handles questions relating to the status of Puerto Rico, criticized the referendum for "purporting to offer guarantees on U.S. citizenship under status options other than statehood." Echoing the arguments of the New Progressive Party, the longtime supporter of statehood for Puerto Rico added that a yes vote would further distance the island from the United States. If Puerto Ricans wanted to be outside the plenary powers of Congress, Lagomarsino stated, they should know that that also meant "no US citizenship." The congressman backed his remarks with a letter from an assistant attorney general of the United States that concluded that only statehood could offer constitutional guarantees to U.S. citizenship. Under independence or a Commonwealth status outside the plenary powers of Congress, the letter argued, even if the United States passed laws allowing Puerto Ricans to retain their citizenship, that citizenship would have only statutory, not constitutional, guarantees. Doreen Hemlock, *Lagomarsino: Referendum Is Unfair Contest*, SAN JUAN STAR, Nov. 26, 1991, at 3.

The Congressional Research Service (CRS) was brought to the fray once again. In answer to an inquiry, the CRS released a memorandum stating that no action taken by the Puerto Rican government would be binding on the U.S. Congress. It also reaffirmed its position that the U.S. citizenship of most Puerto Ricans was not protected by the first sentence of the Fourteenth Amendment to the U.S. Constitution, although it recognized that there could be due process problems if an attempt was made to revoke that citizenship unilaterally. Those due process problems, the CRS opined, would be solved easily if the option favored eventually was independence, since in that case the Supreme Court could find that that was legitimate reason enough to revoke citizenship collectively. U.S. CONGRESSIONAL RESEARCH SERVICE, QUESTIONS RELATING TO DECEMBER 8 REFERENDUM IN PUERTO RICO (1991). See the related discussion of these issues in the previous section of this chapter, *supra* notes 173 to 194 and accompanying text.

[212] See, for example, statements made to the press and published the very day of the referendum by the presidents of the Popular Democratic Party and the Puerto Rican Independence Party. María Judith Luciano, *Pleno de interrogantes el voto*, EL NUEVO DÍA, Dec. 8, 1991, at 5.

[213] A total of 60.7% of registered voters participated in the referendum. Of those voting, 53% favored the no option, while 44.9% voted yes. ESTADO LIBRE ASOCIADO DE PUERTO RICO, COMISIÓN ESTATAL DE ELECCIONES, REFERENDUM 8 DE DICIEMBRE DE 1991: INFORMES DE RESULTADOS 1 (1992).

[214] For a journalistic commentary interpreting the results, see Efrén Rivera Ramos, *Mucho más que un referéndum*, CLARIDAD, Dec. 20–26, 1991, at 8.

[215] Two paradigmatic expressions of that attitude, common especially among statehood supporters,

Concluding Comment

Almost two decades after acquiring Puerto Rico, the U.S. government extended American citizenship to Puerto Ricans. The decision reflected a determination to retain the country—an important military site—under its permanent control. The citizenship provision was conceived primarily as a means of inducing a sense of loyalty to American rule. It was strictly a hegemonic mechanism, in the Gramscian sense. The act of Congress bestowing citizenship cannot be interpreted as anything but an imposition, basically because of the way it was implemented. The U.S. Supreme Court eventually decided that the granting of citizenship had not incorporated Puerto Rico into the United States. In other words, its legal effect on the political status of Puerto Rico was considered to be negligible.

Nevertheless, that legal event—the extension of citizenship—has had important social, cultural, and political effects. It has become a crucial building block in the construction of the American colonial project in Puerto Rico. It has contributed powerfully to shape the social world that Puerto Ricans inhabit. It has been a fundamental force in the constitution of experience and in the production of the social understandings and the world of images that populate that human community we call the Puerto Rican nation. U.S. citizenship created a new context for social practice, facilitating massive migration and other critical processes in the lives of Puerto Ricans. It constituted new political subjects, Puerto Ricans as American citizens, providing a basis for reciprocal demands between the colony and the metropolitan society. Those mutual demands contributed to the vast incorporation of Puerto Ricans into the U.S. Armed Forces, a fact that has had significant ideological consequences, and to the eventual development of a colonial welfare state.

U.S. citizenship has also had an effect on the ways many Puerto Ricans conceive of themselves, on the mode in which they construct their identity. The complex web of legal complications emerging from the fact that Puerto Ricans are American cit-

---

can be found in two articles published in July and August 1992 in the English language daily *The San Juan Star*. In one, the author proclaimed, "It is, therefore, the duty of all loyal U.S. citizens in Puerto Rico to join fellow U.S. citizens throughout the nation in exalting the celebration of its 216th birthday and its values as a great nation. It is also imperative, more than ever before, on this Fourth of July, for loyal U.S. citizens in Puerto Rico to reaffirm their strong determination to continue struggling for real permanent union with the United States. I say more than ever before because of the evident moves these days to separate us from the United States." Guillermo Moscoso, *Our Nation's 216th Birthday*, SAN JUAN STAR, July 1, 1992, at 18.

The second columnist wrote, "My primary loyalty goes to the United States of America. Oh, yes. The nation that helped us raise [sic] from extreme poverty, to the point of now enjoying the highest per capita income of Hispanic America. The nation that helped us have the democratic system we enjoy. The one that helped us improve significantly our life expectancy and our level of literacy; and which established, only five years after arriving (1903), our first university. The one that embraced us and *granted us our much cherished citizenship*. The nation which has helped us look to the future with optimism." G. Pagán, *Independentistas Live in Past*, SAN JUAN STAR, Aug. 28, 1992, at 18 (emphasis added).

A noted journalist and NPP legislator wrote in March 1992, in a Spanish language newspaper, "Maybe what Puerto Ricans treasure most is their American citizenship. And with good enough reason. If we were to value it for its emotional significance, possibly we would not get an electrifying effect. But certainly it is useful in other ways that make us feel proud of being American citizens. Our citizenship offers us security and stability and opens up opportunities." Ismael Fernández, *Lo que vale nuestra ciudadanía*, EL NUEVO DÍA, March 9, 1992, at 4 (translated from the Spanish).

izens is part of the normative context within which any future decision on the political status of the islands must be made. American citizenship has become a value for many Puerto Ricans, a fact that has exerted and will probably continue to exert a specific weight in discussions about changes in the relationship between Puerto Rico and the United States.

U.S. citizenship has become an important factor in the reproduction of consent to American presence and, indeed, American rule in this, otherwise, very Caribbean nation. In short, the way in which the granting of U.S. citizenship has intervened in the construction of social reality in Puerto Rico is a telling example of the force of law in contemporary societies. Another theoretical conclusion may be derived from this case study. What Bourdieu called *symbolic violence*—the imposition of principles of vision and division in a given society, in this case exemplified by the attempt to create an identity and constitute a political subject from the vantage point of power —can and often does have the consequence of becoming the point of departure for a negotiated construction of reality. American citizenship was imposed on Puerto Ricans. But out of the necessity to survive economically, politically, and culturally, most Puerto Ricans have "negotiated" in practice their status. They have appropriated the category imposed on them and have tried to make the most of it in the different social contexts in which they operate, and they have done this in ways that have sometimes puzzled the metropolitan power.

Chapter 8
HEGEMONY THROUGH LEGAL CONSCIOUSNESS:
Rights, Partial Democracy, and the Rule of Law

The four previous chapters analyzed the effects on Puerto Rican social, cultural, and political life of particular legal events related to the relationship between the United States and Puerto Rico. The present chapter focuses on more general features of Puerto Rico's legal and political system. Specifically, it discusses the extent to which the discourse of rights, the system of partial representative democracy, and the ideology of the rule of law may be regarded as part of the complex articulation of factors that have operated to reproduce American hegemony and to legitimate the existing power relationship between the two countries. To address this question is to raise important issues that lie at the core of the interconnection between law and the type of domination called "colonialism."

The approach taken in this chapter differs somewhat from that of the previous ones. It draws more on insights from the author's personal observations and reflections over the years and less on documentary evidence and analogous empirical data. Additionally, it dwells more on theoretical issues, seeking to identify the broader outlines of the problems discussed rather than to describe in detail their factual context.

Such an analysis helps in exploring the general and elusive nature of the phenomena examined here. Very little research, in some cases none at all, has been conducted in Puerto Rico on some of these topics from the perspective of their relationship to the country's colonial situation, the creation of identities and subjectivities, and the reproduction of American hegemony. This is particularly the case with rights and the rule of law. These aspects of Puerto Rico's legal and political culture are key to understanding the manner in which the majority of the population relate to American presence, influence, authority, and power in Puerto Rican society. However, the observations I advance here are proposed not as conclusions, but as suggested lines of inquiry in need of further elaboration and more in-depth study.

Referring to European colonialism, Fitzpatrick pointed out that law was always "a prime justification and instrument" of imperialism, as it was portrayed by imperialists as the means by which to raise the mass of uncivilized millions to "a higher plane of civilisation."[1] This civilizing rhetoric was central to the early colonial project launched by Spanish conquerors in the 15th and 16th centuries. Late-19th-century colonialism responded to new sets of determinants, such as the quest for the establishment of commercial-based domination in an expanding capitalist world economy. But, as Osterhammel noted, the claim that the colonizers were fulfilling a civilizing and liberating mission also formed part of the legitimation strategies of colonial rule during that period.[2] One of the moral "duties" that the rulers proclaimed, added Osterhammel, was "to bring the blessings of Western civilization to

---

[1] Peter Fitzpatrick, The Mythology of Modern Law 107 (1992).
[2] Jürgen Osterhammel, Colonialism: A Theoretical Overview 109 (1997).

the inhabitants of the tropics."[3] As we saw in chapter 1, this was also part of the worldview of the promoters of overseas expansion in the United States during the second half of the 19th century.

This was also the objective openly expressed by American colonizers at the close of the Spanish American War. In an often-quoted statement, General Nelson A. Miles, commanding officer of the U.S. troops that landed in Puerto Rico in 1898, solemnly declared that it was the intention of the occupiers to bring to this newly conquered land "the immunities and blessings of the liberal institutions" of the American government and the "advantages and blessings of enlightened civilization."[4]

In most colonial experiences, however, the importation of European law into colonial societies suffered important transformations. Snyder and Hay pointed out that the law exported to the colonies was not simply metropolitan law: "It comprised the most authoritarian aspects of European law, from which most provisions regarding social welfare, basic rights and other entitlements largely had been excised."[5] The legal system had a "markedly administrative rather than rights-oriented" character, and the ideology of the rule of law "was practically absent in many if not most colonies."[6] In fact, as Ghai has argued, even in the African postcolonial states ideologies other than the rule of law and the idea of legality have proved more fruitful as legitimating discourses.[7] Shivji raised a similar point, claiming that in many African societies "legal ideology has little hegemonic significance."[8] Comaroff argued that the discourse of rights played a greater role in European colonialism in Africa than is generally recognized.[9] His analysis reveals, however, that although the discourse of rights serves at times to create spaces from which to resist colonial domination, often such discourse was greatly distorted to accommodate the colonizers' interests.

In all these respects the modern brand of colonialism exemplified by the Puerto Rican experience, especially after the 1940s, represents a significant departure from previous colonial patterns. In some of their most basic features, the discourse of liberal rights and the ideology of the rule of law have been extended to the colonial society in practically the same mold in which they circulate in the metropolitan state. Of course, this is not an exclusively American phenomenon. The remaining French, British, and Dutch dependencies in the Caribbean exhibit similar characteristics.[10]

---

[3] *Id.*

[4] DOCUMENTS ON THE CONSTITUTIONAL RELATIONSHIP OF PUERTO RICO AND THE UNITED STATES 49–50 (Marcos Ramírez Lavandero Ed. 1988).

[5] Francis Snyder & Douglas Hay, *Comparisons in the Social History of Law: Labour and Crime*, in LABOUR, LAW AND CRIME: AN HISTORICAL PERSPECTIVE 12 (Francis Snyder & Douglas Hay Eds. 1987).

[6] *Id.*

[7] Yash Ghai, *The Rule of Law, Legitimacy and Governance*, in THE POLITICAL ECONOMY OF LAW: A THIRD WORLD READER 253–61 (Yash Ghai et al. Eds. 1987).

[8] Issa G. Shivji, *Equality, Rights and Authoritarianism in Africa*, in ENLIGHTENMENT, RIGHTS AND REVOLUTION: ESSAYS IN LEGAL AND SOCIAL PHILOSOPHY 282 (Neil MacCormick & Zenon Bankowski Eds. 1989).

[9] John Comaroff, *The Discourse of Rights in Colonial South Africa: Subjectivity, Sovereignty, Modernity*, in IDENTITIES, POLITICS AND RIGHTS 193–236 (Austin Sarat & Thomas R. Kearns Eds. 1995).

[10] The British dependencies or crown colonies in the Caribbean region include Anguilla, Bermuda (geographically located in the Atlantic, but historically a part of the region), the British Virgin Islands, the Cayman Islands, Montserrat, and Turks and Caicos Islands. The Dutch possessions are Aruba and a

The revealing fact, in all these cases, is that, in the long run, colonialism seems to have been better served not by excising the discourse of rights and legalism from the metropolitan claim to authority, but by promoting such discourse and ideology in the colonial societies themselves.

Fitzpatrick perceptively noted another important, more fundamental way in which the law of Europe and the law of the colonies differed. While European societies regarded themselves as self-determining subjects (they gave themselves their own law), this quality was denied those subjected to colonial rule. Fitzpatrick quoted Westlake, who in 1894 expressed the opinion that although all rights were not denied "uncivilized natives," the "appreciation of their rights is left to the conscience of the state within whose recognized territorial sovereignty they are comprised."[11]

In this respect there are similarities between classical European colonialism and the newer version of colonial domination exemplified by the American model. Thus, the U.S. Congress, with unswerving support from the Supreme Court, has repeatedly insisted that it has "plenary powers" over U.S. territorial possessions. These powers include the faculty to prescribe the nature and extent of their residents' citizenship rights and of their entitlements to social welfare benefits. It is true that the prerogative to determine what "fundamental rights" would be recognized for the inhabitants of the territories was taken away from Congress in the early part of the 20th century. But such power was accorded to another organ of the metropolitan state—its highest judicial forum. This was one of the effects of the doctrine established in the *Insular Cases.*[12]

In this chapter, I discuss the differences between European colonialism at the end of the 19th and first half of the 20th centuries and the type prevalent in late modern colonial welfare states. Those differences account, to an important degree, for the reproduction of U.S. hegemony over Puerto Rico's population. I analyze the dynamics resulting from the interplay among a rights-oriented as well as repressive state, a regime of partial democracy, the ideology of the rule of law, and the development of legal consciousness in the context of a colonial relationship. The main proposition is that the discourse of liberal rights, the experience of partial democracy, and the ideology of the rule of law have contributed to the reproduction of acquiescence to American rule and American presence in Puerto Rico. They have been key features of the American hegemonic project and constitutive parts of the legitimation process.

---

five-island federation known as the Netherlands Antilles (constituted by Curaçao, Bonaire, St. Martin, Saba, and St. Eustatius). French Guiana (on the Caribbean coast of the South American mainland), Martinique, and Guadeloupe are formally integral parts of the French nation, but their social, economic, political, and cultural conditions resemble very much those of the dependent territories of the region. *See, generally*, C. A. SUNSHINE, THE CARIBBEAN: SURVIVAL, STRUGGLE AND SOVEREIGNTY 163–70 (1980); JOSÉ TRÍAS MONGE, 5 HISTORIA CONSTITUCIONAL DE PUERTO RICO chaps. 8–10 (1994); OSTERHAMMEL, *supra* note 2, at 118–19; G. Oostindie, *The Dutch Caribbean in the 1990's: Decolonization or Recolonization?*, 5 CARIBBEAN AFFAIRS 1 (1992); J. Connell, *Britain's Caribbean Colonies: The End of the Era of Decolonisation?*, 32 J. COMMONWEALTH COMPARATIVE POLITICS 87–106 (1994); Efrén Rivera Ramos, *Colonialism and Integration in the Contemporary Caribbean*, 6 BEYOND LAW 189 (1998).

[11] FITZPATRICK, *supra* note 1, at 108, 109.

[12] See the discussion of the *Insular Cases* in Part II of this book.

Certainly, these discourses have also contributed to the widespread social acceptance of the political system in the mainland United States. They also explain in part the legitimacy enjoyed by the political systems in the most developed democratic societies in Europe. But, precisely, one of the defining characteristics of modern welfare colonialism in the Caribbean region is the extent to which it has relied on legitimating and hegemonic mechanisms prevalent within the metropolitan societies themselves. To a great extent, this parallel legitimacy has been possible due to the fact that the dependent societies have come to resemble in important respects the societies of the metropolitan states.

In chapter 3, I explained how American society and institutions have become an exemplary center for Puerto Rican society, resulting in significant transformations in economic practices, political traditions, legal procedures, educational policies, communication techniques, and other aspects of Puerto Rican social life. In the specific case of Puerto Rico, the parallels between the ways in which legitimation is produced in the colony and in the metropolitan society result from the fact that the political, legal, and economic institutional arrangements and many of the social and cultural life processes of the territory have been structured in accordance with the organizing principles of the metropolitan society.[13] Because needs and aspirations are many times defined in analogous fashion within the Puerto Rican community and in the wider American society, their modes of satisfaction tend to be the same or very similar, despite other cultural differences between the two societies.

To the extent that legitimation and hegemony are linked to the satisfaction of needs,[14] including cultural and political ones, legitimation and hegemonic processes tend to resemble each other in the metropolitan society and in the colonial community. Both share a reliance on the discourse of rights and other features of liberal democracy to buttress legitimacy. The colonial condition adds its own specificity to the process. That specificity must be taken into consideration and accounted for. It includes the situation of political subordination, the imbalance in economic exchanges and cultural power, and the structural dependency for the satisfaction of needs. It also involves geopolitical and regional factors, such as the perception of the majority of the population about the possibilities of embarking on an alternative project in light of the economic and political realities of the Caribbean region.[15]

Diverse sectors of the Puerto Rican population have actively participated in shaping this particular colonial experience. Puerto Rican elites and popular sectors alike have promoted the discourse of rights and adherence to democratic principles for reasons that include conscious valuations of what is best and most desirable. Responses from the population to the development of a liberal colonial state have involved varying degrees of acceptance, resistance, complicity, negotiation, and resignation. In this sense, the relationship between the colonizer and the colonized has not been unilateral.

---

[13] Efrén Rivera Ramos, *Self-Determination and Decolonisation in the Society of the Modern Colonial Welfare State, in* ISSUES OF SELF-DETERMINATION 115, 122 (William Twining Ed. 1991).

[14] *See, generally,* JÜRGEN HABERMAS, LEGITIMATION CRISIS (1988); Rivera Ramos, *supra* note 13. See the related discussion in the previous chapter about citizenship.

[15] *See* Rivera Ramos, *supra* note 10; Ramón Grosfoguel, *The Divorce of Nationalist Discourses from the Puerto Rican People: A Sociohistorical Perspective, in* PUERTO RICAN JAM: ESSAYS ON CULTURE AND POLITICS 57, 66–70 (Frances Negrón-Muntaner & Ramón Grosfoguel, Eds. 1997).

A Note on Coercion and Consent

The Theoretical Problem

Before proceeding, some comments are in order about the relationship between coercion and consent. The problem is posed in much recent sociological writing about law. The discussion has been motivated by a realization that many political systems have relied on mechanisms other than physical repression or the use of force to reproduce themselves and secure a high degree of acquiescence or active consent from the population. Modern industrial and postindustrial societies provide pointed examples.

Hunt has argued that the main trends in contemporary sociological theories of law have not been able to transcend a "dichotomous conception of law organized around the polar opposition between coercion and consent."[16] Although to conceptualize law in terms of the dimensions of coercion and consent may help to capture important characteristics of law, Hunt argued, none of the positions he examined—which included liberal and Marxist approaches—has succeeded in "advancing a coherent presentation of a mode of combination of the apparently opposed characteristics of law so as to produce a unitary conception not reducible to a choice between opposites or a fluctuation between them."[17] Hunt's argument reveals an important insight. However, his formulation fails to express the problem with precision.

First of all, there is the problem of defining "coercion." Certainly the use of physical force to repress—by means of imprisonment, corporal punishment, or execution—is a means of coercion. But other, more insidious forms of imposing someone's will may too be considered coercive: means such as surveillance, discrimination, ostracism, job dismissals, and psychological harassment. Also, certain practices, which Bourdieu would characterize as *symbolic violence*,[18] could be arguably classified as forms of coercion. These practices consist essentially in the imposition of ways of viewing and evaluating the world. Symbolic violence may take the form of explanations, principles, or rules, for example, the handing down of administrative or judicial decisions not subject to question. In other words, coercion shows itself in multifarious forms that range from those that rely on the use of extreme physical force to those that depend on other, nonphysical, yet forceful means of imposing compliance.

Second, in terms of social theory the binary opposition to be transcended is not that of "coercion" and "consent," but "coercion" and "persuasion." In contemporary societies, especially those of the most technologically advanced countries, consent, in the sociological sense, has to be viewed as the result of a complex articulation of coercive and persuasive mechanisms. Consent is not a polar category to be reconciled with its opposite, coercion. Rather, consent is the synthesis: the end result of a complex process in which the different forms of both persuasion and coercion

---

[16] Alan Hunt, *Dichotomy and Contradiction in the Sociology of Law, in* MARXISM AND LAW 95 (P. Beirne & R. Quinney Eds. 1982).

[17] *Id.*

[18] Pierre Bourdieu, *The Force of Law: Toward a Sociology of the Juridical Field*, 38 HASTINGS L. J. 805, 812 (1987).

combine to produce an active acceptance of, or at least a passive acquiescence in, existing social arrangements. Coercion, then, is an active ingredient in the process of producing acquiescence and consent.

Third, in many contemporary societies, to be effective as part of the hegemonic process, coercion must be regarded as legitimate. In other words, it must rely on consent. Coercion may be considered legitimate either because it is viewed as authorized or lawful by those to whom it is directed, or because it is sanctioned by the majority when aimed at selected groups or individuals.

Is law principally a coercive or a persuasive mechanism? This is the question that much sociological literature seems to intend to address when discussing the (mistakenly formulated) coercion–consent dichotomy. Some theoretical approaches at times provide seemingly contradictory answers to this question. Thus, Gramsci at one point stated that "the law is the repressive and negative aspect of the entire positive civilizing activity undertaken by the State,"[19] while in other passages he stressed the educative function of law.[20] This has led Hunt to criticize the Gramscian approach as being riddled with the coercion–consent dichotomy. "The coercion–consent dualism," wrote Hunt,

> finds its most general expression in Marxist theory through the very widespread recent influence of Gramscian theory. . . . Within such a perspective the central focus has been upon the noncoercive face of law. . . . Yet there coexists in Gramsci an emphasis upon the repressive role of law and state.[21]

Cain provided an alternative reading of Gramsci on this matter. She interpreted the Italian thinker as proposing that law can be used both coercively and persuasively:

> It is persuasive because it assists the directive group by *creating* a "tradition" in an active and not in a passive sense. Law has an umbrella effect whereby the standards and ways of thought embodied in it penetrate civil society and become a part of common sense.[22]

One of the virtues of Cain's interpretation is that it helps to rid the problem of essentialist connotations, for it does not suppose that law *is* irremediably one or the other, but rather postulates that law *can be used* in either or both ways, with a multiplicity of possibilities regarding their mode of articulation and combined effects. This conception may also contribute to historicize the analysis, for then the question would become the following: How has law been used by determinate groups in certain places at given moments? This would be more consonant with a social construction of reality thesis, which in turn is theoretically closer to Gramsci's view of the cultural and historical nature of all social phenomena.

However, in Gramsci the relationship between law and "consent," between law and hegemony, goes even further than the fact that law may be used both coercively

---

[19] ANTONIO GRAMSCI, SELECTIONS FROM THE PRISON NOTEBOOKS 247 (Q. Hoare & G. N. Smith Eds. 1971).

[20] *Id.* at 195, 196.

[21] Hunt, *supra* note 16, at 86, 87.

[22] Maureen Cain, *Gramsci, the State and the Place of Law, in* LEGALITY, IDEOLOGY AND THE STATE 102 (David Sugarman Ed. 1983) (emphasis in the original).

and persuasively. For Gramsci, "the function of law" is to assimilate, educate, and adapt the majority of the population to the requirements of the goals that the ruling groups in society set to be achieved.[23] Through law the state "tends to create a social conformism which is useful to the ruling group's line of development."[24] This conformism is part of what he would call consent, and it is, partially, what hegemony is about. The crucial proposition, if Gramsci is read carefully, is that law produces these effects both through persuasion and coercion. For him the "ethical" dimension of hegemony consists in the creation of a "correspondence" between individual conduct "and the ends which society sets itself as necessary."[25] This congruity is achieved as much by persuasion as by coercion through "the sphere of positive law."[26] In other words, it is not that law at times is used to coerce and at others to generate consent. Rather, it is that law produces consent both through persuasion *and* coercion. The coercive effect of law, then, is as much a factor in producing consent as its persuasive capacity. Hegemony, for Gramsci, is the result of the operation of both persuasive and coercive mechanisms. Law is a particular form that combines both means of producing consent.[27]

Another way to look at the question is through the examination of the relationship among persuasion, coercion, consent, and subjectivity and, in turn, at the connection between subjectivity and law. To the extent that hegemony implies a form of consent to social and political arrangements and relations, it involves subjectivity. By *subjectivity* I mean the categories of perception and evaluation social agents use to assess the world. Giving consent to social arrangements and relations involves interpreting and evaluating them. Many social arrangements and relations are sanctioned by law. They are constructed through the effect of legal categories. The categories used by law are infused with meaning. Such is the case, for example, with the category *citizen*. To the extent that concrete social agents identify themselves with those specific categories, the meanings the law embodies tend to become part of their consciousness, in other words, part of a particular subjectivity. As I explained in the previous chapter, this is the way in which people become "subjective legal subjects," which I defined as people who operate under the premise that they possess the rights and obligations prescribed by law.

Usually, self-perception as a legal subject occurs in the context of certain actions that the actor wants to take or of specific acts or consequences he or she wishes to avoid or enjoin. Thus, this mode of construction of subjectivity, which passes through the appropriation by concrete social agents of the meanings ascribed to legal categories, is closely related to social practice. This process of appropriation of the meaning of legal categories may also occur in people who are not themselves or do

---

[23] GRAMSCI, *supra* note 19, at 195.

[24] *Id.*

[25] *Id.* at 196; *see also* Cain, *supra* note 22, at 102.

[26] GRAMSCI, *supra* note 19, at 196.

[27] Gramsci's view, thus understood, is entirely compatible with the constitutive theory of law that underlies this book. In fact, it is one of its supporting theoretical sources. The Gramscian analysis proposes that law has effects. Those effects have to do with the configuration of the prevailing understandings (or common sense) in a particular society and with the production of social practices (as in his assertion that law tends to generate conduct that corresponds with the general goals set by the ruling groups). Finally, Gramsci saw those effects as forming part of the social world, as constituting a particular culture.

not see themselves as subsumed in the relevant categories. For example, noncitizens may accept the meaning of the term *citizen* as defined by law and act according to its contents. In this sense, the legal norm creates an ideological map of what should be considered legitimate and illegitimate by all members of the community.

Many times the addressees of legal discourse willfully adopt the categories of perception and evaluation of reality contained in its statements. That which law considers legitimate is accepted as such by social agents. In other words, the contents of individual consciousness are directly influenced by the contents of legal discourse. For example, a groundbreaking decision by a liberal court declaring the equality of rights of children born in and out of marriage may eventually be accepted as fair by the majority of the population. In that case, we may say that the law has acted persuasively to produce consent.

The effect of law on subjectivity may also occur indirectly. Such is the case when the incorporation of the categories of law into consciousness is mediated through experience. This mediated absorption is the product of a particular mode of operation of normative discourse. This mode of operation results from the fact that norms tend to elicit responses from people. In the case of legal norms, those responses may be in the nature of compliance, resistance, or any of the multiple ways that social actors cope with the context that legal norms create.

Compliance with or accommodation to legal norms, in turn, may be based on a variety of motives, such as convenience, fear, or agreement with the values or purposes contained in the law. When observance of the law results from willful adherence to its substance or from a judgment of expediency, the law may be regarded as acting persuasively. When compliance results from fear of punishment or loss of a good, such as freedom or prestige, law is operating coercively. However, regardless of their nature or motive, as responses to law become generalized and repeated over time, they turn into routine practices. Examples of this would be the habits of stopping at red lights or avoiding entering into another person's property without permission resulting from repeated compliance with traffic laws or anti-trespassing laws. The experiences that said practices generate for those involved in them eventually may affect their subjectivity, because those practices begin to be perceived as "natural" or inevitable or because they end up being judged desirable. The latter may be the result of a mental slippage that gradually turns the perception of what *is* into the belief of what *ought to be*. From social practice—originated as a response to the legal norm—there emerges an intersubjective construction of the world that becomes part of the social understandings (or the common sense, as Gramsci would say) of the community at large or of certain sectors of the community. In this way, law contributes indirectly to constitute consciousness. It does so acting either persuasively or coercively. In sum, law contributes to produce consent through persuasion or coercion or both.[28] Since law usually elicits diverse responses within a given community, it generally operates to generate consent through a combination of coercion and persuasion.

For Gramsci, hegemony is a specific mode of exercising domination. One may, then, reformulate his proposition in other terms: Domination is the result of a complex articulation of technologies of power that include the use of force, insidious

---

[28] For a more extended discussion, see Efrén Rivera Ramos, *Derecho y subjetividad*, 5–6 FUNDAMENTOS 125 (1997–98).

forms of coercion, symbolic violence, regulation, and a host of other practices that work in a persuasive fashion. These practices and technologies of power reinforce each other in a multidimensional process. Law is a particular site in which many of those technologies and practices of power converge.

The Coercive Dimension of the American Colonial Project in Puerto Rico

The way to transcend the mistaken dichotomy between coercion and consent involves two steps. First, it is necessary to theoretically recognize the role of coercion in the production of consent, as I have done in the previous discussion. Second, efforts must be made to identify historical instances in which coercion has been used to reinforce hegemony in a particular case.

The Puerto Rican colonial experience under American rule has been characterized by various combinations of coercive and persuasive mechanisms for consolidating American hegemony. The very acts upon which the colonial relationship was founded were traversed by this complex dynamics of force and inducement. The encounter between colonizer and colonized was mediated by a military occupation touted as a promise of liberation. Legal reforms meant to open up new avenues of individual freedom for diverse sectors of society were imposed by a military government that responded to the strategic goals of the metropolitan power. Limited U.S. citizenship rights were descended upon the population in a unilateral show of force.

Since those early days and throughout the century, metropolitan largesse and self-discipline have coexisted with intense periods of selective persecution and repression of different sectors of the population. Coercion has included the overt use of physical force, more insidious forms of repression, and acts of symbolic violence.[29] Repression and selective persecution have been aimed particularly at the independence movement and against other social and political forces that, at different times, have questioned either the legitimacy of the colonial regime as a whole or some of the discrete and immediate manifestations of colonialism in Puerto Rican life.[30]

However, the effects of that repression have been more generalized, as their exemplary dimension has succeeded in inducing fear of the independence movement. Repressive activities have been conducted by direct agents of the metropolitan state (like the U.S. armed forces, the Central Intelligence Agency, and the Federal Bureau of Investigation [FBI]);[31] by agents of the local Puerto Rican government (such as

---

[29] The imposition of American citizenship in 1917, discussed at length in chapter 7, is a good example of an act of *symbolic violence*, an instance of coercion that, in the versatile manner in which law many times operates, eventually assumed a "persuasive" character, becoming one of the key pillars of American hegemony.

[30] Two examples of resistance aimed at concrete manifestations of colonialism have been the campaign of opposition to the draft in the 1960s and the struggle to expel the U.S. Navy from the island of Vieques.

[31] *See* RONALD FERNÁNDEZ, THE DISENCHANTED ISLAND: PUERTO RICO AND THE UNITED STATES IN THE TWENTIETH CENTURY 206–280 (1992); Leonor Mulero, *Admite la persecución a independentistas el FBI*, EL NUEVO DÍA, March 17, 2000, at 30; Leonor Mulero, *Ordena el FBI investigarse a sí mismo en el caso de las carpetas*, EL NUEVO DÍA, March 22, 2000, at 36.

the Puerto Rican police and the Puerto Rican Justice Department);[32] by political parties; and even by "private" actors operating in the realm of what Gramsci and others would call "civil society."[33] A few illustrations of these repressive practices will provide a rough picture of the coercive dimension of American colonialism during the 20th century. They should dispel any notion that American colonialism has been an entirely benign phenomenon totally devoid of the harshness and the painful, even brutal, effects of European colonialism.[34]

The first three decades of American colonial rule were particularly harsh. Poverty was widespread, despite a relative degree of modernization brought about by a program of public works to develop transportation, communications, and sanitation facilities and by the changes in the economic organization of the country introduced by American capitalism. Absentee American corporations controlled the sugar industry and exploited Puerto Rican workers. The depression of the 1930s aggravated the condition of the Puerto Rican population, providing fertile ground for an upsurge in social agitation. Furthermore, the imperial refusal to solve the colonial problem fostered the radicalization of the independence movement.

The first direct, radical, and organized challenge to the legitimacy of colonial rule came from the Nationalist Party, led by a charismatic Puerto Rican lawyer trained at Harvard University, Pedro Albizu Campos. Initially, the nationalists participated in the electoral process. But after the elections of 1932 they opted for a more confrontational politics aimed at inducing a crisis that would lead the United States to relinquish its control over Puerto Rico. The colonial administration responded violently.

A rapid succession of events eventually led to the incarceration of Albizu Campos and other nationalist leaders. In October 1935, four nationalists and a police officer died in a shootout after police detained four members of the party. In February 1936, the chief of police, an American, was killed. Two young nationalists arrested for that action were, in turn, assassinated while in police custody. As a result of these events, Albizu Campos and others were indicted for attempting to overthrow the government of the United States and were sentenced to jail terms of up to 15 years to be served in a prison in Atlanta, Georgia. In 1936, while Albizu was imprisoned, the police attacked a peaceful nationalist demonstration in the southern city of Ponce. Nineteen people, including two policemen, were killed, and more than 100 were wounded. A report by a commission of the American Civil Liberties Union, presided

---

[32] See ESTADO LIBRE ASOCIADO DE PUERTO RICO, COMISIÓN DE DERECHOS CIVILES, INFORME—DISCRIMEN Y PERSECUCIÓN POR RAZONES POLÍTICAS: LA PRÁCTICA GUBERNAMENTAL DE MANTENER LISTAS, FICHEROS Y EXPEDIENTES DE CIUDADANOS POR RAZÓN DE IDEOLOGÍA POLÍTICA (1989) [COMISIÓN DE DERECHOS CIVILES]; Noriega v. Hernández Colón, 88 J.T.S. 141 (1988) and 92 J.T.S. 85 (1992).

[33] COMISIÓN DE DERECHOS CIVILES, supra note 32; Noriega v. Hernández Colón, supra note 32.

[34] More elaborate descriptions and analyses of the historical events mentioned herein can be found in GORDON K. LEWIS, PUERTO RICO: FREEDOM AND POWER IN THE CARIBBEAN (1963); FERNANDO PICÓ, HISTORIA GENERAL DE PUERTO RICO (1986); JOSÉ TRÍAS MONGE, PUERTO RICO: THE TRIALS OF THE OLDEST COLONY IN THE WORLD (1997); RONALD FERNÁNDEZ, LOS MACHETEROS: THE WELLS FARGO ROBBERY AND THE VIOLENT STRUGGLE FOR PUERTO RICAN INDEPENDENCE (1987); RONALD FERNÁNDEZ, THE DISENCHANTED ISLAND, supra note 31; IVONNE ACOSTA, LA MORDAZA (1987); ARTURO MELÉNDEZ LÓPEZ, LA BATALLA DE VIEQUES (1989); ANN NELSON, MURDER UNDER TWO FLAGS: THE UNITED STATES, PUERTO RICO, AND THE CERRO MARAVILLA COVER-UP (1986).

by the well-known American attorney Arthur Garfield Hays, concluded that the police action had constituted a massacre and put the blame on the American governor.

Nationalist activity subsided until after the return of Albizu to the island in 1947. Another series of events, including a nationalist revolt in several towns in Puerto Rico in 1950 and an armed attack against the Blair House, the residence of President Harry S. Truman in Washington, ended in a new period of incarceration for the nationalist leader. He was released again in 1953. But in 1954 three young nationalists fired gunshots into the floor of the U.S. House of Representatives. Albizu was arrested and imprisoned once more. He was not freed until 1964 and died in 1965.

The events of 1950 triggered a massive wave of persecution against independence supporters of all political shades. Many were detained without trial. McCarthyism showed its face in the colony using as its principal instrument a gag law adopted by the Puerto Rican legislature in 1948 (popularly called "La Mordaza," or "The Muzzle").[35] The law was a Puerto Rican version of the infamous American Smith Act of 1940.[36] Other forms of harassment became common. Many independence followers were routinely denied jobs in government and private firms. Police surveillance and the monitoring of legitimate political activities became common practices. The more militant became subject to visits in their homes by U.S. federal agents as a harassing tactic. At one point even possession of a Puerto Rican flag was sufficient to prompt intervention by the Puerto Rican police.[37]

These measures have had long-lasting consequences in Puerto Rico. The independence movement was, in effect, criminalized. Proindependence advocacy was equated with "lack of patriotism," "communism," and "subversion." Not infrequently, to be an *independentista* in Puerto Rico after 1950 meant to become, for many practical purposes, a political and social outcast. The result was a pervasive fear and rejection among significant sectors of the population of anything that hinted at separation from the United States. Although some changes in that attitude have been noticed in recent years, strong lingering effects of those apprehensions are still evident among many people.

New economic, social, and political crises in the following decades created the conditions for new challenges to the colonial system, which, in turn, were met with new repressive policies. Toward the end of the 1960s, a strong movement against the drafting of Puerto Rican young men into the U.S. military and opposition to the Vietnam war produced a series of confrontations. The FBI and the federal judiciary intervened actively to curb the protests. In the 1970s the role of the U.S. military in Puerto Rico was again put into question by militant movements that called for the withdrawal of the U.S. Navy from Culebra and Vieques. Dozens were arrested and indicted because of their participation in acts of civil disobedience.

In 1978 two young *independentistas* were killed by police at a mountain top known as Cerro Maravilla. The official version of the incident, supported by the Puerto Rican Justice Department and the prostatehood governor, claimed that the police had acted in self-defense. However, a much publicized investigation conducted by the Popular Democratic Party-controlled Senate revealed that the two men had

---

[35] Pub. L. No. 53 of June 10, 1948 (Puerto Rico), repealed by Pub. L. No. 2 of August 5, 1957 (Puerto Rico).

[36] Smith Act of 1940, ch. 439, 54 Stat. 670, 18 U.S.C.A. 2385 (1940).

[37] *See* Ivonne Acosta, La Mordaza (1987).

been led to the site by an undercover agent and that, as many proindependence activists and intellectuals had alleged, they had been murdered after surrendering to the police. The Cerro Maravilla killings shook the public conscience. Their aftermath seems to have motivated a reassessment of the relationship of the colonial state and the population at large to the independence movement.

In the 1980s a new clandestine organization, Los Macheteros, staged a series of dramatic actions against the U.S. military. They included an armed attack against a Navy bus, in which two sailors were killed and nine injured, and the destruction of nine National Guard planes, causing damages estimated at $50 million.

In 1985, in a commando-style operation, hundreds of American enforcement officers arrested a group of Puerto Ricans in their homes in the early hours of the morning and charged them with participating or collaborating in the 1983 multi-million dollar robbery of a Wells Fargo facility in the United States. The Macheteros had claimed responsibility for the robbery, declaring that they committed the robbery as a means to finance their revolutionary activities. Many of those arrested were later convicted in a U.S. court in Connecticut and have served or are serving time in several American prisons. One of the leaders of the group, Filiberto Ojeda Ríos, who has since gone into hiding, was acquitted by a Puerto Rican jury of charges arising from incidents surrounding his arrest by FBI agents, who claimed that he had fired against them and wounded one of them. Ojeda Ríos alleged he was only defending himself and his wife against the gun-wielding officers.

The public hearings conducted to ascertain the truth of the Cerro Maravilla murders opened up new windows for understanding the nature, extent, and dimensions of the decades-long persecution of the independence movement and suppression of other popular struggles. One such discovery was the revelation that the intelligence division of the Puerto Rican police and the Bureau for Special Investigations of the Puerto Rican Justice Department had for many years kept so-called subversive files on persons who were known or suspected to be followers of the independence, socialist, labor, feminist, environmentalist, and other social or political movements or organizations. The information contained in the files had been collected through undercover agents, police informers, and even unsuspecting sources that included job supervisors, coworkers, relatives, and neighbors. A civil action filed in a Puerto Rican court led to the release of thousands of such files.[38] Both the superior court that decided the case and a separate inquiry by the Puerto Rico Civil Rights Commission[39] concluded that, for decades, independence followers and others considered "subversive" for engaging in perfectly legal activities had been subjected to a systematic pattern of persecution.

One illuminating aspect of these inquiries was the evidence suggesting that U.S. enforcement agencies had taken an active, if not a leading, role in these practices. In fact, the interference of the FBI in Puerto Rican political affairs had been substantiated before. Documents obtained from the U.S. Justice Department through the Freedom of Information Act revealed that the FBI conducted a systematic campaign of disinformation and destabilization against the independence movement in the 1960s and 1970s and that the agency meddled in the 1967 plebiscite and the 1968

---

[38] *See* Noriega v. Hernández Colón, 88 J.T.S. 141 (1988) and 92 J.T.S. 85 (1992).
[39] COMISIÓN DE DERECHOS CIVILES, *supra* note 32.

general elections.[40] On March 16, 2000, during a congressional hearing in Washington, DC, answering questions by José Serrano, a representative from New York of
Puerto Rican origin, the Director of the Federal Bureau of Investigations, Louis
Freeh, admitted that the FBI had persecuted independence advocates in Puerto Rico
and promised a full report on the matter.[41] The next day, Freeh created a task force
to investigate.[42] As a result, the FBI has been delivering to the Puerto Rican legislature thousands of files kept on Puerto Ricans over the decades, including volumi-
nous records on Nationalist leader Pedro Albizu Campos and former Governor Luis
Muñoz Marín.

Law has thus clearly been used at various levels and in multiple forms in the
coercive dimension of the colonial state. Laws, legal procedures, legal personnel,
courts, and enforcement agencies have all been deployed against the various sectors
that have suffered persecution and repression. Law has also been used as a site to
contest those practices and seek redress, as the suit seeking enjoinment of the practice
of keeping subversive files demonstrates.

Important sectors of the Puerto Rican population have come to perceive many
of the actions and practices described as illegitimate. But others have "validated"
those actions and practices, at various moments, with reference to the notion that
they are appropriate ways of dealing with "subversives." In that sense, the continuation of those practices has depended on the existence of a social understanding,
of varying degrees of extension and depth, sanctioning their legitimacy.[43]

More than that, those practices may have had the effect of buttressing the very
social consensus on which they have depended for their efficacy.[44] Thus, the persecution of the independence movement after the 1950s was based, to a large extent,
on a strategy of criminalizing the activities of its members in a variety of ways. The
most glaring actions in this sense were detaining people for possessing Puerto Rican

---

[40] *See* FERNÁNDEZ, THE DISENCHANTED ISLAND, *supra* note 31, chap. 8. According to documents
cited by Fernández, the FBI's primary tactics in 1967 and 1968 were to "confuse the *independentista*
leaders, exploit group rivalries and jealousy, inflame personality conflicts, emasculate the strength of
these organizations, and thwart any possibility of proindependence unity." *Id.* at 217. Fernández concluded, "The electoral impact of this harassment and interference was felt in two primary areas. First,
by creating dissension within the groups, agents helped avert the possibility that ... independence
activists would once again become a significant force in island politics. Second, and more important for
any understanding of the island from 1968 until today, the FBI continued a policy of harassment that
"began" with Muñoz's enactment of La Mordaza in 1948. A youngster born in 1950 or 1960 grew up
fearing the consequences of any independence activity. That fear became (and remains) an institution-
alized part of Puerto Rican political life, and the FBI must assume a good degree of responsibility for
helping the Populares strike fear into the heart of anyone considering an independence posture." *Id.* at
217–18.

[41] Leonor Mulero, *Admite la persecución a independentistas*, *supra* note 31, at 30.

[42] Leonor Mulero, *Ordena el FBI investigarse a sí mismo*, *supra* note 31, at 36.

[43] This assertion is supported by the findings and conclusions of the Puerto Rico Civil Rights
Commission in its cited report. COMISIÓN DE DERECHOS CIVILES, *supra* note 33. See also the concurrent
opinions of Associate Justices Federico Hernández Denton and Jaime Fuster Berlingeri in Noriega v.
Hernández Colón, 92 J.T.S. 85, at 9656 and 9658, respectively.

[44] Crenshaw suggested that the "coercion of nonconsenting groups may provide an important reinforcement to the creation of consensus among classes that do accept the legitimacy of the dominant
order," alluding specifically to the "possibility that the coercion of Blacks may provide a basis for others
to consent to the dominant order" in American society. Kimberle W. Crenshaw, *Race, Reform and
Retrenchment: Transformation and Legitimation in Antidiscrimination Law*, *in* CRITICAL LEGAL
THOUGHT: AN AMERICAN–GERMAN DEBATE 274 (C. Joerges & D. M. Trubek Eds. 1989).

flags and keeping police files of independence advocates. Placing many forms of independence advocacy outside the law, formally or symbolically, contributed to create a social space of illegitimacy that had a negative effect on the way many people viewed the movement. This perception of illegitimacy, which translated from the legal to the political and vice versa, generated or promoted attitudes adverse to any proposal of separation from the United States. The coercive dimension of U.S. policy depended on those very attitudes for its effectiveness.

It has taken many years for independence to be viewed again as a legitimate aspiration by the population at large. This has occurred largely as a result of the events surrounding the deaths of the two *independentistas* on the Cerro Maravilla mountaintop. By now, however, American hegemony over Puerto Rican society has developed deeper roots, and independence is rejected on other grounds. Its political and legal legitimacy as a status formula is one thing; its perceived viability as an economic, social, and political project to be embarked upon is quite another.

The Discourse of Rights

It is crucial to remember, in the context of the form of colonialism that the Puerto Rican situation represents, that the coercive dimension of the colonial regime has been interwoven, in a relationship that transcends mere coexistence or contradiction, with a widely accepted discourse of rights, the institutions of representative democracy, and an otherwise generalized observance of the rule of law. In the sections that follow, I discuss how these phenomena have operated to constitute subjectivities and consolidate American hegemony in the island. I will start with the discourse of rights.

The notion of rights is a key feature of modern law. A *right* may be defined as a claim that a subject may make on others with the legitimate expectation of securing compliance through established mechanisms. The central actor in a modern legal system is the legal subject, who is conceived as a bearer of rights and obligations. In classical jurisprudence the debate about rights was mostly confined to an argument about the sources of rights. Positivists would accord the status of rights only to those claims sanctioned by positive law. Natural rights theorists would justify rights by reference to higher principles or norms conceived either as emanating from divine authority or as requirements of "natural" or practical reason. Present-day debates still reflect these tensions. For example, contemporary human rights philosophy locates the source of rights in various conceptions of human nature or by reference to the notion of human needs.

More recently, a new controversy has erupted, largely as a result of the writings of critical legal scholars. The debate hinges on the extent to which rights discourse is linked to diverse forms of domination. Most of the discussion has focused on the dynamics of rights discourse within industrial or postindustrial democratic societies. Little attention has been given to the dynamics of rights discourse in a colonial setting.[45] Because of its relevance, before addressing the particular situation of Puerto Rico I will discuss the main features of what has been called the "critique of rights."

---

[45] For a notable exception, *see* John Comaroff, *supra* note 9. For a discussion of the importance of rights claims among states in the international arena, see Onuma Yasuaki, *Between Natural Rights of Man and Fundamental Rights of States*, *in* ENLIGHTENMENT, RIGHTS AND REVOLUTION, *supra* note 8.

Critique of Rights

As formulated by critical scholars in the United States, Europe, and other countries within the Western legal tradition, the critique of rights has revolved around two fundamental problems: (a) the limits of liberal rights discourse and (b) its (negative) political and ideological effects.

Writing from a feminist perspective, Smart summarized some of the perceived limits of rights discourse, particularly for subordinated groups.[46] The most obvious limit, conceded by liberal theorists, is that the recognition of rights is not a guarantee of their actual enjoyment.[47] This is the famous problem of the ever-present "gap" between formal declaration and "reality."[48] Second, rights do not necessarily solve problems. They tend to oversimplify complex power relations, focusing on one aspect of them and most of the time failing to contextualize that single aspect within the multiple dimensions in which social problems usually occur.[49] Third, although formulated to deal with a social wrong, rights are always focused on the individual, who must prove that his or her rights have been violated.[50] This tends to preclude any formulation of collective right.[51] Fourth, rights may be appropriated by the powerful to further their own interests to the detriment of those who sought protection by the enactment of a particular right.[52] Finally, any claim of rights can be effectively countered by claims of competing rights.[53] This, in fact, is a variant of the indeterminacy critique, which was one of the earlier contributions of the critical legal studies movement and has since become part of much current theoretical writing about law.[54]

---

[46] CAROL SMART, FEMINISM AND THE POWER OF LAW 138–59 (1989).

[47] *Id.* at 143–44.

[48] *See also* E. Denninger, *Government Assistance in the Exercise of Basic Rights (Procedure and Organization)*, in CRITICAL LEGAL THOUGHT, *supra* note 44; Richard D. Parker, *The Effective Enjoyment of Rights*, in CRITICAL LEGAL THOUGHT, *supra* note 44; Shivji, *supra* note 8, at 273.

[49] *See* SMART, *supra* note 46, at 144.

[50] *Id.* at 145.

[51] But see Gerald G. Postema, *In Defence of 'French Nonsense': Fundamental Rights in Constitutional Jurisprudence*, in ENLIGHTENMENT, RIGHTS AND REVOLUTION, *supra* note 8, at 110, arguing that there is "no logical barrier to speaking of rights of groups, classes, states, corporations, nations or families, which rights are not reducible to rights of members considered apart from their membership in the group" and that "it is conceivable, then, that some rights might secure collective goods or interests." Shivji also raised this possibility from a Marxist perspective, claiming that in the specific context of Africa the struggle for rights has to be reconceptualized so that the central demands be cast in terms of collective rights, particularly the "right to self-determination" and the "right to organize." Shivji, *supra* note 8, at 283. In the field of international law there has been, since World War II, an emergence of the recognition of collective rights in the forms of "rights of people." *See* Onuma, *supra* note 45, at 144–45; Anna Michalska, *Rights of Peoples to Self-Determination in International Law*, in ISSUES OF SELF-DETERMINATION, *supra* note 13, at 71, 72–75. From the critics' point of view it may be argued that these arguments and developments represent only an apparent transcendence of classical individualism by replacing it with a new kind of "group individualism" that, ultimately, separates one group from another and precludes the formation of truly universal relations of solidarity. From the perspective of political economy, these phenomena may be explained as made possible by the transformations related, on the one hand, to the development of corporate capitalism and, on the other, to the tendency toward a global economy based both on competitiveness and interdependence among collective units, such as large corporations and states or, even, blocs of states.

[52] SMART, *supra* note 46, at 145.

[53] *Id.*

[54] *See* Frances Olsen, *Liberal Rights and Critical Legal Theory*, in CRITICAL LEGAL THOUGHT,

As Olsen expressed it, "in any important social conflict each side can present equally logical arguments that the concept of protecting individual rights requires that they prevail over the other side."[55]

For many critical scholars law is riddled with a radical indetermination. Its provisions do not have a fixed meaning. Any meaning is provided by the interpreter. Interpretation, especially judicial interpretation, is an exercise of power. Rights discourse, therefore, is a malleable instrument that many times ends up serving the interests of the dominators. This radical ambiguity has been explained in various ways. Its source may be located in the equivocal nature, the pliability, of language, as the legal realists demonstrated long ago. But it may go even further. Picciotto, for example, referred to an inherent contradiction in law arising from the tension between the requirement of generality of application and the need for specificity (as a precondition of predictability).[56] There may be other explanations.

Thus, the ambiguity of law may well reside in the very purpose the liberal ideal ascribes to it: the definition of a sphere of autonomy for the individual. In the liberal worldview, individuals are subjects competing for social goods, and their claims are conflicting demands in an ever-expanding field of commodified relations where needs are satisfied and personality defined. The indeterminacy of law would provide the needed flexibility to accommodate these conflicting demands in continually shifting circumstances.

The question remains whether rights discourse, as a form of referring to social relations, can survive the transcendence of a "liberal" culture and whether, in a different social world, any type of rights discourse would still be afflicted by a radical indeterminacy. If such were the case, we would have to look to deeper causes that extend beyond law and beyond existing social relations. Kennedy, for one, referred to a "fundamental contradiction" between the need and the fear of others that was supposedly reflected in law's provisions and, inevitably, in judicial interpretations of rights.[57] Along these lines, but avoiding the essentialism exuded by the fundamental contradiction thesis, it could be posited that, inasmuch as social life is so often riddled with paradox, any attempt to capture social relations through normative discourse would almost certainly be doomed to bear the burden of indeterminacy. Rights, then, would be, at the very least, an ambiguous value subject to the contingencies of power and other social and historical conditions.

The critique of rights also draws attention to the perceived negative effects of the discourse of rights. Three distinct critiques can be identified from the most recent theoretical debates about the political and ideological effects of rights discourse: (a) the individualism (or alienation) critique; (b) the disciplinary effect of rights claims, and (c) the "rights fetishism" critique.

The individualism or alienation critique can be traced back to Marx. For Marx liberal rights not only defined autonomous zones for individuals, but also set them

supra note 44, at 242; Postema, supra note 51, at 116–19; James Boyle, Introduction, in CRITICAL LEGAL STUDIES xiii, xix–xxi (James Boyle Ed. 1994).

[55] Olsen, supra note 54, at 242.

[56] Sol Picciotto, The Theory of the State, Class Struggle and the Rule of Law, in MARXISM AND LAW, supra note 16, at 178.

[57] Kennedy later "recanted" the fundamental contradiction analysis as a "reified abstraction." Peter Gabel & Duncan Kennedy, Roll over Beethoven, 36 STAN. L. REV. 1, 15–16, 36 (1984).

apart from others and alienated them from their own social nature and their community. In his famous essay "On the Jewish Question," he stated the following:

> Thus none of the so-called rights of man goes beyond egoistic man, man as he is in civil society, namely an individual withdrawn behind his private interests and whims and separated from the community. Far from the rights of man conceiving of man as a species-being, species-life itself, society appears as a framework exterior to individuals, a limitation of their original self-sufficiency. The only bond that holds them together is natural necessity, need and private interest, the conservation of their property and egoistic person.[58]

In sum, the discourse of rights reinforces individualism and alienation from self and from others. Fine replicated this criticism by asserting that "the law seems to engender community and common humanity, but at the same time, it produces mutual isolation, indifference and antagonism."[59] Writing from another political standpoint, Glendon argued that American "rights talk" enhances individualism, insularity, and the neglect of responsibility.[60] Picciotto added to the Marxist critique by suggesting that the channeling of struggles into the form of claims of "bourgeois legal rights" breaks up any movement toward solidarity through the operation of legal procedures that recognize only the individual subject of rights and duties.[61] Merry raised a similar point when, analyzing the cultural impact of domestic violence court cases, she concluded that "the nature of the law and its individualist construction of rights continue to construct the battered woman as an individual subject, enduring an individual injury rather than a collective wrong."[62]

From the perspective of political economy, it may be added that the tendency in market-oriented societies to commodify all relations, and to conceive of all aspirations in terms of value, results in the transformation of "rights" into things owned. This development could be seen as reinforcing what Habermas, following others, called the "possessive individualism"[63] that characterizes the dominant worldview in capitalist societies. But Habermas himself has refuted the thesis that the notion of rights is inevitably individualistic. Rights, according to Habermas, are constructed in the context of intersubjective relations. To assert a claim as a right is to invoke the recognition of the other members of the community as a legal subject.[64] "Rights," argued Habermas, "are based on the reciprocal recognition of cooperating legal persons."[65] He added,

> *At a conceptual level*, rights do not immediately refer to atomistic and estranged individuals who are possessively set against one another. On the contrary, as elements

---

[58] Karl Marx, *On the Jewish Question, in* NONSENSE UPON STILTS: BENTHAM, BURKE AND MARX ON THE RIGHTS OF MAN 137, 147 (Jeremy Waldron Ed. 1987).

[59] BOB FINE, DEMOCRACY AND THE RULE OF LAW: LIBERAL IDEALS AND MARXIST CRITIQUES 145 (1984).

[60] MARY ANN GLENDON, RIGHTS TALK: THE IMPOVERISHMENT OF POLITICAL DISCOURSE (1991).

[61] Picciotto, *supra* note 56, at 175.

[62] Sally Engle Merry, *Wife Battering and the Ambiguities of Rights, in* IDENTITIES, POLITICS, AND RIGHTS, *supra* note 9, at 305.

[63] JÜRGEN HABERMAS, LEGITIMATION CRISIS 77, 82–83 (1988).

[64] JÜRGEN HABERMAS, BETWEEN FACTS AND NORMS: CONTRIBUTIONS TO A DISCOURSE THEORY OF LAW AND DEMOCRACY 88 (1996).

[65] *Id.*

> of the legal order, they presuppose collaboration among subjects who recognize one another, in their reciprocally related rights and duties, as free and equal citizens.[66]

In this view, rights are seen as buttressing the relational aspect of living.

Other authors have also stressed the capacity for rights discourse to build social relations marked by solidarity rather than isolation. Scheingold, for example, has maintained that the claim of a right, particularly through litigation, implies a certain politicization of a demand, which may contribute to the formation of a collective identity to the extent that the claim is made by groups of individuals who view themselves as sharing a common plight.[67] Sherry has argued that many of the most important rights that eventually made their way into the U.S. Constitution "serve a communal or civic purpose." "Certainly many of the rights were necessary or useful to a deliberative republican citizenry (freedom of speech is one such right), and others offered 'protection to various intermediate associations . . . designed to create an educated and virtuous electorate.' "[68]

Building upon a Foucauldian analysis of power, Smart asserted that the claim for rights has another important effect: It generates new mechanisms for surveillance, regulation, and control. The recognition of a legal right immediately calls for the establishment of a machinery to enforce it. This machinery enhances the power of the state and regulatory apparatuses, which claim the need for more information about the subjects entitled to rights.[69] Piven and Cloward, among others, advanced a similar insight almost two decades before in relation to welfare recipients.[70]

The Australian jurist Valerie Kerruish has authored an elaborate formulation of the "rights fetishism" critique.[71] Working from the basic categories of Marxist political economy, Kerruish concluded that liberal legal practices and jurisprudence, operating as ideology, have helped to produce a social phenomenon that may be described as "rights fetishism." One aspect of rights fetishism consists in the attribution of a universal value to rights, much in the same fashion as commodities are ascribed a universal value (of exchange) apart from the specific use value of each object produced. Another aspect is the process whereby "rights" become an abstract reality that begins to command certain veneration. Finally, fetishization involves a process by which the identity of a person is defined by his or her rights—by the fact that he or she is a legal subject.[72] In short, it is having rights that constitutes the person, or more precisely, rights are the source of one's value as a person. This is the most profound effect, in the realm of consciousness, of the discourse of rights.

The critique of rights has elicited vigorous responses. In the United States, particularly, lawyers engaged in activist work and feminist and minority scholars took to task the critical legal studies critique of rights by stressing the benefits that the

---

[66] *Id.* (emphasis in the original).

[67] STUART SCHEINGOLD, THE POLITICS OF RIGHTS: LAWYERS, PUBLIC POLICY, AND POLITICAL CHANGE (1974); *see esp.* chap. 9.

[68] Suzanna Sherry, *Rights Talk: Must We Mean What We Say?*, 17 LAW & SOC. INQ. 491, 498 (1992).

[69] SMART, *supra* note 46, at 142, 143.

[70] *See* F. PIVEN & R. CLOWARD, REGULATING THE POOR: THE FUNCTIONS OF PUBLIC WELFARE (1971); *see also* Anthony V. Alfieri, *The Antinomies of Poverty Law and a Theory of Dialogic Empowerment*, 16 N.Y.U. REV. L. & SOC. CHANGE 659, 667–68 (1987–88).

[71] VALERIE KERRUISH, JURISPRUDENCE AS IDEOLOGY (1991).

[72] *Id., esp.* 139–65.

claim for rights entails for those in subordinated positions in society.[73] For Crenshaw, "rights have been important." "They may have legitimated racial inequality, but they have also been the means by which oppressed groups have secured both entry as formal equals into the dominant order and the survival of their movement in the face of private and state repression."[74] Olsen suggested that one important value of the possibility of claiming rights is the sense of human worth that such claims reinforce in those making them.[75] "On a personal level," Olsen wrote, "to claim a right is to assert one's self-worth, to affirm one's moral value and entitlement. It is a way for a person to make a claim about herself and her role in the world."[76] This reasoning converts into a positive gain the effects of rights Kerruish attributed to the phenomenon she labeled "rights fetishism."

That rights provide benefits to people, including the less powerful, is something that most critics of rights discourse would concede. Marx himself did not rule out "bourgeois rights" as a mere sham. Fine has interpreted Marx's critique as one directed not at individual rights in themselves but at the limited nature of those rights in bourgeois society. The question for Marx, according to Fine, was not the abolition but the enlargement of individual rights, the limitless extension of right until it encompasses the totality of human experience.[77] Picciotto admitted that a right "encapsulated in bourgeois legal form is certainly better than no right at all"; the aim, however, is to transcend the limitations of this form if social transformation on behalf of the working class is to succeed.[78]

Kerruish also proposed that rights "be taken seriously" in at least two senses: (a) the claims of subordinated people are claims for rights and must be attended to, and (b) rights, if properly kept to their specific contexts, have a political use value.[79] There are both political and moral reasons for this attitude. "The political point," she wrote, "is that in a society structured by materially unequal social relations, people on the down side of these relations would be worse off without law than they are with law"; while the "moral point is still the Kantian perception of the ethical value of equal concern and respect for individuals."[80] Her "political point" implies that the valuation of rights has to be contextualized. To the extent that the critique of rights adopts the form of an absolute rejection of rights, without attending to the historical, social, and political context, it slips into abstract, a priori theorizing, with the risk of becoming what Olsen termed a "new Scholastic Orthodoxy."[81]

---

[73] See, e.g., Ed Sparer, *Fundamental Human Rights, Legal Entitlements, and the Social Struggle: A Friendly Critique of the Critical Legal Studies Movement*, 36 STAN. L. REV. 509 (1984); Olsen, *supra* note 54; Crenshaw, *supra* note 44; Mari Matsuda, *Looking to the Bottom: Critical Legal Studies and Reparations*, 22 HARV. C.R.–C.L. L. REV. 323 (1987).

[74] Crenshaw, *supra* note 44, at 293.

[75] Olsen, *supra* note 54, at 244.

[76] *Id.*

[77] See FINE, *supra* note 59, at 129.

[78] Picciotto, *supra* note 56, at 175.

[79] One of the best analyses of the political use value of rights has been provided by the American political scientist Stuart Scheingold. In his now classic THE POLITICS OF RIGHTS, *supra* note 67, Scheingold saw rights as political resources that can be used for the effective activation and mobilization of social groups to achieve social change.

[80] KERRUISH, *supra* note 71, at 145. A question Kerruish does not seem to answer is whether the "moral" reason for taking rights seriously would imply that rights, in the end, do have a universal value, apart from their obvious specific use value in particularized political contexts.

[81] Olsen, *supra* note 54, at 253.

Shivji made a similar point, in the African context, arguing that the "struggle for formal legal equality and democracy," cast in a new language of "collective rights," "has still a role to play in the African formation."[82] Comaroff and Abel have produced case studies that have shown how even in its traditional liberal form rights discourse was useful first in generating resistance against the colonizers in colonial South Africa and, later, in the struggle against the system of apartheid.[83] The Japanese jurist Onuma Yosuaki, emphasizing that the "rights" formulation has a particularly strong appeal to those who are oppressed or alienated from various values and interests in society, predicted that

> as long as there remains an apparent hierarchical structure in terms of power, a frustration resulting therefrom, and a keen desire to express the claims of the powerless in a legitimate and effective manner, the attempts to formulate these claims as rights will continue to exist.[84]

This, he added, is also valid for international society, where there are enormous gaps between a small number of rich and powerful nations and a large number of poor and powerless ones. The poorer nations, he suggested, will benefit from recourse to the discourse of rights.[85]

The debate generated by the critique of rights has produced a new awareness, on both sides of the question, of the ambiguity and even paradoxical character of rights. It has become generally accepted that, from the point of view of political struggles and attempts at social transformation, the claim of rights has limitations but can produce tangible benefits. As Sarat and Kearns expressed it, "We know now that rights can be sources of empowerment and protection for persons against the societies in which they live, yet they can constrain those same persons."[86] "Rights persist and flourish," they concluded, "at least in part, because of, not in spite of, their many-sidedness and their paradoxical qualities."[87]

The Discourse of Rights in Puerto Rican Society

The Puerto Rican experience under American rule has differed in one important respect from many other colonial experiences. The language of rights has been a key feature of the dominant discourses in Puerto Rican society and an important mediating phenomenon between the United States and the Puerto Rican population. Although in other colonial situations the discourse of rights may have been part of the legitimating strategies of both colonizers and colonized, the difference in the Puerto Rican case lies in the centrality of such language in Puerto Rican culture during the course of the 20th century.

---

[82] Shivji, *supra* note 8, at 282–83.

[83] *See* Comaroff, *supra* note 9; Richard L. Abel, *Nothing Left but Rights: Law in the Struggle against Apartheid*, in IDENTITIES, POLITICS, AND RIGHTS, *supra* note 9, at 239–70.

[84] Onuma, *supra* note 45, at 151.

[85] *Id.* at 150, 151.

[86] Austin Sarat & Thomas R. Kearns, *Editorial Introduction* to IDENTITIES, POLITICS, AND RIGHTS, *supra* note 9, at 7.

[87] *Id.* The collection of articles contained in the cited book on identities, politics, and rights, edited by Sarat and Kearns, reflects this approach to rights as ambiguous and paradoxical.

Several factors may have contributed to this development. For example, the discourse of rights was not foreign to Puerto Rican political elites when the United States invaded the country. They were well versed in its nuances. Nineteenth-century Puerto Rican liberals had already made the claim of rights a major element of their political discourse to confront the oppression of the Spanish regime. They soon started to wield its critical edges against the new invader. Thus, a significant number among them began to demand their "right" to self-government.

Another factor may be the extent to which, since the early days of the American occupation, the subordinated sectors of Puerto Rican society felt attracted to the new regime. Many workers, women, and Black and mixed-race Puerto Ricans saw in the forms and symbols of American legal and political discourse an opportunity to shed the state of social oppression they identified with Spanish colonialism and with the Creole elite that had exploited and marginalized them.[88] For example, the founder of the prostatehood Puerto Rican Republican Party was a Puerto Rican physician of African descent who had studied in the United States. The suffragist movement took inspiration in its American counterpart. The labor movement of the early part of the 20th century established close links with U.S. labor unions. In fact, the first Puerto Rican Socialist Party adopted statehood as its goal for the resolution of the colonial problem of Puerto Rico.

A third factor contributing to the development of a rights-oriented political culture may be the fact that, especially since the middle of the 20th century, in many respects Puerto Rican society has come to resemble more and more, in its organizing principles and daily practices, the societies of advanced capitalism. To the extent that the liberal discourse of rights embodies a certain equivalence to the ideological framework of commodity exchange in a capitalist economy, as Pashukanis and other Marxists and neo-Marxists have suggested,[89] it is understandable that a colonial society with a relatively modern market economy would become the site of a normative discourse of social relationships that assumes the form of expanding claims of individual rights.

A related factor was the deepening insertion of Puerto Rican society into the worldview of modernity as the century progressed. By *modernity*, I mean the cultural forms associated with the development of industrialized societies and liberal democratic or socialist states. Rights discourse has been a principal feature of these social and cultural formations, particularly in the version of modernity in American and Western European cultures. Rights discourse, then, has been an important component of modern subjectivity. Puerto Rico gradually became a modern colonial society, with a corresponding reliance on rights discourse to interpret and evaluate the legitimacy of social and political relations.

Finally, another contributing factor to the development of a rights-oriented public and private discourse in Puerto Rico has been the basic conceptual and normative framework the ruling elites of the metropolitan state elaborated to facilitate its exercise of authority over the territory, together with the compromises they made to attend to the material and symbolic demands emerging from the various sectors of

---

[88] *See* Wilfredo Mattos Cintrón, *La hegemonía de Estados Unidos en Puerto Rico y el independentismo, los derechos civiles y la cuestión nacional*, 16 EL CARIBE CONTEMPORÁNEO 21, 27–28 (1988).

[89] *See* EVGENI PASHUKANIS, LAW AND MARXISM (1983); FINE, *supra* note 59; KERRUISH, *supra* note 71.

the territory's population. It is to this conceptual framework that I now turn my attention.

The governing elites of the United States who helped shape the country's colonial policy at the turn of the century had differing views regarding how to treat the populations of the recently acquired territories. A strong current argued that the establishment of a colonial regime in those territories was not incompatible with the recognition of basic fundamental rights of the subjected populations. Indeed, to be successful, the colonial project would have to rely on such recognition. The idea was expressed very clearly by Senator Teller, who saw "no reason . . . why the United States may not have a colony" but felt that the country was bound to extend to any colony the "great principles that underlie the government" and to maintain there "a free government" and "liberty."[90] Senator Teller's remarks synthesized the basic political conceptual framework that would, in due course, be adopted by the three branches of the government of the United States.

This basic framework is clearly evident in the rationale of the *Insular Cases*. Those cases drew a sharp distinction between civil rights and democracy, between "fundamental" individual rights and the rights of political participation. They relied also on another conceptual cleavage that distinguished between the "civil rights" of the inhabitants and the "political status" of the territory. These conceptual differentiations would justify extending certain rights deemed "fundamental" while preserving the basic subordination inherent in a colonial system.

A complex normative structure emerged from this basic conceptual framework. The *Insular Cases* made clear that the inhabitants of unincorporated territories could claim the "fundamental" rights enshrined in the U.S. Constitution. Those guarantees were deemed to be limitations imposed on the actions of the territorial and "federal" governments.[91] Throughout the century that has elapsed since the first group of cases were decided, the Supreme Court has been engaged in determining what those "fundamental rights" might be. The *Insular Cases* themselves established that indictment and trial by jury were not fundamental enough.[92] Either by express holding or by implication, the Court has determined that at least the following constitutional rights should be considered fundamental, and therefore applicable in Puerto Rico: freedom of expression,[93] due process of law,[94] equal protection of the laws,[95] the right to travel,[96] and the protection against unreasonable searches and seizures.[97] It has been

---

[90] Quoted in José Cabranes, *Citizenship and the American Empire*, 127 U. PA. L. REV. 391, 429 n.146 (1978).

[91] The term "federal" is placed here in quotation marks because, strictly speaking, unincorporated territories are not considered to be part of the federation, but territory belonging to the United States. In practice, however, the government of the United States is referred to as the federal government in all its dealings with the territories. In subsequent text, the quotation marks will be omitted both for stylistic purposes and to conform with current usage of the term.

[92] Hawaii v. Mankichi, 190 U.S. 197 (1903); Dorr v. United States, 195 U.S. 138 (1904).

[93] Balzac v. Porto Rico, 258 U.S. 298 (1922); Posadas de Puerto Rico Associates v. Tourism Company of Puerto Rico, 478 U.S. 1046 (1986).

[94] Bianchi v. Morales, 262 U.S. 170 (1923); Secretary of Agriculture v. Central Roig, 338 U.S. 604 (1950); Calero Toledo v. Pearson Yacht Leasing Co., 416 U.S. 663 (1974); Examining Board v. Flores de Otero, 426 U.S. 572 (1976).

[95] Examining Board v. Flores de Otero, 426 U.S. 572 (1976); Califano v. Torres, 435 U.S. 1 (1978); Harris v. Rosario, 446 U.S. 651 (1980).

[96] Califano v. Torres, 435 U.S. 1 (1978).

[97] Segurola v. United States, 275 U.S. 106 (1927); Torres v. Puerto Rico, 442 U.S. 465 (1979).

suggested that, regardless of the rationale of the *Insular Cases*, most of the Bill of Rights of the U.S. Constitution should be considered extensive to Puerto Rico.[98] Puerto Ricans residing in Puerto Rico may also claim against the U.S. government those rights extended to them by congressional legislation creating federal entitlements.

Another dimension of the normative structure of rights in Puerto Rico consists of claims that may be made exclusively to the government of Puerto Rico. These rights constitute what may be called the "internal regime of rights." Their source may be legislation passed by the U.S. Congress that limits the powers of the Puerto Rican government or provisions contained in the Constitution of Puerto Rico and in Puerto Rican laws. A group of such statutory rights created by the U.S. Congress was contained in Section 2 of the Jones Act of 1917,[99] a bill of rights claimable against the government of Puerto Rico. The list included most of the rights found in the Bill of Rights and other provisions of the U.S. Constitution. The provisions of Section 2 were repealed in 1950 by Public Law 600,[100] the U.S. statute that authorized Puerto Ricans to draft their own constitution. The bill of rights contained in the Puerto Rican Constitution of 1952 replaced the statutory scheme of basic civil rights adopted in the Jones Act. The Constitution of the Commonwealth of Puerto

---

[98] Former Associate Justice William Brennan's concurrent opinion in Torres v. Puerto Rico, 442 U.S. 465, 474 (1979), adhered to by Justices Stewart, Marshall, and Blackmun, contained the expression: "Whatever the validity of the old cases such as *Downes . . . Dorr . . .* and *Balzac . . .* , in the particular historical context in which they were decided, those cases are clearly not authority for questioning the application of the Fourth Amendment—or any other provision of the Bill of Rights—to the Commonwealth of Puerto Rico in the 1970's." *Id.* at 476. For more detailed discussions of the matter, see ARNOLD H. LEIBOWITZ, DEFINING STATUS: A COMPREHENSIVE ANALYSIS OF UNITED STATES TERRITORIAL RELATIONS (1989); David Helfeld, *How Much of the United States Constitution and Statutes are Applicable to the Commonwealth of Puerto Rico?*, 110 FED. RULES DEC. 452 (1986); José A. Cabranes, *Puerto Rico and the Constitution*, 110 FED. RULES DEC. 475 (1986); R. Pérez-Bachs, *Applicability of the United States Constitution and Federal Laws to the Commonwealth of Puerto Rico*, 110 FED. RULES DEC. 485 (1986).

One question the Supreme Court has refused to decide is by virtue of what clause of the U.S. Constitution do the "due process" and "equal protection" guarantees apply to Puerto Rico. The Fifth Amendment applies only to the federal government, while the Fourteenth Amendment is addressed to the states. The issue is not without legal significance. For the Fifth Amendment to protect against actions of the Puerto Rican government, the latter would have to be considered no more than an extension of the "federal" government. If the Fourteenth were the source of the protection, then Puerto Rico would be considered a sovereignty akin to a state of the union. In a well-known footnote in Calero v. Pearson, 416 U.S. 663 (1974), Justice Brennan stated, "Unconstitutionality of the statutes was alleged under both the Fifth and Fourteenth Amendments. The District Court deemed it unnecessary to determine which Amendment applied to Puerto Rico . . . and we agree. The Joint Resolution of Congress approving the Constitution of the Commonwealth of Puerto Rico, subjects its government to "the applicable provisions of the Constitution of the United States, . . . and there cannot exist under the American flag any governmental authority untrammeled by the requirements of due process of law as guaranteed by the Constitution of the United States." *Id.* at 668–69 n.5 (citations omitted).

In Examining Board v. Flores, 426 U.S. 572 (1976), Justice Blackmun, writing for the Court, referred to Brennan's footnote thus: "The Court, however, thus far has declined to say whether it is the Fifth Amendment or the Fourteenth which provides the protection. *Calero-Toledo*, 416 U.S., at 668–669, n. 5. Once again, we need not resolve that precise question because, irrespective of which Amendment applies, the statutory restriction [under discussion] . . . is plainly unconstitutional." *Id.* at 601.

[99] Jones Act, ch. 190, 39 Stat. 951 § 2 (1917) (codified at 48 U.S.C. § 731c (1987).

[100] 64 Stat. 319, 48 U.S.C.A. 731b (1950).

Rico[101] provides the current formal framework for the internal regime of rights in the country.

The Puerto Rican Constitution follows closely, in most respects, the American constitutional model, although there are some significant differences. The Puerto Rican Constitution adopts the American institutional arrangement of separation of powers. The judicial system provided for is very similar to that existing in the United States, with the peculiarity that judicial review of legislative acts is expressly established in the constitutional text. Puerto Rican Supreme Court justices enjoy life tenure. Judges of the inferior courts are designated for specified periods of time. The system is predicated on the principle of judicial independence.

Article II contains a bill of rights that in many respects surpasses the provisions of its federal counterpart. It recognizes the familiar rights protecting against the deprivation of liberty and property without due process of law, the guarantees of equal protection of the laws, freedom of speech and assembly, and the rights of the accused in the criminal process. But additionally, it expressly consigns the right to privacy (which protects against state and private action), several important rights relating to employment (such as the right to equal pay for equal work and to a reasonable minimum wage), and a direct condemnation of discrimination on account of race, color, sex, birth, social origin or condition, or political or religious ideas. Since 1952, the Supreme Court of Puerto Rico has made it a point to assert the principle that the Constitution of Puerto Rico, in questions relating to human rights, should be regarded to enshrine a much broader scope of protections than those contained in the U.S. Constitution.[102]

It is evident that the writers of the Puerto Rican Constitution of 1952 wished to go beyond the traditional liberal conception of rights. They drafted a section providing for certain social rights, such as the rights to obtain work; to an adequate standard of living; to social protection in the event of unemployment, sickness, old age, or disability; and to special care during motherhood and childhood.[103] The Puerto Rican electorate approved that section, together with the rest of the constitution. However, the U.S. Congress rejected the provision and excluded it from the approval it extended, with certain conditions, to the remainder of the document drafted by the Puerto Rican Constitutional Convention and ratified by the Puerto Rican people.[104]

The Puerto Rican Constitution of 1952 articulates a particular political vision: a combination of American political theory and the worldview of the Puerto Rican elites that led the process of economic, social, and political reform during the 1940s. Those elites were, in large measure, the biological and political heirs of the creole *hacendados* and liberal professionals who, in the late 19th century and early years of the 20th, had embraced the liberal political creed, first as a response to the ab-

---

[101] See chapter 3 for a brief description of the process that led to its adoption.

[102] *See, for example*, Figueroa Ferrer v. ELA, 107 D.P.R. 250 (1978) (declaring that the right to obtain a divorce on mutual agreement, without stating the reasons for the request, is part of the right to privacy protected by the Constitution); Soto v. Secretario de Justicia, 112 D.P.R. 477 (1982) (recognizing the right to obtain certain information from the government as part of the freedom of speech guarantee).

[103] Constitution of Puerto Rico § 20.

[104] Public Law 447, 66 Stat. at L 327, 48 U.S.C.A. 731d (1952). The requirement imposed by the U.S. Congress on the Puerto Rican Constitutional Convention and on the Puerto Rican people that Section 20 be excised from the Constitution can be considered another instance of symbolic violence. It constituted an imposition, in the manner of rejection, of certain principles of social organization.

solutism of the Spanish regime and later as a way of reaffirming their identification with, and admiration for, American institutions.

Many among the leaders and technocrats who participated in the process that produced the Puerto Rican Constitution had been trained in American universities and professed the basic values of the American political system. Many of them also had a pronounced inclination to take on social questions, influenced by early contacts with the labor-led Puerto Rican Socialist Party or by the social democratic ideals of the Rooseveltian New Dealers. This inclination partly explains the inclusion of certain social rights in the Constitution. The explanation also lies in the fact that, to a certain degree, the Constitution crystallized some of the claims that had been made throughout the first four decades of the century by popular movements, such as the labor and the women's rights movement.

Of course this regime of rights has limits of the type mentioned above in the general discussion of the critique of rights. The most obvious one is the "gap" existing in many instances between the formal declaration of rights and the "reality" of their enjoyment. The profound social inequalities that still exist in Puerto Rican society effectively preclude many people from full enjoyment of their rights.

For example, it is estimated that more than 60% of Puerto Rican families live below the poverty level.[105] Poor communities often bear the brunt of police brutality, and despite the existence of legal aid programs, acute problems of access to the courts are prevalent. In 1991, 72% of the men convicted and under custody had been unemployed at the time of their arrest, 65% did not have an occupation or trade, and half had not obtained a formal education beyond the ninth grade. Among women convicted and in jail, 99.7% were unemployed at the time of their arrest, 93.4% did not have an occupation or trade, and 4 out of 10 had not studied beyond the eighth grade. Among young adults, 81% of those in jail had been unemployed, 65% did not engage in any trade or occupation, approximately half had not studied beyond the eighth grade, the majority had been convicted for crimes against property; and 90% of the crimes had been motivated by economic difficulties.[106]

An increasing number of poor households are headed by women. Working women are still paid less than men for comparable work. Moreover, women are often victimized when they take part in judicial processes.[107] Poor immigrants from nearby Caribbean countries, like the Dominican Republic, have been increasingly subjected to discriminatory practices and are often the object of bigoted remarks, both in private and in public, not only by ordinary citizens but also by government officials. Gay men and lesbians have suffered from discrimination and prejudice in all levels and activities of society. The Puerto Rican situation confirms Smart's insight that rights do not necessarily solve complex social problems. Despite the profusion of

---

[105] See CONSEJO DE DESARROLLO ESTRATÉGICO PARA PUERTO RICO, OFICINA DEL GOBERNADOR, EQUIDAD, CALIDAD DE VIDA Y DESARROLLO ECONÓMICO EN PUERTO RICO: LA CUESTIÓN DE LA POBREZA 28 (1992) [LA CUESTIÓN DE LA POBREZA]. The extent and nature of poverty in Puerto Rico is extensively discussed also in *Desigualdad y pobreza en Puerto Rico* (documentary film, Linda Colón prod. 1988) (copy on file at the Faculty of General Studies of the University of Puerto Rico).

[106] LA CUESTIÓN DE LA POBREZA, *supra* note 105, at 7.

[107] See Esther Vicente, *Las mujeres y el cambio en la norma jurídica*, 56 REV. JUR. U.P.R. 585 (1987); COMISIÓN JUDICIAL ESPECIAL PARA INVESTIGAR EL DISCRIMEN POR GÉNERO EN LOS TRIBUNALES DE PUERTO RICO, EL DISCRIMEN POR RAZÓN DE GÉNERO EN LOS TRIBUNALES (1995).

rights recognized by the legal system, fundamental oppressions and unequal power relations still prevail, including class, gender, racial, and colonial subordination.

Another limiting effect of the discourse of rights in the Puerto Rican context can be detected. The liberal conception of rights prevalent within such discourse exerts an ideological pressure that tends to force the formulation of demands into the mold of individual rights, to the detriment of more collective demands. This tendency, however, seems to be countered by other types of discourses arising from a long tradition of social struggles that bring to the surface a more collective vision, such as when diverse groups claim the protection of the "rights" of a certain community, such as the rights of "workers" or of "women," viewed as distinct groups. A recent expression of this collective vision was contained in the claims made by the residents of Vieques that they have a collective right to be left alone by the U.S. Navy.[108]

The conflict between individual and collective rights tends to emerge especially in the context of discussions about the future political status of Puerto Rico. The demands attendant to a collective right, such as the right of self-determination of the Puerto Rican people, may encounter difficulties when confronted with the individual rights of Puerto Ricans viewed as individual American citizens or as individual voters. The claim of a collective "right" of a people to preserve its identity may clash with the preferences of individuals who assert their individual rights to self-expression.

This clash has become apparent, for example, in debates about the issue of language in Puerto Rico. The goal of preserving the collective right to preserve Spanish as a defining feature of Puerto Rican culture may collide with the expectations of individual Puerto Ricans who do not speak Spanish (for example, some of those raised in the continental United States) not to be discriminated against on account of language. Thus, the Puerto Rican context exemplifies the tensions inherent in claims of collective rights when confronted with those of individual members of the collectivity.

The limitations of rights discourse identified above, however, should not be taken as evidence that such discourse has been only a trap for Puerto Ricans as a community. The discourse of rights has not been a sham, a naked legitimating strategy of the powers that be. The language of rights and the concrete experience of a regime of liberal rights, despite their constraints, have produced opportunities for the vindication of important claims. They have been deployed internally against the Puerto Rican elites who control the state apparatus as well as externally against the policies and actions of the metropolitan state. The many examples include individual victories won in local and federal courts of law, as well as gains more collective in nature, such as the people's right to elect their own legislature and their own governor, however limited the powers of those officials may be.

In this sense, rights in the Puerto Rican context have not been simply an illusion. They have yielded tangible benefits. They have been part of the material experience of negotiating, sometimes on the larger scale of history, most of the time on a day-to-day basis, the conditions of existence of Puerto Ricans, both as individuals and as a national community. Rights, then, within the context of the colonial relationship between the United States and Puerto Rico, have exhibited the ambiguous and par-

---

[108] See the brief discussion of the Vieques issue in chapters 3 and 7.

adoxical character that other authors have described in a variety of situations in other communities.[109]

The regime of rights in place in Puerto Rico has had a variety of constitutive effects on Puerto Rican society. Those effects have touched on all aspects of living and struggling within the community, on all dimensions of the country's social fabric, and on the larger facets of its historical experience as well as on the most minute details of its daily interactions. The regime of rights has helped to shape the relations and practices that compound family life, economic structures, educational systems, artistic expression, political organizing, the dispensation of justice, the electoral process, and many other social phenomena.

The regime of rights is, in turn, supported by a highly developed infrastructure to administer the handling of rights claims. That complex web of institutions includes a sizable organized legal profession, a relatively modern system of courts, a high number of judicial functionaries, several professional law schools, diverse legal services programs, and an increasing number of informational and other support services geared to the legal profession. This infrastructure is part of the material manifestation of a pervasive legal culture and of the importance of the discourse of rights in this particular society. All of these phenomena call for more extensive and in-depth sociological analysis, for they help to define the character of contemporary Puerto Rican society. That fuller inquiry cannot be pursued here, so my examination is limited to those effects of the discourse of rights that most directly pertain to the relationship between the United States and Puerto Rico.

An important effect of the discourse of rights has been the development of a "federal" machinery for the protection of rights. Its workings include the supervision of the local state apparatus by the U.S. federal court system and the operation of the U.S. Supreme Court as ultimate arbiter of many individual and collective conflicts. This supervision has made possible a type of subjection to metropolitan control that many view as legitimate, and even desirable or simply convenient. In fact, independence advocates and other social and political activists who oppose the American regime in Puerto Rico or question some of its adverse consequences have sought remedy in federal courts as a way to exercise leverage against local Puerto Rican officials or against the federal bureaucracy and the U.S. military. Examples include civil rights suits against the Puerto Rico and U.S. governments and court challenges to U.S. Navy activities in Vieques. At different moments, the role of the federal court in Puerto Rico has been criticized and even radically questioned, both politically and in academic writing.[110] However, in a very important way, the view of the federal

---

[109] *See, for example,* the collection of essays in IDENTITIES, POLITICS, AND RIGHTS, *supra* note 9, especially those discussing the place of the discourse of rights in colonial South Africa, in the struggle against apartheid, and in the context of wife battering cases in Hawaii.

[110] *See, e.g.* Carmelo Delgado Cintrón, *El juez federal Bernard Rodey y la crisis de 1909; La oposición de la Cámara de Delegados a la Corte Federal,* 40 REV. COL. ABOG. P.R. 415 (1979); Miriam Naveira de Rodón, *Federal Court Jurisdiction and the Status Commission,* 39 REV. COL. ABOG. P.R. 131 (1978); Roberto Tschudin, *The United States District Court for the District of Puerto Rico: Can an English Language Court Serve the Interest of Justice in a Spanish Language Society?,* 37 REV. COL. ABOG. P.R. 41 (1976).

The most recent political challenge to the U.S. District Court in Puerto Rico has been the refusal of Vieques protesters to recognize the court's authority to judge them for their acts of civil disobedience. The court's orders to incarcerate some protesters pending trial for misdemeanor charges has triggered

court system as a guarantor of rights has served to buttress American hegemony within segments of the population in different periods.

There are still more profound ways, however, in which the discourse of rights has operated to consolidate U.S. hegemony over Puerto Rico. The vision enshrined in the Puerto Rican Constitution has developed a force of its own. The language of rights has become a central feature of political discourse in Puerto Rican life throughout the social spectrum. Because of its visibility and great weight in public life, the legal profession—which to a large measure has taken as its "exemplary center"[111] the American bar—has been instrumental in spreading this vision and transforming it into part of the dominant, hegemonic culture. In this sense, the discourse of rights has been not only a product of an ideological consciousness, but also a primary producer of that consciousness.[112]

The discourse of rights promotes a view whereby social relations and needs are interpreted and articulated in terms of rights possessed, claimed, or denied. Rights discourse is a component of a broader phenomenon that may be called *legal consciousness*, or the awareness of law as a constitutive element of personal and social experience that, in turn, produces a tendency to view the world through juridical lenses. Legal consciousness and rights discourse, therefore, constitute a particular subjectivity. They form part of a subject's perception and evaluation of the world and of the subject's relationship to it. Through those lenses, the world is perceived either as conforming or deviating from law, as fulfilling or frustrating the promises held by rights. The discourse of rights, then, has contributed to produce a certain way of viewing the world, that is, a certain type of subjectivity, within the Puerto Rican community.

I have discussed already how rights are closely associated with notions of personal worth. This is an important feature of the kind of subjectivity that incorporates rights discourse as one of its constitutive elements. On the basis of my observations of Puerto Rican society, I believe that substantial sectors of the Puerto Rican population ascribe a great significance to the notion of rights.[113] For many, having rights constitutes one as a person, as a moral being. In this sense, their identity as people is to a great extent defined by their perceived status as bearers of rights. The extent to which that self-perception outweighs the sense of identity produced by other factors, such as language, ethnicity, or other shared "cultural" practices, is difficult to determine. In fact, it may be that, in many people, there is no felt need to balance them. All those factors may work to reinforce each other. Such would be the case, for example, when a person claims the right to speak a certain language, for example Spanish. In that instance his or her identity is being constructed both as someone who has a right and as someone who speaks and wants to speak that language as his or her own. The notion of the self as a "rights bearer" is, then, another among the multiple identitary factors that coalesce into the making of his or her specific identity.

Certainly, there are bound to be differences in this construction of the self de-

---

harsh criticism from the Puerto Rican Bar Association, law professors, and political and religious leaders, among others.

[111] CLIFFORD GEERTZ, NEGARA: THE THEATER STATE IN NINETEENTH CENTURY BALI (1980).

[112] *See* Robert W. Gordon, *Critical Legal Histories*, 36 STAN. L. REV. 57, 112 n.120 (1984).

[113] This fact is made patently clear in a documentary film sponsored by the Puerto Rican Bar Association under the title *Nosotros, el pueblo de Puerto Rico* (Angelita Rieckehoff prod. c. 1982).

pending on such variables as class or generation. But what seems obvious, in the Puerto Rican case, is that many express a great appreciation for the idea that they have rights. This does not mean necessarily that they can recite with precision the specific rights accorded them by the legal order. Nor does it mean that those rights are effectively enjoyed by them. What it means is that there is a generalized belief that they, as individuals, have rights. Sometimes, the content of those rights deemed to be possessed may coincide with the "objective" definition contained in actual legal texts. Other times, it may not. Nonetheless, people continue to view themselves as legal subjects, that is, as bearers of rights.

The crucial fact, as far as the reproduction of hegemony is concerned, is that, for considerable segments of the population, this source of moral worth is the American legal and political system. It is in the institutions of the metropolis that "safeguards" of this worth are perceived to be located. The paradox that results is that the devaluation that colonialism has historically entailed becomes invisible, concealed, as it is compensated by the sense of worth that is felt to derive from being an American citizen and a bearer of rights. As we have seen, that citizenship and those rights have very serious limitations. But they are accorded enough value to provoke strong reactions in their defense and to stimulate aspirations to see their benefits extended.

Some independence supporters have minimized the relevance of this "reality" of rights, particularly at the individual level, and have stressed the importance of the collective and personal devaluation inherent in a colonial relationship. For the more radical, the discourse of rights has been a mere illusion, a "hoax" that conceals colonial domination and exploitation. In many ways this radically skeptical counterdiscourse has missed the point and is the product of a reductionist view. Its proponents have been unable to see the ambiguous, paradoxical nature of social life. They have failed to acknowledge that recognizing the very real sense in which rights "exist" within this colonial framework does not preclude the possibility and desirability of exposing the devaluation resulting from a relationship of political subordination. Nationalist discourse has operated many times under the assumption that the only, or most important, dimension of freedom is the freedom of collectivities, such as nations. Often the gain of individual rights appears to be considered secondary to the claim of collective liberty.

Set in another location in the spectrum of political discourses within the Puerto Rican community, a recent postnationalist critique has stressed the value of rights for the Puerto Rican people as they have accrued throughout a century under U.S. rule. This perspective acknowledges the subordinate condition that colonialism entails. It explains the ideological attachment of most Puerto Ricans to U.S. citizenship as being the product of a conscious choice based on the appreciation of the democratic gains of the population flowing from a regime of civil and political rights. This position has ended up rejecting independence out of concern that an independent Puerto Rico will become a neo-colonial state deprived of the rights now enjoyed through U.S. citizenship. Some of its members have adhered to statehood as the solution to the status problem. Others have called for a nonessentialist approach to the status question, expressing a willingness to consider any political status as long as it does not imply severing the connection to the United States and losing the benefits of U.S. citizenship.[114]

---

[114] *See, generally,* PUERTO RICAN JAM, *supra* note 15; Juan Duchesne et al., *Algunas tesis democráticas ante el plebiscito de 1998*, DIÁLOGO, March 1999, at 38–39.

As an explanation of Puerto Rican attitudes, this perspective seems to have hit the mark. It shares many of the views expressed in this book. As a political proposition, however, it exhibits a shortcoming that is the reverse of the reductionist view held by some independence advocates. If those in favor of independence tend to naturalize nationhood, the postnationalists tend to essentialize rights. If some independence advocates at times make too much of collective, to the detriment of individual, rights, some fragments of the postnationalist discourse seem to dissolve the collectivity into the maze of individual aspirations enveloped in the liberal discourse of rights. The radical postnationalists appear to have assumed the discourse of rights without problematizing it. Although they acknowledge that the rights presently enjoyed are restricted in range, their solution is to struggle to expand their scope.

In some ways this is reminiscent of Marx's contention that bourgeois rights should be expanded to cover the whole of social experience. Pointing to the limited reach of the content of rights at a given moment, however, is not the same as accounting for the paradoxical effects of rights, as explained in this chapter. The degree to which rights simultaneously liberate and subject is absent from the discussion in their academic writings.

One of the most striking features of this radical postnationalist discourse is its insistence on linking the viability of a regime of rights to the continued connection with the metropolitan state. This conclusion is based, among other things, on the calculation that without the protection of U.S. citizenship, globalized capital would be mercilessly exploitative of Puerto Rican workers and that Puerto Rican elites would manifest a meager disposition to guarantee the enjoyment of rights to many subaltern groups, like women, gay men and lesbians, and others. It relies for this prediction on an assessment of the realities observed in nearby independent countries in the Caribbean.[115] In a substantial manner this position exemplifies the degree to which the discourse of rights has penetrated Puerto Rican consciousness and the historical connection established between such discourse and the American presence in the island.

The sense of liberty associated with the notion that the system is protective of rights has led many Puerto Ricans, from all sectors of society and professing diverse political and religious persuasions, to link the conditions of relative freedom they experience with the colonial relationship itself, or at least with American rule. Many openly attribute the "existence" of rights to the American presence. In Puerto Rico "modernity" has tended to be equated with the particular brand of modernity incarnated in American institutions and the American "life world."[116] In the same fashion "rights" are thought by many people to be equivalent to the particular regime of rights characteristic of American political life. Association—or "permanent union" —with the United States is considered a precondition for the preservation of rights.

Two paradigmatic, and poignant, expressions of this belief can be found in the published statements of two very different members of Puerto Rican society. One, a poor, Black man named Cruz Rivera who lived in a public housing project, stated the following in an interview in a Puerto Rican cultural newspaper:

---

[115] *See* Grosfoguel, *supra* note 15, at 66–70; Ramón Grosfoguel, *Colonialismo puertorriqueñista*, EL NUEVO DÍA, Nov. 9, 1998, at 58.

[116] The term is taken from Habermas, *supra* note 63, at 4.

> I am a statehooder. I believe in permanent union between Puerto Rico and the United States. . . . The United States has made me identify myself with freedom, with the kind of democracy that has always existed in that country, with the capital it generates. I have been a poor person who wants to get ahead, a person who believes in freedom of expression, which is fundamental to democracy. That made me become a statehooder.[117]

In an article penned for the opinion page of the *New York Times*, his well-to-do compatriot, author Rosario Ferré, wrote,

> The majority of Puerto Ricans prize their American citizenship. It represents for us economic stability and the assurance of civil liberties and democracy. On the other hand, we also cherish our language and culture. Thus, Puerto Rico's situation has historically been a paradox. . . . As a Puerto Rican and an American, I believe our future as a community is inseparable from our culture and language, but I'm also passionately committed to the modern world. That's why I'm going to support statehood in the next plebiscite.[118]

As may be readily seen from the two quotes, the conviction that civil liberties may only be preserved by maintaining a close association with the United States partially explains the growth of the prostatehood movement. Some among its leaders, when confronted with the argument about the devaluation inherent in the colonial relationship, propose that the way to overcome it is by becoming "full-fledged" members of the American polity. "Equality of rights" has become the slogan of the movement. According to this rhetoric, the complete dignity of Puerto Ricans can be achieved only through the equality of rights perceived to be the inevitable by-product of incorporation as a state of the union. Arguably, it is within this sector of the Puerto Rican population that the identity created by the rights deemed to be inherent in the condition of being a member of the American union has attenuated with most effectiveness the weight traditionally accorded by nationalists to such factors as ethnicity and language in the formation of a collective identity.

In sum, as much as it has served to vindicate particular claims, satisfy discrete needs, and articulate localized and more overarching resistances to diverse forms of oppression, the discourse of rights has also contributed to reproduce American hegemony within the Puerto Rican population. To the extent that "rights" have been associated with the American presence, that presence has been legitimated.

As of this writing, the goal of establishing a liberal colonial system has been achieved, and the discourse of liberal rights has been an important factor in the reproduction of that colonialism. It is true that in recent decades there has been an increasing critique of the present political arrangement. However, this does not invalidate the conclusion just stated. The results of the several referenda held in the island on the status question and the public discourse on the matter indicate that the majority of the population prefers the present arrangement to severing ties with the United States. Furthermore, most of those who favor statehood are satisfied with remaining under the present subordinate political relationship until statehood is achieved.

The present arrangement seems to be acceptable until a formula is found to gain

---

[117] R. Otero, *Yo soy de Canales: Entrevista a Cruz Rivera*, Piso 13, May 1992, at 2, 3.
[118] Rosario Ferré, *Puerto Rico, U.S.A.*, New York Times, March 19, 1998, at A-23.

greater political power (through greater autonomy or full incorporation into the United States) without losing the connection to the United States. This attitude has very much to do with the perceived connection between the enjoyment of rights and life within the American legal and political orbit. Whether formal colonialism is finally shed or not, the discourse of rights may still operate to contribute to a trans- formed, but still close, entanglement of the Puerto Rican nation with the accouter- ments of American modernity and American political and legal culture. This is what hegemony is about.

The above argument is not based on the attribution of some form of "false consciousness" to the Puerto Rican population. By *false consciousness* I mean a form of misrepresentation that somehow conceals the "true state" of things. False consciousness implies that people have been "brainwashed" to accept their current beliefs. The way in which the concept of hegemony is sometimes explained may produce that impression. What I have attempted to do is to provide a sociohistorical explanation of why most Puerto Ricans accept American presence and American rule.

On the other hand, avoiding the attribution of any form of collective false con- sciousness does not require one to disregard the fact that sometimes people operate under misconceptions about certain phenomena. Thus, there may be popular mis- conceptions about the meaning accorded in the official legal system to concepts such as *citizenship* or *right*. Or they may make decisions based on mistaken calculations about the probable effects of their actions. Identifying these misconceptions and miscalculations is not the same as attributing them to a form of false consciousness, as understood in some theoretical and political literature.

In the same vein, the fact that people associate in their minds certain phenomena does not imply that the link is "true" or "false" in any objective fashion. What may be more important, in explaining behavior, is that the link is made. Those mental associations do not have to be attributed to false consciousness for us to understand that they may be conditioned by particular forms of discourse and experience. Many times those associations are made under conditions that render alternative interpre- tations very difficult to arrive at. Historical conditions and events, including the discourses prevalent in certain moments, all affect those interpretations.

The association that many Puerto Ricans have made between a society ruled by rights and the American presence is such an interpretive phenomenon. It has been made within a given historical context. That context includes having lived during 100 years under American colonialism. U.S. colonialism, as constructed by the im- perial state and as experienced by the Puerto Rican community, has been a prime conditioner of the social, political, and cultural perceptions of Puerto Ricans and of their interpretations of the world, including their calculations about the viability of a regime of rights outside the American sphere and their assessments about the possibility of alternative futures. To deny this would be to set aside an enormous fact of power that has been actively operating in Puerto Rican society for such a long time.

The Regime of Partial Democracy

Puerto Rico's internal governing processes have been organized according to the principles of liberal representative democracies. Officials of the government of Puerto

Rico are elected by popular vote. The system is considered democratic by most of the population. Yet it is a system of only partial democracy in a very important sense. Although the Puerto Rican government is subjected to scrutiny through popular elections, Puerto Ricans residing in Puerto Rico are deprived of full participation in the election of officials of the U.S. government and in decisions taken by that government regarding fundamental aspects of Puerto Rican life. Thus, a regime of internal democracy coexists with a system of undemocratic colonial subordination. That regime of internal democracy, moreover, is riddled with many of the limitations shared by most modern systems of representative democracy that impede the citizenry from fully participating in the affairs of the community.

I examine below the undemocratic character of the political relationship between the United States and Puerto Rico as well as the characteristics and shortcomings of the latter's internal political system. Finally, I look at the extent to which, despite these constraints, this "partial" and limited democratic experience has contributed to a generalized acquiescence, if not active consent, to U.S. rule in Puerto Rico.

The Undemocratic Character of Colonial Subordination

The status of nonincorporated territory, as defined by the U.S. Supreme Court, implies that Congress is invested with plenary powers over Puerto Rico.[119] This means that, constitutionally, Congress has exclusive control over fundamental aspects of life in the territory. The executive branch of the U.S. government also exercises important functions and conducts operational activities in Puerto Rico. The U.S. federal judiciary has jurisdiction over important legal controversies emerging from activities or behavior occurring in or pertaining to Puerto Rico. Despite this massive intervention of the U.S. government in Puerto Rican life, Puerto Ricans residing in Puerto Rico do not vote for the president of the United States or elect representatives to the U.S. Congress, except for a nonvoting resident commissioner for Puerto Rico who sits in the House of Representatives.[120]

This obviously undemocratic arrangement is one of the fundamental reasons for the conclusion that Puerto Rico is a colonial dependency of the United States. This fact has been stressed continuously since the early decades of the century by the independence movement[121] and has been at the core of the claim for admission into the union made by followers of the statehood movement.[122] Even many supporters of the current Commonwealth status, including influential leaders of the Popular Democratic Party, find the situation problematic and have striven to obtain reforms that would, in their assessment, eliminate the most flagrantly undemocratic features of the system.

Thus, during the 1989–1991 plebiscite discussion,[123] the Popular Democratic

---

[119] See the full discussion of the matter in chapters 4 through 6.

[120] *See* chapter 3.

[121] *See* Statement by Rubén Berríos Martínez, President of the Puerto Rican Independence Party, *in* 1 *Political Status of Puerto Rico: Hearings on S. 710, S. 711, and S. 712 before the Senate Committee on Energy and Natural Resources*, 101st Cong., 1st Sess. 143 (1989) [*Hearings*].

[122] *See, e.g.,* Statement by Carlos Romero Barceló, Former Governor of the Commonwealth of Puerto Rico, *in* 1 *Hearings, supra* note 121, at 113.

[123] See chapters 6 and 7 for more detailed discussions of the process that took place during 1989–1991 as a result of the proposal to hold a plebiscite in Puerto Rico to "solve" the status question.

Party proposed various measures to increase the participation of the people of Puerto Rico in decisions of the U.S. government that affect the island.[124] Jaime B. Fuster, former resident commissioner of Puerto Rico in Washington and now an associate justice of the Puerto Rico Supreme Court, explained the matter in the following terms to the U.S. Senate Committee on Energy and Natural Resources during hearings held in San Juan in the summer of 1989:

> That even today the United States should stand accused of being a colonialist power by both those who favor independence and by those who favor statehood is largely due to this question of the applicability of Federal laws to Puerto Rico. . . . To us it is necessary to do away with indiscriminate extension of Federal laws to Puerto Rico which occasionally hamper our development efforts. And we should also like to remove the cloud of doubt that hovers over the legitimacy of the Commonwealth relationship.
>
>   For both these practical and theoretical reasons, we need a mechanism that will allow for adequate consent and participation in Federal legislation not dealing with overriding national interests.[125]

Throughout the 20th century the U.S. government has been adamant in its refusal to augment that participation in any significant way.[126] This attitude surfaced again during the process that led to the scuttling of the plebiscite proposal in 1991.[127] Developments related to the discussion of the plebiscite bill presented in Congress in 1996 by Representative Don Young confirmed congressional reluctance to grant Puerto Rico greater powers of participation in the enactment of federal legislation while it remains a Commonwealth as currently defined.[128] This latter process opened the possibility, however, of exploring a fourth alternative—apart from Commonwealth, statehood, and traditional independence—that would recognize Puerto Rican sovereignty but preserve close legal and political ties between the United States and Puerto Rico. This status option, known variously as "free association" or the "associated republic status," was not openly adopted as its main proposal by any Puerto Rican political party.

But its rather ambiguous inclusion in the Young Bill and the insistence of a close majority of the House of Representatives in defining Commonwealth as an unreformed territorial status forced the Popular Democratic Party to look to the free association alternative more closely and to try to produce a definition of Common-

---

[124] *See* S. 712, 101st Cong., 1st Sess. Title IV (1989).

[125] 2 *Hearings, supra* note 121, at 6, 8. Similar comments were made by such Popular Democratic Party stalwarts as former Resident Commissioner (and former president of the University of Puerto Rico) Jaime Benítez; the president of the Puerto Rican Senate, Miguel Hernández Agosto; and the speaker of the Puerto Rican House of Representatives, José R. Jarabo. *See id.* at 41, 63, 83.

[126] *See, generally,* ANTONIO FERNÓS ISERN, ESTADO LIBRE ASOCIADO DE PUERTO RICO: ANTECEDENTES, CREACIÓN Y DESARROLLO HASTA LA ÉPOCA PRESENTE (1974); TRÍAS MONGE, *supra* note 34.

[127] Before reporting favorably on S. 712, one of the original plebiscite bills, the Senate Energy and Natural Resources Committee eliminated from it a provision to grant nonvoting representation to Puerto Rico in the United States Senate and diluted significantly, almost to the point of obliteration, the Popular Democratic Party proposal that Puerto Rico have a greater say in federal decision making. JUAN M. GARCÍA PASSALACQUA & CARLOS RIVERA LUGO, PUERTO RICO Y LOS ESTADOS UNIDOS: EL PROCESO DE CONSULTA Y NEGOCIACIÓN DE 1989 y 1990 (1990).

[128] H.R. 856, 105th Cong., 2nd Sess. (1998) (enacted).

wealth status more akin to the characteristics of an associated republic. That route began to be seen beyond a small circle of its long-time proponents as a legitimate solution to the democratic deficit of the present relationship, without having to resort to the full integration of Puerto Rico into the American union or to a more radical severance of ties with the United States. Free association was finally included as a separate option on the ballot during the Puerto Rican-sponsored plebiscite held in December 1998. The option was represented in the process by several small autonomist groups that included some known members of the Popular Democratic Party. The free association formula obtained only 0.3% of the votes cast in that plebiscite.

Congressional refusal to increase Puerto Rican participation in federal legislation or to grant a greater degree of autonomy than is now vested in the Puerto Rican government, absent a substantial change in the political status of the island, is grounded in the view that Congress may not relinquish its plenary powers over Puerto Rico as long as the latter remains unincorporated territory of the United States. The reaffirmation of such momentous power has been a constant part of the legitimating discourse deployed to support all varieties of congressional action regarding Puerto Rico. Those actions have ranged from the extension and limitation of citizenship rights to the granting and elimination of tax incentives and the determination of the processes designed to decide the political future of the island.

This stance does, in fact, produce markedly paradoxical results in the context of self-determination claims. There has been a very profound contradiction in the so-called self-determination bills presented in Congress to address the question of the political status of Puerto Rico. Although purporting, however sincerely, to create the conditions for the exercise of self-determination by Puerto Ricans, all the recent proposals have operated under the premise that Congress has the ultimate power of decision regarding the terms of the bills and the procedures to be followed in the self-determination process. Puerto Rican political parties, government officials, and other sectors of Puerto Rican society have been consulted through various means on these matters. But Congress has always claimed the final say. Establishing the rules of the game is as important as making substantial input into the decision-making process, if not more so. Puerto Rican collective self-determination is, consequently, made to depend on an initial act of determination by the metropolitan state directed at defining the content and the form of the available possibilities and the means to attain them.[129]

This view is the direct result of the discourse of power legitimated by the *Insular Cases*. It is a product of the way in which the colonial relationship has been legally constructed since the early days of its establishment. This critique against those congressional processes generally produces the response that, although conceptually correct, the observation fails to grasp the "practicalities" of the situation. Congress, after all, is the real power in this matter. This realist, pragmatic appraisal of the power relationship may be directly on target, especially when referring to the politics of the self-determination process. Yet the truer the response appears to be, the more it reaffirms the adequacy of the critique. For it lays bare the colonial, ultimately undemocratic, character of the relationship.

---

[129] For a similar view, *see* Ediberto Román, *Empire Forgotten: The United States's Colonization of Puerto Rico*, 42 VILLANOVA L. REV. 1119, 1210 (1997).

Internal Government of the Colony

In the early days of the American occupation, Puerto Rican politicians of different persuasions sought to gain control of the internal governmental apparatus of the country. However, despite the proclamations heralding a new age of democracy and freedom, the United States soon showed itself reluctant to entrust the administration of the colony entirely to Puerto Ricans. In fact, the metropolitan state was more inclined to formally recognize certain individual rights than to release its direct control over the island's internal governmental structure. Liberalism and democracy, it must be remembered, are not necessarily identical. The governing elites of the American state always stressed the difference, particularly in the context of territorial possessions. The basic assumption that justified withholding control from the "native population" was that Puerto Ricans were unfit for self-government.[130] This attitude would gradually be modified in the course of the relationship.

After the initial 2-year period during which the country was governed by military commanders, the United States established a civilian government. The first such government consisted of a governor, appointed by the president of the United States; a House of Delegates, whose members were elected by qualified voters residing in the island; and an Executive Council, integrated by appointees of the U.S. president. The Executive Council had both executive and legislative functions, serving in effect as a second legislative chamber, an obvious departure from the traditional American model of separation of powers. This structure would facilitate the goal of devising an internal government with some degree of participation of the native elites while preserving as great a control as possible in the hands of the metropolitan power.[131]

As a result of continued pressure from Puerto Rican political leaders, the Executive Council's legislative functions were abolished by the Jones Act of 1917. This measure established a bicameral legislature elected by popular vote. In consequence, Puerto Rican political leaders gained additional clout. In 1947 Congress authorized Puerto Ricans to elect their own governor. The following year Puerto Ricans chose Luis Muñoz Marín, the charismatic founder of the Popular Democratic Party, as their first elected governor. Since then Puerto Rico has had seven elected governors, all of them Puerto Ricans, three belonging to the pro-Commonwealth Popular Democratic Party and three to the prostatehood New Progressive Party.

The reform movement that culminated in the promulgation of the 1952 Constitution shifted to the Puerto Rican people the power to approve the internal structure of their government, under the supervising eye of the U.S. Congress. The Puerto Rican Constitution established a three-branch government, the basic structure of which remains to this date. The governor, as chief executive officer, and the members of the bicameral legislature are elected by popular vote. The members of the Supreme Court are designated by the governor, with the advice and consent of the Puerto Rican Senate.

Puerto Rico has been engaging in party politics for over a century. The first political party in the modern sense, the Liberal Reformist Party, was founded in 1870. Most political parties since then have forged their identities in great measure around the positions they take regarding the political status of the island. The country

---

[130] *See* FERNÁNDEZ, THE DISENCHANTED ISLAND, *supra* note 31, at chap. 1.
[131] *See id.* at 19–21.

has also had a long experience of general elections,[132] starting from the time of the Spanish colonial regime. From 1809 to 1898 there were 24 such elections to select different types of functionaries, including representatives to the Spanish Cortes when such representation was allowed.[133] During Spanish rule voting was severely restricted to certain classes of people.[134] Under the American regime there have been 29 general elections.[135]

Electoral practices in the first four decades of American colonial rule were fraught with irregularities, the purchase of votes, physical and psychological coercion, and other corrupting activities. Despite this generally recognized fact, voter participation in the 14 elections held from 1900 to 1936 averaged 74.47% of those eligible to vote.[136] In 1940 the newly formed Popular Democratic Party strove to imprint a new meaning onto the voting process, presenting it as the vehicle for the oppressed masses to get rid of the old political bosses and to facilitate the social and economic transformation so many were clamoring for.

The definitive victory of the Popular Democratic Party at the polls in the election of 1944 was repeated in 1948, and the subsequent social, economic, and political reforms the party was able to put in motion, with support from the Roosevelt and Truman administrations, gave credence to the argument advanced by the populist reformers that voting did make a difference. Since then, voter participation in electoral events in Puerto Rico, especially general elections, has been even larger. The 14 general elections held from 1940 to 1992 averaged a registered voter participation of 81.41%.[137] Notwithstanding occasional allegations of fraud, the results of the elections are generally accepted as valid, transitions from one government to another are peaceful, and in cases of controversy, the judiciary's resolution of conflict enjoys a great degree of legitimacy.

Of even more significance is the fact that voting has acquired a special mystique, a particular value, for the majority of Puerto Ricans. One explanation for this phenomenon may lie in the feeling of empowerment that voting has been engineered to produce since the reforms of the 1940s. Additional reasons may be found in the fact that voting in Puerto Rico is closely tied to concrete material interests. The past 50 years have witnessed the development of a colonial welfare state that has become a crucial actor in the economic and social life of the community. The Puerto Rican government employs approximately one-third of the work force in the country and administers a great variety of social and economic programs. It grants permits and licenses. It provides an array of public services such as electricity, water, and telecommunications. It allocates public housing and runs a sizable public education system that extends from kindergarten to graduate university programs. It pays enor-

---

[132] "General elections" are those whose purpose is to elect the officials of the government, be they functionaries of the internal government or representatives or delegates to the government of the metropolitan state. *See* FERNANDO BAYRÓN TORO, ELECCIONES Y PARTIDOS POLÍTICOS DE PUERTO RICO 2–3 (1989).

[133] *Id.* at 3.

[134] *Id.* at 4.

[135] *See id.* at 3. The cited work covers elections held until 1988. The numbers provided here include the general election that took place in 2000.

[136] *See id.* at 348.

[137] *See id.* at 349; ESTADO LIBRE ASOCIADO DE PUERTO RICO, COMISIÓN ESTATAL DE ELECCIONES, RESULTADOS FINALES: ELECCIONES GENERALES 3 DE NOVIEMBRE 1992, at 1 (1993).

mous amounts of money to the private sector for contracts to provide a wide spectrum of goods and services, and it regulates a countless number of activities and relationships.

Municipal governments, which are the most important local government bodies, also render needed services and establish significant links with local communities, groups, and individuals. A notable degree of patronage at both levels of government inspires added interest in the makeup of their administrations. All of this means that the outcomes of electoral events, especially those that determine who controls the government apparatus, always involve high stakes for the many people whose daily lives and enterprises are directly affected by government decisions, particularly those that beget inclusions and exclusions or that grant or withhold benefits. The high turnout to determine who makes those decisions is, therefore, understandable.[138]

These features of Puerto Rican internal democracy—elected government officials, a long tradition of party politics, belief in the power of suffrage, large voter participation, respect for the outcomes of elections, and acceptance of judicial arbitration of electoral disputes—have coexisted with other characteristics that form an important part of the island's political culture. For example, Puerto Rican politics have always exhibited a great measure of paternalism and *personalismo*.[139] Political parties have relied heavily on patronage to preserve the loyalty of their followers. Preference for the strong charismatic leader is still the norm, rather than the exception. On many occasions these traits have worked to muzzle discussion of substantive issues, as the voters' attention is drawn to questions of personality, personal loyalties, and the preservation or conquest of privileged access to public perquisites based on political affiliation. Party allegiance has tended to prevail over independent judgment. There have been growing signs of dissatisfaction in this regard, however, manifested in an increase in the number of "unaffiliated" voters and those who cross party lines to endorse candidates of other parties on the basis of their performance or their proposed programs of action.

Paternalism, *personalismo,* and unconditional party allegiance are not exclusive to the Puerto Rican political system. They are found in many countries of Latin America, the Caribbean, Asia, and Africa as well as in regions and political communities in Europe and the United States. In Puerto Rico, they may be the surviving political traits of a former cultural milieu associated with the world of the *haciendas*. This fusion of the old and the new is not an unfamiliar phenomenon in contemporary societies. As Habermas indicated, the sociocultural systems of many liberal societies have contained diverse blendings of precapitalist and bourgeois elements in their traditions.[140]

---

[138] Referenda and other electoral events not related to the election of officials tend to elicit a lower voter turnout. Thus, for example, the 1952 referendum to approve the Constitution of Puerto Rico drew out 58% of registered voters; the 1967 plebiscite, 66%; the 1970 referendum to lower the voting age to 18 years, 35%; the 1991 referendum on "Democratic Rights Guarantees" (*see* chapter 7), 62%; the 1993 plebiscite on political status, 73.6%; the 1994 referendum to amend the Constitution to abolish the absolute right to bail and to increase the number of justices in the Puerto Rico Supreme Court, 62.9%; and the 1998 plebiscite, 71.3%. *La voz del pueblo en las urnas*, EL NUEVO DÍA. July 28, 1998, at 4; ESTADO LIBRE ASOCIADO DE PUERTO RICO, COMISIÓN ESTATAL DE ELECCIONES, ESCRUTINIO RESULTADOS ISLA. PLEBISCITO 13 DE DICIEMBRE DE 1998 (1999).

[139] *See* LEWIS, *supra* note 34, at chap. 17. *Personalismo* is an attitude that accords greater importance to the personality of the leader than to his or her ideas or program.

[140] HABERMAS, *supra* note 63, at 32–33.

The democratic system established in Puerto Rico for internal governance manifests the limitations of all modern formal democracies. According to Habermas, in these systems citizens are in fact excluded from real substantive participation through various mechanisms and practices. One of those excluding practices is what he termed *structural depoliticization*, which consists in relegating citizen participation to occasional voting, or even the public expression of protest, while entrusting real decisions to political, bureaucratic, or technocratic elites.[141] "The arrangement of formal democratic institutions and procedures," argued Habermas, "permits administrative decisions to be made largely independently of specific motives of the citizens." He added, "This takes place through a legitimation process that elicits generalized motives—that is, diffuse mass loyalty—but avoids participation."[142] In fact, modern formal democracy "counts now as only a method for selecting leaders and the accouterments of leadership."[143] Formal democracy replaces the notion of self-determination of the people by a process intended "to make possible *compromises* between ruling elites."[144]

These same tendencies can be observed in the Puerto Rican political system. Popular enthusiasm for voting and political debate does not necessarily translate into effective power to influence fundamental decisions. Despite the populist discourse that became part of the codes for political communication with the masses since the middle of the 20th century, real decision making (in the limited spheres over which the Commonwealth government can exercise control) has often been withheld from the population.[145] Aware of these shortcomings, many popular movements in Puerto Rico have demanded greater participation in the resolution of issues that affect their constituencies. Thus, communities have organized themselves to press for access to administrative decisions that might have a negative impact on their environment. Women's groups have taken their pressure directly to the legislature to claim specific reforms on their behalf.[146] Workers have struggled to augment their influence in public decision making by promoting legislation recognizing their right to collective bargaining in the government sector. Students and faculty have sought inclusion in the decision making bodies of the public university.

In sum, the internal government of Puerto Rico is based on the institutions of representative democracy and draws on a long tradition of party politics, popular elections, and sustained voter participation. Nonetheless, it is afflicted by traits that, on many occasions, distort democratic politics. Additionally, the shortcomings of

---

[141] *Id.* at 36–37.

[142] *Id.* at 36.

[143] *Id.* at 123.

[144] *Id.* (emphasis in the original)

[145] A recent dramatic example of this phenomenon was the 1997 decision by the Puerto Rican government to partly privatize the government-owned telephone company. A massive wave of opposition surged from a wide spectrum of voices in the Puerto Rican community. Despite a turbulent general strike that pitted the police against demonstrators, the governor went ahead with the sale. Part of the popular backlash was to be felt the following year as some voters apparently decided to "punish" the pro-statehood governor by voting against statehood in a plebiscite promoted by him. The plebiscite had been called by the governor, again despite strong opposition to its realization even by people of his own political party.

[146] *See, e.g.*, Esther Vicente, *Beyond Law Reform: The Puerto Rican Experience in the Construction and Implementation of the Domestic Violence Act*, 68 REV. JUR. U.P.R. 553 (1999).

formal liberal democracies effectively preclude its citizens from important public decision making through various mechanisms.

Puerto Ricans do participate in the election of the officials of the government of Puerto Rico. This makes this internal arrangement democratic in a formal and, to a certain extent, real sense. However, they do not participate in the election of those who govern them or in decision making processes at the level of the metropolitan state; this external setup is thus undemocratic. The political structure designed to govern Puerto Ricans can only be described, then, as an example of partial democracy.

Effects of the Partially Democratic Experience

The effects within the Puerto Rican community of the experience of partial democracy are difficult to ascertain. More detailed, empirical study, using quantitative and qualitative methods of sociological inquiry, would help to produce a better understanding of the phenomenon. This particular experience should be studied especially in connection with the production of identities and subjectivities, in relation to perceptions of the individual and collective self, and in regard to the manner in which notions of self-worth have been generated. As happens with the discourse of rights, arguably those effects also will be found to be multisided, ambiguous, and paradoxical. Following are some suggestions meant to stimulate further research about the ways the regime of partial democracy may have contributed to the legitimation of American rule and the reproduction of American hegemony.

Over the course of a century,[147] the Puerto Rican population has been subjected to norms they have not participated in producing directly or through elective representatives with full voting powers. In this very fundamental sense, the Puerto Rican legal subject has been denied one of the most basic goods promised by the regulating ideals of modernity: the condition of being a self-determining subject. In the modern tradition, manifested politically in the ideals of the French and American Revolutions and expressed philosophically by the Kantian notion of moral autonomy, self-determination has principally referred to the capacity of the subject to give himself or herself his or her own norms. This is, in sum, what is meant by the concept of "self-government."

In this regard, self-determination extends well beyond the act of choosing among different political status alternatives. It refers to the capacity or, normatively, to the right to continuously adopt, or participate in the production of, the norms that regulate the subject's own life, whether conceived as an individual or as a collective subject. Colonialism entails a denial of this self-governing capacity. The plenary powers claimed and exercised by the U.S. Congress over the peoples of the territories subvert the ideal of self-governance. The repercussions of this condition on the questions of identity and the formation of subjectivities should not be underestimated.

In addition to other factors, identities are formed in reference to the norms by which people choose, or are forced, to live. Subjectivities are closely related to identities. Thus, for Americans, their individual and collective identities, especially

---

[147] The analysis is limited here to the period under American rule. If one adds the additional 400 years of Spanish colonialism the country endured, the extension of time to which these considerations apply is obviously substantially longer.

in the political sense, have much to do with the contents and types of norms (including the most basic of them: the Constitution) by which they feel they have chosen to guide their lives. Europeans have always seen in European law a particularly defining feature of the European character. Puerto Ricans, however, are continuously forced to live under norms they have not chosen. In this sense, part of their identity is being shaped not only by the content of norms adopted by others, but also, and most importantly, by the very fact that those norms have been produced by others.

Certainly, many Puerto Ricans find the content of many of those norms desirable. They even feel their tangible benefits. For the purpose of this analysis, however, it is irrelevant whether those norms are deemed to be good or bad, detrimental or beneficial in some particular sense. The question is that they have been determined by others. Living by norms determined by others may lead to feelings of alienation. This may be the case, for example, with subjects ruled by a benevolent dictator. Those who benefit from the generous decrees of the dictator may feel grateful. Yet they may feel that their welfare is not in their own hands, but in those of the ruler. They may feel alienated from the power that produces their welfare or their misery.

Second, accommodating one's daily practices to rules that correspond to cultural codes different from one's own may produce an unsettling gap between action and self-perception. This rift eventually may be mended either by circumventing the norm or by transforming one's own cultural codes. In either case, the subject's identity will have been affected. Additionally, if, for reasons of expediency or other motives, those norms are routinely obeyed, the practice of compliance may engender a disposition to abide by such norms even when they do not respond to the obliging subject's assessment of fairness or necessity.

In Puerto Rico, federal legislation is accepted as legitimate by most of the population. Its application is deemed legally valid and enforceable. For some time, some people advanced the argument that in 1952 Puerto Ricans had given their "generic" consent to be ruled by the U.S. Congress. Therefore, they had no need to participate fully in the passing of federal legislation. The legitimacy of federal legislation was predicated on this alleged generic approval. That argument has long been discredited.

Historically, the legitimacy of the legislative power of Congress over Puerto Rico has been more the effect of the normative consequences ascribed to the acquisition of Puerto Rico by the United States than the product of any democratically based theory of legitimacy. The result has been that this fact of power—the acquisition by force reaffirmed through a treaty—has led to compliance with legal norms that have not been the product of a participatory process. In a conceptual and experiential slippage that goes from practice to normative conclusion, the habit of obeying norms adopted by others seems to have led to a positive normative assessment of the validity of such norms. The validity of metropolitan law is then, as a practical matter, made to depend on the fact of power.

It is true that many people today question the present relationship between the United States and Puerto Rico because of its colonial character. But very few of them are proposing that U.S. legislation does not validly apply in Puerto Rico because it is colonial in nature. Thus, despite the fact that they believe that Puerto Rico is a colony of the United States, no statehooder, autonomist, or free associationist and very few independence advocates would subscribe to the position that U.S. laws should not be generally obeyed because they are colonial laws.[148] The validity of federal law in Puerto Rico is assumed as a consequence of the latter's acquisition by the United States in 1898.

This historical experience, reproduced daily both consciously and unconsciously in myriad instances, must have an effect on notions of the self, particularly regarding the aspiration to become a self-determining subject. In this sense, one of the most profound effects of colonialism seems to be the production of a subject accustomed to conform to norms arising out of the will of an outside power, that is, norms that are the product of a heteronomous definition of obligation. A derivative of this disposition could very well be a psychosociological inclination to accept nonparticipation in obligatory norm-making, particularly in the "metropolitan" spheres of power, as somehow "inevitable," "legitimate," "necessary," or "natural."[149] The power relationship embodied in the situation of political subordination that has been produced through colonialism is thus normatively and practically acquiesced to. In other words, it is legitimated.

The preceding analysis refers to that feature of the colonial system that has made of Puerto Rico a partially democratic polity. That is, it relates to the condition resulting from the lack of participation in decisions made by the metropolitan state. However, the internal government of the territory *has* been structured according to the organizing principles of modern representative democracies and allows a significant degree of participation. In the long run, this too has had important hegemonic effects.

First of all, this limited internal democratic regime has produced a sense of popular participation. The fact that in general elections the population votes for political parties that include in their platforms the traditional alternatives to the status problem has convinced many that the country's present relationship with the United States is the result of popular will. The fact is that in the entire century that Puerto Rico has "belonged to" but not been "a part of" the United States, the latter, as a whole, has not demonstrated any serious intention to terminate that condition by incorporating Puerto Rico as another state of the union, granting independence, or recognizing any other form of sovereignty. In fact, the United States government has not appeared to be willing to relinquish its power over Puerto Rico by facilitating a transition to any other form of relationship less subordinate in nature, even in a formal sense. As long as Puerto Ricans remain divided as to the specific form in which a change of status should occur, the U.S. Congress seems to be more than happy to continue retaining its plenary powers and acting accordingly.

In this scheme of things, the will of the people on which the solution to the status question is deemed to depend must always be expressed within the limits of colonial legality. To a great extent those limits were constructed by the doctrine adopted in the *Insular Cases*. Colonial legality, in turn, has imposed strictures on

---

[148] I am referring to a wholesale rejection of U.S. laws because of their colonial foundation, in the fashion proposed by the nationalist leader Pedro Albizu Campos. There have been discreet instances of civil disobedience to protest specific situations or actions of the U.S. government considered to be particularly outrageous—for example, the civilian occupation of land controlled by the U.S. Navy in the island of Vieques. However dramatic and effective they may have been in calling attention to these situations, these actions do not amount to a radical questioning of the legal validity of U.S. rule.

[149] *In accord, see* Román, *supra* note 129, at 1179 (Puerto Ricans' history "of being ruled throughout their existence has fostered an acceptance of foreign rule").

the ways of transforming the very social and economic conditions that operate to reinforce dependence and consent. Consent has thus been continually reproduced. The will of the people in the colony has been conditioned, through the effect of heteronomously determined needs, by the colonial situation. Therefore, that "will" (as expressed through colonial legality) has, until now, been formulated to reaffirm the relationship.

Acquiescence has become the justificatory principle of the relationship of domination. It has been colonialism by consent in its most elaborate and sophisticated version.[150] On the other hand, the most desirable alternative to the present situation, as expressed at the polls, is one that addresses the question of formal political subordination by seeking full incorporation into the union. If this were to pass, American hegemony over Puerto Rico will have been complete.

This structure of partially democratic participation has provided a context for action. It constitutes the framework within which any "legitimate" discussion and action regarding the colonial question must be conducted. Even the forms of resistance to colonial rule are conditioned by the structures designed to channel political action considered appropriate by the metropolitan state, by those who control the internal governmental apparatus, and by a substantial part of the population. Thus, many forms of revolutionary or "radical" methods of struggle have been delegitimized.

Moreover, there is a tendency to relate the existence of a democratic regime, however limited, to the American presence itself. The experience of democracy, for many, is the direct result of the American occupation of 1898. To the extent that formal democracy, elections, and other features of the political system are associated, accurately or not, with the American presence, that presence is legitimated.[151] Conversely, separation from the United States raises in many minds the specter of an antidemocratic future. The fears expressed by many people during the campaign leading to the 1991 referendum (fostered aggressively by the supporters of statehood) were related not only to the possible loss of economic benefits and American citizenship,[152] but also to the imagined threat that that exercise posed to the continuity of the democratic experience.

This perception of threat has been continuously reinforced by interpretations of Puerto Rican reality put forth by colonial elites that have emphasized, among other things, the desirability of modernization American style, the virtues of American citizenship, the need to keep at bay the "enemies of progress" (for example, those who advocate independence or socialism), and the superiority of the democratic nature of the regime over the dictatorships and corrupt governments of Latin America.

American hegemony, then, is predicated not only on a perceived superiority of the American economic system and its capacity to satisfy needs, but also on the impression that its political system is the best imaginable. For some time, especially at the height of mass support for Commonwealth status, these perceptions seemed to be powerful enough to obliterate the reality of political subordination that is endemic to colonialism, whatever its guise. An increasing awareness of the demo-

---

[150] *See* Rivera Ramos, *supra* note 13, at 120–21.
[151] *See* Mattos Cintrón, *supra* note 88, at 28–29.
[152] *See* chapter 7.

cratic weakness of the present relationship has developed, and different groups are seeking new political articulations. However, the discerned superiority of the American political system over other perceived alternatives is blocking the envisioning of a future that is not, somehow, linked to the United States.

Ideology of the Rule of Law

The ideology of the rule of law has been a mechanism of moral and political persuasion in the context of the relationship of political subordination that has existed between the United States and Puerto Rico. The effects of this ideology must be viewed in conjunction with those of the discourse of rights, the experience of partial democracy, and the repressive dimension of the system. For it is their conjoined operation that partially accounts for the reproduction of the prevalent attitudes of the majority of the population regarding the value of the continued association with the United States, irrespective of the form that that relationship may assume.

The rule of law has been defined in different ways. One view, associated with neoconservative doctrines in the Anglo-American world, seems to equate it with the notion of "law and order," or with the idea that people should obey the law and be ruled by it.[153] The traditional liberal conception, on the other hand, emphasizes that the main purpose of the rule of law is to impose inhibitions on state power: The government should be ruled by law and be subject to it. This is the main sense in which British historian E. P. Thompson used the concept in an attempt to retrieve what he understood to be its original import.[154] From a sociological perspective, the rule of law has been defined as "the use of legal forms to regulate and legitimize state power."[155] In this chapter *rule of law* will encompass both the normative liberal conception, as explicated by Thompson and others, and the sociological definition.

The Theoretical Debate and the Critique of the Rule of Law

The principal contemporary debate regarding the rule of law in the Anglo-American world, particularly among neo-Marxist scholars, was sparked to a great extent by Thompson's defense of the liberal ideal of the rule of law as a universal value.[156] For Thompson,

> the rhetoric and the rules of a society are something a great deal more than sham. In the same moment they may modify, in profound ways, the behavior of the powerful and mystify the powerless. They may disguise the realities of power, but, at the same time, they may curb that power and check its intrusions. And it is often from within that very rhetoric that a radical critique of the practice of the society is developed.[157]

---

[153] See the discussion in Picciotto, *supra* note 56, at 169–70. I have also drawn from M. D. A. Freeman, *The Rule of Law: Liberal, Marxist and Neo-Marxist Perspectives,* lecture delivered during the Anglo-Soviet Symposium sponsored by University College London (July 20, 1990).

[154] E. P. Thompson, *The Rule of Law, in* MARXISM AND LAW, *supra* note 16, at 130–37. The cited work is an excerpt from the concluding chapter in E. P. THOMPSON, WHIGS AND HUNTERS: THE ORIGIN OF THE BLACK ACT (1975). Further references will be to the excerpted piece.

[155] THE POLITICAL ECONOMY OF LAW, *supra* note 7, at 651.

[156] Thompson, *supra* note 154.

[157] *Id.* at 134.

According to Thompson, "the inhibitions upon power imposed by law" are an important legacy, a cultural achievement, of the agrarian and mercantile bourgeoisie of the 17th century and of their supporting yeomen and artisans. Insofar as the rule of law itself imposes "effective inhibitions upon power" and can be invoked for "the defense of the citizen from power's all-intrusive claim," it must be regarded as an "unqualified human good."[158] Even in the colonial context, Thompson argued, the rules and rhetoric of law imposed some constraints upon the imperial power.[159] "Even rulers," Thompson commented, "find a need to legitimize their power, to moralize their functions, to feel themselves to be useful and just."[160]

The most important criticisms of Thompson's position do not deny the benefits and advantages of the rule of law for subordinated groups and peoples. Some of them, in fact, do little more than reemphasize what Thompson himself conceded: that law's effects are contradictory. Others go beyond this critique.

Fine summarized Thompson's contribution as reviving the liberal conception of the rule of law as a weapon against the growth of state authoritarianism, persuasively demolishing the conservative view that the "rule of law" means unconditional obedience to the state and attacking the tendency on the left to dismiss civil liberties as a sham and law as merely a class instrument.[161] However, he criticized Thompson for "reducing" law to one of its functions and neglecting the democratic limits of liberalism.[162]

Kerruish echoed an aspect of Thompson's claim when she asserted that "law can and has conferred benefits on people who are subordinated and devalued within existing social relations and it imposes constraints of some kind on dominant and empowered people."[163] "We need not doubt," Kerruish remarked, "that law is useful or beneficial to some people some of the time. Indeed it is hard to imagine how legal practices and institutions could have the vitality and persistence they do have if that were not the case."[164] Yet that does not warrant according to law a universal value.[165] Picciotto, on the other hand, declared that the strategy for subordinated groups, especially the working class, must be "not to uphold the impossible ideals of the liberal forms of state and the 'rule of law', but to insist on the necessity that it be transcended, in forms which challenge the dominance of capitalist social relations."[166]

What the dispute reveals, once more, are the complexities of the legal phenomenon, the paradoxical quality of law. In that sense, the debate about the rule of law follows closely the developments and perspectives gained as a result of the controversy over the benefits and limitations of rights.

One critique of European imperial law has consisted in exposing how "the ideal of the rule of law" was not extended to many colonial societies.[167] Kerruish percep-

---

[158] *Id.* at 135.

[159] *Id.*

[160] *Id.*

[161] FINE, *supra* note 59, at 8.

[162] *Id.* at 8, 175.

[163] KERRUISH, *supra* note 71, at 3.

[164] *Id.* at 19.

[165] *Id.*

[166] Picciotto, *supra* note 56, at 179.

[167] *See* Snyder & Hay, *supra* note 5, at 12; KERRUISH, *supra* note 71, at 142.

tively noted that some of those criticisms presuppose the notion of "a pure, uncorrupted form" of the law. Nonetheless, insofar as a regime based on the rule of law is better than one based on despotism, this flaw of imperial law had significant consequences for those subjected to the most extreme forms of authoritarian rule in the colonies. Due to the characteristics of the American colonial project in Puerto Rico, this chapter is concerned, however, with another type of critique: the degree to which the ideology of the rule of law, extended as it was to the colony, has operated to reproduce the metropolitan power's hegemony.

The Rule of Law in the Puerto Rican Context

In the course of their struggles against the authoritarian Spanish regime, 19th-century Puerto Rican liberals became attracted to various versions of the ideal of the rule of law. Not surprisingly, the organic intellectuals of the Puerto Rican socially hegemonic classes would be willful recipients of the Anglo-American notion of the rule of law as an organizing principle of the country's political and legal system. Throughout the 20th century the heirs to that liberal tradition, regardless of their position on the status of Puerto Rico, have replicated, refined, and expanded the vision that the best form of government is one subject to law. They have not been alone in the reproduction of this discourse. Many of those in the socially and economically subordinated sectors of Puerto Rican society, in their localized struggles and resistances against the metropolitan state or local elites, have also tended to view the ideal (expressed in various forms) as something close to an "unqualified human good." Law is perceived by many not only as a repressive mechanism, but as a shield against arbitrary power. The ideology of the rule of law has grown strong roots in public consciousness, particularly since the political reforms initiated in the 1940s.

The constraints imposed on the local government and the metropolitan state by this discourse on the rule of law have at times benefited powerless individuals and groups. But the ideology of the rule of law has also legitimated American rule or buttressed American hegemony in two fundamental ways.

First, the metropolitan state has sought to justify its exercise of power by reference to law. This was the primary function of the constitutional doctrine of territorial incorporation developed by the Supreme Court in the *Insular Cases*. The ideology of the rule of law, as a powerful element of the idea of legitimacy in the American political and constitutional order, compelled the American governing elites to obtain an authoritative statement from the highest tribunal of the land sanctioning their decision to install a colonial regime in the territories acquired after the Spanish American War.

Of course, it must not be forgotten that this legal benediction came from an organ of the metropolitan state. The Supreme Court was not an independent arbitrator located in a position of neutrality between the metropolitan power and the people of the conquered territory. Furthermore, the sources used as interpretive guides, the traditions examined, the interests weighed, and the normative principles developed and applied were part of the history and the worldview of the framers and rulers of the metropolitan state itself. It was the shared understanding of the governing elites that the word spoken by the members of the Supreme Court would be the law of the land regarding the power that could be exercised over the new colonial dependencies. If that power could be grounded in the Constitution, it would have to be considered legitimate. It was so found.

Since then, the exercise of congressional power over Puerto Rico has been justified with reference to the notion that the Constitution sanctions it. The law of the metropolitan state itself has become the justificatory basis for the exercise of imperial power.[168] Furthermore, specific exercises of power are considered legitimate only if sanctioned by congressional legislation in accordance with established constitutional norms and procedures, or if they are undertaken pursuant to the constitutional prerogative of the executive or the judicial branch. In sum, the colonial regime is justified with the argument that it is sanctioned by law. In fact, for the metropolitan state, for most of Puerto Rico's political elites, and for substantial, if not most, segments of the population, even processes aimed at dismantling colonialism must follow the law.

There is a second way in which the ideology of the rule of law has operated as a hegemonic mechanism for American rule. Just as a good number of Puerto Ricans associate many of the things they value with the American presence in the island, in the popular imagination, fueled by the legitimating discourses propagated by the ruling elites, the "freedom" that the rule of law guarantees is possible because of that presence. Whether that perception is justified or not, the fact is that it operates as a powerful force in the domain of consciousness. It acts as a forceful mechanism in the process whereby consent to the relationship with the United States is reproduced and American presence and rule are legitimated.

---

[168] *See* Sally Engle Merry, *Law and Colonialism*, 25 LAW & SOC. REV. 889, 890 (1991).

CONCLUSION

One hundred years have elapsed since the United States acquired Puerto Rico as a result of the Spanish American War. Acquiring this Spanish-speaking country in the Caribbean, several centuries old in history and traditions, was part of a movement aimed at extending the physical borders and the military, economic, and political influence of the emerging world power well beyond its immediate periphery. The expansion flowed in different directions: to the Caribbean, the Pacific, and the northwestern tip of the North American continent.

The historic developments that constituted the American imperial venture would have profound effects on the expanding republic and on the populations that came under its control. From the beginning, this expansionist drive would be conceived as a hegemonic project, that is, it would seek to elicit a relative degree of acquiescence from the peoples of the acquired territories through a series of mechanisms that combined different modes of coercion and persuasion. They included the installation of an American military presence, the infusion of American capital, and the application of at least some of the trappings of American modernity in the societies pulled into the sphere of American power. In this process law would be called upon to play a central role.

The case of Puerto Rico is a paradigmatic example of the paradoxical consequences of that historical experience. The legal construction of American colonialism in Puerto Rico has had significant implications for the configuration of identities, subjectivities, and the reproduction of American hegemony within the population. In an effort to explain how this process has operated, this book has sought to document and interpret the social, political, and cultural repercussions within Puerto Rican society of certain legal events and developments. This case study provides important insights into the character of modern law and its social effects and illustrates the deep connection between the workings of law, viewed as a type of social discourse, and a particular form of colonialism.

General Conclusions: The Effects of Law

In general terms, this book substantiates the intricate relationship between law and politics. We have seen how certain legal doctrines and decisions have incorporated the ideologies and worldviews prevalent at the time of their adoption and how they managed to accommodate important interests connected to long-term political, economic, and military objectives.

Furthermore, we have been able to corroborate the constitutive force of law. The capacity of law to fashion social reality has been manifested in a variety of ways. First of all, it has been evident in the manner in which specific legal events have worked to legitimate the power relationship that emerged from the Spanish American War. Second, this constitutive force has been apparent through law's operation in the creation of legal subjects, identities, and subjectivities. We have noted how certain legal categories, such as citizenship, have been engineered to obtain particular results, have been impregnated with conflicting meanings, and have become contested terrain in the struggle to negotiate a given identity.

Law has also had the effect of forging a discursive universe that has set limits on the production of further discourse and established the "legitimate" parameters for the definition of needs and available routes of action. The legal events examined here have constructed a normative context for action that has conditioned and will probably continue to condition strategies, responses, and political practices by all sectors of Puerto Rican society involved in managing the relationship between the United States and Puerto Rico. In all these respects, law has operated through both its coercive and persuasive capacities.

Finally, legal discourse has also been a site for resistance, a circumstance that at times has opened up avenues for respite. At other times legal discourse has functioned to buttress the very power relationship on which its legitimacy has been founded. In the final analysis, law has become an important hegemonic mechanism that has served to induce a generalized acceptance of American rule and American presence.

The Legal Construction of Hegemony: Colonialism, Identities, and Subjectivity

The reproduction of American hegemony within the Puerto Rican population has been the result of a complex articulation of factors that have reinforced each other in a multidimensional fashion. Those factors can be traced back to the years previous to the American occupation, when significant economic connections were already in place between the two countries and when a sector of Puerto Rican intellectuals, well versed in the tenets of liberalism, openly admired American institutions and political traditions. The very first encounter between the occupying forces and the people of the conquered territory was cloaked with promises of redemption and hopes of liberation.

Further down the century, an intricate web of economic ties has effectively made the Puerto Rican economy an adjunct of the American economic system. A key strand of this web is the policy of allowing the Puerto Rican population a certain degree of access to the benefits and entitlements administered by the metropolitan state. The gradual incorporation in Puerto Rico of the accouterments of modernity, American style, has added another dimension to the process.

The United States has become an "exemplary center" for Puerto Rico, whose institutions and life processes have come to resemble more and more those of the metropolitan society. This is particularly so in the legal dimension of social life—that is, the set of ideals, norms, institutions, and procedures that constitute the legal system in a given society. Puerto Rico's institutional framework has been increasingly modeled on that of American society. In part, although not exclusively, due to this dynamics, a regime of partial democracy has developed for the internal governance of the colony, with a corresponding system of rights and a heavy accent on the ideology of the rule of law as a legitimating basis.

The extension of American citizenship, in addition, has become a crucial component of the discourse of rights and a major reference point regarding tangible benefits attributed directly to the relationship with the United States. These features of the association have coexisted with recurrent periods of repression and persecution against independence advocates and other resistance movements. Repression has been unleashed at times by agents of the metropolitan state and at others by officials of the Puerto Rican government. This complex articulation of coercive and persuasive mechanisms has had the effect of producing an enormous degree of acceptance of the American presence and American rule within the population. This is, precisely, what the concept of hegemony refers to. Law has been imbricated in each and every aspect of these processes.

The power relationship between the United States and Puerto Rico has been justified, from the perspective of the metropolitan state, on the basis of a constitutional doctrine developed by the U.S. Supreme Court that holds that the U.S. Congress enjoys plenary powers over the peoples and resources of so-called unincorporated territories. Through the *Insular Cases*, which adopted the doctrine of unincorporation, the Court actually created a new legal and political reality. If before 1901 there were no such things as unincorporated territories, after the *Insular Cases* the American political and constitutional world would include such entities. This has been one of the most perfect examples of the law's "power of naming" and of its capacity to generate new understandings and, therefore, new realities.

Categorizing Puerto Rico and other lands as unincorporated territories would have important normative and political consequences. First, the Court in effect legitimated the exercise of power by the United States over other peoples much in the same way as that of the European imperial powers. A new common sense emerged within the dominant legal and political circles in the United States that it was justified, natural, appropriate, and morally correct to acquire lands inhabited by people who, as in the case of Puerto Rico, viewed themselves as distinct nations, to hold them as territorial possessions, and to govern them as colonial dependencies.

A second important effect of the theory of unincorporation was the enormous flexibility it accorded the political branches of the federal government. In fact, that was the main purpose of the doctrine. In the end, it authorized the United States to exert direct rule over other lands and other peoples without the difficulties inherent in dealing with formally sovereign states and unencumbered by the complications of admitting those "distant and different peoples" into the American federation. More importantly still, the overwhelming fact of power that the military occupation and the subsequent legal justification of its consequences entailed forced the Puerto Rican people to accept being ruled through norms not of their making. Eventually, this situation came to be viewed by many Puerto Ricans as inevitable, convenient, or even desirable. Outside governance has been decried as unjust but has been treated as "legally valid" inasmuch as its normative outputs are obeyed. This acquiescence has been at the core of the construction of the legitimacy of the regime.

Another aspect of the legal construction of American rule in Puerto Rico has been the extent to which the process has encompassed the creation of a legal and political subject. This has been a gradual endeavor that started with the Foraker Act of 1900. Relying on cues offered by Congress, the executive, political leaders, and legal academicians, the Court of the *Insular Cases* defined the new legal and political subject as the inhabitant of unincorporated territory. Certainly, those subjects were legitimated to make certain claims on the U.S. government. At the same time, they became "subject," in another sense, to the plenary powers of the government that had recognized them as legal subjects.

Extension of American citizenship to Puerto Ricans in 1917 redefined in some measure the relationship between individual Puerto Ricans and the American political community. Now the "inhabitant of the unincorporated territory of Puerto Rico" became a U.S. citizen. As the Court made clear in 1922 in *Balzac v. Porto Rico*, that action was not understood to alter in any fundamental way the political status of Puerto Rico. Nor did it modify the conclusion that the rights of its inhabitants would still be conditioned by the fact that they resided in "unincorporated territory." "Objectively," that is, from the point of view of the legal operators of the metropolitan state, this new legal and political subject had limited rights. However, "subjectively," many Puerto Ricans appropriated the category in a form that gave it new political meaning and that was popularly interpreted to justify levying certain demands on the American government. In fact, the conversion of Puerto Ricans into U.S. citizens would facilitate the formulation of reciprocal claims between the metropolitan state and the population of the territory. Those mutual exactions have been instrumental in the production of a colonial welfare state and of close material and symbolic ties between the metropolitan state and significant sectors of the population of the territory.

This new legal and political subject views itself as a bearer of rights, particularly individual rights, claimable against both the internal Puerto Rican government and the government of the metropolis. That self-perception serves to empower, while at the same time it operates to subject. This self-conception has recently heightened the strain between the aspirations of large segments of the population for more complete self-determination and the condition of political subordination that the colonial relationship entails. The tension has been manifested in repeated demands for greater participation in the adoption of the rules by which Puerto Rican life is organized. In one version, the claim translates into calls for limited accession to the rule-making processes of the metropolitan state within a more autonomous variant of the present relationship. In another, it becomes a demand for full inclusion in the union as a state of the federation. In still another, it surges as an exigency of full sovereignty for the Puerto Rican nation. It may well be that the very character of American colonialism—with its reliance on the discourse of rights to construct hegemony— may have sown the seeds of its own delegitimation. This may be read as yet another reflection of the paradoxical nature of legal discourse.

These effects are intimately connected to the question of identity. Puerto Ricans, like all other human beings, construct their sense of identity with reference to a multiplicity of factors. One set of factors has to do with the way they relate, individually and collectively, to the fact that the Puerto Rican community shares a common history that embodies a rich ensemble of political, cultural, and social experiences, including the language most of them speak. A sense of ethnic particularity is part of that embroidery. But this set of factors has been traversed by the legal categories that have been produced to name them as social beings. One of those categories is that of "U.S. citizen." These two sets of identity-related discourses—one referring to "Puerto Ricanness" and another to American citizenship—have interacted historically to produce a variety of results within each individual Puerto Rican. Some people tend to harmonize both discourses and to dissolve any conceivable tension between them. Others emphasize one set of factors over the other, without rejecting either. And yet others respond with an outright rejection of one of those defining discourses, as in the case of those who have tried to relinquish their American citizenship. The legal construction of American colonialism in Puerto Rico, then, has had profound effects on the way that individual and collective identities are forged within the Puerto Rican community.

It has also had a significant effect on the configuration of subjectivities. *Subjectivity* refers to the particular content of a given consciousness. It comprises worldviews and the categories through which those views are filtered. The legal categories that populate the Puerto Rican social world have had an influence on the worldviews prevailing at different moments in this particular community. Those legal categories, as in many other modern societies, refer to an ever-enlarging number of social relations. Some of them, such as the categories "unincorporated territory" and "American citizenship," speak directly to the power relationship between the United States and Puerto Rico and to the connection between individual Puerto Ricans and the metropolitan state. Both of those categories circulate in the world of images that provide meaning to social and political life in the Puerto Rican milieu.

Given the intense public discussion that the political status issue has traditionally generated in Puerto Rico, these two categories have become commonplace in Puerto Rican public and private discourse. Their meanings are not absolutely fixed. Different sectors may ascribe to them different connotations. However, they do tend to condition the way Puerto Ricans talk about the world and the manner in which they interpret and evaluate the relationship between the United States and Puerto Rico. Furthermore, the successive transformations experienced by Puerto Rican society throughout the past century, many of them influenced by contact with the metropolitan culture, have engendered ways of thinking and acting constitutive of a worldview that may be generally defined as "modern subjectivity." This includes a distinctive mode of conceiving and relating to law called *modern legal consciousness,* which is characterized by the fact that people generally take law relatively seriously in their dealings with the rest of the world. *Rights discourse* is part of modern legal consciousness: It refers to the extent to which people view the world and themselves through the language of rights. The kind of colonialism put in place in Puerto Rico by the United States not only promoted, but buttressed itself on, legal consciousness and the discourse of rights, contributing strongly to the production of a modern subjectivity that takes the language of law and rights seriously in the formation of perceptions of the self and of the surrounding world.

The legal construction of American colonialism in Puerto Rico has also created a determinate context for action. It has opened up possibilities for, and placed restrictions on, acts of resistance to the power relationship that emerged from the Spanish American War. Such resistance has been constant throughout the century and has been manifest in many ways, including the emergence of political movements promoting independence, greater autonomy, or full formal equality through statehood. But resistance to colonialism and its effects has manifested itself well beyond these status-related developments, for example, in myriad daily responses to the most diverse dimensions of colonial society. Many of those reactions have been shaped by, and channeled through, law. This book has suggested some of the most salient manifestations of defensive and transformative action in this context. A more detailed analysis is required to gauge the extent and depth to which law has served as a site of defiance of American hegemony as well as the degree to which law and legal processes have conditioned the content and form of such resistance.

Hegemony, Self-Determination, and Decolonization

Another important effect of the legal construction of American colonialism has to do with the perspective from which the U.S. Congress and the federal government in general view the process of self-determination and decolonization for Puerto Rico. That perspective is part of the discourse of power contained in the legal framework established by the *Insular Cases* and related legal events. According to that vision, the U.S. Congress possesses plenary powers over questions relating to the territories, including the absolute power to determine how those territories will be "disposed of." As key decisions regarding the political condition of the territories throughout this century have amply demonstrated, that prerogative is understood to extend to the determination of the political alternatives available to the territories and to the very definition of the process by which their peoples are to exercise their "right to self-determination." As a consequence, the territories may choose among available options but, barring a unilateral declaration of independence that would imply a total rupture with the United States, the election is to be made under conditions specified by the U.S. government.

Recent congressional proposals to provide for a process for "self-determination" for Puerto Rico seem to point in a somewhat different direction. They suggest a complex set of mechanisms involving congressional decisions followed by a series of referenda among the Puerto Rican population that would eventually lead to a resolution of the political status problem. However, close examination of the measures produced so far reveals that Congress would still retain the upper hand in all stages of the process. This is accomplished through the ever-present possibility of resorting to the trump card of the Territorial Clause of the Constitution from which, it was declared 100 years ago, the plenary powers of Congress flow, at least until the territories become fully sovereign entities.

Within Puerto Rico itself, a related effect of this legal construction pertains to the options conceived as available for the resolution of the conflict over political status. Much of the discussion in this regard has hinged on the legitimacy of the present legal and political arrangement—known as the *Estado Libre Asociado,* or Commonwealth in the English version—and on the viability and desirability of alternative solutions. Opponents of the present Commonwealth status point to its colonial nature manifest in the formal and material subordination to the United States that it embodies. The alternatives traditionally proposed have been national independence, American statehood, or some form of "enhanced" Commonwealth status that would address some of the perceived shortcomings of this formula. In recent years, a fourth option has been taking shape in the public debate over the matter: a sovereign Puerto Rico formally linked to the United States through a treaty of free association. This formula is known as "the associated republic status."

The controversy, however, has failed to distinguish between two phenomena that are intimately related but not identical. One is the question of American hegemony over the population, and the other is the legitimacy, either in a sociological or normative sense, of the particular institutional arrangement through which that hegemony is expressed at a given moment. In the case of Puerto Rico, *hegemony* refers to the degree to which substantial sectors of the Puerto Rican population view as acceptable and desirable the very attachment to the United States, whereas the question of the legitimacy of Commonwealth has to do with assessment of the validity or desirability of the specific institutional arrangement through which that bond has been structured since the early 1950s.

Any observer of current Puerto Rican reality would have to agree that the majority of the population values its connection to the United States. Currently, disagreements among that majority revolve around the manner in which that link should be preserved. Some propose that Puerto Rico should evolve toward a greater degree of local autonomy while maintaining the existing basic ties to the metropolitan power. Others argue for conversion into a state of the union. Still others have suggested that Puerto Rico become a "sovereign" nation, but with a close political and economic association with the United States. Those who advocate a radical rupture with the United States are a discrete minority.

The differences among the proposed solutions, even within the framework of a sustained connection to the United States, are substantial. It is undeniable that all the different options could have considerable effects on the future of Puerto Rico and its people. But the basic fact remains that, for the immense majority, preserving a significant link to the metropolitan state, with its attendant material and symbolic consequences, is critical. This is, precisely, the most convincing indication that the hegemonic project of the United States initiated 100 years ago has been successful. American hegemony has been realized. One of the conclusions that can be derived from this basic sociological fact is that delegitimation of the current Commonwealth formula would not necessarily imply the breakdown of American hegemony. There are definitive signs that the sociological and political legitimacy of the present Commonwealth status has been seriously eroded. Yet, at the same time, there is substantial evidence that American hegemony over the population is far from dissolving.

Erosion of the sociological and political legitimacy of the Commonwealth status has been manifested in a progressive decline in support for that formula at the polls.[1] It is also evident from the fact that branding it a "colonial relationship" has become a common and extended feature of normative political discourse throughout the entire spectrum of Puerto Rican society. Several cleavages in the present arrangement could explain this decline in popular support or, at least, have the potential of provoking a further downswing. First of all, there has been a deepening awareness of the democratic deficit of the current status. The repeated refusal of the U.S. Congress to provide for a greater degree of participation in decision making on the part of Puerto Ricans within the Commonwealth status could stimulate growth in the followings of the other alternatives, which address this question in a more substantial way. Second, economic and social fissures have long afflicted the Commonwealth formula, such as the relative failure of the latest economic strategies adopted by Commonwealth governments, changes in the fiscal policy of the United States, and regional and

---

[1] Support for the Commonwealth status at the polls has declined from slightly more than 60% in the 1967 plebiscite to 48.4% in 1993. The results of the 1998 plebiscite, in which the pro-Commonwealth party asked its followers to vote for a "None of the above" column appearing on the ballot, cannot be interpreted as an increase in support for Commonwealth. See the details in chapter 3 in the section on constitutional and political development under the American regime. The most plausible interpretation is that, if anything, support hovers around the percentage obtained in 1993.

global developments that have curtailed the comparative advantages that the present relationship to the United States has provided Puerto Rico over its Latin American and Caribbean neighbors. This may convince many that statehood or some form of national independence could better equip Puerto Rico to face the challenges of a transformed global economy.

A third area of vulnerability has to do with the cultural problem. Despite their positive valuation of American citizenship and of the material benefits associated with the bond to the United States, most Puerto Ricans exhibit a heightened degree of cultural nationalism. This phenomenon has to be viewed within the context of the worldwide resurgence of nationalist discourse in its diverse modalities. In the global rhetorical environment, the satisfaction of needs related to the preservation of cultural and national identities has become an important element of political legitimation. If the Commonwealth formula were to prove unable to shield the Puerto Rican community from the most aggressive features of American cultural penetration, this could provide impetus to those sectors of Puerto Rican society proposing political institutional arrangements characterized by a greater degree of autonomy or even sovereignty.

Of course, these factors would not operate alone in promoting alternatives to the present arrangement. They would do so in conjunction with many other developments and considerations, not least of which would be the willingness of the U.S. government to support alternative solutions that would not jeopardize its fundamental political, economic, and military interests in the region or generate burdensome domestic problems from the U.S. perspective.

The above are scenarios that could contribute to the dismantling and transformation of the present institutional political arrangement. However, by themselves they would not necessarily lead to the demise of American hegemony. Only a crisis with profound material and ideological effects would provoke such a breakdown. Developments like the Vieques issue may spark the process. However, the signs that, at the moment, we are far from that crisis are several. First of all, in recent years there has been an increase in the number of statehood followers, who seek a closer link to the metropolis. Second, there has been a very public refusal by supporters of more autonomous versions of the present arrangement, including the advocates of free association, to relinquish the perceived privileges of American citizenship. Some even consider it a matter of principle. Third, the independence option itself has been significantly nuanced to contain the promise of maintaining a tight political and economic relationship with the United States. This option includes the possibility of allowing a substantial proportion of the population of a sovereign Puerto Rico to preserve their American citizenship and a possible agreement regarding the permanence of some American military installations in its territory.

These developments are a telling clue to the degree to which the Puerto Rican intelligentsia has come to terms with the fact that most of the population prefer to stay close to the regional hegemonic power. As long as the factors that have combined to reproduce American hegemony in the island remain substantially unaltered, any delegitimation of the current institutional arrangement could lead only to a legal and political rearrangement that remains within the confines of a link with the current metropolitan state and continued American presence in the country in one way or the other. This rearticulation of the relationship could even be regarded as formally solving the "colonial problem" but would still leave open to resolution the question of American hegemony. Moreover, all the effects of the way American colonialism has been constructed in Puerto Rico will most probably operate to condition the choice eventually made by the population among the different options offered as alternatives to the current situation.

Postcolonial Puerto Rico: The Legacy of Colonialism

The long-term repercussions of the legal construction of American colonialism in Puerto Rico could arguably extend even well beyond the stage in which Puerto Rico becomes a "postcolonial" society. After all, one of the effects of that construction has been its contribution to the production of a certain subjectivity, of certain institutional forms, and of certain material conditions that have helped to constitute a particular type of society. Worldviews, institutional forms, and conditioning material factors are not easily erased with changes in the formal articulation of political relationships. If anything, they tend to persist in time, as the many studies on post-colonial societies have amply demonstrated. It would take a prolonged historical process to transform those ways of viewing the world, organizing social life, and articulating relationships.

It would be expected, for example, that legal consciousness, the discourse of rights, the experience of partial democracy, and the access to given entitlements prevalent within the former colonial relationship, with their attendant advantages and disadvantages, would condition the manner in which the inhabitants of a postcolonial Puerto Rico would view the world, formulate their claims, and manage their individual and collective lives. Furthermore, none of the alternatives of political status currently proposed to solve the colonial question would entirely dissolve, at least in the near future, some of the problems, tensions, and contradictions that have been hatched during the American colonial regime.

With statehood, self-determination claims would not be exhausted, especially as regards cultural matters. Nor would the strains over national and cultural identity disappear. In fact, they could be intensified. The most evident of these would relate to the question of language. Some have even raised the specter of subsequent secession. The formal equality that the statehood solution offers would not efface the problems posed by cultural differences.

The status of associated republic would enhance Puerto Rican collective autonomy but would still harbor the difficulties of limited sovereignty, struggles over American citizenship, and its own versions of the problems of personal and collective identity within Puerto Rico, vis-à-vis the United States, and in the international arena. Even independence, as it has come to be viewed after a century of American presence, will carry over problems from the past. A substantial number of American citizens of Puerto Rican origin living in a sovereign Puerto Rico; inevitable close economic ties with the United States, if not outright dependence; the pressure to maintain American military installations; the foreseeable debate over "formal" versus "real" sovereignty; the intense demographic links with the United States through the millions of Puerto Ricans who either live or have relatives there—in short, all the material and symbolic effects of a long relationship with the metropolitan state— would create tensions as well as opportunities for the new republic that could only be seen as the legacy of American colonialism. Future studies of Puerto Rican society would have to look back to the American "colonial" period for adequate explanation of the economic, social, cultural, legal, and political phenomena within that community.

Puerto Ricans of the present and future generations can do much to transform the conditions generated by the experience of American colonialism, to the extent that such transformation is thought desirable. But in doing so, those very conditions will serve as their platform for action. This particular insight, of course, is far from novel. It is no more than the now-classical notion that people make their own history, but under the conditions they have inherited. That is why in order to understand the possibilities that the future holds, a penetrating look must be cast at how the present has been made possible by the past. This has been one of the main motives behind the story that this book has sought to tell.

American colonialism and its legal construction have not been unidimensional phenomena. They embody experiences of subjection and oppression as well as the creation of conditions that have enhanced the possibilities of a more dignified life for Puerto Ricans. If any worthwhile transformation is to be undertaken of the relationship of inequality and disempowerment that colonialism entails, it would best be done with the utmost cooperation from the United States, up to now the metropolitan power. Any such transformation should preserve the gains made during a century of struggles and momentous episodes of significant social change. But the process should also provide for the exploration of new ways of conceiving the world, organizing social life, and constructing Puerto Rican identities and subjectivities in accordance with our own needs and aspirations. In other words, any process of transformation should make possible a true, continuing, inexhaustible practice of self-determination to the utmost extent feasible in existing and foreseeable world conditions.

REFERENCES

Abel, Richard L., *Nothing Left but Rights: Law in the Struggle against Apartheid, in* IDEN-
TITIES, POLITICS, AND RIGHTS (Austin Sarat & Thomas R. Kearns, Eds.) (Ann Arbor,
Michigan: University of Michigan Press, 1995).

ACOSTA, IVONNE, LA MORDAZA (Río Piedras, PR: Edil, 1987).

Afirmación Socialista Unitaria, *Plebiscito, estado y lucha popular* (1989) (unpublished manuscript).

Alfieri, Anthony V., *The Antinomies of Poverty Law and a Theory of Dialogic Empowerment*,
16 N.Y.U. REV. L. & SOC. CHANGE 659 (1987–88).

Álvarez González, José Julián, *Law, Language and Statehood: The Role of English in the
Great State of Puerto Rico*, 17 L. & INEQ. J. 359 (1999).

———. *The Empire Strikes Out: Congressional Ruminations on the Citizenship Status of
Puerto Rico*, 27 HARV. J. LEGIS. 309 (1990).

AMERICAN IMPERIALISM IN 1898 (T. P. Greene Ed.) (Boston: D. C. Heath & Co., 1955).

ATENEO PUERTORRIQUEÑO, ESTATUTOS (San Juan: Editorial LEA, 1995).

Baldwin, Simeon E., *The Constitutional Questions Incident to the Acquisition and Government
by the United States of Island Territory*, 12 HARV. L. REV. 393 (1899).

BAR ASSOCIATION OF PUERTO RICO, REPORT OF THE SPECIAL COMMISSION ON NUCLEAR
WEAPONS AND THE TREATY FOR THE PROSCRIPTION OF NUCLEAR WEAPONS IN LATIN
AMERICA (San Juan, 1984).

BAYRÓN TORO, FERNANDO, ELECCIONES Y PARTIDOS POLÍTICOS DE PUERTO RICO (Mayagüez,
PR: Isla, 1989).

Beard, Charles A., *Territorial Expansion Connected with Commerce, in* AMERICAN IMPERI-
ALISM IN 1898 (T. P. Greene Ed.) (Boston: D. C. Heath & Co., 1955).

BENTON, THOMAS H., HISTORICAL AND LEGAL EXAMINATION OF THE DRED SCOTT CASE
(1857).

BERLIN, SIR ISAIAH, FOUR ESSAYS ON LIBERTY (London: Oxford University Press, 1969).

Berríos: Decision on Mari Bras Shows P.R. Still a Colony, SAN JUAN STAR, June 7, 1998,
at 6.

Bickel, Alexander M., *Citizenship in the American Constitution*, 15 ARIZ. L. REV. 369 (1973).

BLANCO, TOMÁS, PRONTUARIO HISTÓRICO DE PUERTO RICO (Río Piedras, PR: Ediciones
Huracán, [1935] 1981).

BOCOCK, ROBERT, HEGEMONY (London & New York: Tavistock Publications, 1986).

BOSCH, JUAN, DE CRISTÓBAL COLÓN A FIDEL CASTRO: EL CARIBE, FRONTERA IMPERIAL
(Santo Domingo, Dominican Republic: Alfa y Omega, 1983).

BOURDIEU, PIERRE, *The Force of Law: Toward a Sociology of the Juridical Field*, 38 HAS-
TINGS L. J. 805 (1987).

———. IN OTHER WORDS: ESSAYS TOWARDS A REFLEXIVE SOCIOLOGY (Cambridge, England: Polity, 1990).

———. OUTLINE OF A THEORY OF PRACTICE (Cambridge: Cambridge University Press,
1977).

Boyle, James, *Introduction, in* CRITICAL LEGAL STUDIES (James Boyle Ed.) (New York: New
York University Press, 1994).

BURGESS, JOHN W., RECONSTRUCTION AND THE CONSTITUTION 1866–1876, *quoted in* ROBIN
F. WESTON, RACISM IN U.S. IMPERIALISM: THE INFLUENCE OF RACIAL ASSUMPTIONS ON
AMERICAN FOREIGN POLICY, 1893–1946 (Columbia: University of South Carolina,
1972).

Cabranes, José, *Citizenship and the American Empire*, 127 U. PA. L. REV. 391 (1978).

———. *Puerto Rico and the Constitution*, 110 FED. RULES DEC. 475 (1986).

Cain, Maureen, *Gramsci, the State and the Place of Law, in* LEGALITY, IDEOLOGY AND THE STATE (David Sugarman Ed.) (London & New York: Academic Press, 1983).

Cardona, Iván, *Joe Franco: ¿Qué hace en la Academia?*, DIÁLOGO, October 1992, at 44.

CASSESE, ANTONIO, SELF-DETERMINATION OF PEOPLES: A LEGAL REAPPRAISAL (Cambridge, U.K.: Cambridge University Press, 1995).

Castro Arroyo, María de los Ángeles, *El 98 incesante: Su persistencia en la memoria histórica puertorriqueña, in* ENFOQUES Y PERSPECTIVAS: SIMPOSIO INTERNACIONAL DE HISTORIADORES EN TORNO AL 98 (Luis González Vale ed.) (San Juan: Academia Puertorriqueña de la Historia, 1997).

Cerezo, Benny Frankie, *Sobre la ciudadanía*, EL MUNDO, June 11, 1989, at 42.

CHAMBLISS, W. & SEIDMAN, ROBERT B., LAW, ORDER AND POWER (Reading, Massachusetts: Addison-Wesley, 2nd ed. 1982).

CITIZENSHIP (Geoff Andrews Ed.) (London: Lawrence & Wishart, 1991)

Clinton Offers Release to P.R. Prisoners, SAN JUAN STAR, Aug. 12, 1999, at 5.

Colombani, Juanita, *Bastión militar.Puerto Rico para EE.UU.*, EL NUEVO DÍA, Aug. 11, 1999, at 6.

Comaroff, John, *The Discourse of Rights in Colonial South Africa: Subjectivity, Sovereignty, Modernity, in* IDENTITIES, POLITICS AND RIGHTS (Austin Sarat & Thomas R. Kearns Eds.) (Ann Arbor, Michigan: University of Michigan Press, 1995).

COMISIÓN ESPECIAL DE VIEQUES, INFORME AL GOBERNADOR DE PUERTO RICO HON. PEDRO ROSSELLÓ, Vol. 1 (San Juan, 1999).

COMISIÓN JUDICIAL ESPECIAL PARA INVESTIGAR EL DISCRIMEN POR GÉNERO EN LOS TRIBUNALES DE PUERTO RICO, EL DISCRIMEN POR RAZÓN DE GÉNERO EN LOS TRIBUNALES (San Juan, 1995).

Connell, J., *Britain's Caribbean Colonies: The End of the Era of Decolonisation?*, 32 J. COMMONWEALTH COMPARATIVE POLITICS 87–106 (1994).

CONSEJO DE DESARROLLO ESTRATÉGICO PARA PUERTO RICO, OFICINA DEL GOBERNADOR, EQUIDAD, CALIDAD DE VIDA Y DESARROLLO ECONÓMICO EN PUERTO RICO: LA CUESTIÓN DE LA POBREZA (San Juan, 1992).

Correa Sutil, Jorge, *Acceso a la justicia y reformas judiciales en América Latina ¿Alguna esperanza de mayor igualdad?*, 2000 REV. JUR. UNIV. DE PALERMO 293 (2000).

COTTERRELL, ROGER, THE SOCIOLOGY OF LAW (London, Dublin, Edinburgh: Butterworths, 2nd ed., 1992).

———. *The Sociological Concept of Law, in* LORD LLOYD OF HAMPSTEAD & MICHAEL D. A. FREEMAN, LLOYD'S INTRODUCTION TO JURISPRUDENCE (London: Stevens, 5th ed. 1985).

———. *Legality and Political Legitimacy in the Sociology of Max Weber, in* LEGALITY, IDEOLOGY AND THE STATE (David Sugarman Ed.) (London & New York: Academic Press, 1983).

Crenshaw, Kimberle W., *Race, Reform and Retrenchment: Transformation and Legitimation in Antidiscrimination Law, in* CRITICAL LEGAL THOUGHT: AN AMERICAN–GERMAN DEBATE (C. Joerges & D. M. Trubek Eds.) (Baden-Baden: Nomos Verl.-Ges, 1989).

CRITICAL LEGAL STUDIES (James Boyle Ed.) (New York: New York University Press, 1994).

Declaración del Colegio de Abogados de Puerto Rico sobre la situación actual del proceso de descolonización de Puerto Rico y del caso de Puerto Rico ante el Comité de Descolonización de la Organización de Naciones Unidas (1979), 47 REV. COL. ABOG. P.R. 265 (1986).

DE DIEGO, JOSÉ, II OBRAS COMPLETAS (PROSA. NUEVAS CAMPAÑAS. EL PLEBISCITO) (San Juan: Instituto de Cultura Puertorriqueña, 1966).

DE HOSTOS, EUGENIO MARÍA, AMÉRICA: LA LUCHA POR LA LIBERTAD (Rio Piedras, Puerto Rico: University of Puerto Rico Press, 1988).

————. AMERICA: THE STRUGGLE FOR FREEDOM (Manuel Maldonado Denis Ed.) (San Juan: Office of Cultural Development of the City of San Juan, 1992).

De la Torre, Beatriz, *Plebiscite Born in Carter Era: Status Seen in Domain of Foreign Policy*, SAN JUAN STAR, July 1, 1989, at 1.

DE OBIETA CHALBAUD, J. A., EL DERECHO HUMANO DE LA AUTODETERMINACIÓN DE LOS PUEBLOS (Madrid: Tecnos, 1985).

Delgado Cintrón, Carmelo, *Hostos ante el 1898*, EL NUEVO DÍA, Jan. 11, 1992, at 51.

————. DERECHO Y COLONIALISMO: LA TRAYECTORIA HISTÓRICA DEL DERECHO PUER-TORRIQUEÑO (Río Piedras, PR: Edil, 1988).

————. *El juez federal Bernard Rodey y la crisis de 1909: La oposición de la Cámara de Delegados a la Corte Federal*, 40 REV. COL. ABOG. P.R. 415 (1979).

Denninger, E., *Government Assistance in the Exercise of Basic Rights (Procedure and Organization), in* CRITICAL LEGAL THOUGHT: AN AMERICAN–GERMAN DEBATE (C. Joerges & D. M. Trubek Eds.) (Baden-Baden: Nomos Verl.-Ges, 1989).

Desigualdad y pobreza en Puerto Rico (documentary film, Linda Colón, prod., 1988) (copy on file at the Faculty of General Studies, University of Puerto Rico).

Díaz Alcaide, Maritza, *Johnston lamenta "mal entendido,"* EL MUNDO, June 17, 1989, at 3.

————. *Polémica por la permanencia de la ciudadanía*, EL MUNDO, June 11, 1989, at 6.

Díaz Quiñones, Arcadio, *Once tesis sobre un crimen de 1899*, 11 OP. CIT. REV. DEL CENTRO DE INV. HIST. 109 (1999).

DICCIONARIO DE LA LENGUA ESPAÑOLA (Madrid: Real Academia Española, 20th ed. 1984).

DIETZ, JAMES L., HISTORIA ECONÓMICA DE PUERTO RICO (Rio Piedras, Puerto Rico: Ediciones Huracán, 1989).

DOCUMENTS ON THE CONSTITUTIONAL RELATIONSHIP OF PUERTO RICO AND THE UNITED STATES (Marcos Ramírez Lavandero Ed.) (Washington, DC: Office for Puerto Rico in Washington, 3rd Ed. 1988).

Duchesne Juan, Georas, Chloé S., Grosfoguel, Ramón, Lao, Agustín, & Rivera, Pedro, *Algunas tesis democráticas ante el plebiscito de 1998*, DIÁLOGO, March 1999, at 38.

DWORKIN, RONALD, LAW'S EMPIRE (Cambridge, MA: Harvard University Press, 1986).

————. TAKING RIGHTS SERIOUSLY (London: Duckworth, 1977).

ESTADES FONT, MARÍA EUGENIA, LA PRESENCIA MILITAR DE ESTADOS UNIDOS EN PUERTO RICO 1898–1918 (Río Piedras, PR: Huracán, 1988).

ESTADO LIBRE ASOCIADO DE PUERTO RICO, COMISIÓN ESTATAL DE ELECCIONES, RESULTADOS FINALES: ELECCIONES GENERALES 3 DE NOVIEMBRE 1992 (San Juan, 1993).

————. COMISIÓN ESTATAL DE ELECCIONES, REFERENDUM 8 DE DICIEMBRE DE 1991: INFORME DE RESULTADOS 1 (San Juan, 1992).

————. COMISIÓN ESTATAL DE ELECCIONES, ESCRUTINIO RESULTADOS ISLA. PLEBISCITO 13 DE DICIEMBRE DE 1998 (San Juan, 1999).

————. COMISIÓN DE DERECHOS CIVILES, INFORME—DISCRIMEN Y PERSECUCIÓN POR RAZONES POLÍTICAS: LA PRÁCTICA GUBERNAMENTAL DE MANTENER LISTAS, FICHEROS Y EXPEDIENTES DE CIUDADANOS POR RAZÓN DE IDEOLOGÍA POLÍTICA (San Juan, 1989).

————. JUNTA DE PLANÍFICACIÓN, INFORME ECÓNOMICO AL GOBERNADOR (1999).

Estrada Resto, Nilka, *Rehúsa Victoria retirar la cuña del publicista Franco*, EL NUEVO DÍA, Aug. 15, 1992, at 24.

Fernández, Ismael, *Lo que vale nuestra ciudadanía*, EL NUEVO DÍA, March 9, 1992, at 4.

FERNÁNDEZ, RONALD, THE DISENCHANTED ISLAND: PUERTO RICO AND THE UNITED STATES IN THE TWENTIETH CENTURY (New York: Praeger, 1992).

————. LOS MACHETEROS: THE WELLS FARGO ROBBERY AND THE VIOLENT STRUGGLE FOR PUERTO RICAN INDEPENDENCE (New York: Prentice Hall, 1987).

FERNÓS ISERN, ANTONIO, ESTADO LIBRE ASOCIADO DE PUERTO RICO: ANTECEDENTES, CREACIÓN Y DESARROLLO HASTA LA ÉPOCA PRESENTE (Río Piedras, PR: Editorial Universitaria, 1974).

Ferré, Rosario, *Puerto Rico, U.S.A.*, NEW YORK TIMES, March 19, 1998, at A-23.

FINE, BOB, DEMOCRACY AND THE RULE OF LAW: LIBERAL IDEALS AND MARXIST CRITIQUES (London & Sydney: Pluto Press, 1984).

Fitzpatrick, Peter, *Imperial Deviations* (unpublished paper; on file with author, 1989).

———. THE MYTHOLOGY OF MODERN LAW (London & New York: Routledge, 1992).

Forbath, W. E. et al., *Introduction: Legal Histories from Below*, 1985 WISC. L. REV. 759 (1985).

FOUCAULT, MICHEL, LA VERDAD Y LAS FORMAS JURÍDICAS (Enrique Lynch trans.) (Guanajuato, Mex: Gedisa 3rd ed. 1988).

Fraser, Andrew, *The Legal Theory We Need Now*, 8 SOCIALIST REV. 147 (1978).

FREEMAN, MICHAEL D. A., LLOYD'S INTRODUCTION TO JURISPRUDENCE (London: Sweet & Maxwell, 6th ed. 1994).

———. *The Rule of Law: Liberal, Marxist and Neo-Marxist Perspectives,* lecture delivered during the Anglo-Soviet Symposium sponsored by University College London (July 20, 1990).

Friedman, Robert, *Mari Bras Says Reversed Ruling Violates His Citizenship Rights*, SAN JUAN STAR, June 7, 1998, at 6.

———. *Renunciation Oath Set Aside in Case of U.S. Citizen Mari Bras*, SAN JUAN STAR, June 5, 1998, at 8.

———. *Senate Status Hearings End in Stalemate*, SAN JUAN STAR, July 17, 1998, at 7.

———. *Vieques Gains Ground on National Front*, SAN JUAN STAR, Aug. 5, 1999, at 5.

FRONTERAS EN CONFLICTO: GUERRA CONTRA LAS DROGAS, MILITARIZACIÓN Y DEMOCRACIA EN EL CARIBE, PUERTO RICO Y VIEQUES (Humberto García Muñiz & Jorge Rodríguez Beruff Eds.) (San Juan: Red Caribeña de Geopolítica, Seguridad Regional y Relaciones Internacionales, 1999).

Fuster, Jaime B., *The Origins of the Doctrine of Territorial Incorporation and Its Implications Regarding the Power of the Commonwealth of Puerto Rico to Regulate Interstate Commerce*, 43 REV. JUR. U.P.R. 259 (1974).

Gabel, Peter & Kennedy, Duncan, *Roll over Beethoven*, 36 STAN. L. REV. 1 (1984).

Gallisá, Carlos, *Ha muerto el plebiscito*, CLARIDAD, Feb. 22 to 28, 1991, at 12, 29.

García, Gervasio Luis, *Strangers in Paradise? Puerto Rico en la correspondencia de los cónsules norteamericanos (1869–1900)*, 9 OP. CIT. REV. DEL CENTRO DE INV. HIST. 27 (1997).

García, P., *Ligera ventaja de la estadidad sobre el ELA,* EL NUEVO DÍA, Aug. 6, 1992, at 11.

García Muñiz, Humberto, *U.S. Military Installations in Puerto Rico: An Essay on Their Role and Purpose*, 24 CARIBBEAN STUDIES 79 (1991).

García Passalacqua, J. M., *100 Years of Secrets about P.R. Must End*, SAN JUAN STAR, July 26, 1998, at 85.

———. *La evolución del nuevo E.L.A.*, EL NUEVO DÍA, Dec. 20, 1990, at 81.

———. *Ligera ventaja de la estadidad sobre el ELA*, EL NUEVO DÍA, Aug. 6, 1992, at 11.

GARCÍA PASSALACQUA, JUAN M. & RIVERA LUGO, CARLOS, PUERTO RICO Y LOS ESTADOS UNIDOS: EL PROCESO DE CONSULTA Y NEGOCIACIÓN DE 1989 Y 1990 (2 vols.) (Río Piedras, PR: Editorial Universitaria, 1990, 1991).

Gautier Mayoral, Carmen, *The Effect of the New U.S. National Security Doctrine—the War on Drugs—on the Process of Self-Determination in the Subsidized Colonies of the Caribbean*, 53 REV. COL. AB. P.R. 31 (1992).

———. *Apathy over Plebiscite*, July/Aug. CARIBBEAN CONTACT 15 (1990).

GEERTZ, CLIFFORD, NEGARA: THE THEATER STATE IN NINETEENTH CENTURY BALI (Princeton, NJ: Princeton University Press, 1980).

Genovese, Eugene D., *The Hegemonic Function of Law, in* MARXISM AND LAW (P. Beirne & R. Quinney Eds.) (New York: John Wiley & Sons, 1982).

Ghai, Yash, *The Rule of Law, Legitimacy and Governance, in* THE POLITICAL ECONOMY OF LAW: A THIRD WORLD READER (Yash Ghai et al. Eds.) (Delhi: Oxford, 1987).

Ghigliotty, Julio, *Firmes en que no hay nada como la Isla Nena,* EL NUEVO DÍA, Aug. 4, 1999, at 5.

GIDDENS, ANTHONY, NEW RULES OF SOCIOLOGICAL METHOD (London: Hutchinson, 1976).

GLENDON, MARY ANN, RIGHTS TALK: THE IMPOVERISHMENT OF POLITICAL DISCOURSE (New York: Free Press, 1991).

GONZÁLEZ, JOSÉ LUIS, LA LLEGADA (Río Piedras, PR: Huracán, 1980).

———. EL PAÍS DE CUATRO PISOS Y OTROS ENSAYOS (Río Piedras, PR: Huracán, 1980).

GONZÁLEZ, LYDIA MILAGROS & QUINTERO-RIVERA, ANGEL G., LA OTRA CARA DE LA HISTORIA (San Juan: CEREP, 1984).

GOODRICH, PETER, LEGAL DISCOURSE: STUDIES IN LINGUISTICS, RHETORIC AND LEGAL ANALYSIS (Houndmills, England: MacMillan, 1987).

Gordon, Robert W., *Critical Legal Histories,* 36 STAN. L. REV. 57 (1984).

GRAMSCI, ANTONIO, SELECTIONS FROM THE PRISON NOTEBOOKS (Q. Hoare & G. N. Smith Eds. & Trans.) (London: Lawrence & Wishart, 1971).

Grosfoguel, Ramón, *The Divorce of Nationalist Discourses from the Puerto Rican People: A Sociohistorical Perspective, in* PUERTO RICAN JAM: ESSAYS ON CULTURE AND POLITICS (Frances Negrón-Muntaner & Ramón Grosfoguel Eds.) (Minneapolis: University of Minnesota Press, 1997).

HABERMAS, JÜRGEN, BETWEEN FACTS AND NORMS: CONTRIBUTIONS TO A DISCOURSE THEORY OF LAW AND DEMOCRACY (Cambridge, England: Polity Press, 1996).

———. LEGITIMATION CRISIS (Cambridge, England: Polity, 1988).

HEALEY, DAVID, DRIVE TO HEGEMONY: THE UNITED STATES IN THE CARIBBEAN 1898–1917 (Madison: University of Wisconsin Press, 1988).

HEATER, DEREK, CITIZENSHIP: THE CIVIC IDEAL IN WORLD HISTORY, POLITICS AND EDUCATION (London & New York: Longman, 1990).

HEGEMONÍA Y ALTERNATIVAS POLÍTICAS EN AMÉRICA LATINA (J. Labastida Martín del Campo Ed.) (México: Siglo Veintiuno Editores, 1985).

Held, David, *Between State and Civil Society: Citizenship, in* CITIZENSHIP (Geoff Andrews, Ed., London: Lawrence & Wishart, 1991).

Helfeld, David, *How Much of the United States Constitution and Statutes Are Applicable to the Commonwealth of Puerto Rico?,* 110 FED. RULES DEC. 452 (1986).

Hemlock, Doreen, *Lagomarsino: Referendum Is Unfair Contest,* SAN JUAN STAR, Nov. 26, 1991, at 3.

HISPANIA RESEARCH CORPORATION, MEMORANDO ANALÍTICO SOBRE EL ESTUDIO DEL IDIOMA EN PUERTO RICO–SOMETIDO A: ATENEO PUERTORRIQUEÑO (San Juan, 1993).

HOBSON, J. A., IMPERIALISM: A STUDY (Ann Arbor: University of Michigan, 4th printing 1972).

Hofstadter, Richard, *Manifest Destiny and the Philippines, in* AMERICAN IMPERIALISM IN 1898 (T. P. Greene Ed.) (Boston: D. C. Heath & Co., 1955).

HOLMES, OLIVER WENDELL, THE COMMON LAW (Boston: Little, Brown & Co., 1881).

HORWITZ, MORTON J., THE TRANSFORMATION OF AMERICAN LAW: 1780–1860 (Cambridge, MA: Harvard University Press, 1977).

Hunt, Alan, *Dichotomy and Contradiction in the Sociology of Law, in* MARXISM AND LAW (P. Beirne & R. Quinney Eds.) (New York: John Wiley & Sons, 1982).

Independentistas insistirán en doble ciudadanía, EL MUNDO, June 11, 1989, at 8.

Informe Especial: Reforma Judicial, 26 BIDAMÉRICA 9 (1999).

ISSUES IN SELF-DETERMINATION (William Twining Ed.) (Aberdeen, Scotland: Aberdeen University Press, 1991).

Jaramillo Edwards, I., *La seguridad interamericana: Una problematización,* Paper delivered at the Fourth Meeting of the Working Group on International Relations of the Caribbean,

Latin American Social Science Council (CLACSO) (St. Thomas, U.S. Virgin Islands, June 9–13, 1992).

Jessop, Bob, *On Recent Marxist Theories of Law, the State and Juridico-Political Ideology*, 8 INT'L J. SOC. L. 339 (1980).

Johnston, Bennet J., *Irrevocable la ciudadanía*, EL MUNDO, June 17, 1989, at 27.

Johnston: Citizenship Safe, SAN JUAN STAR, June 17, 1989, at 1.

THE JUSTICES OF THE UNITED STATES SUPREME COURT 1789–1969: THEIR LIVES AND MAJOR OPINIONS 1781 (Leon Friedman & Fred L. Israel Eds.) (New York: Chelsea House Publications, 1969).

KELMAN, MARK, A GUIDE TO CRITICAL LEGAL STUDIES (Cambridge, MA, & London: Harvard University Press, 1987).

Kennedy, Duncan, *Legal Formality*, 2 J. LEGAL STUD. 351 (1973).

KERRUISH, VALERIE, JURISPRUDENCE AS IDEOLOGY (London & New York: Routledge, 1991).

La voz del pueblo en las urnas, EL NUEVO DÍA, July 28, 1998, at 4.

LABOUR, LAW AND CRIME: AN HISTORICAL PERSPECTIVE (F. G. Snyder & D. Hay Eds.) (London & New York: Tavistock, 1987).

Langdell, Charles C., *Status of Our New Territories*, 12 HARV. L. REV. 365 (1899).

Lao, Agustín, *Islands at the Crossroads: Puerto Ricanness Traveling between the Translocal Nation and the Global City, in* PUERTO RICAN JAM: ESSAYS ON CULTURE AND POLITICS (Frances Negrón-Muntaner & Ramón Grosfoguel Eds.) (Minneapolis: University of Minnesota Press, 1997).

LAS IDEAS ANEXIONISTAS EN PUERTO RICO BAJO LA DOMINACIÓN NORTEAMERICANA (Aarón Ramos Ed.) (Río Piedras, PR: Huracán, 1987).

LAW IN EVERYDAY LIFE (Austin Sarat & Thomas R. Kearns Eds.) (Ann Arbor, Michigan: University of Michigan, 1993).

Lears, T. J. Jackson, *The Concept of Cultural Hegemony: Problems and Possibilities,* 90 AMER. HIST. REV. 567 (1985).

Legal Memorandum of John H. Killian, Senior Specialist, American Constitutional Law, Congressional Research Service, American Law Division, November 15, 1990.

LEIBOWITZ, ARNOLD H., DEFINING STATUS: A COMPREHENSIVE ANALYSIS OF UNITED STATES TERRITORIAL RELATIONS (Dordrecht [Netherlands]: Martinus Nijhoff, 1989).

LEWIS, GORDON K., PUERTO RICO: FREEDOM AND POWER IN THE CARIBBEAN (New York: Harper & Row, 1963).

LISKA, GEORGE, CAREER OF EMPIRE: AMERICA AND IMPERIAL EXPANSION OVER LAND AND SEA (Baltimore, MD, & London: Johns Hopkins University Press, 1978).

LORD LLOYD OF HAMPSTEAD & MICHAEL D. A. FREEMAN, LLOYD'S INTRODUCTION TO JURISPRUDENCE (London: Stevens, 5th ed. 1985).

Lowell, Abbot Lawrence, *Status of Our New Possessions—A Third View*, 13 HARV. L. REV. 155 (1899).

Luciano, María Judith, *Pleno de interrogantes el voto*, EL NUEVO DÍA, Dec. 8, 1991, at 5.

LUSTIG, R. J., CORPORATE LIBERALISM: THE ORIGINS OF MODERN AMERICAN POLITICAL THEORY 1890–1920 (Berkeley: University of California Press, 1982).

LYOTARD, JEAN FRANCOIS, THE POSTMODERN CONDITION: A REPORT ON KNOWLEDGE (Manchester, England: Manchester University Press, 1984).

MACCORMICK, NEIL & WEINBERGER, OTTA, AN INSTITUTIONAL THEORY OF LAW: NEW APPROACHES TO LEGAL POSITIVISM (Dordrecht [Netherlands]: Kluwer, 1986).

Maldonado, A. W., *A Message to Congress on the Eve of the Centennial*, SAN JUAN STAR, July 23, 1998, at 53.

MALDONADO DENIS, MANUEL, PUERTO RICO: A SOCIO-HISTORIC INTERPRETATION (New York: Random House, 1972).

MARI BRAS, JUAN, *La claúsula territorial*, CLARIDAD, Dec. 7 to 13, 1990, at 30.

Markovic, Mihailo, *The Principle of Self-Determination As a Basis for Jurisprudence*, 13 ARCHIV FÜR RECHTS-UND SOZIALPHILOSOPHIE (BEIHEFT NEUE FOLGE) 181 (1980).

Marx, Karl, Crítica de la filosofía del estado de Hegel (P. A. Encinares trans.) (México: Grijalbo, 1961).

――――. On the Jewish Question, in Nonsense upon Stilts: Bentham, Burke and Marx on the Rights of Man (Jeremy Waldron Ed.) (London & New York: Methuen, 1987).

――――. Paris Manuscripts, quoted in David McLellan, Marx before Marxism (London: MacMillan, 2nd ed. 1980).

Matos, R., Drug Interdiction Center Opens, San Juan Star, July 15, 1992, at 3.

Matsuda, M., Looking to the Bottom: Critical Legal Studies and Reparations, 22 Harv. C.R.-C.L. L. Rev. 323 (1987).

Mattos Cintrón, Wilfredo, The Puerto Rican Plebiscite (unpublished manuscript, 1990).

――――. La hegemonía de Estados Unidos en Puerto Rico y el independentismo, los derechos civiles y la cuestión nacional, 16 El Caribe Contemporáneo 21 (1988).

May, E. R., American Imperialism: A Speculative Essay (New York: Atheneum, 1968).

McKim, J., National Guard Training for Low Intensity Warfare: Drug Warriors Hit the Trail in Southern P.R., San Juan Star, July 7, 1992, at 2.

McLellan, David, Marx before Marxism (2nd ed.) (London: MacMillan, 1980).

McPhaul, John, President's Clemency Conditions Blasted, San Juan Star, Aug. 13, 1999, at 4.

Meléndez, Héctor, Gramsci en la de Diego: Tres Ensayos sobre cultura nacional, posmodernidad e ideología (Rio Piedras, PR: Ediciones La Sierra, 1994).

Meléndez López, Arturo, La batalla de Vieques (Río Piedras, PR: Edil, 2nd ed. 1989).

Merry, Sally Engle, Law and Colonialism, 25 Law & Soc. Rev. 889, 890 (1991).

――――. Wife Battering and the Ambiguities of Rights, in Identities, Politics, and Rights (Austin Sarat & Thomas R. Kearns Eds.) (Ann Arbor, Michigan: University of Michigan Press, 1995).

Miaja de la Muela, Adolfo, La Emancipación de los Pueblos Coloniales y el Derecho Internacional (Madrid: Editorial Tecnos, 1968).

Michalska, Anna, Rights of Peoples to Self-Determination in International Law, in Issues of Self-Determination (William Twining Ed.) (Aberdeen, Scotland: Aberdeen University Press, 1991).

Minow, Martha, Identities, 3 Yale J. L. & Human. 97 (1991).

――――. Making All the Difference: Inclusion, Exclusion and American Law (Ithaca: Cornell University Press, 1990).

Morris, Nancy, Puerto Rico: Culture, Politics, and Identity (Westport, CT, & London: Praeger, 1995).

Moscoso, Guillermo, Our Nation's 216th Birthday, San Juan Star, July 1, 1992, at 18.

Movimiento Socialista de Trabajadores, Nuestra posición sobre el plebiscito (Dorado, PR, 1989).

Mulero, Leonor, Carlos Romero Barceló: "Las memorias no son publicables en vida," El Nuevo Día, Aug. 1, 1999, at 4.

――――. Admite la persecución a independentistas el FBI, El Nuevo Día, March 17, 2000, at 30.

――――. Ordena el FBI investigarse a sí mismo en el caso de las carpetas, El Nuevo Día, March 22, 2000, at 36.

――――. Congresistas unidos por Vieques, El Nuevo Día, Aug 5, 1999, at 4.

Naveira de Rodón, Miriam, Federal Court Jurisdiction and the Status Commission, 39 Rev. Col. Abog. P.R. 131 (1978).

Nederveen Pieterse, J. P., Empire and Emancipation: Power and Liberation on a World Scale (London: Pluto, 1990).

Negrón de Montilla, Aida, Americanization, Puerto Rico and the Public School System, 1900–1930 (Río Piedras, PR: Editorial Universitaria, 1975).

Negrón-Muntaner, Frances, English Only Jamás but Spanish Only Cuidado: Language and

Nationalism in Contemporary Puerto Rico, in PUERTO RICAN JAM: ESSAYS ON CULTURE AND POLITICS (Frances Negrón-Muntaner & Ramón Grosfoguel Eds.) (Minneapolis: University of Minnesota Press, 1997).

NEGRÓN PORTILLO, MARIANO, CUADRILLAS ANEXIONISTAS Y REVUELTAS CAMPESINAS EN PUERTO RICO, 1898–1899 (Río Piedras, PR: Centro de Investigaciones Sociales, Universidad de Puerto Rico, 1987).

NELSON, ANN, MURDER UNDER TWO FLAGS: THE UNITED STATES, PUERTO RICO, AND THE CERRO MARAVILLA COVER-UP (New York: Ticknor & Fields, 1986).

NERHOT, PETER, LAW, INTERPRETATION AND REALITY (Dordrecht [Netherlands]: Kluwer, 1989).

THE NEW ENCYCLOPAEDIA BRITANNICA (MICROPAEDIA) (15th ed.) (Chicago: Encyclopedia Britannica, Inc., 1991).

Newberry, J., *Constitutional Law: Political Question Doctrine and Conduct of Foreign Policy*, 25 HARV. INT'L. L. J. 433 (1984).

Nosotros, el Pueblo de Puerto Rico (film, Angelita Rieckehoff prod., c. 1982).

Olsen, Frances, *Liberal Rights and Critical Legal Theory, in* CRITICAL LEGAL THOUGHT: AN AMERICAN–GERMAN DEBATE (C. Joerges & D. M. Trubek Eds.) (Baden-Baden: Nomos Verl.-Ges, 1989).

Onuma, Yasuaki, *Between Natural Rights of Man and Fundamental Rights of States, in* ENLIGHTENMENT, RIGHTS AND REVOLUTION (Neil MacCormick & Zenon Bankowski Eds.) (Aberdeen: Aberdeen University Press, 1989).

Oostindie, G., *The Dutch Caribbean in the 1990's: Decolonization or Recolonization?*, 5 CARIBBEAN AFFAIRS 1 (1992).

OSTERHAMMEL, JÜRGEN, COLONIALISM: A THEORETICAL OVERVIEW (Princeton, NJ: Markus Wiener Publishers, 1997).

Otero, R. *Yo soy de Canales: Entrevista a Cruz Rivera*, PISO 13, at 2, 3 (1992).

Otto, Dianne, *Subalternity and International Law: The Problems of Global Community and the Incommensurability of Difference*, 5 SOC. & LEG. STUD. 337 (1996).

P.R.'s Strategic Position Said Enhanced, SAN JUAN STAR, Oct. 2, 1990, at 5.

Pagán, G., *Independentistas Live in Past*, SAN JUAN STAR, Aug. 28, 1992, at 18.

Parker, Richard D., *The Effective Enjoyment of Rights, in* CRITICAL LEGAL THOUGHT: AN AMERICAN–GERMAN DEBATE (C. Joerges & D. M. Trubek Eds.) (Baden-Baden: Nomos Verl.-Ges, 1989).

PARTIDO POPULAR DEMOCRÁTICO. PROGRAMA DE GOBIERNO 1989–1992: VAMOS POR BUEN CAMINO (San Juan, 1988).

PASHUKANIS, EVGENI, LAW AND MARXISM (London & Sydney: Pluto Press, 1983).

Pastor, Robert, *La migración en la cuenca caribeña*, 6 EL CARIBE CONTEMPORÁNEO 105 (1982).

Pérez-Bachs, R., *Applicability of the United States Constitution and Federal Laws to the Commonwealth of Puerto Rico*, 110 FED. RULES DEC. 485 (1986).

Picciotto, Sol, *The Theory of the State, Class Struggle and the Rule of Law, in* MARXISM AND LAW (P. Beirne & R. Quinney Eds.) (New York: John Wiley & Sons, 1982).

PICÓ, FERNANDO, HISTORIA GENERAL DE PUERTO RICO (Río Piedras, PR: Huracán, 1986).

PIVEN, F. & CLOWARD, R., REGULATING THE POOR: THE FUNCTIONS OF PUBLIC WELFARE (New York: Pantheon, 1971).

Plant, Raymond, *Social Rights and the Reconstruction of Welfare, in* CITIZENSHIP (Geoff Andrews Ed.) (London: Lawrence & Wishart, 1991).

THE POLITICAL ECONOMY OF LAW: A THIRD WORLD READER (Yash Ghai et al. Eds.) (Delhi: Oxford, 1987).

Pomerance, M., *Self-Determination Today: The Metamorphosis of an Ideal*, 19 ISRAEL L. REV. 310 (1984).

———. *The United States and Self-Determination: Perspectives on the Wilsonian Conception*, 70 AM. J. INT'L. L. 1 (1976).

Postema, Gerald G., *In Defense of "French Nonsense": Fundamental Rights in Constitutional Jurisprudence, in* ENLIGHTENMENT, RIGHTS AND REVOLUTION (Neil MacCormick & Zenon Bankowski Eds.) (Aberdeen: Aberdeen University Press, 1989).

PRATT, JULIUS W., EXPANSIONISTS OF 1898: THE ACQUISITION OF HAWAII AND THE SPANISH ISLANDS (Baltimore, MD: Johns Hopkins University Press, 1936).

Prepared Statement of Brigadier General M. J. Byron, Acting Deputy Assistant Secretary of Defense (Inter-American Affairs) in 1 *Political Status of Puerto Rico: Hearings on S. 710, S. 711, and S. 712 before the Senate Commitee on Energy and Natural Resources*, 101st Cong., 1st Sess. at 134 (Washington, DC, 1989).

PROGRAMA DE GOBIERNO DEL PARTIDO NUEVO PROGRESISTA PARA EL CUATRIENIO 1981–84 (San Juan, 1980).

PUERTO RICAN JAM: ESSAYS ON CULTURE AND POLITICS (Frances Negrón-Muntaner & Ramón Grosfoguel Eds.) (Minneapolis: University of Minnesota Press, 1997).

QUINTERO RIVERA, ÁNGEL G., CONFLICTOS DE CLASE Y POLÍTICA EN PUERTO RICO (San Juan: Huracán-CEREP, 1976).

———. PATRICIOS Y PLEBEYOS: BURGUESES, HACENDADOS, ARTESANOS Y OBREROS. LAS RELACIONES DE CLASE EN EL PUERTO RICO DE CAMBIO DE SIGLO (Río Piedras, PR: Huracán, 1988).

Ramírez, Marcos A., *Los Casos Insulares*, 16 REV. JUR. U.P.R. 121 (1946).

Ramírez de Ferrer, Miriam, *Statehood Is Solution to 2nd Class Citizenship*, SAN JUAN STAR, May 1, 1998, at 55.

Randolf, Carmen F., *Constitutional Aspects of Annexation*, 12 HARV. L. REV. 291 (1898).

Rivera, Raquel Z., *Rapping Two Versions of the Same Requiem, in* PUERTO RICAN JAM: ESSAYS ON CULTURE AND POLITICS (Frances Negrón-Muntaner & Ramón Grosfoguel Eds.) (Minneapolis: University of Minnesota Press, 1997).

Rivera Ramos, Efrén, *Colonialism and Integration in the Contemporary Caribbean*, 20 BEYOND LAW 189 (1998).

———. *Derecho y subjetividad*, 5–6 FUNDAMENTOS 125 (1997–98).

———. *Mucho más que un referéndum*, CLARIDAD, Dec. 20–26, 1991, at 8.

———. *La Reforma Judicial en la América Latina y el Caribe*, DIÁLOGO, January 1995, at 44.

———. *Self-Determination and Decolonisation in the Society of the Modern Colonial Welfare State, in* ISSUES OF SELF-DETERMINATION (William Twining Ed.) (Aberdeen, Scotland: Aberdeen University Press, 1991).

———. *The Supreme Court of Puerto Rico and the Separation of Powers Doctrine: Notes on Constitutional Argument and Social Conflict* (unpublished LL.M. paper, Harvard University, 1981).

Rodríguez Beruff, Jorge, *La cuestión estratégico-militar y la libre determinación de Puerto Rico: el debate plebiscitario (1989–1993), in* EL CARIBE EN LA POST-GUERRA FRÍA, ESTUDIO ESTRATÉGICO DE AMÉRICA LATINA (1992–1993) (Humberto García & Jorge Rodríguez Beruff Eds.) (Santiago, Chile: FLACSO, 1994).

———. *Puerto Rico and the Caribbean in the U.S. Strategic Debate on the Eve of the Second World War*, 2 REV. MEXICANA DEL CARIBE 55 (1996).

Rodríguez Beruff, Jorge & García Muñiz, Humberto, *El debate estratégico en Estados Unidos y la revisión de la política militar hacia América Latina y el Caribe* (1994).

Rodríguez Orellana, Manuel, *Young, Craig Paved the Way for a Better Bill*, SAN JUAN STAR, June 7, 1998, at 87.

Román, Ediberto, *The Alien–Citizen Paradox and Other Consequences of U.S. Colonialism*, 26 FLORIDA STATE UNIV. L. REV. 1 (1998).

———. *Empire Forgotten: The United States's Colonization of Puerto Rico*, 42 VILLANOVA L. REV. 1119 (1997).

RONEN, D., THE QUEST FOR SELF-DETERMINATION (New Haven, CT: Yale University Press, 1979).

RÚA, PEDRO JUAN, LA ENCRUCIJADA DEL IDIOMA: ENSAYOS EN TORNO AL INGLÉS OFICIAL, LA DEFENSA DEL ESPAÑOL CRIOLLO Y LA DESCOLONIZACIÓN PUERTORRIQUEÑA (San Juan: Instituto de Cultura Puertorriqueña, 1992).

Sagardía de Alvarado, Ana, *Puerto Rico en la encrucijada del '98: Impacto del cambio de soberanía en la ciudadanía de los puertorriqueños*, 11 CULTURA 14 (1997).

SAMUELSON, PAUL & NORDHAUS, WILLIAM, ÉCONOMIÁ (Madrid: McGraw Hill-Interamericana de España, 16th ed. 1999).

Sánchez, Lisa E., *Boundaries of Legitimacy: Sex, Violence, Citizenship, and Community in a Local Sexual Economy*, 22 L. & SOC. INQ. 543 (1997).

Santos, Boaventura de Sousa, *The Gatt of Law and Democracy: (Mis)Trusting the Global Reform of Courts*, in GLOBALIZATION AND LEGAL CULTURES: OÑATI SUMMER COURSE 1997 (Johannes Feest Ed.) (Oñati, Spain: International Institute for the Sociology of Law, 1999).

Sarat, Austin & Kearns, Thomas R., *Editorial Introduction*, in IDENTITIES, POLITICS, AND RIGHTS (Austin Sarat & Thomas R. Kearns, Eds.) (Ann Arbor, Michigan: University of Michigan Press, 1995).

―――. *Beyond the Great Divide: Forms of Legal Scholarship and Everyday Life*, in LAW IN EVERYDAY LIFE (Austin Sarat & Thomas R. Kearns Eds.) (Ann Arbor, Michigan: University of Michigan Press, 1993).

Sassoon, A. S., *Hegemony*, in A DICTIONARY OF MARXIST THOUGHT (T. Bottomore et al. Eds.) (Cambridge, MA: Harvard University Press, 1983).

SCARANO, FRANCISCO A., PUERTO RICO: CINCO SIGLOS DE HISTORIA (San Juan: McGraw-Hill, 1993).

SCHEINGOLD, STUART, THE POLITICS OF RIGHTS: LAWYERS, PUBLIC POLICY, AND POLITICAL CHANGE (New Haven, CT: Yale University Press, 1974).

Schmalz, J., *With Encouragement of U.S., Puerto Rico Seeks an Identity*, NEW YORK TIMES, July 10, 1989, at A1.

Schurz, Carl, American Imperialism, The Convocation Address Delivered on Occasion of the 27th Convocation of the University of Chicago (Jan. 4, 1899), in AMERICAN IMPERIALISM IN 1898 (T. P. Greene, Ed.) (Boston: D. C. Heath & Co., 1955).

SELF-DETERMINATION: NATIONAL, REGIONAL AND GLOBAL DIMENSIONS (Y. Alexander & R. Friedlander Eds.) (Boulder, CO: Westview Press, 1980).

SELZNICK, P., LAW, SOCIETY AND INDUSTRIAL JUSTICE (New York: Russell Sage, 1969).

Serrano Geyls, Raúl, *Memorandum to the Senate Committee on Energy and Natural Resources*, July 7, 1989.

―――. *El misterio de la ciudadanía*, 40 REV. COL. AB. P.R. 437 (1979).

―――. *The Territorial Status of Puerto Rico and Its Effects on the Political Future of the Island*, 11 REV. JUR. U.I. 385 (1977).

SERRANO GEYLS, RAÚL (Demetrio Fernández Quiñones & Efrén Rivera Ramos, contributors) DERECHO CONSTITUCIONAL DE ESTADOS UNIDOS Y PUERTO RICO: DOCUMENTOS–JURISPRUDENCIA–ANOTACIONES–PREGUNTAS (San Juan: Colegio de Abogados de PR/Instituto de Educación Práctica, 1986).

Sherry, Suzanna, *Rights Talk: Must We Mean What We Say?*, 17 LAW & SOC. INQ. 491, (1992).

Shivji, Issa G., *Equality, Rights and Authoritarianism in Africa*, in ENLIGHTENMENT, RIGHTS AND REVOLUTION: ESSAYS IN LEGAL AND SOCIAL PHILOSOPHY (Neil MacCormick & Zenon Bankowski Eds.) (Aberdeen: Aberdeen University Press, 1989).

Silbey, Susan & Sarat, Austin, *Critical Traditions in Law and Society Research*, 21 L. & SOC. REV. 165 (1987–88).

SILVESTRINI, BLANCA G., & LUQUE DE SÁNCHEZ, MARÍA D., HISTORIA DE PUERTO RICO: TRAYECTORIA DE UN PUEBLO (San Juan: Cultural Puertorriqueña, 1987).

SMART, CAROL, FEMINISM AND THE POWER OF LAW (London & New York: Routledge, 1989).

SMITH, ROGERS M., CIVIC IDEALS: CONFLICTING VISIONS OF CITIZENSHIP IN U.S. HISTORY (New Haven, CT, & London: Yale University Press, 1997).

Snyder, Francis & Hay, Douglas, *Comparisons in the Social History of Law: Labour and Crime, in* LABOUR, LAW AND CRIME: AN HISTORICAL PERSPECTIVE (Francis Snyder & Douglas Hay Eds.) (London & New York: Tavistock, 1987).

Sparer, Ed, *Fundamental Human Rights, Legal Entitlements, and the Social Struggle: A Friendly Critique of the Critical Legal Studies Movement,* 36 STAN. L. REV. 509 (1984).

Statement to the Senate by Roberto Roldán Burgos, General Coordinator of the Instituto Puertorriqueño de Derechos Civiles (Puerto Rico Civil Rights Institute) *in* 2 *Political Status of Puerto Rico: Hearings on S. 710, S. 711, and S. 712 before the Senate Committee on Energy and Natural Resources,* 101st Cong., 1st Sess. 170 (Washington, DC, 1989).

STOYANOVITCH, KONSTANTYN, EL PENSAMIENTO MARXISTA Y EL DERECHO (Madrid: Siglo XXI, 1981).

Suárez, Manny, *260 Reservists Called Up: Assignments Not Yet Known for 3 P.R. Units,* SAN JUAN STAR, Sept. 27, 1990, at 1.

Summers, Robert S., *Pragmatic Instrumentalism in Twentieth Century American Legal Thought—A Synthesis and Critique of Our Dominant General Theory about Law and Its Use,* 66 CORNELL L. REV. 861 (1981).

SUNSHINE, C. A., THE CARIBBEAN: SURVIVAL, STRUGGLE AND SOVEREIGNTY (Washington, DC: EPICA, 1980).

Terdiman, Richard, *Translator's Introduction, in* Pierre Bourdieu, *The Force of Law: Toward a Sociology of the Juridical Field,* 38 HASTINGS L. J. 805–13 (1987).

Thayer, James Bradley, *Our New Possessions,* 12 HARV. L. REV. 464 (1899).

Thompson, E. P., *The Rule of Law, in* MARXISM AND LAW (P. Beirne & R. Quinney Eds.) (New York: John Wiley & Sons, 1982).

THOMPSON, E. P., WHIGS AND HUNTERS: THE ORIGIN OF THE BLACK ACT (Hardmondsworth, U.K.: Penguin, 1975).

THOMPSON, WINFRED LEE, THE INTRODUCTION OF AMERICAN LAW IN THE PHILIPPINES AND PUERTO RICO: 1898–1905 (Fayetteville: University of Arkansas, 1989).

Torres, Eulalio A., *The Puerto Rico Penal Code of 1902–1975: A Case Study of American Legal Imperialism,* 45 REV. JUR. U.P.R. 1 (1976).

TORRUELLA, JUAN R., THE SUPREME COURT AND PUERTO RICO: THE DOCTRINE OF SEPARATE AND UNEQUAL (Río Piedras, PR: Editorial Universitaria, 1985).

TRÍAS MONGE, JOSÉ, EL CHOQUE DE DOS CULTURAS JURÍDICAS EN PUERTO RICO (San Juan: Equity, 1991).

———. LA CRISIS DEL DERECHO EN PUERTO RICO (San Juan: Publicaciones JTS, 1979).

———. 1–5 HISTORIA CONSTITUCIONAL DE PUERTO RICO (Río Piedras, PR: Editorial Universitaria, 1980–1983, 1994).

———. PUERTO RICO: THE TRIALS OF THE OLDEST COLONY IN THE WORLD (New Haven, CT: Yale University Press, 1997).

———. EL SISTEMA JUDICIAL DE PUERTO RICO (Río Piedras, PR: Editorial Universitaria, 1978).

Tschudin, Roberto, *The United States District Court for the District of Puerto Rico: Can an English Language Court Serve the Interest of Justice in a Spanish Language Society?,* 37 REV. COL. ABOG. P.R. 41 (1976).

Turner, Harry, *The Odyssey of Puerto Rico's Plebiscite: 1988–1990,* SAN JUAN STAR, Dec. 23, 1990, at 1, 24.

TWINING, WILLIAM, RETHINKING EVIDENCE: EXPLORATORY ESSAYS (Oxford: Blackwell, 1990).

TWINING, WILLIAM & MYERS, DAVID, HOW TO DO THINGS WITH RULES (London: Weidenfeld & Nicolson, 2nd ed., 1982).

UNGER, ROBERTO MANGABEIRA, THE CRITICAL LEGAL STUDIES MOVEMENT (Cambridge, Massachusetts: Harvard University Press, 1986).

———. LAW IN MODERN SOCIETY: TOWARD A CRITICISM OF SOCIAL THEORY (New York: Free Press, 1976).

UNITED STATES CONGRESS, 144 CONG. REC. H772 (daily ed. March 4, 1998) (statements by Reps. Young, Miller, and Kennedy).

———. 144 CONG. REC. H823, H822, H829 (daily ed. March 4, 1998) (statements by Rep. Young; Res. Comm. Romero Barceló).

———. 144 CONG. REC. H819 (daily ed. March 4, 1998) (statement by Res. Comm. Romero Barceló; recorded vote).

———. HOUSE COMMITTEE ON INTERIOR AND INSULAR AFFAIRS, REPORT TOGETHER WITH ADDITIONAL VIEWS ON PUERTO RICO SELF-DETERMINATION ACT, H.R. 4765, 101st Cong., 2nd Sess. (1990).

———. HOUSE COMMITTEE ON INTERIOR AND INSULAR AFFAIRS, REPORT TOGETHER WITH ADDITIONAL VIEWS TO ACCOMPANY H.R. 4765, 101st Cong., 2nd Sess. at 15–16 (1990).

———. HOUSE COMMITTEE ON RESOURCES, REPORT TOGETHER WITH DISSENTING AND ADDITIONAL VIEWS TO ACCOMPANY H.R. 3024, 104th Cong., 2nd Sess. (1996).

———. Political Status of Puerto Rico: Hearings on S. 710, S. 711, and S. 712 before the Senate Committee on Energy and Natural Resources, 101st Cong., 1st Sess. (Vol. 1 & 2) (1989).

U.S. CONGRESSIONAL RESEARCH SERVICE (CRS), DISCRETION OF CONGRESS RESPECTING CITIZENSHIP STATUS OF PUERTO RICO (1989).

———. QUESTIONS RELATING TO DECEMBER 8 REFERENDUM IN PUERTO RICO (1991).

U.S. DEPARTMENT OF THE TREASURY, THE OPERATION AND EFFECT OF THE POSSESSIONS CORPORATION SYSTEM OF TAXATION: SIXTH REPORT (Washington, DC, 1989).

U.S. GENERAL ACCOUNTING OFFICE, PUERTO RICO: INFORMATION FOR STATUS DELIBERATIONS (Washington, DC, 1989).

Vicente, Esther, Beyond Law Reform: The Puerto Rican Experience in the Construction and Implementation of the Domestic Violence Act, 68 REV. JUR. U.P.R. 553 (1999).

———. Las mujeres y el cambio en la norma jurídica, 56 REV. JUR. U.P.R. 585 (1987).

WEBER, MAX, ECONOMY AND SOCIETY (G. Roth & C. Wittich Eds.) (Berkeley: University of California Press, 1978).

Weston, Nancy A., The Fate, Violence, and Rhetoric of Contemporary Legal Thought: Reflections on the Amherst Series, the Loss of Truth, and Law, 22 L. & SOC. INQ. 733 (1997).

WESTON, ROBIN F., RACISM IN U.S. IMPERIALISM: THE INFLUENCE OF RACIAL ASSUMPTIONS ON AMERICAN FOREIGN POLICY, 1893–1946 (Columbia: University of South Carolina, 1972).

Young, Iris Marion, Difference and Policy: Some Reflections in the Context of New Social Movements, 56 CINCINNATI L. REV. 535 (1987).

———. Polity and Group Difference: A Critique of the Ideal of Universal Citizenship, 99 ETHICS 250 (1989).

Zimmermann, Warren, Jingoes, Goo-Goos, and the Rise of America's Empire, WQ (WILSON Q.) (Spring 1998, at 42).

TABLE OF AUTHORITY

Cases

Other Legal Materials

INDEX

ABOUT THE AUTHOR

Efrén Rivera Ramos, PhD, is a full professor at the University of Puerto Rico School of Law. He currently teaches courses on jurisprudence, sociology of law, the legal profession, law and social change, and evidence. Born and raised in Puerto Rico, he obtained a BA in political science and a JD from the University of Puerto Rico, an LLM at Harvard Law School, and a PhD in law and social theory from the University of London. He has worked as a professional journalist, is a published poet, has practiced and taught law for over 20 years, and has lectured on a wide variety of topics in Puerto Rico, the United States, Europe and Latin America.

Keenly interested in interdisciplinary work, Dr. Rivera Ramos has focused much of his scholarship on the analysis of legal phenomena from the perspectives of social and political theory. He has published in academic journals and collective books on such topics as constitutional law, colonialism, citizenship, self-determination, equality, rights, identities, and subjectivity, as well as on the legal, political, and sociological aspects of the complex relationship between the United States and Puerto Rico.